Royal Heirs

Against the odds, monarchies flourished in nineteenth-century Europe. In an era marked by dramatic change and revolutionary upheaval, Europe's monarchies experienced an unexpected late flowering. *Royal Heirs* focuses on the roles and personalities of the heirs to the throne from more than a dozen different dynasties that ruled the continent between the French Revolution and the end of the First World War. The book explores how these individuals contributed to the remarkable survival of the crowns they were born to wear. Constitutions, family relationships, education, politics, the media, the need to generate 'soft power' and the militarisation of monarchy all shaped the lives of princes and princesses while they were playing their part to embody and secure the future of monarchy. Ranging from Norway to Spain and from Greece to Britain, *Royal Heirs* not only paints a vivid picture of a monarchical age, but also explores how such disparate monarchies succeeded in adapting to change and defending their position.

Frank Lorenz Müller is Professor of Modern History at the University of St Andrews. Between 2012 and 2017, he led a major research project on the role of heirs in nineteenth-century monarchies. His publications include *Britain and the German Question* (2002), *Our Fritz: Emperor Frederick III and the Political Culture of Imperial Germany* (2011) and, as co-editor, *Royal Heirs and the Uses of Soft Power in Nineteenth-Century Europe* (2016). He is founder-editor of the Palgrave Studies in Modern Monarchy.

Royal Heirs

Succession and the Future of Monarchy
in Nineteenth-Century Europe

Frank Lorenz Müller

University of St Andrews

Translation by

Rona Johnston

CAMBRIDGE
UNIVERSITY PRESS

GOETHE
INSTITUT

CAMBRIDGE
UNIVERSITY PRESS

Shaftesbury Road, Cambridge CB2 8EA, United Kingdom

One Liberty Plaza, 20th Floor, New York, NY 10006, USA

477 Williamstown Road, Port Melbourne, VIC 3207, Australia

314–321, 3rd Floor, Plot 3, Splendor Forum, Jasola District Centre,
New Delhi – 110025, India

103 Penang Road, #05–06/07, Visioncrest Commercial, Singapore 238467

Cambridge University Press is part of Cambridge University Press & Assessment,
a department of the University of Cambridge.

We share the University's mission to contribute to society through the pursuit of
education, learning, and research at the highest international levels of excellence.

www.cambridge.org
Information on this title: www.cambridge.org/9781316512913

DOI: 10.1017/9781009071284

Originally published in German as *Die Thronfolger. Macht und Zukunft der
Monarchie im 19. Jahrhundert* by Frank Lorenz Müller

German edition © 2019 Siedler Verlag a division of Penguin Random House
Verlagsgruppe GmbH, Munich, Germany

First translated and published in English by Cambridge University Press 2023 as
Royal Heirs: Succession and the Future of Monarchy in Nineteenth-Century Europe

English edition © 2023 Cambridge University Press

Printed in the United Kingdom by TJ Books Limited, Padstow Cornwall

A catalogue record for this publication is available from the British Library.

*A cataloguing-in-publication data record for this book is available from the Library of
Congress.*

ISBN 978-1-316-51291-3 Hardback

The translation of this work was supported by a grant from the Goethe-Institut.

für Celia

Contents

Figures

Acknowledgements for the German Edition (2019)

For years, I have tested the patience of my friends and family with stories about royal heirs. I have pestered colleagues, archivists and librarians with queries and requests. I have relied on the generous support of institutions kind enough to fund historical research. Now that this book is finished, the least thing I can do is to record my gratitude. It is to this pleasant duty that I would now like to turn.

This book is one of the many fruits of a project financed by the Arts and Humanities Research Council (AHRC) and hosted by the University of St Andrews between 2012 and 2017. The support offered by these two institutions was crucial. Without it, the small band of historians researching the roles of *Heirs to the Throne in the Constitutional Monarchies of Nineteenth-Century Europe (1815–1914)* (http://heirstothethrone-project.net) could never have been formed. I would like to thank my fellow team members – Amelia Carruthers, Jennifer Henderson Crane, Dr Charles Jones, Dr Carmina López Sanchez, Dr Maria-Christina Marchi, Dr Richard Meyer Forsting, Lynneth Miller, Dr Mariko Okawa, Dr Miriam Schneider and, above all, Dr Heidi Mehrkens – for our wonderful time together and for our many cheerful and instructive conversations. That my colleagues have made a huge contribution to this volume will be obvious to any reader, and I am particularly grateful for their help in the course of the final writing process.

I have also benefited enormously from the assistance I have received from other scholars, who kindly responded to my pleas for help and shared their expertise with me. I am indebted to Alma Hannig, Trond Norén Isaksen, Professor Axel Körner, Professor Jes Fabricius Møller, Professor Jane Ridley, Christoph de Spiegeleer, Dr Andrew Thompson and Dr Valentina Villa.

The archival research I undertook for this book would not have been possible without the knowledgeable and patient help offered to me by archivists in Altshausen, Amberg, Berlin, Dresden, Munich, Stuttgart, Oxford and Windsor. I would especially like to acknowledge the assistance I received from Dr Robin Darwall-Smith (Oxford), Dr Albrecht

Ernst (Stuttgart), Dr Eberhard Fritz (Altshausen), Dr Gerhard Immler (Munich) and Dr Gerhard Keiper (Berlin). I am indebted to Her Majesty, Queen Elizabeth II, for her gracious permission to let me consult and quote from material kept in the Royal Archives. My thanks also go to the librarians at St Andrews University Library and at the *Staatsbibliothek* Berlin. I wrote the bulk of this book during a sabbatical year in Berlin in 2016–2017 and I am indebted to Heike Fritz, who looked after me in the glorious new reading room of the *Staatsbibliothek* Berlin/Unter den Linden.

Both for my family and for me, the year in Berlin was a great joy in so many ways. For that, I would like to thank both my many old Berlin friends and also the new ones: Professor Birgit Aschmann and Britt Schlünz as well as the equally charming and musical men, women and youngsters of the *Blechmontage* brass ensemble. I would also like to thank the staff of the IBZ, where we found a welcoming home.

My parents, Hedi and Erhard Müller, lovingly looked after us in Berlin, and they also carefully read and commented on the early drafts of this book. My friends and colleagues Dr Bernhard Struck and – as always – Professor Dominik Geppert lavished much care on my manuscript and improved it in countless ways. I would like to thank them, as well as Dr Saskia Limbach, who compiled the bibliography, for their expertise, meticulousness and encouragement.

Working with Siedler Verlag was a real pleasure. I am indebted to Jens Dehning for his support and feedback. Ditta Ahmadi was a judicious, expert and delightful editor.

Finally, I would like to thank my family: my sons Hugo and Nicholas, who will, I hope, have happier lives ahead of them than the many princes who populate the pages of this book. Without the cheerfulness and affection of these two splendid boys, the years I spent with my royal heirs would have been far less enjoyable. I would especially like to thank my wonderful wife Celia for the almost three decades of loving support of the author. As a small gesture of my appreciation of this kind of dedicated championing of historical research, I dedicate this book to her – with much love.

Acknowledgements for the English Translation (2022)

I am delighted that my 'Royal Heirs' are now also available in English, and I would like to thank the people who have helped to make this happen. At Cambridge University Press, I am indebted to Liz Friend-Smith, Atifa Jiwa, Natasha Whelan and Elliott Beck for their warm support of this project. I am grateful to Steven Holt for his sharp-eyed and professional copy-editing. Above all, I owe a huge debt of gratitude to Dr Rona Johnston Gordon who produced an elegant and sure-footed translation of the German original and lavished meticulous care on my text – removing the numerous glitches that I had failed to spot before. I would also like to thank the Goethe-Institut for its generous contribution towards the cost of the translation.

Introduction

On 21 January 1793, a cold and foggy day, King Louis XVI of France was delivered to the guillotine on what is now the Place de la Concorde. More than 100,000 soldiers lined the snow-covered streets of Paris. The procession took almost two hours to cover the two miles from the Tour de Temple, where Louis had been imprisoned. On reaching the place of execution, the dethroned monarch stepped down from the carriage, took off his overcoat and unbuttoned his shirt collar. As the way up to the guillotine was slippery, he initially took the arm of his confessor, the Irish-born Abbé Henry Edgeworth, but he finished climbing the steps on his own. Sentenced to death by the National Convention for treason, the king turned from the scaffold towards the great crowds, averred his innocence and forgave his enemies. A drum roll ordered by General Antoine Santerre, the commander of the National Guard, drowned out his last words. The executioner seized the Bourbon king and forced him beneath the guillotine. The condemned man's broad neck did not sit well within the notch hollowed out in the executioner's block, and the decapitation turned out messy and very bloody. When, at last, the severed head was held up for the crowd to see, the dam broke for some spectators: a few onlookers sampled the blood that had spurted from the king's neck and argued over its flavour; others dipped their hands into it, and so many wanted to wet handkerchiefs or envelopes that in the end the executioner provided a bucket filled with blood. Nine months later, the king's widow, Marie Antoinette, was executed at the same spot. As the blade fell, again the cry went up: 'Long live the Republic!'[1]

From a monarchical point of view, the long nineteenth century, which stretched from the French Revolution to the end of the First World War, could hardly have started in more apocalyptic fashion. For many contemporaries and their successors, the legally sanctioned public execution of

---

[1] John Hardman, *Louis XVI* (New Haven, CT and London, 1993), pp. 231–233; J. M. Thompson (ed.), *English Witnesses of the French Revolution* (Oxford, 1938), pp. 227–231; Henri Sanson, *Tagebücher der Henker von Paris*, vol. 1, www.projekt-gutenberg.org/sanson/henker1/chap012.html (accessed May 12, 2022).

an anointed king was so outrageous an offence that it seemed to herald the definitive end of an ancient world order. News of Louis's beheading drove some distraught contemporaries into an emotional abyss. According to reports, it triggered suicides and cases of sudden insanity. Even in the twentieth century, the French philosopher and author Albert Camus still rued the execution of the king, which to him seemed to mark 'the irrevocable destruction of a world that, for a thousand years, had embraced a sacred order'. For Camus, on 21 January 1793 a moral code sanctioned by a transcendental God had been lost forever.[2]

In the light of this bloody start to the long nineteenth century, surely no member of the tightly knit network of Europe's ruling families would have dared to dream on that bleak winter's day of so colourful a monarchical spectacle as was mounted in Berlin and Braunschweig 120 years later. In the early summer of 1913 a magnificent gathering of the ruling dynasties of Europe took place in the German capital. The dignitaries could now appear before the lenses of film cameras, which preserved the festive moment in moving images for posterity to enjoy. The occasion was the wedding of Princess Viktoria Luise, the German emperor's only daughter, to Prince Ernst August of Cumberland, of the House of Guelf. The elite of Europe's monarchies were amongst the more than 1,000 guests: Tsar Nicholas II was happy to accept the invitation of Emperor Wilhelm II, his cousin by marriage, as was the British king, George V, who was also a cousin of the German ruler. Both led the young bride in a polonaise. The date of the celebration, 24 May, was a deliberate choice, for it was the birthday of British Queen Victoria, forebear of many of the illustrious guests, who had died in 1901. The wedding was intensely political, for it served to resolve the longstanding conflict between the Guelf and Hohenzollern dynasties initiated by the Prussian annexation of Hanover in 1866. Despite this backdrop, the marriage was successfully presented as an affair of the heart, and thousands of excited Berliners turned out to view the spectacle. Much to the infuriation of the socialist press, which was spitting tacks at the 'cheering rabble' filling the streets of the German capital during the lengthy festivities, the population of the city took a lively interest in the happy fortune of their 'little princess'.[3]

---

[2] Susan Dunn, *The Deaths of Louis XVI: Regicide and the French Political Imagination* (Princeton, NJ, 1994), p. 140; Susan Dunn, 'Camus and Louis XVI: An Elegy for the Martyred King', *The French Review* 62 (1989), p. 1032.

[3] Hennig Holsten and Daniel Schönpflug, 'Widersprüche eines dynastischen Gipfeltreffens im Jahr 1913', in Ute Daniel und Christian K. Frey (eds.), *Die preußisch-welfische Hochzeit 1913. Das dynastische Europa in seinem letzten Friedensjahr* (Braunschweig, 2016), pp. 50–68; Jörg Kirschstein, 'Kaisertochter und Welfenprinz. Die glanzvolle Hochzeit von Victoria Luise und Ernst August im Jahr 1913', in Stiftung

The royal wedding took place amid a bumper crop of splendid monarchical anniversaries: 1913 was not just the centenary of Napoleon's defeat at the Battle of Leipzig but also Wilhelm II's Silver Jubilee, marking twenty-five years since his accession to the German imperial throne. In addition to the Berlin nuptials, both these occasions were celebrated with great pomp. Eventually, in November 1913, greeted by the cheers of the population, the freshly married couple arrived in Brunswick, where Ernst Augustus ascended the throne of the duchy. More than four decades after the Kingdom of Hanover had ceased to exist, a Guelf prince returned to the German Empire as a ruling duke. 'You, ancient clan, shall always be renewed in the ranks of noble princes, just as at all times your people vow to you the ancient German fealty', read one commemorative postcard printed specially for this great day. 'The populace greeted us at the train stations, which had been decorated with flowers and with the blue and yellow colours of the land', Duchess Viktoria Luise would later recall. 'It was not just the inhabitants of the town who participated. From near and far more than 100,000 people had come ... all those who heard the rejoicing gained a sense of the power of tradition in the hearts of the people.'[4]

One hundred and thirty years earlier the French revolutionary Maximilien Robespierre had called out at the National Convention: 'Louis must die for the fatherland to live!' Yet in 1913 the monarchs of Europe could still bask in the warm glow of public approval, stage high politics as a family affair and tap into a dynastic loyalty beating deep in the hearts of the people. A broad monarchic seam ran through the nineteenth century and characterised that era in manifold ways. That phenomenon is the subject of this book.

The survival of the European monarchies in the nineteenth century seems all the more remarkable because this age is largely viewed as a period of accelerating, profound and often revolutionary change. This interpretation is reflected in the titles of the master narratives of the era. Eric Hobsbawm's classic trilogy identified a sequence of three epochs, with the age of revolution followed by the age of capital and then by the age of empire; in the volumes of the majestic history of Europe published by Propyläen, Eberhard Weis and Theodor Schieder identified first the 'breakthrough of the bourgeoisie' and then the establishment of the 'state

---

Residenzschloss Braunschweig (ed.), *Europas letztes Rendezvous. Die Hochzeit von Victoria Luise und Ernst August* (Braunschweig, 2013), pp. 14–55.
[4] Wulf Otte, 'Zwischen Welfenstolz und Preußenmacht. Die braunschweigische Thronfolgefrage 1866–1918', in Meike Buck, Maik Ohnezeit and Heike Pöppelmann (eds.), *1919 – Herrliche moderne Zeiten?* (Braunschweig, 2013), p. 52; Herzogin Viktoria Luise, *Ein Leben als Tochter des Kaisers* (Göttingen, 1965), pp. 118–119.

system as global hegemon' as characteristic of the century. According to Jürgen Osterhammel's magnum opus this century witnessed nothing less than a 'transformation of the world'. And, indeed, the circumstances in which the people of Europe lived changed vastly over the course of the nineteenth century: accelerating industrialisation reached more and more areas of the continent; the growth of the population and the related migration from the countryside to the cities and beyond, out of Europe and overseas, were vast; communications and mobility were galvanised by rapid progress in both knowledge and technology; literacy rates grew rapidly, generating a broader public sphere; increasingly larger groups within the population benefited from the introduction of constitutions and the step-by-step expansion of the franchise; new horizons opened up as a number of European powers extended an imperial grip across the rest of the world.[5]

Despite all these changes, Europe remained a profoundly monarchical continent during this era. Every new European state established in the nineteenth century entered independence with a crowned head, from Greece (1821) and Belgium (1830) to Bulgaria (1878) and Norway (1905). When the nations of Europe went to war in 1914, the continent was still overwhelmingly monarchical. France, Switzerland, Portugal and tiny San Marino were the few republican exceptions that proved the monarchical rule.[6] Certainly, anti-monarchical movements were active in several states, and individual rulers were subject to sharp, and some-times vitriolic, public criticism. Moreover, a number of crowned heads – amongst them Tsar Alexander II, Empress Elisabeth of Austria and King Umberto I of Italy – fell victim to a wave of nihilistic assassinations at the turn of the century. But there was no significant broad anti-monarchical current. On the contrary, the monarchical regimes – in the various forms that they had taken on in the decades since 1793 – continued to be widely accepted. Sometimes they were even downright popular in this new age of radio sets, airplanes, X-ray machines and Charlie Chaplin films. Self-congratulatory references to the 'power of tradition in the hearts of the people' were not entirely fanciful.

The appeal of exploring the monarchical dimension of the age lies precisely in that contrast between the profound transformation of

---

[5] Eric Hobsbawm, *The Age of Revolution: Europe 1789–1848* (London, 1962); Eric Hobsbawm, *The Age of Capital: 1848–1875* (London, 1975); Eric Hobsbawm, *The Age of Empire: 1875–1914* (London, 1987); Eberhard Weis, *Der Durchbruch des Bürgertums. 1776–1847* (Berlin, 1990); Theodor Schieder, *Staatensystem als Vormacht der Welt, 1848–1918* (Berlin, 1986); Jürgen Osterhammel, *The Transformation of the World: A Global History of the Nineteenth Century* (Princeton, NJ, 2014).

[6] Dieter Langewiesche, *Die Monarchie im Jahrhundert Europas. Selbstbehauptung durch Wandel im 19. Jahrhundert* (Heidelberg, 2013), p. 6.

Europe and the seemingly improbable tenacity of the monarchical order. In Arthur Conan Doyle's short story *Silver Blaze*, master detective Sherlock Holmes has to direct the attention of a dim-witted policeman to the 'curious incident' that, on the night in question, the guard dog did not raise the alarm. Therein lay the key to catching the wrongdoer. This admonition to pay attention to what did *not* happen although it could have been expected also impels us here: regardless of the shocking symbolism of 21 January 1793 and despite the monumental political, social, economic and cultural changes that followed, monarchy did not die out in nineteenth-century Europe. The period that the American historian Robert Roswell Palmer named the 'Age of the Democratic Revolution' did not lead to an era of republicanism.[7] Even the next great wave of revolutions, which swept Europe in 1848–1849, hardly thinned out the ranks of the continent's monarchs. The underlying theme of this book is the 'curious incident' that in the course of the long nineteenth century, which followed the French Revolution, the monarchies of Europe did *not* disappear. At the heart of our story lies the remarkable manifestation of tenacity, transformation and survival that made the celebrations of 1913 possible.

This book depicts and analyses Europe's monarchical nineteenth century. It asks what made the late flowering of European royalty possible and how this unfolding came about. How did the dynasties and their supporters manage to safeguard a form of government in which the head of state routinely inherited that office for life? Its survival was surely not a simple matter. It happened in the midst of the rapid change that devoured so many elements of the Ancien Régime and in the face of the challenges posed by a post-revolutionary age that insisted on greater popular participation in the exercise of power, on the dismantling of privilege and on extensive civil liberties. What was the nature of the transformation of the princely system which enabled, in the words of Dieter Langewiesche, monarchy's 'self-assertion in the nineteenth century'?[8]

For a long time historians failed to give due attention to the monarchical dimension of this age. The topic seemed too nostalgic, too

---

[7] Robert R. Palmer, *The Age of the Democratic Revolution: A Political History of Europe and America, 1760–1800*, 2 vols. (Princeton, NJ, 1959 and 1964).

[8] For the sake of completeness, we must also acknowledge that in a few instances – the Vatican, the Holy Roman Empire before 1806, Poland-Lithuania until 1795 – there existed monarchical systems in which the head of state was determined not by birth but by the decision of an exclusive electoral college. See Tobias Friske, *Staatsform Monarchie. Was unterscheidet eine Monarchie heute noch von einer Republik?* (Freiburg, 2007), pp. 40–44, https://freidok.uni-freiburg.de/data/3325 (accessed 10 August 2017); Langewiesche, *Die Monarchie*.

apologetic or too reactionary, and even when they did address it, they often approached it with insufficient analytical rigour. In 1989, the British historian David Cannadine, one of the fathers of modern monarchical history, complained about 'too much chronicle and too little history, a surfeit of myth-making and a dearth of scholarly scepticism'. The situation has changed decisively over recent years, and outstanding studies have taught us a great deal about the development of European monarchy during the nineteenth century. Scholarly interest has focused, on the one hand, on royal public-relations activities, analysing media, self-representation and communications, and, on the other hand, on the development and capacities of the constitutional-monarchical system. Beyond these two broad themes, a clearer picture of the monarchical century has emerged from numerous new biographies of the rulers themselves. The leading lights of the monarchical scene, figures such as Queen Victoria of Great Britain, King Ludwig II of Bavaria, Archduke Franz Ferdinand of Austria and the bombastic and mercurial Emperor Wilhelm II, have all been the subjects of numerous biographies.[9]

This study adopts a new perspective to help to shed light on the ability of European monarchy to adapt and survive. Its focus is on the royal heirs. These individuals, the many men and few women at the heart of this story, were essential to the survival of hereditary monarchy. The future of their dynasties depended upon the heirs to the throne. Great importance was attributed to these august figures from the very moment of their birth, an event that naturally attracted great attention.

One such child was born in Laxenburg near Vienna on 21 August 1858. He was at the centre of attention from the moment he took his first breath.

---

[9] David Cannadine, 'The Last Hanoverian Sovereign? The Victorian Monarchy in Historical Perspective, 1688–1888', in A. L. Beier, David Cannadine and James M. Rosenheim (eds.), *The First Modern Society: Essays in English History in Honour of Lawrence Stone* (Cambridge, 1989), pp. 129–130; a short overview of published research on the history of monarchy in Europe can be found in Frank Lorenz Müller, 'Stabilizing a "Great Historical System" in the Nineteenth Century? Royal Heirs and Succession in an Age of Monarchy', in Frank Lorenz Müller und Heidi Mehrkens (eds.), *Sons and Heirs: Succession and Political Culture in Nineteenth-Century Europe* (Basingstoke, 2015), pp. 1–16; Martin Kohlrausch, 'Die höfische Gesellschaft und ihre Feinde. Monarchie und Öffentlichkeit in Großbritannien und Deutschland um 1900', *Neue Politische Literatur* 47 (2002), pp. 450–466; and Torsten Riotte, 'Nach "Pomp und Politik". Neue Ansätze in der Historiographie zum regierenden Hochadel im 19. Jahrhundert', *Neue Politische Literatur* 59 (2014), pp. 209–228; on the (self-)representation of the German monarchy in the second half of the nineteenth century see also Anja Schöbel, *Monarchie und Öffentlichkeit. Die Inszenierung der deutschen Bundesfürsten 1848–1918* (Cologne, Weimar and Vienna, 2017). A Europe-wide approach to the role of the monarchy in the nineteenth century can be found in Benjamin Hasselhorn und Marc von Knorring (eds.), *Vom Olymp zum Boulevard. Die europäischen Monarchien von 1815 bis heute – Verlierer der Geschichte?* (Berlin, 2018).

Figure 1. 'The Emperor's Pride – The Hope of His Peoples':
a contemporary print portrays the baptism of the Austrian Crown
Prince Rudolf in 1858 as an ethereal act, surrounded by saints and
ancestors, transcending the centuries. Johann Schmickl, *Baptism of
Rudolf, Crown Prince of Austria, 1858* [*Taufe von Rudolf, Kronprinz von
Österreich, 1858*], ÖNB Bildarchiv und Grafiksammlung, Sign. Pk
3001, 270.

'The Pride of the Emperor – The Hope of His Peoples' read the title of
a 'pamphlet to commemorate Austria's happy day', here shown as
Figure 1. Garlanded with all the insignia of power and majesty, it portrayed the baptism of Crown Prince Rudolf (1858–1889) by Cardinal
Josef Rauscher at Laxenburg Castle on 23 August 1858. At the centre of
the depiction is the two-day-old infant boy, held above the baptismal font
by his father, Emperor Franz Joseph (1830–1916), while the cardinal
administers the sacrament. The scene is framed by pillars mounted with
busts of Emperor Rudolf I (1218–1291) and Empress Maria Theresa
(1717–1780), great ancestral figures of the House of Habsburg.
Additionally, the baby, the emperor and the cardinal are surrounded by
the patron saints of the Austrian Crown lands, numerous additional

dignitaries, and – somewhat unexpectedly – a lion, who looks on genially. The three crowns that the child was born to wear – the imperial crown of Austria and the royal crowns of Hungary and Bohemia – are displayed for the onlookers on a cushion at the base of the font. Many similar images were crafted at the time of the birth of this heir to the throne. Bearing the title 'The Habsburgs' Youngest Flowering' (*Habsburgs jüngste Blüte*), a lithograph by Eduard Kaiser showed the new-born child in a crib decorated with a personification of Austria. A coloured chalk lithograph with the title 'The most illustrious imperial family with his Serene Highness Crown Prince Rudolf Carl Josef' depicts the heir to the throne's small bed below a commanding image of Rudolf I and a trumpet-blowing angel, who gestures towards the child. Joseph Kohn's *Crown Jewel for the Habsburg Dynasty*, a 'festive album' published in Lemberg in 1858, 'on the occasion of the happy birth of his Imperial and Royal Highness the most august Crown Prince Rudolf', provided its reader with a full thirty-five pages of loyal imperial edification.[10]

The baroque-like splendour of such propaganda images and the glorifying texts that explained them are an indication that securing the succession – the transfer of monarchical rule from one individual to that individual's successor, usually from one generation to the next – continued to place high demands on dynastic systems. With the principle of inheritance remaining a core element of European monarchical rule, royal heirs were essential to the system. Additionally, they provided the monarchies, whose future they embodied, with a unique political resource that proved particularly valuable in the nineteenth century. Someday in the future they would serve as the next generation of ruler, but they already existed in the present, in a visible, directly communicable and malleable form, years and even decades before they would come to power. Within monarchical systems, royal heirs formed a flesh-and-blood medium that prepared and heralded the future of the dynasty, one that could be fashioned according to the needs and inclinations of the relevant elements of the population.

Heirs to the throne personified a message about the fundamental continuity of monarchical rule – precisely that reassuring and awe-inspiring steadfastness of tradition that was emphasised by Rudolf I, the founding father of the Habsburg dynasty, gazing down on his descendent and namesake, born 650 years later. At the same time, however, they were a sign that, in accordance with the law of nature, change at the head of the system was inevitable. While the men and women who were predestined

---

[10] Werner Telesko, *Geschichtsraum Österreich. Die Habsburger und ihre Geschichte in der bildenden Kunst des 19. Jahrhunderts* (Vienna, 2006), pp. 282–286.

to wear the crown one day were certainly influenced by their ancestry and by their dynastic and courtly surroundings, they were more than just products of traditional influences. Future rulers needed to be able to react to the political, medial, cultural and constitutional dynamics of their present. Additionally, they served as a screen onto which the people could project their hopes, all the more so when their media presence was growing. During times of rapid change, the people's wish for a better future was often all the more accompanied by a need for familiar continuity. Royal heirs promised both.

The role of future ruler was not determined by longstanding convention alone. It was also shaped by new factors such as the introduction of constitutions and demands for greater participation from a constantly growing public. Increasingly, therefore, heirs to the throne had to live in the public eye, where the statesman-like qualities and social graces of the future ruler could be scrutinised. What the future under the ruling dynasty might hold could be divined from whether the next-in-line appeared industrious or feckless, morally upright or debauched, well-equipped or overwhelmed, committed or lacklustre, whether he was decried as a lecherous skirt-chaser or admired as a loving husband and father. We have good reason, then, to explore the experiences, depictions, performances and functions of the future monarchs precisely in the years they spent under the public spotlight preparing themselves for the office of ruler. They did so in a multiplicity of roles: as tender infants, as hardworking schoolchildren, as devoted parents, as world travellers, as parliamentarians, as guardians of the constitution, as dashing soldiers and as patrons of culture and learning.

A lens focused on royal heirs can also capture the monarchical century as a whole. Their biographies illustrate both what remained unaltered and what did change: the royal houses' adaptation to the supposedly bourgeois lifestyle of the many is just as evident as their efforts to preserve the magic and remain at heart proudly different and unique. The peoples of the European monarchies on which we concentrate here were experiencing rapid social, political, medial, cultural and economic modernisation. In response to the resulting challenges, monarchies from Spain to Sweden and from the Netherlands to Greece sooner or later moved to a form of constitutional rule. This constitutionalisation was the most significant shared characteristic of the monarchies of Europe. According to the constitutional historian Martin Kirsch, it was this step that allowed 'monarchical constitutionalism' to prevail across the continent.[11] Amongst the

---

[11] Martin Kirsch, *Monarch und Parlament im 19. Jahrhundert. Der monarchische Konstitutionalismus als europäischer Verfassungstyp – Frankreich im Vergleich* (Göttingen, 1999).

larger European states only two held out against this trend. Initially, at least, the monarchies of Russia and the Ottoman Empire on the eastern edge of Europe resisted the effects of post-revolutionary modernisation. Russia's Romanovs succeeded in maintaining their autocratic form of rule largely undiminished until 1905, and in significant respects even beyond that date. Similarly, after the suspension of the short-lived constitution of 1876, the Turkish sultans were able to delay the constitutional age until the Young Turk Revolution of 1908. These two singular cases are omitted here.

Although this book seeks to provide a panoramic European perspective, it makes no claim to be encyclopaedic. The monarchies and their heirs in this era were too numerous for every single ruling dynasty and every heir to the throne even to be mentioned, let alone treated in detail. Instead its central themes are illustrated using examples of dynasties, individuals, developments and events drawn from more than a dozen European monarchies. While this study is principally concerned with the monarchical systems in Great Britain, the German lands, Austria and Italy, it also considers the monarchies in Spain, Greece, France, the Netherlands, Belgium and Scandinavia. The colourful and arresting biographies of the heirs discussed here are tied into larger contexts and broader developments. These future rulers were significant and revealing components of a system of rule, but their individual human fates must not disappear behind an analysis of their functions.

Whether specific heirs to the throne were able, and indeed willing, to fulfil the onerous duties they had been assigned at birth and how they went about doing so depended on numerous factors. Happenstance was just as significant as individual preference or aptitude. With all the variety of human character in play here, we cannot expect each instance to follow the same pattern. Nor did the monarchical actors of the nineteenth century all speak from a single script. Repeatedly, exceptions broke – and proved – the rules of a broader development. Nevertheless, it is important that we first sketch the essential features of the world in which most heirs in the constitutional monarchies of nineteenth-century Europe claimed and performed their roles.

1 'Pledge of a Blessed Future'?

Royal Heirs in the Nineteenth Century

On 14 July 1891, an article in the *Herald Democrat* cast an unusual light on the circumstances that defined the life of a European heir to the throne. Heloise, a ten-year-old American girl travelling in Europe, provided the readers of this provincial newspaper, which served the mining town of Leadville, Colorado, with an extensive description of the opening of the Italian parliament. The 'very fine affair' had seemed almost fantastical to the young traveller. King Umberto I (1844–1900) and Queen Margherita (1851–1926) had arrived in the state carriage, drawn by six horses in ceremonial trappings. Footmen in silk stockings and powdered wigs accompanied the royal couple. To the cheers of the people, the King, sporting a magnificent full dress uniform and a richly decorated brass helmet, entered the parliamentary chamber, where he gave a speech. Then, one by one, the members of parliament swore an oath of allegiance to him. On this occasion, his son, the twenty-one-year-old Vittorio Emanuele, prince of Naples (1869–1947), also pledged his fealty, 'which everyone seemed to think very interesting'.[1]

Even with its deliberately childish perspective, this vignette touched on many of the elements that dictated the life and work of those who were next-in-line to the throne in nineteenth-century Europe: the occasion for all the ceremony was the opening of the elected and constitutionally guaranteed parliament by the king; according to that constitution, on turning twenty-one the crown prince became a member of the Senate, the first chamber of the parliament, and swore the oath of loyalty that bound him to king and constitution. He did so before a captivated public that reached from Rome all the way to Colorado and surrounded by his family. All of this took place in the midst of a carefully choreographed pageant full of beplumed and ensilked court pomp, which, by 1891, would have appeared to many people – not just to ten-year-old American girls – like something out of a fairy tale.

This ceremony epitomised a political system that coupled transformation with inertia in an effort to secure the survival of the European monarchies in

---

[1] 'Opening of Parliament at Rome', in *The Herald Democrat*, 14 July 1891, www.colorado historicnewspapers.org/cgi-bin/colorado?a=d&d=THD18910714.2.24 (accessed 18 November 2016).

the post-revolutionary era. For the royal houses, the transition into the constitutional age arguably formed the most profound caesura between the Ancien Régime and the nineteenth century. It also defined the celebratory scene in Rome. The constitutions that were promulgated throughout Europe soon after the defeat of Napoleon provided for the continuation of divinely ordained monarchical rule and proclaimed that all the authority of the state was to remain with the monarch. Yet, the introduction of fundamental laws also changed everything: the hereditary and absolute ruler sanctified by God had turned into an organ of the state who could now be held to account and functioned within defined areas of responsibility. A once-radiant majesty emerged more sober and more functional; the monarchical authority that had previously been accepted as the will of God now had to argue its own merits on the basis of political success and effective government.

If royal families wanted to protect their identity – the culture for which they stood and the system of rule that they embodied – they would have to safeguard surviving traditions and continuities. A good measure of all the things that had made the monarchies of Europe seem extraordinary and astonishing in the royals' own eyes and in the eyes of their subjects would need to survive. The magic had to be cultivated through public appearances, at court and within the network of dynastic families. In *The Leopard*, Giuseppe di Lampedusa's great novel about aristocratic persistence and decline, Prince Tancredi Falconeri wrily concludes, 'If we want things to stay as they are, things will have to change.' Both parts of this famous aphorism applied to the monarchies in nineteenth-century Europe: they transformed to protect their continuities; they remained unchanging to survive their alteration.[2]

With the French Revolution's calls for freedom and democracy continuing to echo, Europe's heirs faced new and dynamic expectations and responsibilities that could not easily be reconciled with the continuities that doggedly persisted at court and within the family. In the first place, this tension applied to the institutional framework within which monarchs and their families existed, acted and ruled. Strict guidelines set out what was legitimate for members of the royal family, what was desirable and what was proscribed. Even a monarch who headed the institutions of the state had to abide by these rules, no matter the executive and leadership possibilities commanded by the crown. For junior dynastic figures – and for heirs to the throne in particular – leading lives within institutions that shifted constantly, metamorphosed or remained rigidly fixed formed a particular challenge – private and public, as personal as it was political.

---

[2] Giuseppe Tomasi di Lampedusa, *The Leopard*, trans. Archibald Colquhoun (New York, 1960), p. 40.

The happiness and success of future monarchs in nineteenth-century Europe depended largely on their ability to negotiate this tough and at times oscillating course. How well they held up would influence how secure the monarchical system would be in future. The wide dissemination of an attractive image of the future ruler enabled the public to recognise in the heir to the throne what the *Norddeutsche Allgemeine Zeitung* celebrated in the German crown prince, Friedrich Wilhelm, in October 1881: 'the pledge of a blessed future'. In the nineteenth century, the image of the crown prince, projected at and perceived by the public, was of central importance for the survival of the monarchy.[3]

The challenge was thus to tie the heir to the throne as productively as possible into the monarchical institution. The crown sought to tackle the 'crisis in the legitimation of the European monarchy' by promising political and social usefulness, and for this task, the heir – by definition the future monarch – could naturally be very valuable.[4] A closely related issue concerned the development of the constitutional state, in which the rights of the crown and those who wore the crown, on the one hand, and the right of subjects of the crown, on the other, had to be demarcated, with their relationship balanced out on legal foundations. Additionally, heirs to the throne also needed to be portrayed as part of the institution of a royal family, just as it became increasingly visible to the public and measured by bourgeois standards. Notwithstanding these changes, the decision-making monopoly of the head of the family, often codified in house rules, continued to intrude deep into the private life of every family member and shaped these family units. Last but not least, the heir to the throne had to perform at the court. This highly structured and carefully constructed context provided the monarch with a powerful means of communicating monarchical rule and of disciplining various groupings. Constitution, family and court determined the world in which Europe's heirs to the throne had to carve out their path and confront the task of guaranteeing the future of the monarchical system.

'Monarchs Need Majorities': Ways out of the Crisis of Legitimation

When Duchess Viktoria Luise entered Braunschweig in the autumn of 1913, she recognised in the loyal population an affection for her husband and herself. She believed this feeling to be strongly rooted in tradition. On their own, such sentiments would not have been sufficient, though, to

---

[3] *Norddeutsche Allgemeine Zeitung* of 18 October 1881.
[4] Gaby Huch, *Zwischen Ehrenpforte und Inkognito. Preußische Könige auf Reisen. Quellen zur Repräsentation der Monarchie zwischen 1797 und 1871*, vol. 1 (Berlin, 2016), p. 3.

shore up monarchy through the nineteenth century. A sufficient number of contemporaries had to be convinced that monarchy was an effective form of rule that could carry the politics and culture of the continent and provide viable solutions. 'In most countries, monarchy is stronger today than it was 50 years ago', summarised Willem Hendrik de Beaufort, a leading Dutch liberal, in 1900. 'If one previously thought or feared that the constitutional and parliamentary monarchy could only be a transitional form for the republic, so one can say today that the constitutional monarchy has a secure footing. Democracy, other than a few socialists, does not want to change that.'[5] This result had not come about without effort. In order to survive the demands of the age that had dawned with the French Revolution, Europe's crowned heads had acquiesced to far-reaching innovations.

This transition had turned out well for the monarchies despite – or even because of – the challenging conditions after 1789. After the storming of the Bastille, popular demands for greater participation in political power could no longer be contained. In 1848–1849, these calls were heard again. They shook the foundations of the monarchical model, which had also been weakened by a further development: the waning of the belief in the divine origins of royal power. The rationality of the Enlightenment had already dented the idea of rule by divine grace and the doctrines of Enlightened Absolutism had fostered new expectations for the performance of a ruling prince. This resulted in a further disenchanting of monarchs. The idea that a prince's legitimacy rested on his ability to master the royal craft had famously been formulated as early as 1752 by King Friedrich II of Prussia in his political testament, where he stated that the monarch must function as the 'first servant and official of his state'. Subsequently, with the entry of monarchy into the constitutional age, the religious and mystical legitimation of the right to rule was spent. Inclusion in the constitutional state deconsecrated the Crown and ultimately rendered it a mere organ of the secular state.

Romantic ideas about the sacredness of royal rule survived amongst parts of the population in a few places – for example, in the Vendée, in western France and in Alpine Bavaria – and were also entertained by individual monarchs and their closest advisers – Friedrich Wilhelm IV of Prussia (1795–1861), for example, or the Bavarian king Ludwig II. Additionally, almost everywhere the crowns clung stubbornly to the nostalgic formulation 'by the grace of God'. Yet none of this changed

---

[5] Coen A. Tamse, 'Die niederländische Monarchie', in Horst Lademacher and Walter Mühlhausen (eds.), *Freiheitsstreben. Demokratie. Emanzipation. Aufsätze zur politischen Kultur in Deutschland und den Niederlanden* (Münster and Hamburg, 1993), p. 125.

the fact that, in the nineteenth century, the monarchical principle lacked a broadly accepted religious justification. Certainly, princes could continue to insist upon the Christian obligation, enshrined in the Gospels, to render obedience to a legitimate temporal ruler, but duty provided far less protection than had the belief in the monarch's personal anointment by the grace of God. 'It was not just the educated classes who found these notions outdated', Heinz Gollwitzer concisely concluded, 'the population as a whole no longer really believed in them.'[6]

With the traditional and once axiomatic bond between ruler and ruled now loosened, monarchy required other forms of legitimation. In the modern state, an entirely new justification was needed for the monarch's exercise of power. This inevitably had implications for the civil lists that financed the royal court. An appeal to the hearts of the people was no longer sufficient; monarchical power had to be tied to effective government and leadership of the state. This power could not be unlimited, though. It was subject to oversight by elected parliaments and by an increasingly self-confident public.[7] The task the crowned heads had to confront was urgent and so the first steps towards a re-legitimisation of monarchy were taken immediately following the European monarchies' defeat of Napoleon. Arousing both admiration and fear, the French emperor, who had acted as the executor of the Revolution of 1789, would prove a decisive influence on the transformation of monarchy.

In the course of the nineteenth century, European monarchs eventually achieved broad popular approbation by aligning themselves with the preferences of the greater part of their politically engaged contemporaries. In 1912, the German journalist and politician Friedrich Naumann summarised the logic of this step in a pithy phrase: 'monarchs need majorities'.[8] In that search for majorities, constitutional developments

---

[6] Otto Brunner, 'Vom Gottesgnadentum zum monarchischen Prinzip. Der Weg der europäischen Monarchie seit dem hohen Mittelalter', in *Das Königtum. Seine geistigen und rechtlichen Grundlagen* (Lindau and Constance, 1956), pp. 293–303; Katharina Weigand, 'Die konstitutionelle Monarchie im 19. Jahrhundert im Spannungsfeld von Krone und Staat, Macht und Amt', in Wolfgang Wiese and Katrin Rössler (eds.), *Repräsentation im Wandel* (Ostfildern, 2008), pp. 36–37; Heinz Gollwitzer, 'Die Endphase der Monarchie in Deutschland', in Heinz Gollwitzer, *Weltpolitik und deutsche Geschichte*, ed. Hans-Christof Kraus (Göttingen, 2008), pp. 367–369.

[7] Weigand, 'Die konstitutionelle Monarchie', pp. 37–38; Hans-Michael Körner, 'Die Monarchie im 19. Jahrhundert. Zwischen Nostalgie und wissenschaftlichem Diskurs', in Winfried Müller and Martina Schattkowsky (eds.), *Zwischen Tradition und Modernität. König Johann von Sachsen 1801–1873* (Leipzig, 2004), pp. 26–27; Ernst Rudolf Huber, *Deutsche Verfassungsgeschichte*, vol. 3 (Stuttgart, 1963), pp. 20–22.

[8] 'Monarchen brauchen Mehrheiten', from Friedrich Naumann, 'Monarchie und Demokratie' (1912), in Friedrich Naumann, *Werke*, vol. 2 (Cologne and Opladen, 1964), p. 443.

marked the first step, and not just chronologically. 'Constitution' had served as a potent incantation at the beginning of the century, and for many crowns the ostensibly magic powers of this concept now seemed indispensable. In 1814, when the Bourbon king Louis XVIII, younger brother of Louis XVI, who had been beheaded in 1793, returned to France, he presented himself to the French nation not only as rightful king by the grace of God but also as 'consummator of the Revolution'. As such, he ratified the nation's attainments since 1789, issuing a constitution that provided for an elected parliament and guaranteed civil liberties. According to Dieter Langewiesche, contemporaries recognised this as the 'monarch's pact with reform', as a 'revolution in its true sense', and thus as a 'promise to the nation to provide it with the reforms that the times demanded but without endangering order'.[9]

Although of indisputably fundamental importance, constitutionalism was only one sphere in which monarchs worked to establish a leading position; they sought a similar role when it came to national identity, imperial power and military strength and in embodying a social morality.

Even at an early stage, Europe's rulers succeeded in defusing the contradiction between the emergent ideology of nationalism and the dynastic principle. The monarchies of the Ancien Régime had been created through inheritance, conquest, purchase and land exchange. They were identified with the legal norms these processes represented. The often scattered, heterogeneous and loosely integrated territories produced by these means of acquisition now confronted the 'nation', a political and cultural concept that required commonality and cohesiveness as well as uniformity in language, culture, religion and politics. The nation, which rapidly pushed all other reference points to the margins, was invested with certain rights, and the defence of national interests gradually became the key task for any form of legitimate government. The monarchies were forced back to the drawing board. Dynastic ambitions were replaced by national goals, which the crowns proved remarkably skilled at pursuing. The more nationalism established itself as an essential and unassailable independent political force over the course of the nineteenth century, the more willing monarchs grew to wrap themselves in the national flag and act as representative-in-chief of the nation. In the vanguard was the British king George III (1738–1820), who sought to ensure that the royal house was identified with the achievements

---

[9] 'Über Verfassungsvertrag, Verfassungsformen und die Würksamkeit ständischer Versammlungen', in *Rheinische Blätter* no. 154, 27 September 1817, p. 638; Dieter Langewiesche, 'Die Monarchie im Europa des bürgerlichen Jahrhunderts. Das Königreich Württemberg', in Landesmuseum Württemberg (ed.), *Monarchie und Moderne* (Stuttgart, 2006), p. 26.

of the nation. At the end of his decades-long reign, which climaxed with the victorious campaign against Napoleonic France and thus with the successful defence of British liberty and exceptionality, the monarch underwent national deification. In the festivities marking his Golden Jubilee in 1809 and in the mourning that accompanied his death eleven years later, the nation celebrated its freedom and the triumph over what was understood as the military despotism of the French emperor. As the irreproachable head of a large family and located at the heart of a carefully staged display of magnificence, 'our Georgie' became the touchstone for the nation. 'How are we to manifest our patriotism?' the Reverend Henry Gauntlett asked his congregation in October 1809, 'Surely, my friends, one principal mode of proving its reality is to pray for our King.'[10]

The monarchs on the European continent also resolutely grasped the coattails of nationalism – which had once powerfully buttressed the throne of their greatest adversary, Emperor Napoleon. The reason is not hard to detect: by embracing the idea of the nation, the crowns ensured that nationalists could also be monarchists. According to Minister Élie Decazes, on Louis XVIII's return to France in 1814, the king's prime intention was 'to make the nation royal and to make what is royal national'. That idea took off on both sides of the Rhine. In 1840, when, in response to French ambitions to win back the Rhine border, nationalism flared up in Germany, the crowned heads had no intention of turning away from the flames. The 'Rhine Song Movement' (*Rheinliedbewegung*) ensued, during which thousands of Germans raised their voices in a patriotic chorus. Nikolaus Becker, whose stirring poem 'They Shall Not Have It, the Free, German Rhine' made him the man of the moment, received extraordinary royal recognition: Friedrich Wilhelm IV of Prussia granted the Rhenish wordsmith an honorary pension for life. Ludwig I, king of Bavaria (1786–1868), presented him with a precious cup; in return, in his letter of thanks the honouree lauded Ludwig as 'the staunch protector of what is it to be German'. The creation of unified national states in Italy in 1861 and in Germany ten years later was celebrated above all as the achievement of the foremost dynasties. King Vittorio Emanuele II (1820–1878) of the House of Savoy became 'the father of the fatherland'. Similarly, in an allusion to the legendary

[10] W. M. Spellman, *Monarchies 1000–2000* (London, 2001), p. 209; Volker Sellin, *Gewalt und Legitimität. Die europäische Monarchie im Zeitalter der Revolutionen* (Munich, 2011), p. 217; Hagen Schulze, *Staat und Nation in der europäischen Geschichte* (Munich, 1994), p. 208; Linda Colley, 'The Apotheosis of George III: Loyalty, Royalty and the British Nation 1760–1820', in *Past & Present* 102 (1984), pp. 102, 121, 124–125; Volker Sellin, 'Die Nationalisierung der Monarchie', in Benjamin Hasselhorn and Marc von Knorring (eds.), *Vom Olymp zum Boulevard. Die europäischen Monarchien von 1815 bis heute – Verlierer der Geschichte?* (Berlin, 2018), pp. 241–253.

medieval emperor Frederick Barbarossa, the Red Beard, the aged
Hohenzollern emperor Wilhelm I (1797–1888) was adorned with the
honorary title 'Barbablanca', or White Beard, celebrating that he had
fulfilled an ancient yearning by awakening German glory from its
slumber.[11]

Throughout Europe, dynasty and nation came together. Monarchs
performed as the symbolic heart of the nation in elaborately staged
national pageants. In June 1867, the Austrian emperor, Franz Joseph
(1830–1916), was crowned king of Hungary in a splendid ceremony
lasting several days. A coronation mound was raised specifically for the
occasion, with farmers from all the provinces of Hungary each contributing a cubic foot of soil. After Franz Joseph had been anointed, he received
the crown of St Stephen. He then vowed to uphold the constitution and
rode up onto the mound to draw the Sword of St Stephen. 'High it flashed
in his raised fist and the anointed arm directed four thrusts to the four
regions of the world', reported the *Pester Lloyd* from the Hungarian
capital, 'and now the enthusiasm of the people no longer knew any
bounds. The tumultuous shouts of rejoicing roared out to the monarch
without ceasing.' The mood was similar when, in 1887, the English queen
Victoria celebrated her Golden Jubilee. 'Not London alone, but all
England transformed itself for the time into a huge Court at which the
nation and empire rendered fealty to its Sovereign', the London *Times*
declared at the end of the festivities.[12]

The example of the British queen receiving homage from nation and
empire shows that the monarchs of nineteenth-century Europe proved
their legitimacy not just by means of constitutionalism or nationalism but
also through their contribution to the imperial ambitions of state and
society. Amongst the dignitaries who filled Westminster Abbey in 1887 to
honour the woman who had also borne the title 'Empress of India' for
a decade, the reporter for the *Times* recognised 'Asiatic princes gleaming
with jewels, forms and faces as fair as they were Royal and noble'. David
Cannadine reminds us that here 'an imperialized monarchy merged with
and moulded a monarchicalized Empire'. Benjamin Disraeli, the British
Prime Minister and architect of Victoria's elevation to Empress of India,

[11] Sellin, *Gewalt und Legitimität*, p. 217; Heinz Gollwitzer, *Ludwig I. von Bayern. Eine
politische Biographie* (Munich, 1997), p. 637; Otto Hintze, *Die Hohenzollern und ihr
Werk 1415–1915. Fünfhundert Jahre vaterländische Geschichte*, 5th edn (Berlin, 1915),
p. 520; Frank-Lothar Kroll, 'Zwischen europäischem Bewußtsein und nationaler
Identität. Legitimationsstrategien monarchischer Eliten des 19. und frühen 20.
Jahrhunderts', in Hans-Christof Kraus and Thomas Nicklas (eds.), *Geschichte der
Politik. Alte und neue Wege* (Munich, 2007), pp. 360–366.
[12] Michaela Vocelka and Karl Vocelka, *Franz Joseph I. Kaiser von Österreich und König von
Ungarn, 1830–1916* (Munich, 2015), pp. 203–204; *The Times* of 22 June 1887.

had already promoted the ties between national pride, empire and monarchy in his celebrated speech given at the Crystal Palace in 1872: 'I say with great confidence that the great body of the working class of England [...] are for maintaining the greatness of the kingdom and the empire, and they are proud of being subjects of our Sovereign and members of such an Empire.' Indian princes and the Queen of Hawaii took part in the Jubilee procession in 1887, honouring the 'Mother of the Empire' and embodying the imperial relationship that bound her oversees subjects to the queen and empress. At the same time, the spectacle strengthened the pride of eager onlookers within the Mother Country in the powerful colonial empire over which the Union Jack flew – it spanned six lakes named after Victoria, two Victoria Capes, the Victoria Falls on the Zambesi, the Victoria Nile in Uganda and the Australian Colony of Victoria.[13]

The German longing for colonial power and a place in the sun was similarly displayed in Emperor Wilhelm II (1859–1941). With his loud enthusiasm for the navy, his restlessly energetic omnipresence and his self-confident insistence on Germany's imperial interests, the last Hohenzollern emperor offered, as Rüdiger vom Bruch has noted, a unique proposition – the 'Prussified anointing of the young nation state with ambitions for global power'. The monarch thus answered the contemporary need so clearly expressed in Max Weber's oft-quoted inaugural lecture of 1895, in which he called for the unification of Germany to become the 'point of departure for a policy of German world power'. Five years later Friedrich Naumann linked this aspiration directly to the German emperor: 'In no other area is the will of the emperor so clear, so absolutely historically necessary to his whole nation as in this one. With his thoughts on the navy he will prevail, thus he will become the tutor of the nation', he stated in his handbook *Demokratie und Kaisertum* (*Democracy and the Imperial Idea*). Perspicacious contemporaries had already noted that with his advocacy of a forceful German imperialism Wilhelm II was feeding a contemporary appetite – or was even a product of that craving. Looking back, in 1919 Walther Rathenau observed that 'these people at this time consciously and unconsciously

---

[13] *The Times* of 22 June 1887; T. E. Kebbel (ed.), *Selected Speeches of the Late Right Honourable the Earl of Beaconsfield*, vol. II (London, 1882), p. 528; David Cannadine, *Ornamentalism: How the British Saw Their Empire* (London, 2001), pp. 101–120; Jane Ridley, *Victoria: Queen, Matriarch, Empress* (London, 2015), p. 110; Duncan Bell, 'The Idea of a Patriot Queen? The Monarchy, the Constitution and the Iconographic Order of Greater Britain, 1860–1900', in *The Journal of Imperial and Commonwealth History* 34 (2006), pp. 3–22.

wanted him as he was, and not otherwise, and they themselves wanted to be as he was, and not otherwise.'[14]

Such goodwill was not only enjoyed by the monarchs of the great powers, which forcefully pursued their imperial ambitions, but also coloured perceptions of the rulers of the smaller European states. In the summer of 1900, Prince Valdemar (1858–1939), a naval officer and son of the Danish king Christian IX (1818–1906), returned from an extended tour aboard the corvette *Valkyrie*, a world trip extensively covered by the press. In Copenhagen, he was enthusiastically welcomed home by thousands of spectators. Henrik Cavling, a journalist who had accompanied him, had predicted at their departure that the prince's undertaking would 'bring certain advantages for a small and peaceable land'. He noted that 'European governors and native princes' would lay on 'oriental festivities' in Valdemar's honour and thereby serve 'civil interests'. In July 1900, Cavling, writing for the *Politiken* newspaper, covered the magnificent reception for the prince laid on by the Danish capital: 'No emperor has ever on his arrival brought more people onto the promenade at Toldboden', for the people had recognised, he wrote, that Prince Valdemar 'has been of the greatest possible service to the country that can or should be obtained from a royal house, by representing the country in distant lands'.[15]

The Spanish king Alfonso XIII (1886–1941) also capitalised on imperial possibilities, but the role he constructed was far more militaristic than was the Danish venture. Alfonso XIII had exhibited an early interest in events in Morocco, and in 1909 he travelled to North Africa, the first Spanish ruler to do so since the sixteenth century. Wearing the uniform of a captain general, he inspected Spanish troops in the field who were fighting against the local Berber tribe, and he subsequently championed officers who had served to extend Spanish rule in North Africa. On his return, Alfonso, too, was celebrated by his people. The president of the Spanish Senate compared him to the legendary Emperor Charles V (1500–1558), on whose empire the sun had never set, and paid tribute to him by bestowing the title 'Don Alfonso el Africano'.[16]

---

[14] Schulze, *Staat und Nation in der europäischen Geschichte*, pp. 262–263; Rüdiger vom Bruch, 'Kaiser und Bürger. Wilhelminismus als Ausdruck kulturellen Umbruchs um 1900', in Rüdiger vom Bruch, *Bürgerlichkeit, Staat und Kultur im Kaiserreich. Ausgewählte Aufsätze* (Stuttgart, 2015), pp. 25, 30; Friedrich Naumann, *Demokratie und Kaisertum. Ein Handbuch für innere Politik* (Berlin, 1900), pp. 213–214.

[15] *Politiken* of 13 October 1899 and 22 July 1900; Miriam Schneider, *The 'Sailor Prince' in the Age of Empire: Creating a Monarchical Brand in Nineteenth-Century Europe* (London, 2017), pp. 17, 242. I am grateful to Miriam Schneider for the reference for Prince Valdemar.

[16] Carolyn P. Boyd, 'El rey-soldado. Alfsonso XIII y el ejercito', in Javier Moreno Luzón (ed.), *Alfonso XIII. Un politico en el trono* (Madrid, 2003), p. 221; Javier Moreno Luzón, 'Alfonso *el Regenerador. Monarquía escénica e imaginario nacionalista español*, en

When King Vittorio Emanuele III of Italy ordered the invasion of Libya, a Turkish province at the time, he too received the enthusiastic endorsement of his people. On 19 September 1911, after a nationalist propaganda campaign had depicted Libya as a land flowing with milk and honey whose Arab population would welcome the Italians as their liberators, the usually somewhat cautious and sceptical king declared war on the Ottoman Empire. The monarch had finally been convinced, reported Gioacchino Volpe, that Italy must resist the encirclement by other powers on the Mediterranean. Additionally, Volpe noted, the king had been pleased to have an opportunity to raise the morale of the army. The public were promised a speedy victory, with little or no cost in Italian lives. The rejoicing was great. Nationalist and Catholic newspapers as well as the government-controlled press pushed for a bold intervention that would forestall a possible French annexation of Tripoli. Liberal politicians and even several socialists joined in with the imperialist enthusiasm. 'Not more than fifty years after it reawakened into life', declared the poet Giovanni Pascoli in a widely distributed speech after Italian troops had invaded Libya, 'Italy, the great martyr amongst the nations, has performed its duty and has contributed to the progress and the civilisation of the people, and has asserted its right not to be corralled and suffocated behind its own coasts.' In October 1912, the Ottoman Empire agreed a peace and withdrew its troops from Libya, which effectively fell to Italy.[17]

The fighting in North Africa was brutal, with cruelties perpetrated by both sides. In spite of this ruthlessness, the Libyan experience drew numerous Italian intellectuals to a phenomenon that also benefited the monarchs – militarism. 'I have come to the firm conviction that Italy can only say that it has avenged one and a half millennia of shameful history and can face the future with confidence when it has achieved a manly victory by its people over an enemy, whatever enemy that may be', wrote the historian Giustino Fortunato in November 1912. 'For the first time in my life I have a perception of the sanctity of war.'[18] Monarchies would profit from such sentiments, for the crowns' embodiment and representation of military power struck a chord of the age. The monarchs

---

perspectiva comparada', in *Hispania* LXXIII (2013), p. 339. I am grateful to Richard Meyer Forsting for the reference for Alfonso XIII.

[17] Denis Mack Smith, *Italy and Its Monarchy* (New Haven, CT and London, 1989), pp. 182–191; Christopher Duggan, *The Force of Destiny: A History of Italy since 1796* (London, 2007), pp. 381–384; Andrea Ungari, 'The Role of the Monarchy in the War in Libya', in Luca Micheletta and Andrea Ungari (eds.), *The Libyan War 1911–1912* (Cambridge, 2013), p. 37; Martin Clark, *Modern Italy 1871–1982* (London, 1984), pp. 153–156.

[18] Duggan, *The Force of Destiny*, p. 384.

successfully adapted the archaic role of the ruler as warrior and military commander to the demands of an era identified with constitutions, mass armies, complex military technology and a growing public for mass communications.

The triumphal march of nationalism in the nineteenth century meant that societies and states sought to assert their often-aggressive foreign policy interests by military means – or at least by threatening their deployment. Soon a phenomenon that Johannes Paulmann described as a 'valorisation of matters military' became apparent. Thanks to their traditional role at the head of the army and their close association with armed power, monarchs could easily translate this valorisation into a confirmation of their own role, for they were the visible embodiment of national military power.[19] On commemorative postcards printed in 1912, Vittorio Emanuele III was depicted hovering above an angel of victory, even though he had barely been actively involved in the leadership of the Italian campaign in Libya. Many nineteenth-century monarchs presented themselves similarly to their people: they were the fathers of their nations, constitutionally ratified, and they successfully championed the interests of the fatherland both at home and overseas – almost always in uniform and, if necessary, at the head of the army.

Monarchs reaped the benefits of this role above all because they did not hide the light of their political achievements under a bushel, regardless of whether it actually burned bright or was little more than a dim flicker. They proved shrewd strategists when it came to self-promotion and made skilful use of a range of media – initially, coins, proclamations, ceremonials, monuments, paintings and engravings; later, newspapers, photographs, walkabouts and even moving images. Moreover, they were now prepared to travel, and to appear to their subjects away from the court, surrounded by the sounds of patriotism. As a new mass market for communication approached, they had to find a way of responding to its demands, indeed of using it in their favour. Presenting a *bella figura* and charming various publics would help the crowns hold their ground through the course of the century. Now that the monarchs' work was understood as a public business, they needed to blow their own trumpet – ideally as loudly and melodically as possible.

---

[19] Dieter Langewiesche, 'Nation, Nationalismus, Nationalstaat. Forschungsstand und Forschungsperspektiven', in *Neue Politische Literatur* 40 (1995), pp. 205–210; Dieter Langewiesche, 'Nationalismus im 19. und 20. Jahrhundert. Zwischen Partizipation und Aggression', in Dieter Langewiesche, *Nation, Nationalismus, Nationalstaat in Deutschland und Europa* (Munich, 2000), pp. 35–54; Johannes Paulmann, *Pomp und Politik. Monarchenbegegnungen in Europa zwischen Ancien Regime und Erstem Weltkrieg* (Paderborn, 2000), pp. 160–164.

The logic of this kind of music making dictated that princes had to extend their staging as leaders beyond the strictly political and military spheres. They also had to present themselves as paragons for society on account of their cultural activities, their philanthropy and their moral rectitude. Building on archetypes, sometimes 1,000 years old, of kings performing – and being depicted – as saviours of the poor, defenders of the faith and patrons of the arts, the monarchies of the nineteenth century developed a beguiling narrative that told of the all-encompassing virtue of the institution and appealed carefully to the inclinations of contemporaries. Nothing that Empress Eugénie, wife of Napoleon III, did was more celebrated in the press than her carefully staged visits to the cholera hospitals of Paris and Amiens in 1865 and 1866. Soon anecdotes were circulating that suffused the empress's actions with compassion: in Paris she had been delighted when a patient addressed her as 'sister'; in Amiens she had adopted two cholera orphans; and when a senior officer had advised her against such dangerous visits, Eugénie had supposedly interrupted him to state, 'Marshall, this is how we go into battle.'[20]

Expressions of princely virtue did not always involve such courage. 'I would not be a scion of the art-loving House of Wittelsbach, which everywhere or almost everywhere that it has ruled has left evidence of its support for the arts', declared Prince Ludwig (1845–1921), heir to the Bavarian throne, in the Bavarian chamber in April 1890, 'I would not be the grandson of the unforgettable King Ludwig I, rejuvenator of German art, I would not be the son of the keen friend and promotor of art and artists, His Royal Highness the Prince Regent, if I were not to greet with joy all that is intended to promote art.'[21] Almost all members of ruling houses in the nineteenth century joined this son of the Wittelsbach dynasty in vaunting their family's venerable cultural, charitable and moral traditions, which continued into the present. They also sought to justify their place at the apex of nation, state and increasingly bourgeois-dominated society by staging themselves as the most brilliant stars within the firmament of bourgeois values.

The crisis of legitimation facing monarchies as a result of the French Revolution and the waning belief in divine right was not easy to resolve. The need to win over those majorities was a considerable challenge for princes and their successors and led them into uncharted waters. That Prince Ludwig of Bavaria, subsequently King Ludwig III, voiced his paean to his dynasty's cultural commitment in parliament, and indeed

[20] Matthew Truesdell, *Spectacular Politics: Louis-Napoleon Bonaparte and the 'Fête Imperiale', 1849–1870* (New York and Oxford, 1997), pp. 121–135.
[21] J. M. Forster, *Ludwig. Königlicher Prinz von Bayern* (Munich, 1894), p. 54.

as a member of that parliament, is no coincidence. The setting is indicative of an obstacle that had to be surmounted if monarchy was to survive: the transition to the constitutional state.

'For the Sovereigns There Is No Longer Any Other Way': Monarchy Turns Constitutional

Soon after the outbreak of the Franco-German war of 1870–1871, it became apparent that one consequence of the bloody conflict would be the formation of a German constitutional nation-state under Prussian leadership. The Prussian crown prince, Friedrich Wilhelm (1831–1888), sought to familiarise himself – with a certain degree of self-assurance – with the role for which he seemed destined. He would fulfil the needs of this new age, he confided to his diary in March 1871, for he believed he was the first prince to appear before his people 'unreservedly and faithfully devoted to the institutions of the constitution'.[22] The future German emperor Friedrich III thus documented his intention to assimilate himself to the institutional framework that had most significantly transformed the European monarchies since the time of Napoleon and had recently also arrived in Prussia – constitutionalism.

The beginnings of monarchical constitutionalism – the form of constitutionalism that became established throughout almost all of Europe in the course of the nineteenth century – can be dated to the constitutional decree of King Louis XVIII (1755–1824) of France. The Bourbon king, who left his English exile in 1814 to return home after the defeat of Napoleon, rejected the constitution formulated by the French Senate before his arrival but consented to the decree known as the 'Charter'. The text still proclaimed divine-right kingship and conferred sovereignty on the monarch alone. Additionally, however, the document took up the demands and achievements of the Revolutionary and Napoleonic eras, which were to be constructively integrated into the configuration of monarchical rule in the nineteenth century. 'We also believe', Louis declared in the preamble, 'that we must acknowledge the new circumstances that have brought forth this progress within bourgeois society, the direction they have given to the human spirit over the last half century, and the deep-seated changes that have resulted.'[23]

---

[22] Kaiser Friedrich III., *Das Kriegstagebuch von 1870/71*, ed. Heinrich Otto Meisner (Leipzig and Berlin, 1926), pp. 415f. (7 March 1871).

[23] Martin Kirsch, *Monarch und Parlament im 19. Jahrhundert. Der monarchische Konstitutionalismus als europäischer Verfassungstyp – Frankreich im Vergleich* (Göttingen, 1999), pp. 299–411; Dieter Gosewinkel and Johannes Masing (eds.), *Die Verfassungen in Europa 1789–1949* (Munich, 2006), p. 281.

The Charter launched a process that would eventually be realised in almost all European states in the course of the nineteenth century: the transition from absolutist princely rule to a system of constitutional monarchy. The power of the ruler was thus limited by statute and tied to the cooperation of other organs of the state – in particular to elected popular representative assemblies. Additionally, constitutions guaranteed central basic rights and civil liberties. Sometimes monarchies did not respond quickly enough to demands for constitutionally framed progress, and reforms were introduced only when revolutionary pressure had built up or had already been released. In 1830, the July Revolution in Paris forced an end to Bourbon rule and brought in the 'July Monarchy' of King Louis Philippe (1773–1850). This transition was accompanied by a revision of the constitution and an expanded franchise. Soon after, constitutions were introduced in Braunschweig, Saxony and Hanover, while Britain witnessed constitutional reform and the expansion of the franchise. The Europe-wide revolutions of 1848–1849 produced short-lived republics in France, Venice, the Palatinate and the Grand Duchy of Baden, but in many other places, they were the impetus for a broader and sustained thrust towards constitutionalism. It was then that the monarchies in Prussia and Piedmont-Sardinia and also temporarily in Austria entered the constitutional age.

Sooner or later, and driven to varying degrees by public opinion, the monarchical states on the continent were modernised as the century progressed. Princely rule was repeatedly reconfigured in constitutional terms – in a process that was largely peaceful and orderly. Monarchs often portrayed themselves as the fathers of the constitution and as august guarantors of the rights it enshrined. As can be seen in Figure 2, one year after the constitutional decree of 26 May 1818, the 'grateful estates' of Bavaria had a coin struck in honour of King Maximilian I Joseph (1756–1825), to commemorate the granting of the *Charta Magna Bavariae*. Numerous monuments were erected within the kingdom to keep alive the memory of that royal act. Additionally, Maximilian's successors, the kings Ludwig I and Ludwig II (1845–1886), deployed consummate dynastic public relations to ensure that the good deed would not be forgotten. Their efforts paid off. In March 1891, on the occasion of a celebration to mark the seventieth birthday of Luitpold, the Bavarian prince regent (1821–1912), the mayor of Nuremberg, Otto von Stromer, looked back with gratitude at the achievements of the Bavarian royal house: 'Do we not have His Majesty King Maximilian I to thank for our constitution, which remains binding today, which is splendidly composed and whose principal intent is to offer what the Bavarian people want?', he asked in the presence of the Bavarian heir to the throne. According to the report that appeared

Figure 2. 'To the Giver of the Constitution [, from] Bavaria's Grateful Estates, 26 May 1829': like many other European monarchs, King Maximilian I Joseph of Bavaria allowed himself to be venerated as the generous father of the constitution and as guarantor of the freedoms enshrined in it. Wikimedia Commons Berlin-George CC https://com mons.wikimedia.org/wiki/File:Medal_Bavarian_Constitution_1819,_ obv.jpg. CC BY-SA 4.0 and Wikimedia Commons Berlin-George CC https://commons.wikimedia.org/wiki/File:Medal_Bavarian_Constitut ion_1819,_rev.jpg. CC BY-SA 4.0.

in the *Münchner Neueste Nachrichten*, Stromer's speech was followed by jubilant applause.[24]

Such celebrated monarchical–constitutional decrees had frequently been the basis for the reconciliation of crown and nation in the early nineteenth century: they answered the call for reform while also ensuring the peace and order that were so necessary after decades of war. Here lie the origins of the 'monarchical principle', which in the course of the century became a political rallying cry. This classic formulation conceived the entirety of the power of the state to be located in the sacrosanct and inviolable person of the monarch, who – in accord with the relevant constitutional agreement – undertook to exercise that power only in cooperation with other organs of the constitution. While the powers of the crown remained considerable in several areas – as commander of the armed forces or in foreign policy, for example – the very notion of

---

[24] Frank Lorenz Müller, *Royal Heirs in Imperial Germany: The Future of Monarchy in Nineteenth-Century Bavaria, Saxony and Württemberg* (London, 2017), pp. 141–142; *Münchner Neueste Nachrichten* of 13 March 1891.

a constitutional system implied an incontrovertible curb on monarchical power, a limitation that tended to grow over the years.[25] After the transition to the constitutional state in 1814, the king of France's exercise of executive power required the cooperation of the relevant ministers, while legislation and allocations from the public purse depended on the agreement of the elected parliament. Additionally, the Charter and subsequent European constitutions affirmed the basic rights of the subjects, another significant legacy of the Enlightenment and the Revolutionary era. This constitutional decree of 1814, the historian Volker Sellin has proposed, launched a dynamic process that would leave its mark on the monarchies of Europe for the next 100 years. Sellin writes of a 'century of restorations', during which monarchical rule was repeatedly re-established and re-legitimised from above by means of constitutional reforms that responded to the specific demands of the moment. This kind of 'restoration' should not be understood as a reactionary attempt to rewind the clock, perhaps using force, to return to a *status quo ante*. Rather, these repeated restorations sought to ensure that, while power would indeed remain formally with the monarch, a legally confirmed right to political participation would be extended to ever broader strata of the population. The assertion of monarchical sovereignty thus went hand in hand with homage to the revolution. The changes associated with constitutional solutions were less dramatic than revolutionary upheaval and also proved longer lasting.[26]

The monarchs' generally consistent – if sometimes grudging – willingness to make concessions meant, as Sellin has noted, that the chasm between the monarchical and democratic principles began to narrow. These endeavours at restoration were not one-time events but formed steps in a continuous policy of reform. The letter of the constitutional text usually remained almost entirely unaltered after it had been codified. Such was the case, for example, for the constitutions of Bavaria and Württemberg, which had been inspired by the Charter, and for the *Statuto Albertino* of 1848, the constitution of Piedmont, which would subsequently serve as the constitution of the Kingdom of Italy. The constitutional realities, however, steadily and patently changed with the times. When King Ludwig III of Bavaria,

---

[25] Volker Sellin, 'Die Erfindung des monarchischen Prinzips. Jacques-Claude Beugnots Präambel zur *Charte Constitutionelle*', in Armin Heinen and Dietmar Hüsen (eds.), *Tour de France. Eine historische Rundreise. Festschrift für Rainer Hudemann* (Stuttgart, 2008), pp. 489–497.

[26] Volker Sellin, 'Restorations and Constitutions', in Kelly L. Grotke and Markus J. Prutsch (eds.), *Constitutionalism, Legitimacy, and Power* (Oxford, 2014), p. 91; Volker Sellin, *Das Jahrhundert der Restaurationen. 1814–1906* (Munich, 2014), p. 139.

Wilhelm II (1848–1921) of Württemberg and Vittorio Emanuele III of Italy ruled at the end of the nineteenth and the beginning of the twentieth centuries, the constitutional basis of their rule had remained unchanged. Yet all three monarchs understood their roles very differently from their much more autocratic predecessors two generations earlier, Ludwig I (1786–1868), Wilhelm I (1781–1864) and Vittorio Emanuele II (1820–1878). Several prominent exceptions prove the rule of the advancing process of Europe's explicit or silent monarchical constitutionalisation – the 'Swan King' Ludwig II of Bavaria, for example, or Willem III of the Netherlands (1817–1890), dubbed 'King Gorilla', or Emperor Wilhelm II, whose comparison to Caligula in a pamphlet that appeared only a few years after he had ascended the throne caused great public commotion. Significantly, these neo-absolute or backwards-looking rulers struck their contemporaries as scandalous, threatening or mentally ill, and certainly not fit for the modern age.[27]

Evidently, these black sheep failed when it came to meeting what would emerge as the public's central requirement for a European sovereign – that the monarch be a good constitutional ruler. What this meant can be gleaned from the obituary for King Karl I (1823–1891) that appeared in the *Staats-Anzeiger für Württemberg* in October 1891. His constitutional sensitivities were cited as part of his 'noble virtues of a ruler' – 'the king abided loyally by the constitution, this secure bond that always unites the prince and the people of Württemberg', extolled the official gazette. For the ruler to have a friendly attitude towards elected representatives of the people was better still: the obituary also noted that 'throughout the whole of his reign, a beautiful relationship of undiluted harmony joined the king to parliament'.[28]

Nine years before his assassination, *L'Illustrazione Italiana* similarly celebrated King Umberto as a 'model constitutional monarch'. 'From him emanated the most profound and absolute devotion to the institutions of the fatherland', and the essence of the modern constitution was, the newspaper reported, well-nigh 'etched in his soul'. The following year, Catalan architect José Grases i Riera composed a memorandum on the erection of a monument to Spanish king Alfonso XII (1857–1885), who had died at the age of twenty-seven. This

---

[27] Sellin, *Das Jahrhundert der Restaurationen*, pp. 139–140; Heinz Häfner, *Ein König wird beseitigt. Ludwig II. von Bayern* (Munich, 2008); Sicco Ernst Willem Roorda van Eysinga, *Uit het leven van Koning Gorilla* (The Hague, 1888), pp. 1–91; Coenraad A. Tamse, 'König Wilhelm III. und Sophie', in Coenraad A. Tamse (ed.), *Nassau und Oranien. Staathalter und Könige der Niederlande* (Göttingen and Zurich, 1985), pp. 308–328; Martin Kohlrausch, *Der Monarch im Skandal. Die Logik der Massenmedien und die Transformation der wilhelminischen Monarchie* (Berlin, 2005), pp. 118–154.

[28] *Staats-Anzeiger für Württemberg* of 7 October 1891.

sovereign, whose reign had been accompanied by hopes for peace, order and freedom, this cultivated, tolerant, liberal, indeed democratic man had embodied the fatherland, wrote Riera, as a 'constitutional king of the modern era'. The standards prescribed by this ideal increasingly tied the hands of heirs to the throne.[29]

It is hardly surprising that the idea of the model constitutional monarch – which says nothing about the reality of any individual monarch's attitude towards the constitution or parliament – was so widely celebrated. Its popularity was an almost inevitable consequence of the success of monarchical constitutionalism, understood as rule by an individual whose power was limited by (usually codified) law. In the course of the century, this political order emerged, in Martin Kirsch's phrase, as a 'European constitutional type'. Great Britain, where the constitutional containment of royal power had continued to advance after the Glorious Revolution of 1688, had previously been the exception. Now, in the course of the nineteenth century, almost all European monarchies followed in its tracks.

Monarchical constitutionalism usually developed in line with Sellin's model of restoration. The monarch approved a written constitutional agreement, securing his authority by submitting the exercise of his sovereign rights to conditions and limitations. By the time the Russian Empire eventually took its first step in this direction with the Fundamental Laws of 23 April 1906, the other European great powers had already been living in the constitutional age for a long time. The various French monarchies had given themselves constitutions in 1814, 1830 and 1851–1852, while the Austrian Habsburg dynasty had taken action in 1848, 1849, 1862 and 1867. Prussia or Germany adopted constitutions in 1848–1850, 1867 and 1871. Piedmont-Sardinia had been a constitutional state since 1848 and transferred its constitution to the Kingdom of Italy, united under its leadership, in 1861. Since its first constitution of 1808, Spain had seen a multitude of constitutions and revisions to existing constitutions (1812, 1834, 1837, 1845 and 1869), until a more enduring solution was found with the restoration of the monarchy under the constitution of 1876. And Europe's numerous smaller monarchies – from Bavaria in the years 1808–1818 to the newly founded principality of Bulgaria in 1879 – also embraced this development, almost without exception.[30]

[29] *L'Illustrazione Italiana* XXVII, no. 31, 5 August 1900; José Grases i Riera, *Memoria del anteproyecto de monumento que ha de erigirse en Madrid a la gloria del Rey Don Alfonso XII, el Pacificador* (Madrid, 1901), p. 7.
[30] Kelly L. Grotke and Markus J. Prutsch (eds.), *Constitutionalism, Legitimacy, and Power* (Oxford, 2014), pp. 3–19, 69–103; Werner Daum, Peter Brandt, Martin Kirsch and Arthur Schlegelmilch (eds.), *Handbuch der europäischen Verfassungsgeschichte im 19.*

Kirsch has attributed the success of this model to a 'functionalisation of the monarch'. Limited by the constitution, the royal ruler fulfilled a recognisable and practical function within the political system: as a font of national integration, as intermediary between competing parties, as a bulwark against excessive innovation. He could thus justify his existence – if he was successful. Royal rule in the nineteenth century was increasingly judged according to whether the man or woman on the throne accomplished the tasks that they had been assigned on behalf of state, nation and society. Recent research has scored the performance of the European monarchies rather highly. A number of historians have acknowledged that Europe's constitutional monarchs contributed considerably to solving significant problems, above all by completing the Revolution. This process proved broadly peaceful because many of its promises were honoured. In the post-revolutionary era, the crowns brought about significant political, legal and social reforms, such as the integration of new sections of the population into the political decision-making process, the realisation of national independence and the broadly peaceable transformation of Europe into a system of great powers.[31]

For Europe's crowned heads and for those in training for the monarchical role, the constitutionalisation of princely rule meant accepting a multitude of innovations. Even formalities left no room for doubt: a law of 17 March 1861 ensured that Vittorio Emanuele II of Piedmont-Sardinia accepted a dualistic legitimation of his status as king of Italy, with the wording of his title 'by the grace of God' now followed by 'and according to the will of the nation'.[32] Other changes were more tangible: the financing of the monarch's court now depended on the civil list granted by elected popular representation. If – as was the case at the accession of King Friedrich August III of Saxony in 1904 – the mood was testy and the topic fraught, requesting an increase in the sum established at the beginning of each new reign might not appear advisable. Parliament also had oversight of the funds raised through taxation, and the people's representatives could therefore derail a government initiative by tightening the purse strings. In the early 1860s, the liberal majority in the Prussian parliament refused to finance the military reforms sought by

---

Jahrhundert. Institutionen und Rechtspraxis im gesellschaftlichen Wandel, vol. 2: *1815–1847* (Bonn 2012), pp. 165–207.
[31] Martin Kirsch, 'Die Funktionalisierung des Monarchen im 19. Jahrhundert im europäischen Vergleich', in Stefan Fisch, Florence Gauzy and Chantal Metzger (eds.), *Machtstrukturen im Staat in Deutschland und Frankreich* (Stuttgart, 2007), pp. 87, 97; Langewiesche, 'Die Monarchie im Europa des bürgerlichen Jahrhunderts', pp. 26, 28.
[32] Gosewinkel and Masing (eds.), *Die Verfassungen in Europa*, p. 1373.

the king; in the political crisis that followed, King Wilhelm I came close to abdicating.[33]

Any monarch wishing to keep a hand on the helm of the ship of state could not decide the course at will but had to act within the limits set by the constitution. Willem II of the Netherlands, whose constitutional loyalty blew hot and cold, provided a wonderfully pithy formulation: 'One must step out boldly along the constitutional path', he is said to have declared at his accession in 1840, 'for sovereigns there is no longer any other way.' The implications were very real: monarchs now had to come to a political understanding with parliaments, for without the cooperation of parliament, the ministers appointed by the king would be hard pressed to govern. Monarchs were required to open parliamentary sessions and give the official opening speech from the throne. When they appointed their ministers, the rulers increasingly had to take account of public opinion, parliamentary majorities and election results. They had to attempt to cultivate a particular attitude for which the king of Württemberg was expressly praised in 1916: 'King Wilhelm never exercised personal politics or attempted to exercise them. He manoeuvred strictly within the boundaries of his constitutional status', judged no less a figure than Wilhelm Keil, leader of Württemberg's Social Democrats. Keil continued, 'In presenting himself to the public, he adopted the restraint that must be desired of the most senior servant of the state who is above all parties.'[34]

Not every ruler was able to accept the constitutionally required limitations with discernment and equanimity. King Ludwig I of Bavaria, son of Maximilian I Joseph, who had issued the Bavarian constitution of 1818, disdained the idea of a partnership between people and monarch. Government and leadership of the people were his alone, the king claimed, and he refused to allow the rights of the crown to be disturbed. Willem I, the first constitutional king of the Netherlands, had great difficulty reconciling himself to the realities created by the constitution of 24 August 1815, and in his conflicts with the chambers always held his royal rights to be both greater and older. In the early phase of her reign, Queen Victoria – with the support of her husband, Albert – was determined to deploy her monarchical powers aggressively and to defend them against any constraints. In the 1840s, she was certainly not going to

---

[33] Müller, *Royal Heirs in Imperial Germany*, pp. 32–35; Huber, *Deutsche Verfassungsgeschichte*, pp. 275–377; Otto Pflanze, *Bismarck and the Development of Germany*, vol. 1 (Princeton, NJ, 1990), pp. 164–217.

[34] H. T. Colenbrander (ed.), *Gedenkstukken der Algemeene Geschiedenis van Nederland van 1795 tot 1840*, Deel 10, vol. 3 (The Hague, 1920), p. 665, http://resources.huygens.knaw.nl/ged enkstukken (accessed 30 November 2016); 'Regierungsjubiläum', in *Schwäbische Tagwacht*, 5 October 1916.

content herself with the right to be consulted, the right to warn and the right to encourage, the three rights that Walter Bagehot famously recognised as still granted to the British monarch in the 1860s. King Friedrich Wilhelm IV of Prussia had decreed the constitution of his realm and affirmed it by oath, yet he still kept his distance: in his political testament he called on his successors to refuse to repeat that oath.[35]

In the course of the nineteenth century, constitutionalism outgrew many of its teething problems. Tellingly, none of Friedrich Wilhelm IV's successors on the Prussian throne followed the instruction contained in his political testament: Wilhelm I and then also Friedrich III and Wilhelm II all took the constitutional oath on their accessions, and Wilhelm II even destroyed his forefather's testament with his own hands in order to erase this embarrassing evidence of constitutional infidelity. Monarchical systems were able to develop a less antagonistic relationship with the constitution over time because the next generation of rulers had largely been socialised politically within the framework of the constitutional system while they were still heirs to the throne. Whether through repetition, conviction or resignation, they had come to terms with the situation and accepted that, if they were to rule, they could do so only as good constitutional rulers.

Royal heirs were still children or young adults when they first experienced the institutions of the constitutional state and the constitutional duties of the ruler. This usually happened when they accompanied the monarch to the opening of parliament or were present for the monarch's speech from the throne. The meticulously planned ceremony, its form dictated by published decree, with which the king of the Belgians opened parliament explicitly provided for the participation of his family. In 1847, the heir to the Belgian throne, the twelve-year-old Prince Leopold, rode with his father and namesake in the annual procession to the parliament. His own son having died young, King Leopold II would later be accompanied on this ride by his younger brother Philippe, as heir to the throne. Vittorio Emanuele, the Italian crown prince, was even younger when he was at the side of his father, King Umberto I, at the opening of parliament in Rome in February 1880. According to press reports, the ten-year-old

---

[35] Heinz Gollwitzer, 'Fürst und Volk. Betrachtungen zur Selbstbehauptung des bayerischen Herrscherhauses im 19. und 20. Jahrhundert', in *Zeitschrift für bayerische Landesgeschichte* 50 (1987), p. 731; Tamse, 'Die niederländische Monarchie', p. 115; David Cannadine, 'The Last Hanoverian Sovereign? The Victorian Monarchy in Historical Perspective, 1688–1888', in A. L. Beier, David Cannadine and James M. Rosenheim (eds.), *The First Modern Society: Essays in English History in Honour of Lawrence Stone* (Cambridge, 1989), pp. 127–165, 139–144; Walter Bagehot, *The English Constitution*, ed. Paul Smith (Cambridge, 2001), p. 60; Huber, *Deutsche Verfassungsgeschichte*, p. 165.

boy was met with great cheers both within the chamber and on the streets outside the parliament.[36] In most cases, the constitutions of the European monarchies provided for an even earlier and more fundamental connection between the heir to the throne and the new ordering of the state. Alongside the standard practice whereby the rules for accession to the throne – usually succession in the male line – were laid out in each constitutional text, the heir's future claim to the throne, and often the heir's current claim to an apanage too, were written into public law and confirmed alongside the civil liberties of the subjects. That accession to the throne was conditional and sanctions might be applied is demonstrated by the Spanish constitutions of 1837, 1845, 1869 and 1876. According to these texts, the parliament, the *Cortes*, was explicitly permitted to exclude from the succession individuals 'who are incapable of governing or have done something on account of which they deserve to lose the right to the crown'.[37] Succession to the throne outside the constitutional framework was thus inconceivable.

In general, however, the ties that developed in the nineteenth century between heirs to the throne and parliaments were more amicable than the articles of the Spanish constitutions suggest. In many constitutional monarchies, princes of the blood – and therefore the heirs to the throne – were entitled by birth to membership of the relevant first chamber of the parliament. In exercising this right, future monarchs participated as parliamentarians in law making. Such provisions existed in many German states – for example in Prussia, Bavaria, Württemberg, Saxony, Baden, Hessen-Darmstadt and Hanover – and also in Austria, France, Spain, Greece and Italy. In Belgium, the heir's involvement in parliamentary business was not limited to accompanying the king each year to the ceremonial opening of the parliament. Prince Leopold, the future King Leopold II, joined the Belgian Senate in April 1853, and by the time of his succession to the throne twelve years later, he had given more than a dozen speeches on trade and colonial policy. As a senator, he participated forcefully in debates and even interrupted speeches by ministers. Leopold's nephew Albert, the future King Albert I, was also a member of the Senate, from 1906 to 1909, where he gave speeches and participated in votes.[38]

[36] Gita Deneckere, 'The Impossible Neutrality of the Speech from the Throne: A Ritual between National Unity and Political Dispute. Belgium, 1831–1918', in Jeroen Deploige and Gita Deneckere (eds.), *Mystifying the Monarch: Studies on Discourse, Power, and History* (Amsterdam, 2006), pp. 208–209; *Illustrated London News*, 21 February 1880, p. 174.

[37] Gosewinkel and Masing (eds.), *Die Verfassungen in Europa*, pp. 555, 563, 582, 595.

[38] Veronique Laureys, 'Les princes de Belgique au Sénat', in *L'histoire du Sénat de Belgique de 1831 à 1995* (Brussels, 1999), pp. 292–309.

On becoming a member of the relevant chamber, the future monarch usually took an oath that bound him to the constitution of the nation long before his accession to the throne, which often involved a further constitutional oath. Thus after the French Revolution of 1830 and the subsequent creation of the July Monarchy under King Louis Philippe, the monarch's two oldest sons, the dukes of Chartres and Nemours, took the same oath as other members of the Chamber of Peers, solemnly swearing loyalty to the king and obedience to the *Charte Constitutionelle* and the laws of the land. In March 1887, when twenty-one-year-old Prince Friedrich August, the future king, became a member of the upper chamber in the Kingdom of Saxony, he swore 'to safeguard the constitution of the nation', an oath required of him by Paragraph 82 of that same constitution. Four years later, also aged twenty-one, on his admission to the Italian Senate in the presence of his royal father and watched by young Heloise from America, Vittorio Emanuele similarly pledged his loyalty to the constitution. In Württemberg the members of the chamber – and thus also the heir to the throne – even had to promise 'to keep the constitution sacred', while Hohenzollern princes who came of age and entered the Prussian upper house had to swear, along with their loyalty to the king, their 'diligent observation of the constitution'. In Bavaria, independently of any membership of parliament, when they came of age, all princes had to take an oath promising 'close observation of the constitution'.[39]

The existence of these regulations certainly did not mean that all crown princes felt bound to the principles and ideals of the constitutional state. Only a small number were enthusiastic about their work on parliamentary committees, with most avoiding the opportunity to embed themselves within the institutions of the constitutional state. By seizing this opportunity, however, a future ruler could earn public praise. At the accessions of Wilhelm II of Württemberg in 1891, Friedrich August of Saxony in 1904 and Ludwig III of Bavaria in 1912, the press praised the fact that, as heirs to the throne, each of these men had garnered valuable experience as parliamentarians. The Bavarian prince, in particular, one of the few heirs who performed his duties as a member of parliament with earnestness and commitment, was repeatedly lauded. Munich's *Volks-Zeitung* commended

---

[39] Session minutes: 'Chambre des Pairs. (Présidence de M. le baron Pasquier.) Séance publique du 9 août', in *Journal des Débats Politiques et Littéraires*, 10 August 1830, pp. 2–3; http://landt agsprotokolle.sachsendigital.de/protokolle/ansicht/20028441Z/10 (accessed 15 May 2022); www.documentarchiv.de/nzjh/verfsachsen.html (accessed 16 November 2016); 'Opening of Parliament at Rome', in *The Herald Democrat*, 14 July 1891, www.coloradohistoric newspapers.org/cgi-bin/colorado?a=d&d=THD18910714.2.24 (accessed 18 November 2016).

the 'praiseworthy and productive enthusiasm' with which the prince practised his 'parliamentary responsibilities as a member of the Bavarian
Chamber of *Reichsräte*'. The words of welcome spoken by the president
of the Saxon First Chamber to Crown Prince Georg when he became
a member of the parliament have a self-possession indicative of the significance ascribed to the institutions of the constitutional state for the training
of a future monarch. 'But we also allow ourselves to hope', declared
Friedrich Graf Vitzthum von Eckstädt after he had required both enthusiasm and interest of Georg, 'that the parliamentary activity in this Chamber
and the close contact established as a result with the honourable other
House [the elected Chamber] will have a part in preparing Your Royal
Highness for your lofty calling.'[40]

Acceptance of the importance of constitutions, familiarity with the
principles, processes and institutions of the constitutional state, even to
the extent of 'close contact' with the elected parliament, and a desire to
become a good constitutional monarch – these were all requirements of
the changed contexts of nineteenth-century monarchy. The next generation of monarchs had to grow up and prepare the future of their crowns
under these novel circumstances. The heir to the throne had to sport this
new, tightly cut constitutional coat, but below, closer to the skin, heirs
wore considerably older garb: they were swaddled in the authority
wielded by the head of the dynasty over the family. Often, this power
was laid down in a codification of the laws of the dynastic house.

'Familial Tyranny in Lieu of Absolutism': The Royal House

According to Romeo Maurenbrecher, who taught constitutional law at
Bonn University in the 1830s, the 'familial power of the ruler' amounted
to the 'the quintessence of those rights over all members of the family that
are due each monarch as head of the family'. This legal phenomenon had
two distinct roots. On the one hand, it grew out of the age of absolute
monarchy and meant, for example, that, having received the title of king
in 1701, the Prussian monarch could now exercise authority over his
family on the basis of his sovereignty: 'he viewed its members as his
subjects'. On the other hand, the princely family power reached still
further back. It referenced Roman law, the *patria potestas* – that is the
power exercised by the Roman father over his family. The purpose of this

---

[40] Müller, *Royal Heirs in Imperial Germany*, pp. 109–110; *Volks-Zeitung* (Munich) of 20/
21 February 1893; *Mittheilungen über die Verhandlungen des Landtags*, I. Kammer, 10.
Sitzung, 21 January 1914, http://digital.slub-dresden.de/id20028367Z/190 (accessed
18 November 2016).

oversight by the head of the family was, according to Hermann Schulze, another nineteenth-century jurist, 'to grant the king a decisive influence over the outward demeanour and conduct of those closest to the throne, in order that the dignity of the crown and the wellbeing of the state be upheld in every way and the so-necessary union and unity of the royal family also be maintained in their external appearance'.[41]

This 'mix of family authority and the authority of sovereignty', as Maurenbrecher termed it, produced a tight web of paternal jurisdictions over individual family members: oversight of their education, confirmation of their wardship, approval of their travel and acquisitions abroad and consent for their choice of spouse, without which their marriage would be invalid. Additionally, the head of family could act as a judge within the family, a role that included imposing punishments as well as issuing house rules, which contained measures to maintain the honour of the family as a whole. The Austrian 'Family Statute' of 1839, which brought together all the rules issued by the Habsburgs to date, was a particularly robust version of this patriarchal order. According to Paragraph 25, the head of the family had authority not only over the education and travel of family members but also over 'the creation of households for each individual member of the family' and the 'selection of their retinue, that is the people who will be closest to them'. Thus the emperor, who naturally controlled the finances of all members of his family, had the right to dictate whom his relatives would marry, where they would live and who might make up their staff. After a run of scandals and quarrels with Emperor Franz Joseph, Archduke Leopold Ferdinand of Austria–Tuscany formally left the imperial family in 1902, but then struggled to make a living in his new bourgeois existence, under the name Leopold Wölfling. Embittered, he recognised in the Family Statute and its application a 'familial tyranny in lieu of absolutism'.[42]

The provisions of the Habsburg Family Statute were by no means unusual. Bavaria's 'Royal Family Law' of 1816 similarly prohibited the princes of the House of Wittelsbach from marrying or travelling abroad

---

[41] Romeo Maurenbrecher, *Grundsätze des heutigen deutschen Staatsrechts*, 2nd edn (Frankfurt am Main, 1843), p. 474; Ferdinand von Prittwitz und Gaffron, *Die Königlichen Hausgesetze in Preußen* (dissertation) (Leipzig, 1908), pp. 19, 32; Hermann Schulze, *Die Hausgesetze der regierenden deutschen Fürstenhäuser*, vol. 3 (Jena, 1883), p. 614.

[42] Maurenbrecher, *Grundsätze des heutigen deutschen Staatsrechts*, pp. 474–475; 'Familienstatut (1839)', www.heraldica.org/topics/royalty/hg1839.htm#Familienstatut_1839 (accessed 21 November 2016); Matthias Stickler, 'Dynastie, Armee, Parlament. Probleme staatlicher Integrationspolitik im 19. Jahrhundert', in Winfried Müller and Martina Schattkowsky (eds.), *Zwischen Tradition und Modernität. König Johann von Sachsen 1801–1873* (Leipzig, 2004), p. 114.

without the permission of the king and reserved for the head of the family 'all measures that serve to maintain the peace, honour, order and well-being of the royal house'. The 'Royal Saxon House Law' of 1837 emphasised that 'all members of the royal house [...] are subject to the sovereignty [...] and legal powers of the king' and required the king's approval for the appointment of all court personnel. In the Kingdom of Württemberg, Wilhelm I issued a comprehensive 'Royal House Law' in 1826. It set out what constituted the 'highest oversight of the king', whose competences were similarly widely conceived, so that the selection of a spouse, the manner in which children were educated and any time spent abroad all required the king's approval.[43]

The exercise of 'familial authority' by the ruler as head of the family was ultimately not tied to the existence of codified house laws, which were most common in German-speaking Europe. No such legal foundations existed for the British royal family, for example, and yet Queen Victoria's position as sovereign and the conventional authority of the head of the family were entirely sufficient to secure her almost absolute authority over her family. The existence of a house law was not a necessary condition in Germany either. 'Even though these sovereign powers are not formulated in a modern house law in Prussia as is the case in the other constitutional German states', Hermann Schulze declared in 1883, 'it is undoubtedly proper for the king [of Prussia] to adopt all measures that serve to maintain the peace, honour, order and wellbeing of the royal house.' Schulze's characterisation of the monarch's authority over the members of the family as self-evident is a reminder that codified house laws were an innovation. Initiated by the Bavarian House Law of 1808 and increasingly found throughout Germany, these codifications were a reaction to the dissolution of the Holy Roman Empire in 1806, which ended the princely families' status as subordinate only to the Holy Roman Emperor. Moreover, the introduction of house laws was seen as supplementing the constitutions that were being enacted everywhere.[44]

Coercive and controlling royal fathers had certainly not been unknown in earlier centuries – we need think only of the bullying of the future King Friedrich II of Prussia by his father. Now that the monarch's familial power was formally enshrined, though, the phenomenon gained a new intensity, with which heirs to the throne had to come to terms. With an eye to developments at the beginning of the nineteenth century, legal historian Dorothee Gottwald has concluded that 'never before had the

---

[43] Hermann Schulze, *Die Hausgesetze der regierenden deutschen Fürstenhäuser*, vol. 1 (Jena, 1862), pp. 1, 323, 325, 326; Schulze, *Die Hausgesetze der regierenden deutschen Fürstenhäuser*, vol. 3, pp. 253–254, 513–514.
[44] Schulze, *Die Hausgesetze der regierenden deutschen Fürstenhäuser*, vol. 3, p. 614.

position of the head of the family in relation to family members been so strong'.[45]

We cannot be sure that the expansion of this patriarchal role and the often-strict exercise of monarchical oversight over lower-ranked family members was indeed, as Leopold Wölfling suggested with psychoanalytical overtones, a compensation for the monarchs' loss of absolute authority within the state. After all, the domineering father-ruler was not unknown to the age of absolutism. In the course of the nineteenth century, though, as the result of two interconnected developments, the ties that bound the heir to the institution of the royal family, with the monarch at its head, tightened in practice and were also perceived as more intense. First, each dynasty portrayed itself more strongly as a family in the bourgeois sense and was therefore obliged to adopt certain ideals and modes of behaviour. Secondly, the 'well-nigh ceaseless publicity of their existence', as Heinz Dollinger described it, meant that whether the royal family achieved these standards was now subjected to much more intensive external monitoring than ever before. After all, the 'principal requirement' the people set for their monarch, a report amongst the cabinet papers of the king of Bavaria noted, was that he must 'be visible'.[46]

The British journalist and economist Walter Bagehot penned a particularly trenchant analysis of the benefits which a monarchy might derive from the portrayal of its leading personalities as a family. 'A *family* on the throne is an interesting idea also', he ironically remarked in his famous study *The English Constitution*, published in the mid 1860s: 'It brings down the pride of sovereignty to the level of petty life.' Moments common to all families, events such as weddings and births, made people – and especially women – happy, and all the more so when they were 'brilliant'. Only a small number of cynics could ignore the magic of an appealing story, he proposed, which explains why the spectacle provided by the royal family could have such an effect: it 'sweetens politics by the seasonable addition of nice and pretty events'. For Queen Victoria, Bagehot's finding was nothing new. As early as 1844, with more than a touch of self-congratulation she had informed her uncle, the king of the Belgians, that the newspapers were reporting that 'no Sovereign was more

---

[45] Christopher Clark, 'Fathers and Sons in the History of the Hohenzollern Dynasty', in Frank Lorenz Müller and Heidi Mehrkens (eds.), *Sons and Heirs: Succession and Political Culture in Nineteenth-Century Europe* (Basingstoke, 2016), pp. 22–26; Dorothee Gottwald, *Fürstenrecht und Staatsrecht im 19. Jahrhundert. Eine wissenschaftsgeschichtliche Studie* (Frankfurt am Main, 2009), pp. 46–47.

[46] Heinz Dollinger, 'Das Leitbild des Bürgerkönigtums in der europäischen Monarchie des 19. Jahrhunderts', in Karl F. Werner (ed.), *Hof, Kultur und Politik im 19. Jahrhundert* (Bonn, 1985), p. 336; Anja Schöbel, *Monarchie und Öffentlichkeit. Zur Inszenierung der deutschen Bundesfürsten 1848–1918* (Cologne, Weimar and Vienna, 2017), p. 75.

loved than I am'. And she believed she knew the reason for this agreeable state of affairs: it stemmed 'from our happy domestic home – which gives such a good example'.[47]

By referencing her family idyll, Victoria evoked, with good reason, her grandfather King George III, who had died in 1820; the king's virtues as a husband and caring father had earned him great sympathy from the English people. The origins of the staging of a happy, bourgeois family life reached back to the eighteenth century on the other side of the Channel too. The carefully cultivated story of King Friedrich Wilhelm III (1770–1840) of Prussia, the head of a wholesome family who enjoyed an idyllic family life at the palace and estate of Paretz, with his wife, Luise, and their eight children, found a receptive audience. In 1798, the Romantic poet Friedrich von Hardenberg, known as Novalis, commented: 'The more the royal house, suffused with the value of true domesticity, raises it up to the rare height of the throne, the more the great family of the people recognises itself in this image [...] and unites in ever greater strength to protect it.'[48]

If they wished to enjoy the fruits of the popularity they might thus attract, then royal families would need to conform to the 'values of true domesticity' so praised by Novalis and embrace – at least in part – the catalogue of virtues of a bourgeois family. Even on 'the rare height of the throne', families had to live together devotedly and in tender proximity; they had to consist of doting parents and loving children; they had to display kindness and respect. Almost all the royal houses of Europe adopted the popularisation strategy that involved what Monika Wienfort has called the 'transferral of a dynastic tradition into a modern family realm'. Numerous carefully staged and widely distributed photographs from the decades after 1840 show representatives of the royal houses as blissful couples and parents, surrounded by a crowd of lovingly cared-for children and basking in the warmth of a happy home. The result was an interweaving of the institutions of the bourgeois family and of the dynasty.[49]

While it was hard enough to live up to the bourgeois family ideal in regular life, the challenge was all the greater in royal households. The heirs to the throne faced particular hurdles, for unlike the adult sons of

[47] Bagehot, *The English Constitution*, p. 37; Queen Victoria to King Leopold, 29 October 1844, in Arthur C. Benson and Viscount Esher (eds.), *The Letters of Queen Victoria*, vol. 2 (London, 1908), p. 27.

[48] Angelika Lorenz, *Das deutsche Familienbild in der Malerei des 19. Jahrhunderts* (Darmstadt, 1985), p. 184.

[49] Monika Wienfort, 'Dynastic Heritage and Bourgeois Morals: Monarchy and Family in the Nineteenth Century', in Frank Lorenz Müller and Heidi Mehrkens (eds.), *Royal Heirs and the Uses of Soft Power in Nineteenth-Century Europe* (London, 2016), p. 165.

bourgeois families, they remained under the family authority of the monarch. If a monarch was particularly long-lived, the next-in-line might still have to endure the limitations imposed by the head of the family when he was a grandfather himself, as was the case for the later Edward VII of Great Britain and Emperor Friedrich III. Their position within the dynastic unit robbed heirs of many of the freedoms that their future subjects enjoyed as a matter of course. Thus, for example, in the 1820s the future Emperor Wilhelm I failed to wring permission from his father for his marriage to the woman he loved, despite years of intensive effort, because she was not considered his social equal. In the late 1870s, Crown Prince Rudolf of Austria was denied his heartfelt wish to attend university. The parents of the future King Edward VII of Great Britain forbade their son the career in the military he desired, and in 1883 the fifty-two-year-old German crown prince Friedrich Wilhelm had his request to take his son Wilhelm with him on a visit to Spain rejected by his father. 'I am bluntly denied all my wishes', the Crown Prince complained resentfully, 'like a very young man still dependent on his superiors.'[50] In some cases the monarch's harsh exercise of familial power could be explained by a spiteful stubbornness that had set in with age or reflected a poor relationship between ruler and heir, but other reasons also account for the idiosyncratic character of the royal family. The family was expected to demonstrate bourgeois virtues – ideally in so perfect a form that it could serve as a model for the bourgeoisie – but it could not itself be bourgeois or conventional. On the one hand, to be so would hardly be compatible with the deeply rooted self-image of noble exceptionality, and on the other hand, it was precisely the mixture of apparent bourgeois affability and magical–majestic distinction that provided the royal families of Europe with their public potency.

To maintain appearances and keep the public enamoured, Walter Bagehot had noted, the marriage of a prince must be 'the brilliant edition of a universal fact'. A run-of-the-mill wedding held little interest. The one thing the emperor's new clothes could not be was ordinary. Perceptive pro-monarchy observers such as Baroness Hildegard von Spitzemberg therefore reacted vehemently to royal families who looked like they were neglecting the majestic dimension of their exceptional existence. On a visit to Württemberg in October 1897, she reprimanded the royal couple for living practically in a hovel – namely, the modest country estate

[50] Guntram Schulze-Wegener, *Wilhelm I. Deutscher Kaiser – König von Preußen – Nationaler Mythos* (Hamburg and Bonn, 2015), pp. 130–142; Brigitte Hamann, *Kronprinz Rudolf. Ein Leben* (Vienna, 2006), p. 90; Jane Ridley, *Bertie: A Life of Edward VII* (London, 2012), p. 42; Frank Lorenz Müller, *Our Fritz: Emperor Frederick III and the Political Culture of Imperial Germany* (Cambridge, MA, 2011), pp. 26–27.

of Marienwahl in Ludwigsburg – and not in the magnificent palace with its courtyards, gardens and sumptuous décor. 'They are simply no longer princes in their attitude, these lords', Baroness von Spitzemberg recorded in her journal with resignation. 'They no longer want to rule and protect and are surrendering themselves.'[51]

Oversight by the monarch, who ensured that, in the words of the Bavarian House Law, the 'peace, honour, order and wellbeing' of the royal house were maintained, therefore served a thoroughly political purpose. The duty to marry within one's social class, royal enforcement of behaviour befitting one's rank and demonstrative submission to the authority of the head of the family and monarch were intended, Martina Fetting writes, 'to project distinction, exclusivity, in short, majesty'. Given the constant growth of the power wielded by the media, this message was deemed necessary to secure the continued existence of the institution of the royal family against internal and external threats.[52]

The role that fell to the heir to the throne within the institution of the royal family was thus clearly defined: regardless of any purported or actual convergence with the ideal of the private, bourgeois family, the relationship between father and son, between monarch and royal heir, must above all reflect the intended relationship between sovereign and subject. 'A monarchical state has always only one master and it is he who decides', declared Prince Ludwig, the heir to the Bavarian throne, in 1886, 'and those who are closest to him must be his subjects just as is the lowliest day labourer.'[53]

What made this already challenging task even more difficult was the fact that the life of the royal family increasingly played out on a public stage. 'Monarchical performance', as Martina Fetting has termed it, gained increasing significance. Thomas Mann incorporated this reality into *Königliche Hoheit* (*Royal Highness*), his satirical novel published in 1909, when he described the crucial tasks of the fictional Prince Klaus Heinrich of Grimmburg: 'whether he succeeded in giving a greeting, a gracious word, a winning and yet dignified hand wave was important and decisive'. Constantly visible, the royal family had to fulfil its duty 'to appear' before an ever-larger public, in a performance that included a myriad of acts: Klaus Heinrich's dignified waving, the annual

---

[51] Bagehot, *The English Constitution*, p. 37; Rudolf Vierhaus (ed.), *Das Tagebuch der Baronin Spitzemberg, geb. Freiin v. Varnbüler. Aufzeichnungen aus der Hofgesellschaft des Hohenzollernreiches*, 3rd edn (Göttingen, 1963), p. 360.

[52] Martina Fetting, *Zum Selbstverständnis der letzten deutschen Monarchen. Normverletzung und Legitimationsstrategien zwischen Gottesgnadentum und Medienrevolution* (Frankfurt am Main, 2013), p. 68.

[53] Stefan März, *Ludwig III. Bayerns letzter König* (Regensburg, 2014), p. 65.

procession to the parliament by the Belgian king accompanied by his heir, the 'brilliant' wedding of the Prince of Wales in 1863, with the public informed in advance of every detail of the bride's fashionable gown, and also the daily appearance in the 'historical corner window' opposite the Berlin guard house with which Emperor Wilhelm entertained tourists and passers-by.[54]

Because the palace of a prince was, as Berlin's *National-Zeitung* explained in January 1883, 'always more or less a glasshouse', the public could peer into its private corners.[55] The sensational royal scandals and tragedies of the nineteenth century – the accidental death of the heir to the French throne in 1842, the gambling and amours of the Prince of Wales, the long-drawn-out death of Emperor Friedrich III, the homosexual relationships of the King of Württemberg, the flight of the Saxon crown princess from the Dresden court – all revealed that the public gaze, focused and intensified by the press, reached into the most intimate concerns of the royal family. Future rulers needed to distinguish themselves by conforming to certain behavioural standards on the political and legal stage of the constitutional state, but even that was insufficient. Having entered an 'age of boundless publicity' – a characterisation provided in 1893 by Bernhard von Bülow, who would subsequently become imperial chancellor – they needed to meet those performance standards as members of the similarly public institution of the 'royal family', which trapped them within a web of dynastic and bourgeois duties.[56]

'In That Second, Artificial World': Royal Courts

When it came to the dynastic duties he had to fulfil, Crown Prince Rudolf, the son of the Austrian emperor Franz Joseph, could hardly complain about a lack of stern guidance. Earnest admonishments flowed primarily

---

[54] Fetting, *Zum Selbstverständnis der letzten deutschen Monarchen*, p. 68; Thomas Mann, *Königliche Hoheit* (1909), www.gutenberg.org/files/35328/35328-h/35328-h.htm, paragraph 235 (accessed 25 November 2016); Juliane Vogel, *Elisabeth von Österreich. Momente aus dem Leben einer Kunstfigur* (Frankfurt am Main, 1998), p. 161; Imke Polland, 'How to Fashion the Popularity of the British Monarchy: Alexandra, Princess of Wales and the Attraction of Attire', in Frank Lorenz Müller and Heidi Mehrkens (eds.), *Royal Heirs and the Uses of Soft Power in Nineteenth-Century Europe* (London, 2016), pp. 210–211; Alexa Geisthövel, 'Wilhelm I. am "historischen Eckfenster". Zur Sichtbarkeit des Monarchen in der zweiten Hälfte des 19. Jahrhunderts', in Jan Andres, Alexa Geisthövel and Matthias Schwengelbeck (eds.), *Die Sinnlichkeit der Macht. Herrschaft und Repräsentation seit der Frühen Neuzeit* (Frankfurt am Main, 2005), pp. 163–185.

[55] *National-Zeitung* (Berlin) of 25 January 1883.

[56] John C. G. Röhl, *The Kaiser and His Court: Wilhelm II and the Government of Germany* (Cambridge, 1994), p. 104.

from the pen of Field Marshall Archduke Albrecht of Austria–Teschen (1817–1895), a grandson of Emperor Leopold II. On the occasion of Rudolf's majority, in 1877, the éminence grise of the Habsburg court presented the heir to the throne with several 'aphorisms' on the deeper meaning of court etiquette and strict ceremony. Their purpose, Albrecht stated, was to obscure the individuality and possible personal weaknesses of the ruler, who would thus withdraw entirely behind his high office. 'On ceremonial occasions', the archduke wrote, 'the people saw the pomp and splendour of his majesty, but not as a remote half-god but as a Christian who both confessed to God and humbled himself before God.' The field marshal insistently warned against any relaxation of ceremony, for such 'softening' would be accompanied by 'lessened moral decorum', and the 'prestige of the dynasty' would suffer as a result of 'the increasingly uninhibited manifestation of the weaknesses of the individual princes'.[57]

The strict rules of the Viennese court with its rigid order of precedence and prioritising of the higher court nobility certainly had a deeper, system-sustaining rationale. Behind the barriers that had protected the whole imperial palace complex since the Revolution of 1848, the institutions of the court – led by the holders of arcane courtly offices, such as the Supreme Master of the Court, the Supreme Chamberlain, the Supreme Marshal of the Court and the Supreme Master of the Horse, all of whom also exercised political influence – experienced a late flowering. Beneath these four 'highest offices of the court' bustled an almost incalculable throng of privy councillors, stewards, ladies-in-waiting and pages, who surrounded and observed the emperor and his immediate family while also isolating them from the outside world. In addition to the constitution and the royal family, the court provided the third of the institutional frameworks that dictated the life of an heir to the throne in the nineteenth century. Within this highly regulated, exclusive and privileged semi-public sphere, the paramount political concerns of the constitutional state were bound in with the monarch's pivotal role as decision-maker for the royal family.

Royal courts – regarded by most observers as the epitome of monarchical rule and culture – also changed over the course of the nineteenth

[57] Brigitte Hamann, 'Erzherzog Albrecht – Die graue Eminenz des Habsburgerhofes. Hinweise auf einen unterschätzten Politiker', in Isabella Ackerl, Walter Hummelburger and Hans Mommsen (eds.), *Politik und Gesellschaft im alten und neuen Österreich. Festschrift für Rudolf Neck zum 60. Geburtstag*, vol. 1 (Munich, 1981), pp. 75–77; Brigitte Hamann, 'Der Wiener Hof und die Hofgesellschaft in der zweiten Hälfte des 19. Jahrhunderts', in Karl Möckl (ed.), *Hof und Hofgesellschaft in den deutschen Staaten im 19. und beginnenden 20. Jahrhundert* (Boppard am Rhein, 1990), pp. 61–67 (also for the following paragraph); see also Jean-Paul Bled, 'La cour de François-Joseph', in Karl F. Werner (ed.), *Hof, Kultur und Politik im 19. Jahrhundert* (Bonn, 1985), pp. 169–182.

century. In the Ancien Régime, the historian Philip Mansel has noted, the French royal court was one of the most important institutions in Europe. It was the centre of power for the country as a whole, but it also exercised profound influence over the manners and customs of the European elites, and over their fashion preferences, artistic expression and leisure activities. As the spring that fed national pride, the court was essential to French national identity. In the palace complex at Versailles, these high aspirations found a suitable architectural expression and also a stage. In the pre-revolutionary era, however, courts had been more than just cultural and social centres. Volker Press has described how these ancient frameworks of government brought forth the institutions which would eventually connect the courts with the apparatus of the early modern state: in particular the chancelleries, cabinets and law courts. Additionally, the nobility had not distinguished between their role at court and their role within the princely government of the country, and traditionally power had been exhibited to the court public through pageantry and grandiose display. As a result, early modern courts had become central instruments of government.[58]

By the nineteenth century, the relative significance of the European royal courts, now financed by constitutionally guaranteed civil lists, had shrunk with regard to both cultural leadership and political hegemony. Despite all the remaining pomp, which occasionally experienced a remarkably exuberant late flowering, the courts were no longer alone in setting the tone when it came to the culture and taste of European society. New cultural, artistic or social centres such as public museums, galleries, theatres and concert halls, universities, conservatories and academies now stood alongside the courts, competing successfully for the attention of the changing elites. Modern forms of communication provided a constantly growing and increasingly more diverse public, with spectacles now performed on new stages. To see what was happening within the palace walls, an individual no longer had to be presentable at court. Curiosity could now be satisfied by peering into these glasshouses through the prism of the press.

The court's function as a political powerhouse underwent a similar development: in tandem with the transfer of state power to institutions that supplemented, or even competed with, the crown, the role of the royal court as the sole or central instrument of rule was also modified. Where monarchs still possessed, and exercised, broadly defined political

---

[58] Philip Mansel, *The Court of France 1789–1830* (Cambridge, 1988), p. 3; Karl F. Werner, 'Fürst und Hof im 19. Jahrhundert. Abgesang oder Spätblüte', in Karl F. Werner (ed.), *Hof, Kultur und Politik im 19. Jahrhundert* (Bonn, 1985), pp. 9, 11–13.

power – for example in Wilhelmine Germany, in the Habsburg Empire or in the Second French Empire – the court and the court elites retained greater direct political importance than was the case in Britain or the Kingdom of Saxony.

Yet neither the unflattering comparison with the lustrous court of the French Sun King nor Thomas Mann's satirical depiction of the court of the fictional Grand Duchy of Grimmburg as a shabby and scurrilous anachronism should lead us to underestimate the significance of courts in the nineteenth century. They remained of enormous importance to the exercise, defence and communication of royal authority – precisely because constitutional developments had ensured that the authority they retained was retrenched and focused on the instruments they still commanded. Additionally, as the formerly exclusive court society was opened up in many places to admit ambitious and successful members of a now augmented upper stratum of society, new elites were incorporated into a sphere of influence that was entirely at the behest of the monarchy. As Karl Möckl has recognised, the court was no longer the sole centre within society, but it was at the court that all trails met.[59]

On that count, the lengths to which many nineteenth-century European courts went to defend or reinstate their grandeur and exceptionality are hardly surprising. In the early years of France's July Monarchy, King Louis Philippe, who owed his throne to the Revolution of 1830, permitted a liberalisation of his court. The livery worn by footmen was abandoned and, if they had served as officers in the National Guard, even artisans could attend his court. However, the king soon reinstated stricter forms and reintroduced a dress code, hoping, not least, that the court would become more splendid and more attractive to the elites whom he wished to attract. His successor, Napoleon III, who reigned as emperor of the French from 1852, was also conscious of the significance of a brilliant court. With an annual outlay of eight million francs, his court swallowed a third of the hefty imperial civil list. Borrowing from the style of the court of Napoleon I, he staged what Roger Price described as a glittering 'act in the theatre of power'. As is illustrated in Figure 3, on particularly extensive celebratory occasions, up to 4,000 members of the political and social elite of France – the men wearing the knee breeches reintroduced by Napoleon and the women in wide crinolines – gathered around the monarch and his family. All this effort served a political purpose. The Earl of Malmesbury, the British

---

[59] Karl Möckl, 'Hof und Hofgesellschaft in den deutschen Staaten im 19. und beginnenden 20. Jahrhundert. Einleitende Bemerkungen', in Karl Möckl (ed.), *Hof und Hofgesellschaft in den deutschen Staaten im 19. und beginnenden 20. Jahrhundert* (Boppard am Rhein, 1990), p. 10.

Figure 3. Jean-Léon Gérôme's sumptuous painting captures the pomp of Napoleon III's court and documents a carefully staged 'act in the theatre of power'. *The Reception of Siamese Ambassadors by Emperor Napoleon III (1808–73) at the Palace of Fontainebleau, 27 June 1861* (oil on canvas), Gérôme, Jean-Léon (1824–1904)/Château de Versailles, France/Alamy Images.

foreign secretary, who visited Paris in the spring of 1853, prophesied the ascendancy of 'a magnificent Court, with a Sovereign who will command the attention of all Europe'. The impact made by Napoleon III's court on Alexander Graf von Hübner, the Austrian ambassador, the following year confirmed Malmesbury's evaluation: 'the brilliant ballroom, the throne with Their Majesties, the number and splendour of the uniforms and the appearance of the ladies left an overwhelming impression', wrote the diplomat.[60]

Even when the staging was not as lavish as for the last French emperor, the distinctive character of court culture, with all its practices that shored up the authority of the monarch, was closely observed. Such was the case, for example, for the unassuming Prince Regent Luitpold, who ruled Bavaria from 1886 to 1912 and was seen as immensely affable in his dealings with the people. Karl Alexander von Müller, son of the Bavarian minister of culture, recorded a perplexing contradiction in his memoirs: 'The unpretentious regent, spartan in some respects when it came to himself, retained at his court all the ritual prescriptions of the protective Spanish–Burgundian ceremonial [. . .] We children also soon heard, sometimes ironically and sometimes also respectfully, of the insurmountable, holy barriers of the five ranks at court, of officials of the crown and senior court dignitaries, supreme master of the court, supreme master of the horse, supreme master of ceremonies, captain-general of the royal life guards, adjutants general, aides-de-camp and chamberlains – who on ceremonial occasions still bore a golden key, just as under Charles V or Philip II.' In these striking figures, von Müller recognised 'a magic guard dressed in white-and-blue' who protected 'in that second, artificial world of the court, the dream of dynastic divine grace on which the forms of the life of our state continued to rest'.[61]

Court rituals were not only maintained, intensified or invented on the continent. At the British Court, Albert, Victoria's husband, took on the transformation of the royal household as one of his first tasks. He established that men could only be seated in the presence of the queen if they were dining together. Even if the prime minister was convalescing after a long illness, as was Lord Derby, or suffered from gout, as did Benjamin Disraeli, he had to remain standing before the seated monarch. In return, Victoria ordered that the younger ladies-in-waiting were to stand when

[60] H. A. C. Collingham, *The July Monarchy: A Political History of France 1830–1848* (London and New York, 1988), p. 103; Roger Price, *The French Second Empire: An Anatomy of Political Power* (Cambridge, 2001), pp. 46–47; William H. C. Smith, *Napoleon III: The Pursuit of Prestige* (London, 1991), p. 39–40.

[61] Karl Alexander von Müller, *Aus Gärten der Vergangenheit. Erinnerungen 1882–1914* (Stuttgart, 1951), pp. 123–124.

Prince Albert was present. Women were forbidden to address the prince consort, who set store in being accompanied at all times by an equerry, to enhance his own dignity.[62] A practice introduced at the court of Carl XV of Sweden in the mid 1860s combined the tactical liberalisation of access with stricter control of outward appearances. With a strategy that Angela Rundquist has recognised as nigh-on Machiavellian, the monarch sought to bind the world of industry and finance to himself by offering daughters from these social circles the opportunity to be presented each year at court. This 'ostensible democratisation' aroused fierce protest from noblewomen who did not wish to share this privilege with the daughters of the bourgeoisie. Their protests did not prevail, and bourgeois debutantes were allowed to wear the traditional black-and-white court dress with broad puffed sleeves. All debutantes now sported this court uniform, which both provided homogeneity for the group of debutantes and sharply distinguished its members from those who did not attend court, until the tradition was ended in the 1960s.[63]

The Wilhelmine Empire provides the most thoroughly researched example of political ends being served by an almost hypertrophic nineteenth-century court. Court institutions around the last German emperor – such as Wilhelm II's civil and military 'cabinets' – increasingly exercised governmental functions that were deliberately kept as far away as possible from parliamentary involvement or control. Alongside this development, there was an astonishing expansion and militarisation of the whole court apparatus, with its sixty-two carefully demarcated court rankings: from the 'Supreme Chamberlain' and the 'field marshals' in first and second positions respectively, down via cardinals (ninth), the lord mayor of Berlin (thirty-ninth) and university rectors (forty-seventh), to 'second lieutenants' in sixty-second, and therefore last, place. Members of the bourgeoisie who held neither military rank nor public office were ranked fifty-seventh at best, as 'gentlemen presented at court', no matter how influential or important they were. The historian John Röhl has identified in this 'efflorescence of a sumptuous neo-absolutist court culture' a characteristic trait of the German Empire, in which the Hohenzollern court constituted the focus of political life up until 1914. For Röhl, the ostentatious court and the creation of a large court society served three significant political ends: the intensification of the charisma of monarchy, the integration and ordering by rank of the German elites – including the industrial

---

[62] E. S. Turner, *The Court of St James's* (New York, 1959), pp. 308–309.

[63] Angela Rundquist, 'Pompe en noir et blanc. Présentation officielle des dames à la cour de Suède', in *Actes de la Recherche en Sciences Sociales* 110 (December 1995), pp. 65–76.

bourgeoisie and the civil service – and a demonstration of German power to the wider world.[64]

As the example of the British court in the Victorian period illustrates, royal courts were extremely influential even below the threshold of high-level politics and the directing of society as a whole. It was here that heirs to the throne – as members of court society – were involved. The historian Michael Bentley encourages us to understand power – and specifically the power of the court – in more subtle terms, not simply as the ability to compel through the use of force. If power is instead understood in terms of a historically evinced expectation of submissiveness by the inferior members of a stratified society, then an analysis of the power exercised by nineteenth-century courts becomes all the more rewarding. When subordinates had immediate contact with Queen Victoria, they found themselves exposed to the authority, persuasion and rehearsed experience that enabled the crown to continue its exercise of power despite all constitutional restrictions. This effect was even more pronounced when such encounters occurred in person rather than in writing, and above all when they took place within the hierarchical court atmosphere at Windsor Castle, Osborne House or Balmoral Castle. The pitiful fate of ministers who were bored rigid yet did not dare leave the palace in case the queen might call for them, for they knew they would not be invited back should they not be ready and waiting, casts a telling light on the disciplining power of the institution of the court. For the royal heir, who was directly and entirely subject to the power of the head of the family, the court proved even more oppressive. The tensions that were the result of these constellations could often not be resolved by the kind of stern advice that Archduke Albrecht like to dispense.[65]

For Crown Prince Rudolf, the admonitions to abide dutifully by the discipline of the court were of little avail. Rudolf, like his mother, Empress Elisabeth, recoiled from the concern with rank and the insistence on protocol, and he became, as Jean-Paul Bled has commented, not just an alien presence within the court system but also its adversary. He began to avoid the institution altogether: he did not attend court and kept his distance from the emperor, he took up interests that were decidedly not of the court, such as oppositional journalism or the natural sciences, and

---

[64] Röhl, *The Kaiser and His Court*, pp. 70, 79–83, 103–106; see also Martin Kohlrausch, 'Zwischen Tradition und Innovation. Das Hofzeremoniell der wilhelminischen Monarchie', in Andreas Biefang, Michael Epkenhans and Klaus Tenfelde (eds.), *Das politische Zeremoniell im Deutschen Kaiserreich 1871–1918* (Düsseldorf, 2008), pp. 31–51.

[65] Michael Bentley, 'Power and Authority in the Late Victorian and Edwardian Court', in Andrzej Olechnowicz (ed.), *The Monarchy and the British Nation, 1780 to the Present* (Cambridge, 2007), p. 163.

he deliberately cultivated an entirely different style for his own milieu. A deliberate nonchalance reigned amongst the men who surrounded the crown prince and who, unlike his father's retinue, were not required to wear tails. Archduke Franz Ferdinand, heir presumptive to the throne following Rudolf's scandalous suicide in 1889, equally refused to submit to the authority of the emperor at the Vienna court on which Archduke Albrecht had insisted. He deliberately distanced himself from the court, above all on account of the affront to his wife afforded by court protocol. The emperor had permitted Franz Ferdinand to marry Sophie Chotek, a member of the high nobility but not his social equal, only after a prolonged conflict and under strict conditions, which included the requirement that the couple not appear at court together. The heir therefore preferred not to attend at all, fuelling the – correct – impression of political tensions and differences between those who governed in the name of the emperor and those who gathered around his successor.[66]

The woes of heirs at court were not limited to Vienna. The Prussian–German Crown Prince Friedrich Wilhelm found the atmosphere at the imperial court, dominated by his aged father's strict regimentation, almost unbearably restrictive. He dated a letter to his wife, Vicky, 'Berlin Cage, 23 October 84' and complained to his 'beloved little wife' that, with his return to the capital, he was now again incarcerated in the 'repugnant prison'. The relationship of the British heir to the throne, Albert Edward ('Bertie', later King Edward VII), to the court of his mother was anything but easy and remained problematic after the death of his father, the prince consort, in 1861. 'The respectability of the Queen's and the Prince's Court, [...] was universally acknowledged to be a great safeguard to the Throne and Country', Queen Victoria wrote with unconcealed asperity to the comptroller of her son's household in 1866, and therefore it was 'absolutely necessary', she noted, that the heir to the throne and his wife receive no unsavoury guests or be themselves the guests of anyone questionable. It was precisely this self-righteous and controlling attitude by his parents that had driven Bertie from the court and turned him into a bon vivant beset by scandal. Following the death of his mother in 1901, the new king therefore made many changes: palaces were decluttered, personnel swapped out and a livelier style admitted. Yet Edward did not refrain from stamping the court with evidence of his own pre-eminence. Thus, for example, he commanded that women at court

---

[66] Hamann, 'Der Wiener Hof und die Hofgesellschaft', pp. 67–68; Bled, 'La cour de François-Joseph', pp. 179–180; Günter Kronenbitter, 'The Opposition of the Archdukes: Rudolf, Franz Ferdinand and the Late Habsburg Monarchy', in Frank Lorenz Müller and Heidi Mehrkens (eds.), *Sons and Heirs: Succession and Political Culture in Nineteenth-Century Europe* (Basingstoke, 2016), p. 216.

kiss his hand, an act of acknowledgement he also required of his grand-children, who were to address their royal grandfather as *Sir*, and even of Prince George, the thirty-five-year-old heir to the throne.[67]

***

Prince George, later George V, is said to have insisted, 'My father was frightened of his father; I was frightened of my father, and I'm damned well going to see to it that my children are frightened of me.'[68] These frequently cited words cannot be verifiably ascribed to him, but they do encapsulate how difficult it was to create a fruitful relationship between heir and monarch. This was already a real challenge within the quasi-public institution of the royal family, but the task was all the more difficult in the context of the essentially semi-public court. In the nineteenth century, this institution remained almost entirely under the control of the monarch and continued to serve primarily to sustain the power of the ruler. It did so through public displays of splendour and by prompting society's desire for acknowledgement by the monarch. Michael Bentley's observations on the establishment of highly ordered spaces in which those on a lower social rung felt compelled to submit should also be considered in this context. The heir to the throne had to defer publicly and with dignity, while kissing hands and sporting the compulsory tails, using such demonstrative obedience to confirm the very monarchical authority on which his own position would one day rest. At the same time, he was under pressure to lead his own life and to develop a personal image that held out to contemporaries the prospect of a future ruler whose under-standing of the functions of the monarch would be modern, productive and constitutional.

The expectations and tensions generated by the task assigned to European heirs in the nineteenth century existed within four concentric circles outlined here: the need to acquire majorities for monarchy formed the outside ring; then came the provisions of the constitutional state; then the rulebooks, old and new, of the ruling family; and finally the etiquette of the court. These typical features of monarchical Europe in the nine-teenth century dictated how the representatives of the next generation of rulers had to act and how they might contribute to the future of the monarchy. How, and indeed whether, they succeeded in individual instances will become evident when we turn now to their conduct within the dynastic family, to which they belonged both as children of ruling parents and as marriage partners.

---

[67] Müller, *Our Fritz*, p. 150 (and n. 4); Ridley, *Bertie*, pp. 112, 350.
[68] http://news.bbc.co.uk/2/hi/uk/1802875.stm (accessed 5 December 2016).

2 'And This Comedy That I Have to Perform before the World'

Royal Heirs as Sons and Husbands

Leo Tolstoy's great novel *Anna Karenina* opens with one of the most famous lines in world literature: 'All happy families are alike; each unhappy family is unhappy in its own way.' Even though psychologists, biologists and economists now celebrate that dictum as the 'Anna Karenina principle', Tolstoy's adage appears to apply only in part to the royal families of nineteenth-century Europe.[1] If we consider the dynasties who were denied a happy private family life, it quickly becomes apparent that they were not all unhappy in their own way. Rather, the elements of each family's misery – mistrust between monarch and heir, coldness between married couples – were evidently more or less the same across generations and national boundaries. The patterns of conflict and the factors that produced such family fissures were depressingly alike. We readily arrive at the sobering conclusion that, despite awareness of what had happened previously and regardless of all the transnational networks and communication, hardly anyone learned from past mistakes.

That no proper remedy for the widespread dysfunctionality of dynastic families could be found and the whole, sad story just kept repeating itself is surprising. After all, ensuring the cohesion, reputation and orderliness of the dynasty was a central objective for the head of a royal family. Nor is that goal at all remarkable, for hereditary monarchy was a family business. The dynasty surrounded its central biological task – reproduction along an uninterrupted, carefully protected bloodline – with ornate layers of political, legal, ideological and cultural fabric. Thus exalted, the process of succession was used to justify a dynasty's claim to rule. The French Revolution and the associated political ruptures meant, though, that Europe's monarchical systems had to look for entirely new ways to retain their authority. These ancient family enterprises, now increasingly under the spotlight of the media, also had to garner public acclaim and the support of the bourgeoisie. This required them to present themselves as morally upright and happy families. In the nineteenth century, a well-ordered, joyful and affectionate

---

[1] https://en.wikipedia.org/wiki/Anna_Karenina_principle (accessed 13 December 2016).

family life – a creation often labelled the 'bourgeois family' – was deemed a cardinal virtue, and the first families of the state had little choice but to display it.[2] It therefore became essential for the royal dynasties to present themselves as model families, and thus conform to the ideals of the age.

The explanation for the repeated failure of Europe's royal houses to achieve exemplary levels of family bliss is both ironic and tragic: the two most important prerequisites for a successful dynastic family life could not be reconciled. The old system with its exclusive and authoritarian dynastic hierarchy and the new ideal of the modern family constantly clashed, repeatedly producing conflicts and sometimes even scandals and tragedies. Commenting on the catastrophic relationship between Frederick the Great and his predecessor, Reinhold Schneider declared in his novel *The Hohenzollerns* that 'Kings are not fathers, kings-to-be are not sons.' Although the rawness of the specific example on which Schneider was drawing had even alarmed contemporaries, in the first half of the eighteenth century this kind of father–son relationship was still broadly acceptable. Over the course of the next 100 years, both the significance of public opinion and popular expectations for the relationship between fathers and sons were to change markedly. It was no longer sufficient for monarchs to present themselves in the ermine-trimmed, crimson robes of kings or the gleaming armour of the victorious soldier. The monarchical cult of the nineteenth century required that the king could be depicted as the 'father of the nation', whose affectionate firmness towards the children of his realm mirrored his behaviour as the head of his own family. His subjects should be able to envisage a ruler who was not only resplendent in his majestic garb but also soothingly domestic, wearing a comfortable house coat.[3]

Like other aspects of monarchical rule in the nineteenth century, family relationships within the walls of the royal palaces were encumbered by what the philosopher Ernst Bloch described as 'the simultaneity of the non-simultaneous'. Periods of transition are often characterised by this 'coexistence of deep-reaching societal modernisation and traditional social formations'. When it came to royal fathers and sons or to princely husbands and their wives, this phenomenon was closely associated with the various expectations and needs of the broad public that observed these family relationships.[4]

---

[2] Gunilla Budde, *Blütezeit des Bürgertums. Bürgerlichkeit im 19. Jahrhundert* (Darmstadt, 2009), p. 25.

[3] Reinhold Schneider, *Die Hohenzollern*, 2nd edn (Cologne, 1953), p. 146; Simone Mergen, *Monarchiejubiläen im 19. Jahrhundert. Die Entdeckung des historischen Jubiläums für den monarchischen Kult in Sachsen und Bayern* (Leipzig, 2005), pp. 115–117.

[4] Rudolf Schlögl, *Alter Glaube und moderne Welt. Europäisches Christentum im Umbruch 1750–1850* (Frankfurt am Main, 2013), p. 158.

These contrasts between old and new could create severe tensions and conflicts. Essentially, royal families could not evade this dilemma, for it was not open to them to abandon traditional arguments and patterns of behaviour to resolve such contradictions in favour of their own modernisation. Like so many members of European princely houses, Klaus Heinrich, the unhappy prince in Thomas Mann's novel *Königliche Hoheit* (*Royal Highness*), could only dream of 'being called Dr Fischer and pursuing a serious profession'. That dream could not be realised, for to disenchant the crown in the eyes of the public would surely mean the end of the dynasty.[5] As fathers, sons and husbands, Europe's heirs were condemned to live in an unresolvable dichotomy that made so many of them unhappy in such similar ways.

The more urgently the palace-dwellers felt the need to access the public, the 'people', the more tightly they were constrained by their collaboration with the media, which afforded them such contact. The 'logic of the mass media', the term used by Martin Kohlrausch, dictated that journalists, writers and – eventually – photographers trained their guns on the masses' centre of attention. As the target of such interest, royal celebrities had to ensure that they appeared as advantageously as possible – at all times and on all occasions.[6] Via the media, the public now infiltrated even the most private, even intimate, spheres, including the personal relationships of members of royal families.

All told, the media were willing to collaborate in the royal families' efforts to present a morally upright example. They continued to disseminate the piously patriotic image of a model ruling family even long after things had turned sour, as, for example, in the case of the marriage of Emperor Wilhelm I and his wife, Augusta.[7] However much the bourgeois press preferred to continue to buttress the state and paint over such fractures – a practice sharply criticised by anti-monarchical socialist journalists – some things were simply beyond whitewashing. When a breakdown in family relationships became public knowledge, the Faustian pact with the well-disposed public, which the media had created, presented the royal dynasties with tremendous difficulties. What was worse, these problems were now on display for all the world to see. In the most egregious cases – such as

---

[5] Thomas Mann, *Königliche Hoheit* (1909), www.gutenberg.org/files/35328/35328-h/3532 8-h.htm, paragraph 235 (accessed 9 December 2016).

[6] Martin Kohlrausch, *Der Monarch im Skandal. Die Logik der Massenmedien und die Transformation der wilhelminischen Monarchie* (Berlin, 2005), p. 45–83; Kristina Widestadt, 'Pressing the Centre of Attention: Three Royal Weddings and a Media Myth', in Mats Jönsson and Patrik Lundell (eds.), *Media and Monarchy in Sweden* (Göteborg, 2009), p. 47–58.

[7] Alexa Geisthövel, 'Den Monarchen im Blick. Wilhelm I. in der illustrierten Familienpresse', in Habbo Knoch and Daniel Morat (eds.), *Kommunikation als Beobachtung. Medienwandel und Gesellschaftsbilder 1880–1960* (Munich, 2003), pp. 59–80.

the so-called 'marriage perturbation' that rocked the ruling family in Saxony in 1902–1903 – the monarchical system itself seemed to be in jeopardy. In February 1903, a few weeks after the Saxon crown princess had eloped with her lover, leaving behind her husband and children, the Prussian envoy nervously reported to Berlin that even 'the educated circles loyal to the monarch could not look to the future without concern'.[8]

Yet the future was the very issue at stake where the upbringing and role of the royal heir as well as the heir's public portrayal and reception were concerned: the future of the monarchical system, which was guaranteed by the transfer of princely power from the occupant of the throne to the next-in-line, a transfer that was inconceivable without the birth of legitimate heirs. The crucial importance of family relationships, and also of their disruption, for the political system and for the state meant that hereditary monarchies had to operate as strongly regulated family enterprises. In the nineteenth century, relationships within the ruling houses of Europe experienced new strains, though, in part as a result of the contradictory demands of the ideal of the modern family, with marriage partners selected freely, on the one hand, and the tradition-bound hierarchical clan that was the dynasty, on the other. The pressure was then significantly heightened by the media and the public that they helped shape. At the heart of this complex were two relationships central to the future of the monarchy: that of the ruler and the ruler's direct heir (usually, but not always, a male monarch and his son) and that of the heir and the heir's spouse, the biological unit on which the future of the dynasty rested.

Princes as Sons

Paul's words in his letter to the Galatians would have struck a chord with many nineteenth-century heirs: 'Heirs as long as they are minors are no better than slaves, though they are the owners of all the property; but they remain under guardians and trustees until the date set by the father.'[9] For heirs to the throne, their minority usually ended only with the death of the reigning monarch, and even though guardians and trustees rarely played a role, some crown princes will have experienced the painful feeling that they were indeed little more than servants at the court of their predecessor. The head of a monarchical family's particular *patria potestas* and status as sovereign doubtless exacerbated the tensions and conflicts that

---

[8] Dönhoff to Bülow, no. 19, 1 February 1903 (Politisches Archiv des Auswärtigen Amtes, R3264).
[9] Galatians 4:1–3 (NRSV).

can arise within any family when children seek to set their own course, veering away from their fathers.

This almost inevitable tension resulted in a decisive problem for the monarchical system of the nineteenth century. The increased expectations for the performance and constitutional surefootedness of the 'functionalised' monarch made the training of a future monarch by the current ruler more necessary than ever. In spite of this, the relationship between ruler and heir was often so dysfunctional that the preparation usually failed. In many cases, no attempt was ever made or the endeavour was in effect sabotaged by the ruler. For the House of Savoy, which from 1861 ruled the newly created Kingdom of Italy, one leading historian has diagnosed a veritable tradition of distrust between generations. As a result, no heir to the throne was initiated into the business of the state or could even gather substantial experience of public life.[10] The exclusion from the business of government could only be painful and humiliating for the royal heir – and not just in Italy. Yet we might wonder whether the break that therefore accompanied the unavoidable transition to a new ruler might not in the end have been an advantage for the monarchical system, for it held out the prospect of a new beginning. Additionally, the gaps in the future ruler's training by his predecessor were progressively offset by the more thorough education that heirs experienced in the nineteenth century, increasingly in the public eye.

The dysfunctional relationship between ruler and heir therefore always revolved around more than just personal fates and family frictions, for it also distilled distinctive features of the monarchical system and its development in the nineteenth century. As we shall see, noteworthy examples are provided by three high-profile heirs who had extremely problematic relationships with their predecessors: the Prussian–German crown prince Friedrich Wilhelm, who in 1888 would rule as emperor for just ninety-nine days; the British heir to the crown Albert Edward, who would succeed his mother, Queen Victoria, in 1901 as King Edward VII; and, finally, Crown Prince Rudolf, the only son of the Austrian emperor Franz Joseph, whose life was ended in 1889 by the shots he fired at Mayerling.

'Dutiful Deference out of Filial Respect': King Wilhelm I of Prussia and His Son Crown Prince Friedrich Wilhelm

After a fight with his oldest son, later Emperor Wilhelm II, Crown Prince Friedrich Wilhelm wrote in a letter to his wife that 'the unedifying tension between father and son that is traditional in the Prussian family has now

[10] Denis Mack Smith, *Italy and Its Monarchy* (New Haven, CT and London, 1989), p. 71.

also appeared for us'. The resigned and embittered words of the fifty-two-year-old heir to the throne resonated with his experiences as the father of a difficult son, but they also reflected his fraught relationship with his own father, the eighty-six-year-old Emperor Wilhelm I.[11] The bleak tradition of the Prussian Hohenzollern dynasty that beset the relationship between ruler and heir was well known to those concerned. It had long seemed, however, that Friedrich Wilhelm and his father would be spared the misery of their family's antagonistic father–son relationship that reached back into the seventeenth century. During the first three decades of the son's life – Friedrich Wilhelm was born in 1831 – their relationship remained healthy. Prince Wilhelm was delighted that his son not only met the comparatively advanced educational demands raised by his mother, Princess Augusta of the House of Saxony–Weimar, but also cut a fine figure as a soldier. The son had uncomplainingly entered into the marriage orchestrated for him by his parents and had wed a British princess, Victoria, the oldest daughter of Queen Victoria and her husband, Prince Albert. After soundings had been taken and with arrangements drawn up long in advance, the couple were married in London in January 1858, in the presence of the groom's father, who represented the Prussian royal family. In an extensive testament written one year earlier, Prince Wilhelm had noted the 'greatest parental happiness' he was able to experience as a result of both of his children 'turning out well'.[12]

Initially, then, the relationship between Prince Friedrich Wilhelm and his father was evidently untroubled. It may have helped that, although Friedrich Wilhelm was the heir presumptive, his father was not in fact the ruler, but rather the younger brother of the childless King Friedrich Wilhelm IV. We know from Prince Wilhelm's own hand that by his sixtieth birthday he no longer had significant expectations for his future: 'I'll perhaps still be able to hang on for a few more years, but what is good is probably now already in the past', he recorded in April 1857. Looking back on his life, he recorded in his testament his gratitude to 'the king, my brother, who is at the same time my trusting friend' for having adopted 'this stance towards him'. A short while later, his daughter Luise gave birth to a son and the sixty-year-old Hohenzollern became a grandfather for the first time. However, Prince Wilhelm would not be granted the tranquil and uneventful old age to which he had seemingly resigned

---

[11] The depiction of the relationship between Emperor Wilhelm I and his son, later Emperor Friedrich III, is based on Frank Lorenz Müller, *Our Fritz: Emperor Frederick III and the Political Culture of Imperial Germany* (Cambridge, MA, 2011), pp. 13, 16–29.

[12] Monika Wienfort, *Verliebt, Verlobt, Verheiratet. Eine Geschichte der Ehe seit der Romantik* (Munich, 2014), pp. 171–177; Guntram Schulze-Wegener, *Wilhelm I. Deutscher Kaiser – König von Preußen – Nationaler Mythos* (Hamburg and Bonn, 2015), p. 269.

himself. In July 1857, his older brother experienced the first in a series of strokes that would leave him incapable of ruling. In October 1857, Prince Wilhelm stood in for the ailing king for a short period, but the following year he became regent in the long term. Then, on the death of Friedrich Wilhelm IV in January 1861, he finally inherited the crown and ruled as King Wilhelm I.[13]

The beginning of Prince Wilhelm's regency in 1858 did not immediately strain his relationship with his son and heir. Indeed, they remained on good terms and his father integrated Friedrich Wilhelm closely into the work of ruling. 'I found unending happiness in the great trust with which my father inducted me into all the circumstances without exception both during the preparations for the regency and also during all the time afterwards', Friedrich Wilhelm wrote in January 1859. Crucially, he expressly supported the regent's principal objective – the reform of the Prussian army – for which he was publicly rewarded by his father. In June 1860, the regent appointed his son colonel of the first regiment of the Grenadier Guards. The 'joy-induced daze' that the young man experienced on that account still lingered on six months later, when Prince Wilhelm acceded to the throne on his brother's death. In that moment Friedrich Wilhelm recorded, 'May God help me act as should the worthy son of such a father and have him find me to be the support that I so greatly wish to be for him.'

It was not long before this deep reciprocal trust was gone for good. The problems began when, having initially conceded to the policies of the new ruler, the liberal majority within the Prussian parliament finally refused to approve the financing of the unpopular army reforms. As a constitutional state, Prussia found itself in the midst of a major crisis. The liberal majority was bolstered by repeated election success, but its refusal to yield was matched by King Wilhelm I's determination that the prerogatives of the crown should not be curtailed when it came to military affairs. Reshuffled several times, the king's ministerial team became increasingly resolute, and in late summer of 1861, the crisis escalated: the parliament refused to pass the budget and Wilhelm I toyed with the idea of abdicating. In September 1861, in a final attempt to have his position prevail, the king appointed Otto von Bismarck as head of his government. Bismarck had assured the king that he was prepared to take on the constitutional conflict and would conclude it with a victory for the crown.

The crown prince was more open to compromise and supported a less rigid response to the heightening crisis. His attitude may have influenced Wilhelm I's decision not to abdicate in favour of his son. Influenced by his

---

[13] Schulze-Wegener, *Wilhelm I.*, pp. 267, 269–270.

father-in-law, Prince Albert, and, after Albert's death in December 1861, by the even more liberal arguments of his own wife, Victoria, Friedrich Wilhelm was less dismissive of the rights of parliament than was his father. He even discreetly encouraged politicians who were open to finding a middle ground. Manifestly under great pressure, the monarch saw his son's response as evidence of unacceptable disloyalty. Dramatic scenes played out in 1862, with the king sharply rebuking his son, on occasion in front of witnesses. During a confrontation in March 1862, Wilhelm I reproached the crown prince for being painted in the democratic press as an adversary of the king who associated with unreliable politicians: 'You will hardly believe how I wailed and sobbed before going to bed', Friedrich Wilhelm subsequently wrote to his wife.

Despite his tears and supported by Victoria, the crown prince remained critical of his father's unwillingness to compromise. He responded to the appointment of Otto von Bismarck, whom he found highly suspect, first with extensive travels and then with a demonstrative silence. 'He sits like a statue and a *memento mori* at the Council of Ministers', a trusted friend commented in February 1863. 'This silence is intended on the one hand to prevent any compromising with those below, and on the other hand to prevent a break with his father.' Mention of the mortality of the almost sixty-six-year-old king and of the crown prince's embodiment of the future hardly helped patch up the relationship between father and son. Instead, as the political crisis intensified over the course of 1863, both the king's need for loyalty and his anger at his son's attitude continued to grow. The final straw came in June 1863, when the crown prince publicly voiced a cautious criticism of Bismarck's restrictions on the freedom of the press. After Friedrich Wilhelm had given a short speech in Danzig in which he distanced himself from the course adopted by the government, the king came close to having his son arrested and brought before a military tribunal. Wilhelm I still harshly rebuked the crown prince for 'publicly setting himself up in opposition to the orders of the king' and thereby presenting the people with a choice between father and son.

Friedrich Wilhelm climbed down immediately. Although he was still not prepared to support Bismarck's reactionary course, he abstained from exerting any political influence in the eventful years that followed. The once-harmonious relationship between father and son could not be restored, though. Despite great moments of solidarity – when the two men met on the battlefield at Königgrätz, the father embraced his victorious son and presented him with his own *Pour le Mérite* order – the relationship remained fundamentally antagonistic. When he was under great political strain, during outbursts of anger Wilhelm I would return to the theme of his son's unreliability and disloyalty – so, for example, in

1866, during the row over the ending of the war, and then again in 1871, when the imperial crown was forced upon him. The monarch even openly criticised his apparently liberal son, who was courted by opposition circles, to third parties. The crown prince, he wrote to his daughter in 1869, neglected his 'dutiful deference out of filial respect', and in 1880, in a conversation with his wife, he termed Friedrich Wilhelm a dangerous supporter of elements hostile to the state. Finally, in the mid 1880s he rebuked his son for displaying a lack of respect for the monarch.

Full of mistrust, for the remainder of his long life Wilhelm I ensured that the crown prince was kept well away from the business of the state whenever possible and denied him any access to pertinent information. Friedrich Wilhelm learnt of the peace with France concluded in March 1871 from a newspaper. Seven years later, the emperor put a halt to Bismarck's initiative to propose the crown prince as governor of Alsace–Lorraine. In March 1887, Friedrich Wilhelm complained about his continuing isolation to the former German ambassador to Paris: 'I find out about everything only from the newspapers and that with the emperor ninety years old.'

Wilhelm I did not content himself with forcing his successor onto the political sidelines. He also rigorously deployed the oversight he exercised as head of the family to control the household and private life of his son. As early as the autumn of 1864, the crown prince had been left at a loss when he received a letter from his father dictating the maximum length of a planned holiday in Switzerland, forbidding his children from being including in the travels, and also ordering that his new-born son, Sigismund, be nursed by a wet nurse and not by his mother. 'How am I supposed to tell this to my poor wife?', he recorded in his diary. His father's prescriptive intervention in the family life of his eldest son – which was by no means exceptional amongst the dynasties of Europe – remained standard practice into the 1880s. It led Victoria and Friedrich Wilhelm to resent the emperor deeply. 'He is alas! very autocratic and tyrannical and very obstinate in these matters', the crown princess wrote to her mother in 1876, 'and Fritz takes it dreadfully to heart and it makes him very bitter and excites and distresses him very much.'

Friedrich Wilhelm grew increasingly disgusted by the 'geriatric idio-syncrasies' exhibited by his parents, 'which traditionally hurt children and descendants most'. His father's longevity left him struggling with pro-found resignation and undisguised impatience. The crown prince talks 'about the expected death without reservation', his trusted friend Albrecht von Stosch reported. The elderly monarch responded with indestructible health and dark humour. At the celebration of his ninetieth birthday in March 1887, Wilhelm I is said to have joked that he could not die yet as his son was still alive. He could not have known that only a few weeks later his son would be diagnosed with terminal cancer. Wilhelm I died on 9 March 1888, just shy of his ninety-first birthday; his son outlived him by only ninety-nine days.

'To See Him Resemble His Angelic Dearest Father in Every, Every Respect': Queen Victoria and Her Son Albert Edward, Prince of Wales

Given that Emperor Wilhelm I and his son had at least enjoyed a few harmonious early decades, the Prussian drama compared favourably with the relationship between Queen Victoria of Great Britain and her oldest son, the future Edward VII. Even when the prince was still an infant, the queen had been dismayed by his character and intellectual faculties. Her frustrations would subsequently grow to something approaching hysteria. In 1921 – two decades after the queen's death and eleven years after that of her son – the shockingly bad relationship between mother and son was still so immediate for contemporaries that the renowned caricaturist Max Beerbohm was inspired to create a sketch entitled 'The rare, the rather awful visits of Albert Edward, Prince of Wales, to Windsor Castle', here shown as Figure 4: wearing her black widow's weeds, a rotund and grim Queen Victoria sits in the foreground; behind her, with his back turned on his mother and his hands clasped sulkily behind him, stands her similarly corpulent son.[14]

The future King Edward VII was born on 9 November 1841, not quite a year after his sister Victoria. Britain had not been able to welcome a direct male heir to the throne since 1762 and the relief was so great that Dr Locock, the Queen's obstetrician, was presented with an exorbitant honorarium of 1,000 pounds sterling to thank him for the providential birth of the future monarch. The newly founded magazine *Punch* celebrated the happy event in pompous and patriotic verse:

> Huzza! we've a little Prince at last,
> A roaring Royal boy;
> And all day long the booming bells
> Have run their peals of joy.

The royal son was baptised as Albert Edward, in honour of Prince Albert, the child's father, who was so idolised by his mother, and in memory of Victoria's late father, Edward, Duke of Kent. Just a few weeks after the birth, the queen recorded her expectations for her son in almost frenzied

---

[14] N. John Hall, *Max Beerbohm Caricatures* (New Haven, CT and London, 1997), p. 171.

Figure 4. 'The rare, the rather awful visits of Albert Edward, Prince of Wales, to Windsor Castle': Max Beerbohm's cartoon pokes fun at a problem that carried significant risks for the monarchy – the deeply dysfunctional relationship between the British queen and her oldest son. Granger Historical Picture Archive/Alamy Stock Photo.

terms: 'You will understand *how* fervent my prayers and I am [sure] *everybody's* must be', she wrote to her uncle Leopold, King of the Belgians, 'to see him resemble his angelic dearest Father in *every, every* respect, both in mind and body.'[15]

Meeting such high and eager expectations was nigh on impossible. 'Bertie', as he was known to his family, was only eighteen months old when disappointment set in, 'I don't think him worthy of being called

---

[15] Sir Sidney Lee, *King Edward VII: A Biography*, vol. 1 (London, 1925), pp. 5–6; Jane Ridley, *Bertie: A Life of Edward VII* (London, 2012), pp. 3–4; Queen Victoria to Leopold, King of the Belgians, 7 December 1841, in Arthur C. Benson, and Viscount Esher (eds.), *The Letters of Queen Victoria*, vol. 1 (London, 1911), p. 366.

Albert yet', the Queen informed her uncle.[16] And he never would prove worthy, adds Bertie's biographer Jane Ridley, signalling the core issue in the relationship between the monarch and her heir: her son's inability, at least in his mother's eyes, to meet the demands his parents made of him and the implications of that failure. Unlike in the Prussian case, no explicit political crisis poisoned their personal relationship for good. The falling out between Victoria and Bertie was personal and stemmed from the queen's decades-long refusal to allow her son's life to have a political dimension.

Prince Albert was the product of a systematic and highly structured upbringing. In turn, he developed a demanding and even overly rigorous pedagogy for his own children, which his wife fully accepted. Bertie's precocious and highly intelligent older sister, Princess Victoria, delighted her father with her outstanding accomplishments and soon became the apple of his eye. The heir to the throne, however, buckled under Albert's system, designed to train the optimally qualified constitutional monarch. He came up short in comparison with his sister, admitted her superiority with resignation, and responded to the humiliation he felt at his parents' hands with obstreperousness and by acting out. Rather than recognise his actions as a plea for his parents' attention, Victoria and Albert had their son seen by the renowned phrenologist Andrew Combe, who examined the shape of the prince's skull and diagnosed him with a defective development of the brain. In 1850 another phrenologist, Dr George Combe, was consulted. Although he sensibly proposed that the young boy be raised with greater consideration and kindness than had been the case to date, his diagnosis corresponded to that of the younger Combe: Bertie's brain was weak and its form abnormal. For the queen, already lacking in instinctive motherly love, that verdict proved fatal – her hypercriticism of her son now veered into a somewhat disgusted rejection. The diarist Charles Greville, a well-connected and avaricious collector of tittle-tattle, had determined as early as 1848 that 'The hereditary and unfailing antipathy of our sovereigns to their Heir Apparent seems ... early to be taking root, and the Queen does not much like the child.'[17]

Little would change over the course of the years – at least not for the better. In early 1858, on the occasion of her heir's confirmation, the queen observed rather unflatteringly that fundamentally he had a good heart and was loving but that these virtues were overshadowed by his all-too-many weaknesses. Victoria faulted her son in particular for his limited intellect, his boundless laziness, his poor behaviour, his disobedience and his lack of independence.[18] Under Prince Albert's indefatigable direction,

---

[16] Ridley, *Bertie*, p. 15.   [17] Ibid., pp. 17–23.
[18] Ibid., p. 40; Karina Urbach, *Queen Victoria. Eine Biographie* (Munich, 2011), p. 98.

Bertie's early upbringing was now followed by a series of educational experiments, in the hope that a satisfactory outcome might still be achieved. Neither his success overseas during a tour to Canada and the USA nor the modest progress in his studies at home could dam the stream of parental fault-finding and reproofs with which his efforts were received.[19] 'I never in my life met such a thorough and cunning lazy-bones', the prince consort complained to his daughter Victoria about Bertie. 'It does grieve me when it is my own son, and when one considers that he might be called upon at any moment to take over the reins of government in a country where the sun never sets.' The much-maligned heir also turned to his older sister, in the hope of eliciting some sympathy for his difficult situation as the constant and comprehensive admonishments continued: he should part his hair differently, he should not fall asleep on the sofa; he should not eat heavy meals; he should not take risks while hunting. But Bertie found no solace with his sister, who instead urged him to comply with their parents' wishes. Then all would be well, and 'dear Mama will be pleased and satisfied'.[20]

Talked down to by his closest family but flattered by many contemporaries, the young man soon appears to have stopped caring whether he was making his father and mother happy. Understandably in need of opportunity for relaxation and amusement and perhaps also rebelling against a regime of disparaging criticism and petty admonitions, Bertie kicked over the traces. He became a pleasure-seeker who met his pronounced sensual needs with an abandonment that was partly naïve and partly foolhardy. The implications for his relationship with his parents, who found his behaviour utterly incomprehensible, could only be grave.

A highpoint in the drama occurred in September 1861, as the prince was enjoying another of the education projects carefully planned for him by his father – on this occasion, military exercises at a garrison in Ireland. With the knowledge of several fellow officers and certainly not as part of his father's educational designs, the prince repeatedly slipped out through a window for trysts with Nellie Clifden, an attractive actress who also offered other services. On 10 September 1861 he recorded in his diary 'N.C. – third time' (after earlier encounters on 6 and 9 September) and then left for Germany. Ironically, the purpose of Bertie's journey was to meet Princess Alexandra of Denmark, whom his father, after close scrutiny of the matrimonial market, had selected as his future bride. To the displeasure of his parents, the heir to the throne was not particularly

---

[19] Christopher Hibbert, *Edward VII: A Portrait* (London, 1976), pp. 27–36; Ian Radforth, *Royal Spectacle: The 1860 Visit of the Prince of Wales to Canada and the United States* (Toronto, 2004).

[20] Hibbert, *Edward VII*, pp. 30–31; Ridley, *Bertie*, pp. 44–46.

taken with the Danish 'pearl' and showed absolutely no interest in marrying soon. He returned hotfoot to London, where in the meantime Clifden had also shown up.[21]

Two months later, on 12 November 1861, rumours about Bertie and his accommodating 'Princess of Wales' reached the ears of Victoria and Albert. Albert's first response was to write his son an almost apocalyptic letter on 'a subject which has caused me the deepest pain I have yet felt in this life'. As A. N. Wilson explains in his recent life of the prince consort, Bertie's transgression undermined the whole edifice of his father's political concept. 'Albert's entire picture of what a constitutional monarch should be', Wilson observes, 'was that the monarch of the modern age should be someone who commanded the respect of the emergent middle-class voters.' As 'models of family rectitude', the royal couple and their offspring were central to this, but 'Bertie's antics showed all too clearly how little the son and heir intended to follow in the father's footsteps.' Immediate action was required. On 25 November the prince consort, whose physical health and mental state were fragile, paid an unexpected visit to his son in Cambridge. In the course of a long and rainy walk, they sought to clear the air. By the time the two men returned, they were drenched and shivering with cold. Albert would never recover from this exertion. For the queen there was no question that Bertie's scandal had caused his father's collapse. On 7 December, the royal physician diagnosed Albert with typhoid. He died a week later. During Albert's final days, neither the prince consort nor Victoria expressed a desire to see Bertie. He was, however, called to his father's sickbed in Windsor by a telegram from his sister Alice and therefore saw Albert alive one last time. Should the queen have had any doubts about whether her son was in fact responsible for the death of her beloved husband, these were quashed by the doctors. In the face of growing criticism of their inability to save the prince consort, they confirmed that mental agitation brought on by Bertie's transgression, the depression that resulted and the strains of the journey to Cambridge had led to Albert's premature end.[22]

The relationship between mother and son was irreparably damaged, and the course had been set for the heir's future life. His father had been tasked with a significant role in affairs of state but not even part of his responsibility was passed on to Bertie; instead the royal heir was forced into an entirely apolitical private life. Not only did his mother disdain him, she also held him responsible for the death of his father. 'Oh, that Boy',

---

[21] Philip Magnus, *King Edward the Seventh* (London, 1964), pp. 43, 46–47; Ridley, *Bertie*, pp. 54–57.
[22] Ridley, *Bertie*, pp. 58–63; A. N. Wilson, *Prince Albert: The Man Who Saved the Monarchy* (London, 2019), pp. 376–377.

the queen wrote in December 1861 to her oldest daughter, 'much as I pity, I never can or shall look at him without a shudder.'[23] She was certain that as the future monarch Bertie represented a major risk. His dutiful willingness to marry Princess Alexandra in early 1863, in accordance with his late father's plans, made no difference. As a result, Victoria monitored the married life of the young couple even unto the smallest detail, and she openly shared her views with other members of the family. Her judgement was withering, 'Oh, what will become of the poor country when I die!', she wrote to her daughter Alice in summer 1863. 'I foresee, if Bertie succeeds, nothing but misery, and he would do anything he was asked and spend his life in one whirl of amusements.' He increasingly showed, she wrote, 'how *totally totally* unfit he is for ever becoming King'.[24]

Over the following decades, the queen seemed to throw herself into ensuring that her estimation would prove a self-fulfilling prophecy. She had absolutely no intention of sharing her power or her knowledge of the affairs of state with her son. He was constantly denied all access to state papers and diplomatic intelligence. When in the early 1870s the heir requested that he might be allowed to peruse this material in order to prepare himself for his future duties, the monarch refused, noting that 'Any preparation of this kind is quite useless, & the Prince of Wales will not do it.' Only in 1892 would Foreign Secretary Rosebery be given permission to hand over to the heir to the throne, now aged fifty, the gold key that had been used by Prince Albert to access diplomatic files. And the queen still turned down the suggestion by Prime Minister Gladstone that Bertie be sent to Ireland as representative of the crown.[25]

His mother's attitude ensured that the heir to the throne had much time on his hands, which he dedicated to the unbridled pursuit of his hedonistic inclinations. Despite his marriage and his responsibilities as head of his own family, he had numerous affairs, proved as attached to congenial dining as he was to gambling at the races and on the tables, enjoyed opulent hunts and plunged himself into Paris nightlife. The future king was the centre of the Marlborough House Set, a clique named after his London residence whose members were of morally dubious character and behaved so scandalously that Bertie's prim father can hardly have rested peacefully in his grave.

---

[23] Magnus, *King Edward the Seventh*, p. 52; Ridley, *Bertie*, p. 66.

[24] Magnus, *King Edward the Seventh*, p. 73; Ridley, *Bertie*, p. 79.

[25] Jane Ridley, 'Bertie Prince of Wales: Prince Hal and the Widow of Windsor', in Frank Lorenz Müller and Heidi Mehrkens (eds.), *Royal Heirs and the Uses of Soft Power in Nineteenth-Century Europe* (London, 2016), p. 128; Magnus, *King Edward the Seventh*, pp. 111–112, 116–117.

His resolutely dissolute lifestyle could not stay hidden from the public, whatever the attempts at discretion and secrecy. Some of his highjinks were comparatively harmless – in March 1868 Bertie and his hunting party chased a deer across London before shooting it in the goods yards at Paddington Station in front of train conductors and porters and then rode home in high spirits through Hyde Park. More serious were the public scandals that revealed the discrepancy between Bertie's lifestyle and the prevailing moral climate. In 1871 he was called as a witness by Sir Charlies Mordaunt in his divorce proceedings against Lady Mordaunt, which brought the sexual licentiousness of the Marlborough House Set to public attention in shocking detail. There followed the Aylesford Affair of 1876 – which included adultery, divorce, the love letters of the crown prince and the threat of a duel – and the Beresford Scandal of 1891, in which Bertie was threatened by Lord Charles Beresford with public exposure after he had stolen away Beresford's lover.[26]

The Tranby Croft Affair of 1891 proved even more of a scandal. It pivoted on an accusation of cheating during an illegal game of baccarat at a house party on the Tranby Croft estate. The prince was again called as a witness, this time in slander proceedings, which revealed how Bertie entertained himself by participating in illegal gambling during a private party. The lawyer Sir Edward Clarke, representing Sir William Gordon-Cumming, the alleged cheat, used every trick in the book as he grilled the heir to the throne. Before a public that was extraordinarily interested in the trial, Bertie was accused of impropriety and disloyalty. The publicity was devastating for the prince's reputation. 'We profoundly regret that the Prince should have been in any way mixed up, not only in the case, but in the social circumstances which prepared the way for it', the *Times* of London recorded in an editorial on 10 June 1891. According to the newspaper, the heir was 'next to the Queen, the most visible embodiment of the Monarchical principle; and any personal default of his gives a shock to the principle which in these democratic days is mischievous, even dangerous'. Victoria thought similarly: 'It is a fearful humiliation to see the future King of this country dragged (and for a second time) through the dirt, just like anyone else, in a Court of Justice', she wrote to her oldest daughter. 'It is very painful and must do his prestige great harm.' For the heir to the throne to be so humiliated and despised put the monarchy itself at risk, according to the queen.[27]

---

[26] Ridley, 'Bertie Prince of Wales', pp. 126–127, 129–130; Magnus, *King Edward the Seventh*, pp. 98, 143–150.
[27] Ridley, 'Bertie Prince of Wales', pp. 133–134; Ridley, *Bertie*, pp. 281–291; Magnus, *King Edward the Seventh*, pp. 222–229; *The Times* of 10 June 1891, p. 9.

The attention-grabbing uninhibited and daringly hedonistic virility of the heir was in complete contrast to the cultivated ideal of the strait-laced grieving widow of Windsor. In 1891, the British newspaper *Truth* depicted the contrast for its readers in a drawing, shown here as Figure 5. For 1841 – the year the year the heir was born – the royal house is portrayed as a stronghold of justice and virtue; fifty years later it is under threat from a monarch devoted to playing cards and gambling at the races.[28]

Although age mellowed the antagonism between monarch and heir somewhat in Victoria's final decade, the gulf between mother and son could not be bridged. When the queen died in 1901, her successor, now almost sixty years old, lost no time and immediately altered the style of the royal court with numerous highly symbolic changes. The prohibition of smoking that had been closely observed in the royal palaces for decades was lifted, and while waiting at Windsor for the funeral ceremonies to begin, the German emperor and the kings of the Belgians and of Portugal could now calm their nerves with a cigar. As the queen's body was conveyed from the Isle of Wight, where Victoria had died, to the British mainland, Edward VII asked the ship's captain why the royal standard was flying at half-mast. 'The queen is dead, Sir', he answered. 'The king of England lives', Edward responded, and the flag was hoisted up to the top of the mast.[29]

'You Are Not Worthy to Be My Successor': Emperor Franz Joseph and His Son Crown Prince Rudolf

At almost seventy-one years of age, Emperor Franz Joseph of Austria felt too old to pay his final respects to the dead British queen in person. At the funeral ceremonies in London in 1901, Austria-Hungary was represented by his nephew, Archduke Franz Ferdinand, who had been designated heir to the throne. Crown Prince Rudolf, born in 1858 and the only son of Franz Joseph and his late wife, Elisabeth, had died more than a decade earlier. The circumstances surrounding his demise, at age thirty, form one of the bleakest and most shocking events in the history of European monarchy in the nineteenth century. In late January 1889, Rudolf secluded himself with his seventeen-year-old lover, Baroness Mary Vetsera, who was entirely in thrall to the crown prince, in the royal hunting lodge at Mayerling, twenty kilometres southwest of Vienna. On a tragic night – the exact course of events is not clear – the couple appear

---

[28] Ridley, 'Bertie Prince of Wales', p. 134.
[29] Hibbert, *Edward VII*, p. 187; Ridley, *Bertie*, p. 348.

Figure 5. The monarchy as 'Society's Idol 1841–1891': having epitomised the very essence of propriety and virtue a few years after Victoria's accession, fifty years later the monarchy heralded a vice-ridden future under the Queen's wayward son Bertie. According to this cartoon from *Truth* magazine, Victoria's dedication to learning, justice and charity was about to be supplanted by a king indulging in horseracing, gambling and drink. picture-alliance/Mary Evans Picture Library.

to have carried out a suicide pact: the crown prince shot first Mary and then himself.[30]

Only with the greatest difficultly and with scant concern for the family of Baroness Vetsera did the Viennese court manage to conceal the excruciating details of Rudolf's death. After the first explanation – death caused by a stroke – proved unsustainable, the crown prince was diagnosed posthumously with 'mental confusion' caused by a 'flattening of the convolution of the brain'. This falsification of the records assured the prince a Christian burial even though he had died by his own hand.[31]

A complex web of physical, psychological and political factors lay behind the crown prince's actions. Above all, this dramatic event marked the highpoint and final act in his long-standing conflict with his father, with whom the heir to the throne had fought bitterly shortly before his death. The nature of the emperor's presence in the last hours of his son's life was made evident by a bundle of letters of farewell that Rudolf addressed to, amongst others, his wife Stephanie, his mother, his sister Marie Valerie, his longstanding lover Mizzi Caspar and the banker Moritz Hirsch. It seems that Rudolf could not bring himself to write even a few lines to his father. On the day before his death, however, as the crown prince took his leave of Prince Philipp von Coburg, who was on his way to the emperor, he had commissioned his friend to 'offer my imperial father many kisses on the hand'. Right up until his final confrontation with his father, whose rule Rudolf had previously criticised as ill-fated, the political dimension of the struggle between father and son had dominated. 'When Papa eventually closes his eyes, it will become very uncomfortable in Austria', Rudolf wrote tellingly in his farewell letter to his sister. 'I know all too well what will follow, and I advise you to emigrate then.'[32]

Franz Joseph and Rudolf's tragic father–son relationship ended in the Capuchin Crypt, the traditional burial place of the Habsburgs, where Rudolf was interred on 5 February 1889. He had kept his composure on the day of the funeral, the emperor subsequently wrote to his daughter Marie Valerie, but once in the crypt, 'there it couldn't be done any more'.[33] While the relationships of Wilhelm I and Friedrich III and of Victoria and Edward VII were each dominated by a single area of conflict, namely political disagreement for the former and different lifestyles for the latter, Franz Joseph and Rudolf's relationship was encumbered in

[30] Brigitte Hamann, *Kronprinz Rudolf. Ein Leben* (Vienna, 2006), pp. 454–472.

[31] Michaela Vocelka and Karl Vocelka, *Franz Joseph I. Kaiser von Österreich und König von Ungarn, 1830–1916* (Munich, 2015), pp. 300–301.

[32] Karl Vocelka and Lynne Heller, *Die private Welt der Habsburger. Leben und Alltag einer Familie* (Graz, 1998), p. 290; Hamann, *Kronprinz Rudolf*, pp. 446–449, 456.

[33] Vocelka and Vocelka, *Franz Joseph I.*, p. 302.

both respects. Add in the particular mental fragility of the crown prince and the unusually rigid hierarchy of Viennese court culture, and the result was a toxic mixture that goes a long way to explaining that night at Mayerling.

The political fault between father and son reflected – perhaps more strongly than was the case for Rudolf's friend, the Prussian–German Crown Prince Friedrich Wilhelm, – the polarisation that accompanied the gradual introduction of monarchical constitutionalism. Archduke Rudolf was a typical representative of what we might term 'crown prince liberalism'. His progressive views on constitutional development, on the politics of nationality, on religion, culture and education stood in sharp contrast to those of his father and other leading representatives of the archconservative politics of the imperial house.[34] That the heir to the throne moved in this political direction would have greatly chagrined Rudolf's father, who had constantly trusted that a male heir would play an important role precisely in the continuation of neo-absolutist politics.

The birth of a son in 1858, after two daughters, had therefore delighted Franz Joseph. The Viennese were informed of the happy event by a 101-gun salute, and the emperor marked the occasion by endowing the city with the new 'Rudolf Hospital' and by giving 20,000 Gulden to the poor. In an act unusual even by the standards of the militarised monarchies of the nineteenth century, Franz Joseph named Rudolf a knight of the Order of the Golden Fleece and colonel of an infantry regiment on the very day of his son's birth. The proud father's declaration read, 'I wish that the son given to me by the grace of God should from the time of his entry into this world belong to my brave army.' The close tie between army and dynasty was literally embodied by the future ruler. Thus, the nature of the young archduke's upbringing was set. Franz Joseph wanted a courageous and physically strong son who would one day make a fine soldier. The precocious intelligence and sensitivity of the young boy, his rich imagination and search for affection and attachment were not what his father expected, and instead gave Franz Joseph cause for concern. In line with family custom, at age six Rudolf was removed from the care of a nursemaid and consigned to a military tutor and court chamberlain (*Obersthofmeister*), who was to make a real man out of the delicate child. Once selected for this task, Leopold Graf Gondrecourt, who had no children of his own, pulled out all the stops to toughen up Rudolf: drills lasting hours, ice-cold baths, pistol shots in the night to awaken him suddenly. He abandoned the young boy in the Lainzer Tiergarten, a park where the Habsburgs hunted, and then shouted to him from the

---

[34] Vocelka and Heller, *Die private Welt der Habsburger*, pp. 289–290.

other side of the wall that a wild boar was approaching, apparently remaining unmoved as the frightened and tearful child hammered on the locked door. The terrified six-year-old, who dared not complain to his father and was repeatedly left on his own by his restless and constantly travelling mother, eventually became so unwell that it was feared he might die.[35]

Only then did the empress intervene and present her husband and his mother, who wielded great influence at court, with an ultimatum – an unheard-of act at the time. In an extraordinarily sharply formulated letter, Elisabeth demanded in August 1865 that she be given oversight of her son's education until he reached the age of maturity. Devoted to his wife and recoiling at the risk of a scandal, the monarch acceded. Gondrecourt was replaced by First Lieutenant Joseph Latour von Thumberg. Although this officer and lawyer, who was thought a liberal, had powerful enemies at court, he was protected by the emperor in accord with his agreement with the empress. Working together with Latour, Elisabeth ensured that Rudolf's upbringing became more compassionate and more broad-minded. His lessons followed the curriculum of the elementary school and then of the grammar school. His tutors were chosen for their skills as teachers and scholars, such that the future monarch was predominantly taught by bourgeois intellectuals who represented the various national-ities within the Habsburg Empire and were largely the product of more modest circumstances. Additionally, they were inclined to be anti-aristocratic and anti-clerical. Within this pedagogical bubble, reviled as an alien entity at the court but protected by the empress, the crown prince developed into a convinced liberal, a critic of court society and the aristocracy, and a fervent advocate of scientific investigation.[36]

Set against his academic education, Rudolf's military training certainly did not come up short. The adolescent archduke proved eager to ensure he lived up to his father's demands – as a fine huntsman, horseman and soldier. A moving scene played out in public on the threshold of Rudolf's majority is evidence that as yet no cloud hung over the relationship of father and son: on the twenty-fifth anniversary of his accession, Franz Joseph spoke of his confidence that the army 'would dedicate themselves to his son with the same love and loyalty they have always shown me'. His words caused the profoundly affected fifteen-year-old crown prince to break into loud sobs, which deeply moved the emperor, who struggled to

---

[35] Hamann, *Kronprinz Rudolf*, pp. 13–15, 29–30; Jean-Paul Bled, *Franz Joseph. 'Der letzte Monarch der alten Schule'* (Vienna, 1988), p. 181; Brigitte Hamann, *Elisabeth. Kaiserin wider Willen*, 4th edn (Munich, 2014), pp. 173–179; Vocelka and Vocelka, *Franz Joseph I.*, pp. 190–191.

[36] Hamann, *Kronprinz Rudolf*, pp. 57–85.

continue to speak. This harmony would disintegrate once the crown prince had come of age and his schooling had ended. With Empress Elisabeth no longer seeking to influence his education, the pendulum swung in favour of the conservative party at court. Rudolf's wish to attend university was denied. Instead, his coming of age was celebrated with a service of thanksgiving, the grand cross of the Order of Saint Stephen, and – truly no great joy – the harsh 'aphorisms' of the flinty Archduke Albrecht. The nineteen-year-old heir to the throne was at least permitted to undertake several educational trips – to Corfu, Silesia, Britain and Switzerland.[37]

During his journey to Britain, Rudolf began what Günter Kronenbitter has identified as the crown prince's 'opposition'.[38] Together with his former teacher, the economist Carl Menger, the heir to the throne subsequently composed a pamphlet entitled *Der österreichische Adel und sein constitutioneller Beruf (The Austrian Nobility and Its Constitutional Calling)*. The work was an avowal of the constitutional state. With its almost contemptuous criticism of the nobility and its abundant praise of the bourgeoisie, it caused a stir and provoked objections in the conservative press. Rudolf's role remained a secret, though. Over the next decade, the crown prince would continue to deploy the method established with this his first intervention: using intermediaries and confidants drawn from anti-government circles – often journalists and publicists – Rudolf repeatedly authored anonymous texts. He criticised the political and social situation in the Habsburg Empire, the halting constitutional progress and above all the politics of the current minister president, the conservative Eduard Count Taaffe, who was supported by the emperor. Rudolf's conviction that the survival of the Danubian Monarchy depended on a stronger, more liberal state headed by a progressive monarch did not, however, amount to a direct attack on his father. Despite all efforts, though, the crown prince's increasingly intense oppositional activities and his related personal contacts did not remain a secret.[39]

It was hardly surprising that Rudolf, whose hatred of the Viennese court and government elites met with hardly concealed disdain from those circles, was kept at a distance from political decision-making. His father continued to ensure, however, that his son was well prepared for his future military duties. Having first commanded an infantry regiment, the

---

[37] Ibid., pp. 86, 90.
[38] Günter Kronenbitter, 'The Opposition of the Archdukes: Rudolf, Franz Ferdinand and the Late Habsburg Monarchy', in Frank Lorenz Müller and Heidi Mehrkens (eds.), *Sons and Heirs: Succession and Political Culture in Nineteenth-Century Europe* (Basingstoke, 2016), pp. 211–225.
[39] Hamann, *Kronprinz Rudolf*, pp. 104–107.

heir to the throne was appointed Inspector General of this branch of the service in 1888. Yet he remained barred from accessing any state papers. Wounded by his exclusion, Rudolf complained that 'The lowest court counsellor has greater influence than do I; I am condemned to doing nothing.' He wrote with resignation to his former teacher Latour that he was never permitted to have his own opinion. The crown prince's despondency at the political realities grew with the news in 1887 that the German heir to the throne, Friedrich Wilhelm, whose eventual rule Rudolf associated with a hope for new liberal impulses, had been diagnosed with an incurable cancer. In a frenzied diplomatic reversal, Rudolf now sought to join Britain and Russia against Austria-Hungary's German ally. This intervention intensified the political opposition between the emperor, who remained firmly attached to the alliance with the German Empire, and his successor, who had ventured into foreign policy, territory traditionally reserved for the monarch.[40]

It was against this backdrop that a fierce struggle between father and son broke out in January 1889. The immediate cause, Jean-Paul Bled suspects, was a letter sent by the crown prince to Pope Leo XIII in which Rudolf had requested the annulment of his dysfunctional marriage. Both the idea of a divorce and the disregard of his authority as head of the family were anathema for the Catholic emperor and staunch dynast. Although details of the confrontation on 26 January 1889 are unknown, a lady's maid who saw the crown prince in the Vienna Hofburg immediately afterwards described him as 'terribly distraught, almost destroyed'. A valet to whom she turned reckoned that 'something terrible' had happened during the audience. 'You are not worthy to be my successor', Franz Joseph had apparently hurled at his son. Only a few days later, Rudolf and Mary Vetsera would make their way to Mayerling.[41]

The prince, who would die by his own hand at the age of thirty, was ruined politically, but he was also prematurely aged and physically wasted. At the beginning of 1889, his wife described him as a sick man, 'His skin was pallid and slack, his stare was flickering and his features were completely changed.' Already suffering from gonorrhoea, the crown prince had been further weakened by months of morphine use and an escape into alcohol. He was paying the price of a hedonistic and, in the end, self-destructive way of life.[42] First in Vienna and then during his time in Prague, where he had moved in 1878 to serve as colonel of the 36th Infantry Regiment, Rudolf had entertained numerous lovers, including

---

[40] Bled, *Franz Joseph*, pp. 434, 436–437; Vocelka and Vocelka, *Franz Joseph I.*, p. 296.

[41] Bled, *Franz Joseph*, pp. 437–438; Hamann, *Kronprinz Rudolf*, p. 434.

[42] Bled, *Franz Joseph*, p. 438; Jean-Paul Bled, *Rodolphe et Mayerling* (Paris, 1989), pp. 142–143.

Baroness Helene Vetsera, Mary's mother. His later instability must also be understood, however, in the light of his failed marriage. In March 1880, the crown prince had entered without protest into an engagement with the daughter of the Belgian king, arranged by the two courts. Far from a novice when it came to the company of women, the crown prince was never particularly enamoured with Princess Stephanie, who was generally thought to be somewhat bland and charmless. Rudolf regarded his marriage as little more than a quickly concluded act of dynastic acquiescence. On the day of their engagement, he wrote of his bride – with little passion but with a characteristic reverence to his father – that she would make 'a loyal daughter and subject of our emperor and a good Austrian'. It seems not to have occurred to Rudolf, who had travelled to Brussels to court his future spouse in the company of one of his alluring mistresses, that Stephanie would also be required to play the role of wife.[43]

After Stephanie had arrived in Vienna, court society tore into the crown prince's plain bride. 'The numerous ladies who knew and loved him were overjoyed', sneered Countess Larisch, 'for with this bride it was not to be feared that he would ever become a model husband.' Nor did he. While Rudolf initially extolled the domesticity that his marriage to Stephanie offered him and demonstrated a tender care for his daughter Elisabeth, born in 1883, he soon lost interest in his wife. He returned to a dissolute love life, entertaining paramours, some of them professionals, in his bachelor apartment in the Hofburg in Vienna and frequenting brothels. Having become infected with gonorrhoea, probably in 1885, and subsequently passing it on to his wife, he believed it unlikely that Stephanie would again become pregnant, eliminating the possibility of the birth of a male heir. His marriage therefore became simply a formality. After 1886, the crown prince even entered into a long-term relationship with the high-class Viennese prostitute Mizzi Caspar, frequenting wine taverns on the edge of the city with Caspar and his coachman Josef Bratfisch.[44]

Rudolf's escapades were eagerly seized upon by the international tabloid press. As the public was constantly entertained with new sensational accounts, Rudolf's emotional state unravelled catastrophically. In the summer of 1888 he had already attempted to convince Caspar to join him in a suicide pact. Their planned death together at the Temple of the Hussars in Mödling, a much-visited edifice that bore the dedication 'For Emperor and Fatherland', was surely designed to send a message. Caspar, as sensible

---

[43] Hamann, *Kronprinz Rudolf*, pp. 142, 152–154.
[44] Ibid., pp. 159, 408–419; Bled, *Franz Joseph*, p. 436; Bled, *Rodolphe et Mayerling*, pp. 143–147.

as she was resolute, refused his request and even managed to inform Minister President Taaffe of Rudolf's plans. Taaffe took no steps to protect his strident political opponent and did not send word to the emperor, cynically preferring to allow matters to take their course.[45]

As the 1880s unfolded, Rudolf and the emperor, whom the crown prince always approached with a mix of awe and fear, had become entirely alienated. Their personal contact was sporadic and amounted to no more than what etiquette required. Their estrangement was evident in their irreconcilable political differences, but the emperor also had absolutely no knowledge of his son's mental and physical deterioration, and he had not the slightest understanding of Rudolf's considerable academic activities. Alongside his political efforts and erotic escapades, the crown prince also found time for scholarly interests, to which he dedicated himself with great commitment. From 1884 on, he was editor and co-author of a multi-volume ethnographic and topographic encyclopaedia covering the whole of the Danubian Monarchy. In December 1885, when the first volume of this work was published, Rudolf presented his father with a copy. In a scene depicted in Figure 6, he deferentially kissed the emperor's hand and, wearing the uniform of a lieutenant field marshal, addressed his father with a heartfelt speech, glowing with authorial pride. The emperor responded by encouraging his son to show some stamina and then asked the Hungarian author Mór Jókai, who was also present, 'So did my son really write this introductory article by himself?'[46] The scene illustrates how alienated father and son had become.

Franz Joseph's failure to comprehend his son's concerns and character did not result from a lack of fatherly affection. The emperor's biographers agree that, irrespective of their political disagreements and temperamental differences, he loved his son deeply. Yet this brittle man, almost pathologically rigid in his conduct, was so bound in with the strict ordering of the court and the imperial family that he could produce little understanding of his son's very different needs, and, at the end, had no knowledge of his condition. Countess Marie Festetics, lady-in-waiting to Empress Elisabeth, believed that, as a result of their elevated position, Rudolf's parents discovered the truth 'only seldom and never completely'. From the Olympian heights occupied by the monarchy, founded on court and dynasty, Franz Joseph was unable to see what should have been closest to him, and those same heights left his son awestruck by his father. The discipline of court etiquette, which Archduke Albrecht had so

[45] Hamann, *Kronprinz Rudolf*, pp. 419–421; Bled, *Rodolphe et Mayerling*, pp. 170–171.
[46] Vocelka and Vocelka, *Franz Joseph I.*, pp. 295–296, 298; Hamann, *Kronprinz Rudolf*, pp. 118–141, 232–240.

Kronprinz Rudolph überreicht Sr. Majestät dem Kaiser das erste Heft von
„Oesterreich-Ungarn in Wort und Bild."

Figure 6. Displaying a mixture of authorial pride and filial deference, Crown Prince Rudolf presents his father with the first volume of his encyclopaedia of the Habsburg Empire in 1885. Emperor Franz Joseph would never understand his son's scholarly ambitions, though. ÖNB Bildarchiv und Grafiksammlung, Sign. Pf 1.299: E (5).

urgently exhorted the young Rudolf to follow, intensified the divide between emperor and heir and helped pave the way to Mayerling.[47]

Thus, in three of the most powerful monarchies of nineteenth-century Europe, the relationship between monarch and first-born son and heir

[47] Vocelka and Vocelka, *Franz Joseph I.*, p. 298.

proved profoundly dysfunctional. Neither Wilhelm I, nor Victoria, nor Franz Joseph succeeded in forming a personal relationship with their successor that was characterised by closeness, affection and trust. Additionally, all three denied their sons the opportunity to prepare themselves for their future office under their own initiative and with access to information. Contradicting Tolstoy's famous assertion, these unhappy parent–child relationships were marked by great similarities. The persistence of dynastic hierarchical demands played a decisive role in all three instances. Wilhelm I, Victoria and Franz Joseph all had precise notions of how their sons and heirs should behave in order to safeguard the future of the dynasty and the crown. The relationship between monarch and heir stood or fell with the ability and willingness of the latter to submit to these notions with demonstrative obedience throughout an extended childhood that lasted until the death of his predecessor. If that willingness was limited, the relationship might suffer irreparable damage. The danger grew when news of such dissonances reached the public. In the end, each of these three monarchs declared their heir incapable of one day being a worthy and capable bearer of the crown.

It might seem cynical, but a poor relationship between monarch and heir that caused both parties such grief could also be useful – at least for the monarchical system. This was not the case for the Habsburg dynasty, for here the failure of the relationship between father and son would also prove harmful to the future of the monarchy. The crown prince died long before his father, and the system did not benefit from the blast of fresh air delivered by the accession of a new ruler. There was no new beginning, which would have proved the empire's capacity for change. According to Rudolf's biographer Jean-Paul Bled, Rudolf's death only fed the uncertainty about the future of the monarchy.[48]

For Crown Prince Friedrich Wilhelm and the Prince of Wales the situation was different. Both suffered under their predecessors and neither man was systematically prepared for the office they would inherit. Precisely as a result of this constellation, though, their succession was an opportunity for a pronounced transformation in style, for a welcome change after the death of an aged monarch who had ruled for decades. Because their predecessors had kept them isolated and at a distance from the levers of power, the new rulers were not identified with the old monarchs, which could prove invigorating, both in political terms and for the monarchy's reception by a broader public. While monarchical succession was all about continuity, inner-dynastic differences and contrasts across generations prevented the system from becoming entirely

---

[48] Bled, *Rodolphe et Mayerling*, p. 275.

inelastic. Although Emperor Friedrich III was already terminally ill when he ascended the throne in 1888, his reign released a pro-monarchical wave within the left-liberal camp and generated great enthusiasm within the population.[49] The succession of Edward VII, who as king demonstrated a surprisingly secure political instinct, revitalised the monarchy. However paradoxical it may sound, that regeneration may have emanated from his scandalous reputation: for a good number of Britons this virile bon vivant was a refreshing break from the dusty, fusty and virtuous widowhood of his seemingly immortal mother. In 1901, the British poet Wilfrid Blunt praised the amiability of the new king and his tolerance of the sins and vulgarity of others. In thus securing the affections of the common man, Blunt believed Edward would 'make an excellent king for twentieth century England'.[50] That unhappy royal families were often so alike was not necessarily a disadvantage for the monarchical family business.

Princes as Husbands

August 1880 was a joyous month for the royal house of Württemberg. Princess Marie, the young wife of Prince Wilhelm, the heir to the throne, gave birth to a healthy boy, Prince Ulrich. Eighteen months after the birth of the couple's daughter, Pauline, the country now had the long-hoped-for Protestant son and heir. The central and centuries-old task of hereditary monarchy had been accomplished yet again. In an almost automatic response, the *Neues Tagblatt* in Stuttgart quoted the final line of a well-known ballad in which the Swabian bard Ludwig Uhland had sung of the victory of Count Eberhard of Württemberg (1315–1392), known the 'the Jarrer'. The son of the elderly count had fallen in the battle of Döffingen in 1388, but that same day Antonia Visconti, the wife of the count's grandson, had given birth to a great-grandson. 'A little lad, bold and fine' had secured the future of the House of Württemberg, then as now. The birth of young Ulrich bridged the gap between the middle ages and the present. 'The whole land celebrates with the great family', the *Neues Tagblatt* declared, and repeats the shout of joy given by Count Eberhard the Jarrer, 'The finch again has its seed, all praise and glory to the Lord.'[51]

When it came to the future of the monarchical system, the bond between monarch and heir was not the only significant family relationship to which the public directed its attention. Even before succeeding to the throne, the future monarch usually also had another vital task to perform – to ensure

---

[49] Müller, *Our Fritz*, pp. 208–209.   [50] Ridley, 'Bertie Prince of Wales', p. 136.
[51] *Neues Tagblatt* (Stuttgart) of 3 August 1880.

through the birth of a legitimate heir that the family tree could continue to grow. Before that step came marriage with a fertile woman or – in the rare case the heir was a woman – with a man able to father a child. Biological suitability was not the only factor at play in this moment, as a marriage partner would also need to meet legally defined standards. Dynastic law determined that for a princely marriage to be legitimate, the approval of the head of the family had to be secured. That permission depended above all on whether the prospective couple were of equal social standing. Political considerations also had a bearing and, additionally, by the end of the nineteenth century some perceptive contemporaries had recognised that marriage within a circle of close relatives was not advisable. Religion or confession was only rarely mentioned in the codified law of the land, as in Britain, where the Act of Settlement of 1701 had explicitly excluded Catholics and their spouses from ascending the throne, but confessionally mixed marriages remained rare and generally undesirable exceptions.

As a result, in the nineteenth century future monarchs were caught in a tightly woven web of traditional rules, significantly limiting their freedom of choice when it came to whom they might wed. Princely marriages, especially that of the heir, remained sovereign acts; they created dynastic connections whose primary rationale was not the happiness of the couple involved. This ancient practice confronted a new development that reached a climax in 1905 with the marriage of the Prussian Crown Prince Wilhelm and Cecilie of Mecklenburg-Schwerin. According to *Der Deutsche*, a weekly newspaper, 100,000 German women were anxiously asking: 'Do they really love one another?' The 'simple and sincere truth', the newspaper could reassure the women of Germany, was 'yes, with all their hearts'.[52] The public's growing interest in the private emotional life of the ruling family was set within an ever more sprawling media landscape, where it was both assuaged and fuelled. Having already cleared the hurdles of social equality, religious confession and political acceptability, the royal couple still needed to convince an audience of millions of their deep love and devotion for each other.

When it came to their public image, ever since the romanticism of the early-nineteenth-century royal marriages had been measured against the ideal of a love match. As a consequence, marriage was no longer understood primarily in pragmatic terms, for example as a source of mutual support, but was instead viewed as a covenant rooted in love. This

---

[52] Daniel Schönpflug, 'Heirs before the Altar: Hohenzollern Marriages in a Bourgeois Age', in Frank Lorenz Müller and Heidi Mehrkens (eds.), *Sons and Heirs: Succession and Political Culture in Nineteenth-Century Europe* (Basingstoke, 2016), pp. 67, 70.

modern conception, writes Monika Wienfort, was characterised by the freedom to choose whom to marry, erotic attraction and the union of body and spirit. In fulfilling this ideal, the royal couple provided much more than just an example of pure marital love; in the case of the future heir it was also a matter of symbolising and reflecting the mutual love and faithfulness that bound together royal house and people, and – extending into foreign policy – the harmony between two dynasties or even two nations. Using the Prussian Hohenzollern dynasty as an example, Daniel Schönpflug has shown how the alleged authenticity of the love between bride and groom was publicly staged at the dynasty's weddings from the late eighteenth century and then with even greater vigour from the 1850s. Thus in 1881 the conservative newspaper *Neue Preußische Zeitung* saw in the pairing of the future Emperor Wilhelm II with Auguste Viktoria of Schleswig-Holstein a 'sign that love can choose freely when the arm of God weaves the band that unites the souls'.[53]

The public appreciation of such stagings and their performance by the royal house are indicative of how new categories were created within dynasties under the pressure of the public gaze. That process affected royal married life in particular. The dynasty remained the 'state family', which continued to represent the body politic, but the public now also believed in the existence of a 'private family', which corresponded in principle to its non-royal counterpart. It was composed of individuals bound together by feelings and personal responsibilities for one other and was judged in the light of that romantic ideal. In public debate, a contrast was readily drawn between the exemplary nature of what was perceived as the bourgeois marriage and the older aristocratic model, now in decline. Thus, for example, Emperor Friedrich III, who died in 1888, was posthumously praised for his 'married life, firmly grounded in loyalty and in its most sincere faithfulness still pure even up until his painful end', a marriage untarnished by 'the scheming of court politics'. As the antithesis of this faithful and pure institution, marriages made at court certainly did not receive good press. As would become evident, however, generating love matches constituted no small challenge for state families.[54]

Heirs to the throne Friedrich Wilhelm, Edward and Rudolf all entered into dynastic marriages. The marriage of the Hohenzollern prince and Princess Victoria had long been planned by the parents of the bride and was a carefully engineered political calculation. In 1851, the eleven-year-old princess was introduced to the nineteen-year-old prince for the first

---

[53] Wienfort, *Verliebt, Verlobt, Verheiratet,* p. 20; Daniel Schönpflug, *Die Heiraten der Hohenzollern. Verwandtschaft, Politik und Ritual in Europa 1640–1918* (Göttingen, 2013), pp. 235, 239, 241.

[54] Schönpflug, 'Heirs before the Altar', pp. 54–55; Müller, *Our Fritz,* p. 121.

time; four years later his proposal of marriage was accepted. The bride was seventeen years old when she stood at the altar, in January 1858. Princess Alexandra of Denmark had been filtered out from the pool of candidates with calculated precision by Prince Albert, Queen Victoria and their oldest daughter and had been commended to Bertie, heir to the British throne, as a correctional measure. That the young man felt no flicker of passion when he saw the princess made no difference to the course already set. After Princess Stephanie had been selected as his future wife, Crown Prince Rudolf undertook his courtship perfunctorily, as an incidental but dutiful act.

It nevertheless goes without saying that all three marriages – Vicky and Friedrich Wilhelm in 1858, Alexandra and Bertie in 1863 and Stephanie and Rudolf in 1881 – would be staged in accordance with the ideal of the love match. The wedding tale crafted by English versifier Henry Robert Lumley in 1858 declared that 'Love is triumphant and has bound,/In two young hearts and hands, two lands.' Five years later, on the occasion of the wedding of the Prince of Wales to Alexandra, the *Illustrated London News* observed that through this marriage 'two hearts are thereby brought into closest contact, and, wherever love is in the ascendant, each becomes the complement of the other'. When sixteen-year-old Stephanie arrived in Vienna in 1881, a waltz composed especially for the occasion by Johann Strauss rang out, 'Royal child of Belgium, northern rose, the south greets you aglow with love.'[55] These effusive words contained no sign of what the future would in fact hold. Rudolf and his wife were certainly not set aglow by love, and Bertie and Alexandra's hearts complemented each other only insofar as she endured his constant and flagrant lack of faithfulness with astonishing forbearance and dignity. But not all couples were casualties of dynastic marriages: Friedrich Wilhelm and Victoria lived in a happy intimacy through the decades – despite the many political and personal burdens that their marriage was forced to bear.[56]

What opportunities could the monarchical system of the nineteenth century derive from the marriages of future rulers, and what risks were run? What did these new expectations mean for the individuals, or rather couples, involved? To address these questions, we turn now to three more European heirs: the Italian crown prince Umberto, Prince Wilhelm of Württemberg and, finally, Prince Friedrich August of Saxony, who was entangled in what was certainly the most sensational marriage scandal of the fin-de-siècle.

[55] Schönpflug, *Die Heiraten der Hohenzollern*, pp. 243–244; 'Marriage of His Royal Highness the Prince of Wales', in *The Illustrated London News* of 24 January 1863, p. 85; Hamann, *Kronprinz Rudolf*, p. 156.

[56] Wienfort, *Verliebt, Verlobt, Verheiratet*, pp. 170–186; Müller, *Our Fritz*, pp. 29–48.

'You Know How Proud I Am to Belong to the House of Savoy': Crown Prince Umberto of Savoy and Crown Princess Margherita

In 1861, the House of Savoy experienced its greatest triumph, but it came with a huge challenge. The ruling dynasty of the Kingdom of Piedmont-Sardinia became head of the newly founded Kingdom of Italy, which was anything but a united country. After decades of unrest, rebellion and revolution, after wars, diplomatic machinations, propaganda and plebis-cites, the dream of the Risorgimento seemed to have been fulfilled: in place of a multitude of separate smaller countries, there now existed the Italian nation-state, led by the king of Piedmont-Sardinia. Vittorio Emanuele II was now 'father of the fatherland'. The patriotic self-adulation and the almost cultish veneration of Giuseppe Garibaldi, Camillo di Cavour and Vittorio Emanuele II as heroes of the Risorgimento could not disguise, however, that the political, linguistic, cultural and geographical fragmentation of the peninsula stood in stark contrast to the patriotic idea of the *unità* of the nation. In the south, the implementation of the hated new order, spoken of locally as 'Piedmontisation', was the catalyst for a brutal civil war. It was clear that the external unification of the country, achieved through the war against Austria in 1859, the campaign by Garibaldi's 1,000 soldier volun-teers the following year and the cool diplomatic savvy of Piedmont prime minister Cavour, was not yet matched by internal agreement. Cavour's predecessor in office, the author, painter and romantic Massimo d'Azeglio, expressed that need in a famous aphorism: 'We have made Italy, now we have to make *Italians*.'[57]

The diverse population of the Italian peninsula was to be nationalised, and in this endeavour the royal house had a vital contribution to make. By winning the hearts of the people from Sicily to Turin, from Milan to the southern tip of Apulia, the monarchy would help overcome the fragmen-tation of the country. Those who still felt bound to their erstwhile ruling families were to become loyal subjects of the new, national dynasty. The royal house that was the focus of hopes for national unity suddenly received support from an entirely unexpected quarter: in 1864, Francesco Crispi, a former revolutionary from Sicily, declared in parlia-ment that 'The monarchy unifies us, and a republic would divide us.'[58] The dream of a nation-state had turned him, as it would many other

[57] Kathrin Mayer, *Mythos und Monument. Die Sprache der Denkmäler im Gründungsmythos des italienischen Nationalstaates 1870–1915* (Cologne, 2004), p. 64, n. 123.
[58] Christopher Duggan, 'Francesco Crispi, the Problem of the Monarchy, and the Origins of Italian Nationalism', in *Journal of Modern Italian Studies* 15, 3 (2010), p. 339.

Italians, into a monarchist. For this dream to become reality, the House of Savoy would need to change, to become more national, more Italian, more exemplary. And a good marriage within the royal family could be extraordinarily useful for that project.

The Piedmont dynasty was by no means well equipped for the task of winning over the hearts of these future Italians. What was the case for the majority of the population of the Kingdom of Italy also applied to the royal family in Turin: Italian was not its first language. It would take until the reign of Vittorio Emanuele III, the grandson of the first king of Italy, for the national monarch to speak Italian without a foreign accent. Additionally, for centuries, Piedmont, which lay at the extreme north-west limits of Italy, had looked culturally and politically to France. The southern climes of the Italian peninsula, above all the Kingdom of the Two Sicilies, once ruled by the Bourbons, seemed alien and hardly inviting to the Piedmontese elites. Although he was lauded as 'father of the fatherland', Vittorio Emanuele II embodied this reservation, for as king of Italy he retained his old Piedmont numbering – as Vittorio Emanuele II – and preferred to speak French or Piedmontese. He was extremely uncomfortable about having to speak Italian in public and found the southern Italian dialect almost incomprehensible. The king favoured continuing to spend his time in Piedmont and made every effort to avoid a stay in Florence, the first Italian capital, or, after 1870, in Rome. Henry Elliott, the British ambassador, was astonished by the 'hatred between the Piedmontese and the *foreigners* as they call the other Italians' and found this feeling particularly marked within the context of the royal court.[59]

That Vittorio Emanuele II had obvious deficits when it came to a comprehensively Italian patriotism could be largely concealed by his styling: he was presented as part of the cult of the Risorgimento, as a war hero, a royal gentleman (*Il Re Galantuomo*) and a simple lover of nature. When it came to the softer role of the royal family as a model bastion of virtuous happiness that might be used to charm the bourgeoisie, the challenges proved harder to meet. The king was a widower and therefore lacked the female figure by his side that was integral to any portrayal of a happy family and an essential component of magnificent court festivities. Adelheid of Piedmont-Sardinia, the king's wife, had died aged just thirty-two, following the birth of her eighth child. Even well-meaning contemporary authors such as the German under-secretary of state and banker Paul David Fischer noted that the marriage of the Piedmontese prince with this pious member of the Habsburg family in 1842 had served

---

[59] Mack Smith, *Italy and Its Monarchy*, pp. 18, 22–23, 63–64.

a particular purpose. It was meant to rein in the young man's 'fiery temperament and untameable love of life'. The plan failed, however, for Vittorio Emanuele's 'hot blood desired a headier excitement' than could be provided by a wife 'of unmatched kindheartedness'. The future king cheated constantly on Adelheid and with so little inhibition that his friend Cavaliere Francesco Casale, a military officer, had to take on the task of discretely providing for the many children Vittorio Emanuele fathered outside marriage. After 1847, in addition to a number of more fleeting affairs, Vittorio Emanuele entertained a long-term mistress in Rosa Vercellana, the voluptuous and down-to-earth daughter of a soldier, with whom he lived at times much as if they were married.[60]

After Adelheid's death in 1855, the king's family circumstances became even more complicated. Although he was under pressure to enter into a second marriage that would both benefit his country and bolster the image of his house, he refused to marry again for dynastic purposes. His plan to wed Rosa Vercellana foundered on the vehement objections of Cavour, for whom the presence of the daughter of a soldier on the throne of Italy was an impossibility. The confrontation between the two men would prove so intense that the king later described it as one of those affairs 'that one should settle with a knife'. Vittorio Emanuele initially conceded, but in 1869 he did indeed marry 'La bella Rosina', although only in a religious ceremony. The civil ceremony followed eight years later, shortly before his death, turning the king's mistress into his morganatic wife.[61]

In the light of these unedifying family circumstances, in 1868 the marriage of the heir to the throne, the twenty-four-year-old Prince Umberto, attracted great attention. The monarchy required an impressive and presentable princess who would restore the tattered dignity of the dynasty and could help the royal heir to form what contemporaries would deem a happy marriage. According to the newspaper *L'Opinione*, word of the heir's engagement spread throughout the Italian peninsula like a 'rapid spark ... along a metal track'. The future king of Italy was to marry his cousin, the seventeen-year-old Princess Margherita of Savoy. The young woman had not been the first option. The initial choice was Archduchess Mathilde of Austria–Teschen. A union with her would have been both politically and financially beneficial to the dynasty. Following the tragic accidental death of the young archduchess in 1867, Prime

---

[60] Paul David Fischer, *Italien und die Italiener. Betrachtungen und Studien über die politischen, wirthschaftlichen und sozialen Zustände Italiens*, 2nd edn (Berlin, 1901), pp. 42–43; Martina Winkelhofer, *Eine feine Gesellschaft. Europas Königs- und Kaiserhäuser im Spiegel ihrer Skandale* (Vienna, 2014), p. 130.

[61] Winkelhofer, *Eine feine Gesellschaft*, pp. 130–131.

Minister Luigi Federico Menabrea had to restart the search. When he proposed the king's own niece Margherita to Vittorio Emanuele II, the nonplussed monarch is said to have exclaimed, 'But she is still a child.' The minister assured him that Margherita was by no means just a girl, but rather a gracious and virtuous young woman of sixteen. After further investigation, the matter was settled and on 28 January 1868 – some seven months after Mathilde's death – Prince Umberto proposed to his cousin.[62]

The young couple's brief exchange betrayed the essence of their future marriage: Umberto is said to have asked, 'Margherita, will you be my wife?', to which the sixteen-year-old responded with a remarkable answer: 'You know how proud I am to be a member of the House of Savoy. I will be made even more so by becoming your wife.' The dynasty to which they both belonged would indeed be at the centre of their union, along with the dynastic responsibilities that entailed. The royal House of Savoy quickly reworked the failure to achieve a good international match into a patriotic virtue. Margherita, like her husband, was a scion of the House of Savoy, and she was also the daughter of Prince Ferdinando of Savoy, the hero of the Battle of Novara. Her heritage intensified the monarchy's national and Italian standing. Years later, after meeting Margherita, the Romanian lady-in-waiting and woman of letters Elena Văcărescu recorded that in the nineteenth century hardly any queen could rival Margherita's claim to embody the fate of her people and also that of her dynasty. 'She is the only one amongst royal consorts who has no need to search for a throne in another country than her own; she alone can speak to her subjects in the language of her childhood, and she treasures in her heart all the faults and qualities of her race. She alone has given them a king of pure native descent.'[63]

The political staging of the couple, shown here in Figure 7, before the eyes of the nation began with the large-scale celebration of their marriage, which took place quickly, in April 1868. After the civil ceremony but before the church service, the couple, apparently at Margherita's suggestion, appeared on the balcony of the royal palace in Turin, presenting themselves before the jubilant crowds. According to reports, more than 50,000 people had travelled to the Piedmontese capital to witness the

[62] *L'Opinione* of 7 February 1868, No. 38, 1. I am grateful to Maria Christina Marchi for this reference and for further insights into the history of the Savoyard Queen; for a fuller discussion of the role of the Savoyard heirs see Maria Christina Marchi, *The Heirs to the Savoia Throne and the Construction of 'Italianità', 1860–1890* (London, 2022); Carlo Casalegno, *La regina Margherita* (Bologna, 2001), pp. 38–39.

[63] Casalegno, *La regina Margherita*, p. 40; Hélène Vacaresco [Elena Văcărescu], *Kings and Queens I Have Known* (New York, 1904), p. 169.

Figure 7. The crown princely couple Umberto and Margherita was the charismatic centrepiece of the Italian royal family. Their happy union was meant to advance and symbolise the unification of the country. News of their engagement, a newspaper report claimed, had raced through the nation like 'a rapid spark ... on a metal track'. Alamy Images.

wedding. After the celebrations came a carefully planned honeymoon, during which the newly married couple criss-crossed the country and displayed their closeness to the people with great gusto. The poor and sick received particular attention, with visits to charitable institutions. In Bologna Princess Margherita was greeted by a group of orphaned children, whom she hugged and kissed; in Genoa she wore the traditional attire of a dark woollen dress with a light muslin veil. Towards the end of the following year, the couple visited Naples, the southern city that had, until recently, served as the capital of the Bourbon-ruled Kingdom of the Two Sicilies. *L'Opinione* welcomed this step. The presence of Prince Umberto and his 'very attractive bride' was, it suggested, 'very effective propaganda on behalf of the principles for which they stand: youth and grace will result in a conquest much more concrete and more substantial than reason and discourse could produce'.[64]

Soon after, Margherita gave birth to a son in Naples – the future King Vittorio Emanuele III. Three months later, the baby's grandfather, King Vittorio Emanuele II, arrived in the city to inspect his grandson. The princess met her father-in-law at the train station and placed the child in his arms, but then the baby was proudly presented to the women of the city's market. In various ways, the northern royal family was thus anchored in the south. Although the baby's father was still 'Prince of Piedmont', the new-born child was given the title 'Prince of Naples'. The future king was baptised Vittorio Emanuele Ferdinando Maria Gennaro. Thus, alongside the typical Savoyard name Vittorio Emanuele and the name of the Blessed Virgin, an indication of the significance of Catholicism, the future heir also bore a name – Ferdinando – that was traditional in the Bourbon family that had ruled in the south of Italy until 1861 and the name of the patron saint of the city of Naples, Saint Gennaro. The future of the Italian monarchy rested with the crown prince's family, which now, with the birth of an heir, was complete and fully aligned with its national and integrating role.[65]

After two years in Naples, Umberto, Margherita and the Prince of Naples moved to Rome, where they took up residence in the Quirinal Palace. They thus embodied the royal family's absorption of the Italian capital, which only shortly before had been under the control of the Pope and French troops. In June 1871, the couple were seen at the *Festa dello Statuto*, the official celebration honouring the transfer of the Italian constitution, once Piedmontese but now applicable to the whole Kingdom of Italy. On this occasion, a nursery school in Rome was named after the princess. Margherita did not limit herself to the roles of mother and carer, though. Her cultural engagement was also remarkable – she held salons, for example – and she had technical and scholarly interests that would subsequently earn her a reputation as a 'monarch of modernity'. In 1894, the German ambassador to Italy, Bernhard von Bülow, was asked by the

---

[64] Fanny Zampini Salazar, *Margherita of Savoy: First Queen of Italy. Her Life and Times* (London, 1914), pp. 47–51; Maria-Christina Marchi, 'The Royal Shop Window: Royal Heirs and the Monarchy in Post-Risorgimento Italy, 1860–1878', in Frank Lorenz Müller and Heidi Mehrkens (eds.), *Royal Heirs and the Uses of Soft Power in Nineteenth-Century Europe* (London, 2016), pp. 23–24, 29, 31.

[65] Maria Christina Marchi, 'Margherita: Italy's First Heir', AHRC Project *Heirs to the Throne in the Constitutional Monarchies of Nineteenth-Century Europe (1815–1914)*, 'Heir of the Month' (February 2014), http://heirstothethrone-project.net/?page_id=843 (accessed 27 January 2017); Romano Bracalini, *La regina Margherita* (Milan, 1983), p. 65.

emperor to provide an assessment of Queen Margherita. His verdict was unambiguous: her motivations were profoundly political. The queen, he wrote, 'is interested only in the glory and honour of her country and of her house. She embodies, one might say, the Italian raison d'état, and does so with spirit and grace.'[66]

Umberto and Margherita's marriage enhanced the public image of the Italian monarchy during the reign of Vittorio Emanuele II and also buttressed the crown following the king's death in 1878. In this charismatic princess, the royal house possessed a central female figure whose beauty, grace, maternal warmth, common touch and patriotic devotion soon became the focus of a fully fledged cult. The princess's public persona was only one factor, though. The Prince of Naples, the only son of the crown prince and crown princess also played an important role. He provided the future monarchs with the opportunity to prove their paternal and maternal qualities, to appeal to the Italians' strong sense of family and thus draw people and dynasty closer together. Umberto and Margherita's private life was depicted accordingly, as happy and warm. When, shortly after the death of Vittorio Emanuele II, Giuseppi Ugliengo sought to provide his fellow Italians with a stronger sense of the new royal couple, he emphasised that both of them dedicated themselves unstintingly to their domestic responsibilities. This image, which had formed while the masculine- and militaristic-connotated king was still alive, had implications for the configuration of the role of the crown prince.[67]

Notwithstanding his truly spectacular moustache, Prince Umberto did not find it easy to develop an image of his own alongside his bright and engaged wife, who on occasion was lauded as the 'only man in the House of Savoy'. He lacked both creativity and stature. It often seemed that Margherita had to spur on her 'lazy and not always available spouse' to ensure their joint dynastic project was realised. However, Umberto developed one aspect of his public persona that would stand the Italian monarchy in good stead. Initially the second king of Italy, like his father, held a reputation that was primarily militaristic and martial, a product of his performance as commander of a division that had fought in the battle between Italian and Austria troops at Custoza in 1866. 'Forming his regiments into squares, and himself taking up his position with the most

[66] Marchi, 'The Royal Shop Window', p. 32; Catherine Brice, 'Königin Margherita (1851–1926). "Der einzige Mann im Hause Savoyen"', in Regina Schulte (ed.), *Der Körper der Königin. Geschlecht und Herrschaft in der höfischen Welt seit 1500* (Frankfurt am Main, 2002), pp. 201, 203; Bernhard Fürst von Bülow, *Denkwürdigkeiten*, vol. 4 (Berlin, 1931), p. 660.

[67] Axel Körner, 'Heirs and Their Wives: Setting the Scene for Umbertian Italy', in Frank Lorenz Müller and Heidi Mehrkens (eds.), *Sons and Heirs: Succession and Political Culture in Nineteenth-Century Europe* (Basingstoke, 2016), p. 42.

exposed one, he withstood with splendid obstinacy the repeated charges of the Austrian cavalry', the London *Times* recalled decades later, in an obituary of the assassinated king. Yet, although Umberto displayed a strong interest in military matters throughout his life, this narrative captures only one part of his public image. His portrayal as a patriotic soldier-king was successfully augmented by the *leggenda del re buono*, the legend of the good king.[68]

The notion of Umberto as a compassionate father to his nation who shared the suffering of his people and brought them solace was based on many small and gracious acts performed on behalf of the poor and the common people. Most effectively, it was inspired by the king's eye-catching presence in the wake of natural disasters. In 1882, he travelled to inundated areas in the north-east of Italy, where heavy floods had left 200,000 residents homeless and would ultimately cause more than 60,000 people to emigrate. The following year he visited the island of Ischia, where a powerful earthquake had destroyed the municipalities of Casamicciola, Forio and Lacco. More than 2,000 people had died, and the damage was so extensive that international relief measures had been activated. Umberto arrived on Ischia within four days of the quake, bringing words of consolation and encouragement to continue the search for those who had been buried under the rubble. In 1884, he hurried to Naples, to be with the residents of that city as they faced a severe cholera epidemic. In a telegram exchange made public through official channels, he had replied to a request that he honour the horse races in Pordenone with his presence by cabling back: 'In Pordenone they celebrate, in Naples they die. I am travelling to Naples. Umberto.' He visited the city's hospitals and despite the risk of infection remained until the situation eased. The impact of his actions was so great that even socialists and republicans spoke in praise of the monarchy. While Umberto could display laurels won in battle, it was, above all, as the husband of an enchanting wife and the father of a propitious heir that he turned into the 'good king'.[69]

It was thus possible to warm the Italians to the idea of the House of Savoy as embodying their monarchy. Paternalism, maternalism and charisma were all significant for this message, writes the historian Axel Körner, for they allowed broad layers of society to identify more readily with the royal family than with the nation's political class. Here Körner correctly identifies a political process, not the quasi-natural result of the charisma of two prominent and exemplary individuals within a truly

---

[68] *The Times* of 31 July 1900, p. 10; Axel Körner, *Politics of Culture in Liberal Italy: From Unification to Fascism* (London, 2009), p. 201.

[69] Körner, *Politics of Culture in Liberal Italy*, p. 201; *Morning Post* (London) of 2 August 1883, p. 5; Körner, 'Heirs and Their Wives', p. 44.

happy marriage. The dynastic and national partnership in which Margherita and Umberto were engaged was certainly based on something else than the purely romantic core identified by Baroness Savio, a leading member of Turin society, at the time of the couple's marriage in 1868. To Savio the princess had appeared 'gracious, smiling and happy', and she noted that Margherita 'clings to her Umberto, each happy with the other and together a godsend for the soul and for the eye'.[70]

Whatever the official staging suggested, the marriage of the crown prince and crown princess was in truth rather cold and distant. After the difficult birth of a son in 1869, the couple were to have no more children. Savoy tradition had a hand in this, for although Umberto appeared somewhat more cultivated than his father, and also more financially responsible and less ready to give his libido free rein, a number of parallels were still apparent. The 'good king', journalist Giovanni Gigliozzi reported, had two passions: horses and women. It was rumoured that, after every extra-marital escapade, he would give his wife a pearl necklace, which explains the description of Margherita as the 'pearliest' (*più imperlata*) queen of Italy. Umberto had several mistresses and a particularly long-lasting relationship with Eugenia, wife of the Duke of Litta-Visconti-Arese. Conveniently, she took up residence very close to the palace in Monza, where Umberto and Margherita spent the majority of their time. Umberto arranged for Eugenia to become a lady-in-waiting to Margherita, and he did not hide his affection for the child he had with her.[71]

When the king eventually steered the monarchy into a crisis, his hardly model behaviour may have been partly to blame. During a difficult phase in the late 1890s, marked by political scandals, a serious banking crisis, military failures and social disquiet, Umberto had unwisely displayed himself in a questionable light, supporting tough action against strikers and overstepping his constitutional position by naming two heads of government. His reputation was badly damaged, and was rescued only by the outrage that followed his murder by the anarchist Gaetano Bresci, in July 1900. The bloody deed turned the ham-fisted monarch back into the 'good king' whom the Munich newspaper *Die Jugend* extolled in lofty verse in August 1900:

> Untainted man, who conquered every heart!
> A noble prince, majestic, plain and strong
> Who lived but for his duty all day long
> And for his country's joy in every part.

[70] Körner, *Politics of Culture in Liberal Italy*, p. 204; Casalegno, *La regina Margherita*, p. 41.
[71] Giovanni Gigliozzi, *Le regine d'Italia* (Rome, 1997), pp. 30, 35; Körner, 'Heirs and Their Wives', p. 40; Mack Smith, *Italy and Its Monarchy*, p. 72.

Who helped, where good intentions help can bring
And vanquished sorrow, where love finds a way
Whom selfishness has never led astray
Onto the path of pride – every inch a king![72]

Margherita had always looked past her husband's infidelity and had maintained a distance from the politics of the day. As queen, widow and queen-mother, she remained highly esteemed first during this difficult period and then beyond the death of her husband. She continued her mission and still had significant impact. On her death, in 1926, the historian Antonio Monti looked back in tribute: 'Margherita of Savoy's particular task, first as wife of the heir and then as queen, lay in providing cohesion and assimilation in a land like Italy that for historic and ethnic reasons tended towards division and fracture rather than uniting under the strong but gentle pressure of a national consciousness.' Monti praised the queen's radiance, which had conquered the hearts of poets, members of all parties and even the opponents of the monarchy. She had, he wrote, 'been able to fulfil a great national duty in a special way'. The curiously distanced and precocious answer given by the sixteen-year-old princess to Prince Umberto's proposal – that marriage with him would make her more proud of the dynasty to which she already belonged – suggests that even at that time she had already been aware of what really counted: her marriage would not necessarily be happy but it must be successful. And she had played her part.[73]

'I Do Not Wish to Give My Country the Example of a Cold, Loveless Marriage!': Prince Wilhelm of Württemberg and the Dilemma of Public Bliss

No nineteenth-century heir seems to have commented as explicitly on the significance of the connection between love and marriage for his future as did Prince Wilhelm of Württemberg. Although he was only distantly related to his predecessor, King Karl I of Württemberg, who was his father's cousin, it soon became clear that Wilhelm, born in 1848, would one day succeed the childless monarch. The consequences of this

---

[72] Christopher Duggan, *The Force of Destiny: A History of Italy since 1796* (London, 2007), pp. 338–349; Mack Smith, *Italy and Its Monarchy*, pp. 121–139; 'Ein reiner Mensch, der jedes Herz gewann!/Ein Fürst voll Hoheit, edel, stark und schlicht,/Der nie auf And'res, denn auf seine Pflicht/Und seines Landes Glück und Ruhe sann!/Der half, wo guter Wille helfen kann/Und Sorgen brach, wo Liebe Sorgen bricht!/Den Selbstsucht nie geblendet hat und nicht/Berauscht die Macht hat – jeder Zoll ein Mann!' – Fritz von Ostini, in *Die Jugend* 33 (August 1900), p. 567.

[73] Brice, 'Königin Margherita', p. 201.

constellation for his personal path were clear, but the young prince still clung with considerable tenacity to a relationship that went back to his student days in Göttingen. There, in the late 1860s, he had fallen in love with Marie Bartling, the daughter of a professor, and he fought a long battle for a future with her. In December 1874, the twenty-six-year-old prince reported to his friend Detlev von Plato on a conversation with his mother. When she had earnestly sought to make him realise the futility of such a relationship, Wilhelm insisted that a marriage with Marie was, in his eyes, the only way in which he could 'imagine a marriage worthy of a genuine true love'. Eventually the two had agreed that he could return to his mother a year later to ask for her approval again. The heir to the throne was optimistic after the meeting. The decision was as good as made, he reported, 'for after a year I must hold her in my arms as my bride if my miserable existence is to mean anything at all'. Yet, in the following autumn, he had to give up Marie Bartling for good. 'The battle is now over', Wilhelm wrote resignedly to Plato in September 1875, 'I am defeated and done with the world, for I can no longer expect anything, neither happiness nor unhappiness – it makes no difference.'[74]

His resignation is understandable, for not only did Wilhelm have to put aside any thoughts of the bourgeois woman whom he had chosen, but he was also under great pressure to enter quickly into a suitable marriage. In a letter of September 1875, he was already mentioning several candidates who had been introduced to him – ostensibly with no ulterior motives. He struck lucky surprisingly promptly and blindsided his family in November 1876 with a request to be permitted to marry Princess Marie von Waldeck-Pyrmont. According to a report from the Bavarian envoy, Wilhelm's telegraphed request was the first the king had heard of his successor's decision.

The news of the marriage of the heir to the throne was received with great delight in Württemberg and celebrated accordingly. At the ceremonial reception of the newlyweds held in the capital, the mayor of Stuttgart, Theophil von Hack, conveyed the good wishes of the citizenry to the young couple with elaborately crafted words: 'Made only more beautiful by the bonds of love and more honourable by the inalienable gifts of the spirit and the heart, may the life of Your Royal Highnesses be formed in undimmed bliss as a joy to the royal house and as a blessing to this land.' Reporting from the 'richly beflagged city', the *Schwäbische Kronik* praised the 'lovely naturalness' of the young bride and noted that at the very moment the princess left the carriage 'a sunbeam had

---

[74] Wilhelm von Württemberg to Plato, 27 December 1874 and 13 September 1875 (Hauptstaatsarchiv Stuttgart, Q, NL Plato).

doused the hall with rose-coloured light'. The omens were apparently very good.[75]

Prince Wilhelm seems to have got over the loss of Marie Bartling surprisingly well indeed, for he was soon enjoying a happy marriage and family life with his young wife. 'After a stormy life, this clear and tranquil peace seem like a delightful sunshine', he wrote to Plato in July 1876, 'and in her love I have become a new person.' Ten months after their wedding, Princess Marie gave birth to a healthy daughter, Princess Pauline, followed, in July 1880, by Prince Ulrich, the long-awaited heir. 'One can imagine the heartfelt delight of the happy parents', the *Schwäbische Kronik* rejoiced, 'and here it is universally shared. Flags are out in much of the city ... Multiple expressions of congratulations are being prepared.' As the Stuttgart *Neues Tagblatt* reported, when receiving a congratulatory deputation from the town of Ludwigsburg, Prince Wilhelm demonstrated a talent for conveying his marital and family happiness to the people: 'His Royal Highness conversed for some time most graciously and delighted them with the news that mother and child are in the best of health.'[76]

The family idyll came to a tragic end. In December that same year, Ulrich, still a baby, died after a short illness. His parents were deeply affected, and the country mourned with them. 'The sympathy of the population of Stuttgart is splendid', commented the Prussian envoy to Württemberg. 'For the last two days the entrance to the prince's palace has never been empty of people of all ranks who want to confirm for themselves at the very location the sad news that has spread like lightning through all of Stuttgart.' For Prince Wilhelm it would only get worse. A little over a year later his young wife died following the stillbirth of her third child. 'Her death destroyed the most beautiful marital happiness', summed up *Der Beobachter*, a Stuttgart newspaper, in May 1882, 'and in heartfelt and sincere mourning the whole country stands at her early grave alongside her deeply bereaved husband, the heir presumptive to the throne of Württemberg.' Something of the 'unpretentious, almost bourgeois family life' of the couple was known to the broader public and had, according to the newspaper, bound the princess more closely to the 'hearts of the people'.[77] The loss had touched Wilhelm to the quick; the

---

[75] Count Tauffkirchen to King Ludwig, no. 81, 1 December 1876 (Bayerisches Hauptstaatsarchiv, MA 3036); Stadtarchiv Stuttgart, 2024, NL Hack, no. 84; *Schwäbische Kronik* of 23 February 1876.

[76] Wilhelm von Württemberg to Plato, 24 July 1876 (Hauptstaatsarchiv Stuttgart, Q, NL Plato) ; *Schwäbische Kronik* of 30 July 1880; *Neues Tagblatt* (Stuttgart) of 3 August 1880.

[77] Graf Dönhoff to Bismarck, no. 63, 28 December 1880 (Politisches Archiv des Auswärtigen Amtes, R3361); *Der Beobachter. Ein Volksblatt aus Schwaben* (Stuttgart) of 2 May 1882.

shock was so great that he exhibited signs of paralysis, causing concern that he had suffered a stroke.

Although, in practical terms, the marriage ended with the death of the princess, it remained politically significant, for the mourning for the dead Princess Marie could be translated into a 'politics of emotion' that served the reputation of the monarchy and, above all, of the heir. The process began at Christmas 1882. 'Most movingly, the memory of the royal and never-to-be-forgotten Princess Marie was recently renewed in neighbouring locations', the *Schwäbische Kronik* reported. 'Just as previously she personally brought the poorest widows and their children rich Christmas gifts, so this year again the princely carriage drew up and the delighted people received imaginatively selected gifts from the hands of the young princess [Pauline].'[78]

Shortly before Holy Week the following year, a publisher in Ludwigsburg produced an elaborate small book with the title *In Remembrance of Her Royal Majesty Princess Wilhelm of Württemberg, Who Died Too Soon*. The anonymous and hagiographic description of the life of Princess Marie highlighted her unpretentious humanity and the tender wholesomeness of her familial happiness. The Bavarian envoy Tauffkirchen judged that the work left 'a deep impression on the whole country'. The book is all the more interesting because Tauffkirchen could report that, while Prince Wilhelm had not written all of the text, it originated with him and was based on communications from him. Fittingly, then, Marie's grieving parents were praised in the book for continuing to care for their other children even after they had lost their child. The parallel to Prince Wilhelm, who had an especially close and loving relationship with his young daughter, Pauline, could hardly be ignored.[79]

However, the heir to the throne, not yet forty years old, could not perform the carefully cultivated role of grieving widower and loving father forever. Yet again Wilhelm was placed under pressure to present the country with a future queen. The insistence that he should remarry came not just from the king and the government but also from the public. Initially, the unwilling prince played for time and stressed the importance of marrying for love, all the more so for a ruler. 'I have never lost sight of what I owe to my position as prince and to my country', he explained, 'but I was too happy with my first wife to render myself unhappy for the rest of my life with a marriage of convenience; even a prince cannot be expected

---

[78] *Schwäbische Kronik* of 29 December 1882.
[79] Count Tauffkirchen to King Ludwig, no. 39, 26 March 1883 (Bayerisches Hauptstaatsarchiv, MA 3043).

to endure that. I do not wish to give my country the example of a cold, loveless marriage! I think too highly of this holy estate to wish to de-sanctify it in this way and thereby to debase myself.'[80]

Such unambiguous words gave the people of Württemberg every rea-son to believe that Wilhelm's second marriage – with Princess Charlotte of Schaumburg-Lippe – was a true love match. That would be all the more gratifying because, as everyone knew, the heir had acted under pressure from the broader public. In January 1886, when the news of their engagement circulated, 'all hearts rejoiced and knew to thank the prince for a decision that fulfilled an urgent wish by the whole country', the *Schwäbische Kronik* recalled three months later, at the time of the royal couple's wedding. As would be apparent at the reception of the newly married couple in Stuttgart, Mayor von Hack had lost none of his relish for highfalutin verbosity: 'In the manifold demonstrations with which the capital greets your Royal Highnesses', he assured them, 'there reigns and grapples to be expressed a single wish, that the union of hearts forged by Your Royal Highnesses may be and may remain a wellspring of steadfast happiness, a never-failing source of the richest blessing.'[81]

If the couple succeeded in giving this impression outwardly, then at least one goal had been met. Sadly, though, the second marriage of the king of Württemberg was by no means the 'wellspring of steadfast happi-ness' that the mayor had anticipated it would be. 'This night too I was again banished from my marriage bed', the Prince complained to his friend Plato a few months after the marriage. 'That's fine by me, for then at least I can sleep, but these are remarkable circumstances! And this comedy that I have to perform before the world, always making coquettish jokes, it's often enough to make one climb the walls. However, the guests went out from here today with the impression of a tender loving couple, and that's the main thing.' A letter written the following year indicates that nothing had changed. The couple were unhappy, but they went to great efforts to perform a princely love match for their eager audience. 'Outwardly, indeed, everything is splendid. We often appear together at the theatre, drive out together or walk together when the mood is right. But, but!!! – if only I had never in my life met her: she could have had a happy life at someone else's side, and I could have carried on along my own path quietly and in time even contentedly.'[82]

---

[80] Anon. [E. Schweizer], *Wilhelm II. König von Württemberg. Ein Lebensbild* (Ludwigsburg, 1891), pp. 27–28.

[81] *Schwäbische Kronik* of 9 April 1886; Stadtarchiv Stuttgart, 2024, NL Hack, no. 84.

[82] Wilhelm von Württemberg to Plato, 10 July 1886 and 9 February 1887 (Hauptstaatsarchiv Stuttgart, Q, NL Plato).

Despite all these efforts, soon rumours began to circulate that all was not well with Wilhelm and Charlotte's marriage. Moreover, although the prince was only in his late thirties and at the time they married his wife was twenty-one, the couple remained childless. Wilhelm was even rumoured to be having an affair with the wife of his friend and chamberlain Detlev von Plato. When the king and queen and the heir to the throne became aware of these rumours, a public campaign to limit the damage was launched immediately. That Wilhelm had recently feigned an illness in order to avoid having to attend the funeral of the Bavarian king was not allowed to hamper the plans. 'Their royal highnesses came to Stuttgart precisely in the days when the prince had sent his apologies for being unable to travel to the obsequies in Munich on account of being indisposed', the Prussian envoy, Wesdehlen, reported back to Berlin in June 1886. 'They appeared in public in the city and went shopping together.' Additionally, smaller stories were launched in the press to dispel the rumours. The government too made efforts to halt the 'malicious gossip' about the future king.[83]

Wilhelm and Charlotte's marriage remained unhappy. The decades-long careful staging of their idyll made no difference. Insiders were fully aware of the reality. In January 1891, the Prussian envoy Eulenburg confirmed that the relationship between King Karl and his heir was cool, before maliciously adding, 'almost as cool as that between Prince Wilhelm and his current wife'. And yet, over the years, the image conceived for the public of the happy marriage of Wilhelm, who ascended the throne of Württemberg in 1891, and his wife prevailed. In April 1911, the whole country joined in the celebrations to mark the royal couple's silver wedding anniversary. A zeppelin flying high over Stuttgart showered flowers on the palace. The donations to mark the couple's anniversary – which were, naturally, donated to a good cause – amounted to more than half a million marks. The less-than-sincere staging of his 'private family' meant that the popular king could indeed avoid presenting his county with a 'cold, loveless marriage' as a model, and, at the same time, it reinforced the state family. Wilhelm's misery that left him on occasion ready to 'climb the walls' was the price he had to pay.[84]

---

[83] Count Wesdehlen to Bismarck, no. 43, 28 June 1886 (Politisches Archiv des Auswärtigen Amtes, R3395); Wilhelm von Württemberg to Karl von Varnbüler, 28 June 1886, Anna Varnbüler to her father, 28 June 1886 (Hauptstaatsarchiv Stuttgart, NL Varnbüler, P10, Bü 568); Wilhelm von Württemberg to Hermann von Mittnacht, 13 June 1887 (Hauptstaatsarchiv Stuttgart, NL Mittnacht, Q1/51, 5).

[84] Philipp von Eulenburg to Adolf Marschall von Bieberstein, 9 January 1891, in John C. G. Röhl (ed.), *Philipp Eulenburgs politische Korrespondenz*, vol. 1 (Boppard am Rhein, 1976), p. 623; *Im Lichte neuer Quellen. Wilhelm II. – der letzte König von Württemberg* (exhibition catalogue), ed. Albrecht Ernst (Stuttgart, 2015), p. 46.

'My Husband and I Were Complete Opposites': Crown Prince Friedrich August, Crown Princess Luise and the Saxon 'Marriage Perturbation'

Nothing suggested that the marriage of Prince Friedrich August, the heir presumptive to the Saxon crown, might be the cause of a scandal that shook the foundations of the very idea of monarchy. Born in 1865, this offspring of the House of Wettin had, as was usual, concluded his carefree youth, university studies and military service by looking for a wife. In June 1891 he became engaged to the twenty-one-year-old Luise of Austria–Tuscany. For a member of the deeply Catholic Wettin dynasty, only a Catholic princess would do – and the Austrian Imperial house was Europe's most exclusive Catholic dynasty. Friedrich August seemed to have achieved an admirable catch, particularly as the much sought-after Luise had already snubbed a number of suitors. The young prince's entry into marriage with the attractive archduchess had been sweetened with an increase in his annual apanage, financed from tax revenue, from 120,000 to 600,000 Marks. 'All our people certainly endorse and believe it to be a happy event that his royal highness has selected a wife and returns home with her', declared the conservative member of parliament Richard von Oehlschlägel in November 1891, and the chamber certainly did not want to appear parsimonious.[85]

To all appearances, it was a love match. Indiscrete comments by the prince's sister led the Prussian envoy Count Dönhoff to believe that the prince's choice had been 'decided by an attraction of the heart'. An exuberant letter sent in August by the heir to the throne to his former military tutor confirmed this assessment: 'Certainly two months ago I would not have thought it possible that I might change so entirely as has been the case ... I am positively swimming in a sea of happiness.' In retrospect, however, several other passages in this letter appear somewhat concerning. The prince claimed that now he thought only of his bride, horse riding and military service, and that he was delighted that his marriage enjoyed 'heavenly protection'. Initially, however, all was sunshine.[86]

After the wedding in Vienna in November 1891, the newly married couple travelled to Saxony, where they received the enthusiastic reception

---

[85] The uplift in the apanage was then expressed in the older currency of the Taler (from 40,000 to 200,000; a Taler was worth three Marks); *Mittheilungen über die Verhandlungen des Landtags*, II. Kammer, 3. Sitzung, 18 November 1891, pp. 21–22, http://digital.slub-dresden.de/id20028419Z/35 (accessed 9 May 2022); see also Staatsarchiv Dresden, 10697, GesMin, F22825.

[86] Dönhoff to Leo von Caprivi, no. 94, 24 June 1891 (Politisches Archiv des Auswärtigen Amtes, R3254); Friedrich August to Ernst von Oer, 8 August 1891 (Staatsarchiv Dresden, 10716, Verein Haus Wettin, no. 329).

typical of such occasions. The president of the civic committee, member of parliament Paul Mehnert, offered a poem:

> A fresh shoot on an ancient tree,
> A maiden young and fine,
> The prize of purest love is she,
> It's truly God's design.

The *Leipziger Zeitung* expressed its enthusiasm, and not just at the 'geniality and skilfulness with which the young wife of a prince who is so revered by all mastered the difficult tasks of her high position', but also at the behaviour of Friedrich August himself, 'The radiantly happy young illustrious husband performed in the most loving and easy manner the services of a 'cavaliere servente' for his illustrious wife. One really had the impression: 'That is a truly happy couple!' They would soon be richly blessed with children: Prince Georg was born in January 1893, Prince Friedrich Christian followed in December the same year. They were joined by Prince Ernst Heinrich (1896), Princess Margarete (1900) and Princess Maria Alix (1901). When King Georg succeeded his older brother Albert as monarch in June 1902, Georg's son Friedrich August advanced in turn to be crown prince, which came with a further increase in his apanage of an additional 100,000 Marks. Moreover, in the light of the new king's advanced years and poor health, it seemed likely that the throne would be passed on again in the not-too-distant future.[87]

The events of mid December 1902 must then have come as a bolt from the blue for outside observers. Under the pretence of visiting her ailing father in Salzburg, the crown princess, pregnant again, left Dresden on 12 December. She travelled to Switzerland, where she met up with André Giron, her children's French tutor, with whom she had been involved for some months. The couple took up residence in the Hotel d'Angleterre in Geneva. They promenaded publicly along the lakeside and in extensive and candid press interviews, Luise explained what had caused her to flee: the dreadful life at the Saxon court and her bleak marriage to a stupid and bigoted Philistine.

Within a few days, the royal house was embroiled in an unprecedented scandal. After the Dresden court had failed to return the princess to Dresden with the help of the police, it seemed that the crown had no choice but to make its own version of the story public. On

---

[87] 'Am alten Stamm ein junges Reis,/Thaufrisch und maidenhold,/Der hehrsten Liebe höchster Preis!/So hat es Gott gewollt.' – *Dresdner Anzeiger* of 25 November 1891; *Leipziger Zeitung*, first supplement of 26 November 1891; *Mittheilungen über die Verhandlungen des außerordentlichen Landtags*, II. Kammer, 2. Sitzung, 5 July 1902, pp. 5–11, http://digital .slub-dresden.de/werkansicht/dlf/11504/49 (accessed 18 January 2017).

22 December 1902 the *Dresdner Journal*, a government-controlled news-paper, reported that Luise 'had suddenly left Salzburg while suffering from emotional agitation and had gone abroad, breaking all ties to Her Highness's family members here'. The Saxon royal family stuck to a strategy of explaining the crown princess's behaviour to the public as a product of illness, confusion or moral depravity. Three months later King Georg followed suit: 'Believe the words of your king, whom you have never found false, that the unending hurt that has befallen us is solely the result of the unbridled passions of a woman who for a long time has been inwardly deeply sinful.'[88]

His dramatic exhortation fell on deaf ears. The public largely preferred not to believe the monarch, whose unpopularity was already evident in his sobriquet 'Georg the Grisly'. Luise became their idol. The cult that developed around the ostensibly misunderstood, loveable and cast-out crown princess was eagerly nurtured by those whose politics led them to make trouble for Saxony's Catholic royal house and the conservative government it supported. Additionally, the mass media ensured that 'Our Luise' had a powerful public presence in newspaper articles, poems, postcards, photographs and songs. The phenomenon lasted for months and years. 'And forgive us our trespasses', pleaded an anonymous versifier in February 1903:

> She left her home so suddenly, the reason no one knew.
> The rumours started flying soon, but none of them was true.
> She left behind her family, her riches and her state.
> She raced towards her liberty, compelled by mighty fate.

All that Luise retained, the prolix poem eventually concluded, was 'her loving mother's heart'. In September 1904, a front-page image in the radical *Dresdener Rundschau* would even depict 'Our Luise as an Angel' – complete with wings and in heavenly garb. The 'Song of Luise' described the fugitive Habsburg princess as the 'pearl of the land of Saxony', and declared, 'Whoever returns this treasure, they will conjure for the people their vanished pleasure.'[89]

The flipside of this glorification of the crown princess was the aversion with which the royal house, and the crown prince in particular, was

---

[88] Quoted after Martina Fetting, *Zum Selbstverständnis der letzten deutschen Monarchen. Normverletzung und Legitimationsstrategien zwischen Gottesgnadentum und Medienrevolution* (Frankfurt am Main, 2013), p. 255; *Dresdner Journal* of 17 March 1903.

[89] 'Sie ging dereinst von Hause,/Weiß niemand recht, warum?/Geschwätzig ist die Fama,/Doch bleibt die Wahrheit stumm./Sie ging von Mann und Kindern,/Von Reichtum, Glanz und Pracht,/Sie stürmte in die Freiheit,/Gepeitscht von Schicksals Macht.' – *Dresdener Rundschau* of 14 February 1903 and 17 September 1904; Staatsarchiv Dresden, 10789, Polizeipräsidium, no. 28, p. 44.

greeted. Admittedly, the Saxon press could not let rip with as little inhibition as *Die Volkswacht* in Moravia, which wrote of Friedrich August as a 'souse and lecherous skirt chaser' and saw in him 'the real culprit for the great fall of his unhappy wife'. The newspapers of the Saxon opposition did, however, use their sympathy for Luise to offer sharp criticism of the Saxon court, claiming that its bigoted and clerical atmosphere and narrow-mindedness had led to the scandal. Soon the atmosphere in the country was openly antagonistic. According to a report by the Prussian envoy in 1903, when the crown prince walked in Dresden it was evident that 'the unrest amongst the lower ranks of the people about the sad events at the court of the crown prince is not yet laid to rest. Unlike in earlier times, when the crown-princely couple were greeted affectionately and joyfully as they walked together in the town, now the prince is seldom greeted and instead a curious crowd hustle him constantly, starring at him and sometimes making disapproving comments about him.' The *Dresdener Rundschau* summed up the situation, noting that the 'intrinsic connection between sovereign and people that has existed for so long has given way to an alienation that has seized all levels of the population with an elementary force'.[90]

It was not just critics on the left of the political spectrum who recognised a systemic crisis in the scandal at the Dresden court. Voices urging caution were also raised in the pro-monarchy camp. 'If princely women forget themselves thus and make a mockery of all that otherwise, even in misfortune, would be held to be proper, genteel and Christian', commented the renowned diarist Hildegard von Spitzemberg in December 1902, 'then they are denying their own right to exist.' The *Sächsische Volkszeitung*, which as a Catholic newspaper was more likely to be Wettin-friendly, declared disapprovingly that the 'higher the position from which the offence emanates, the greater the injury to decency'. For such transgressions, it noted, brought 'a heightened danger of imitation amongst the common people'. The conservative *Dresdner Anzeiger* was opposed to granting the crown princess too much sympathy, since it was not acceptable to 'whitewash an act that every bourgeois family perceived with indignation as a contravention of the rules of morality, which are the foundation of the family, and that was unreservedly to be described as such'.[91]

---

[90] *Die Volkswacht* of 26 February 1903; Graf Dönhoff to Bernhard von Bülow, no. 33, 19 February 1903 (Politisches Archiv des Auswärtigen Amtes, R3264); *Dresdener Rundschau* of 21 March 1903.

[91] Rudolf Vierhaus (ed.), *Das Tagebuch der Baronin Spitzemberg, geb. Freiin v. Varnbüler. Aufzeichnungen aus der Hofgesellschaft des Hohenzollernreiches*, 3rd edn (Göttingen, 1963), p. 424; *Sächsische Volkszeitung* of 28 December 1902; *Dresdner Anzeiger* of 13 January 1903.

Here lay the particular threat to the viability of constitutional monarchy from what was stiltedly termed the Saxon 'marriage perturbation' (*Ehe-Wirrung*). In laying bare the reality of marital and family life inside the palace walls, the scandal called into question the royal 'right to exist'. The revelations about the princely marriage at the Saxon court thus found a receptive audience amongst the socialist opponents of monarchy and bourgeois society. The Social Democratic *Leipziger Volkszeitung* was certainly delighted 'to see the obnoxious whining about Social Democracy's supposed destruction of marriage and family illuminated for once from the other side'. The paper diagnosed a 'repellent rotting of marriage and the family' precisely amongst circles within bourgeois society that wanted to preserve these institutions 'in all their patriarchal magnificence'.[92]

When the crowned family at the head of bourgeois society was unable to set an example of bourgeois values, when it caused doubt to be cast on the moral condition of the bourgeoisie itself, then its own position was in danger. The real heart of the scandal concerned such moral values, inasmuch as Luise was happy to vent openly about the impossibility of living a pure, loving and trusting married life under the conditions set by a very hierarchical court. Both the *Sächsische Arbeiter-Zeitung* and the *Leipziger Volkszeitung* gleefully cited from comments made by the crown princess: 'As you know, we princesses are married off almost without being asked', Luise had declared to a journalist. 'I was twenty-one years old; I was told about the lustre of a crown; my parents coaxed me; and so I agreed, very much against my instincts.' There could be little talk of true love or the union of body and spirit. 'My husband and I were complete opposites', Luise stated regretfully. 'He is a rough military man, for whom feeling is alien.' Certainly, she stated, he had never ill-treated her, but 'His tenderness seemed to me too crude and its complete unabashedness was agonising for me.' Additionally, married life at court was dull and uncultured. 'My husband loves the army', the crown princess reported, 'and otherwise he is very religious. Learning and the arts, music, theatre, literature, they are all perilous territory for him. As he was educated by priests, he always looked at my liking for such things as if it was a dangerous and sinful inclination.' Even if the prince had been otherwise, on account of the power structures at court it would have meant little, Luise proposed, for 'He was weak and in himself powerless, and obedience was so deeply ingrained in him that he was never in a position to accomplish anything that was counter to the court.' It read as if Luise wanted to disprove point by point that her princely marriage lived up to

---

[92] *Leipziger Volkszeitung* of 27 December 1902.

the ideal of the bourgeois love match. 'A woman like me must love her husband', she added, 'That is for a nature such as mine simply how life must be. Otherwise everything seems to me to be insincere, untenable and purposeless. We, however, we princesses, we are ordered to marry, we are meant to be without feeling, without animation, without a will of our own.'[93]

The dangers of such passages were very evident. 'Social Democracy, which in terms of its moral values is here entirely in line with anarchism, intends to take an axe to the roots of the established order when, with devilish reckoning, it undermines and destroys the sanctity of family life, this foundation of human society', raged the *Dresdner Nachrichten*. And indeed, the 'established order' appeared to teeter. In late January 1903, *Die Zeit* in Vienna reported rumours that the disgraced crown prince would relinquish his place in the line of succession for 'the husband in such a marriage-related matter could never purge himself of his share of the blame'. The *Leipziger Volkszeitung* eagerly seized on this news, reporting worries at the highest level that 'a stain would indeed always adhere to the person of the crown prince', and the paper commented on the supposed plans for relinquishing the throne. The rumours also reached the ears of Count Dönhoff, the Prussian envoy in Saxony. The diplomat did not believe them. Such a step would be politically unwise, he reported to Berlin, 'for it could be conceived as confirmation of the rumours spread by the enemies of the monarchy that blamed the crown prince for the sad events of his marriage'. Admittedly, Dönhoff was by no means optimistic when it came to the effect of the marriage scandal: 'For the heir to the throne, whose already limited popularity has hereby suffered severely, it will require a longer time and a particular dexterity that he unfortunately does not possess to win over the affection of the masses.'[94]

Those who doubted the Saxon royal house and the person of the somewhat less than imposing figure of Crown Prince Friedrich August were in for a surprise. The heir to the throne did not forgo his place in the line of succession and, in the short time available to him before the death of his father in October 1904, he largely succeeded in rehabilitating himself in the eyes of the public. Strikingly, he did so precisely where the marriage scandal had hit both him and the royal dynasty – in terms of family virtue. In December 1902, when the crown princess fled from Dresden to Switzerland, she left behind not just her husband and the expectation that she would wear the Saxon crown, but also the five

---

[93] *Leipziger Volkszeitung* of 3 January 1903; *Sächsische Arbeiter-Zeitung* of 3 January 1903.
[94] *Dresdner Nachrichten* of 18 January 1903; *Die Zeit* (Vienna) of 24 January 1903; *Leipziger Volkszeitung* of 26 January 1903; Dönhoff to Bernhard von Bülow, no. 19, 1 February 1903 (Politisches Archiv des Auswärtigen Amtes, R3264).

children they had had together. Although Luise's pain at the separation
from her children took up much space in the press and she did attempt to
visit her son Friedrich Christian when he fell ill, it was soon evident that in
future she would no longer perform her role as her children's mother. As
part of the legal separation, which turned out to be highly lucrative for
Luise, she even agreed to give up her daughter Anna Pia Monica, who had
been born five months after her flight, to the Saxon royal family. The
obvious question of the little princess's paternity was discreetly skirted
but – as Figure 8 shows – there was great public interest in the matter.
Additionally, the lifestyle of the former crown princess gave rise to doubts
about whether she could really serve as model of moral respectability: she
soon separated from Giron and within a short time married an Italian
musician, whom she also subsequently divorced.

Into the breech stepped Crown Prince Friedrich August, who untir-
ingly presented himself to the public as a devoted and genial single father.
Together with his children, he took walks, went on outings, politely
acknowledged those whom he encountered, carefully and successfully

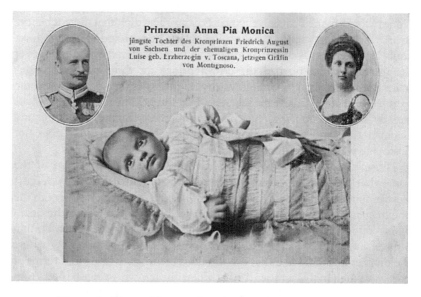

Figure 8. The public eagerly seized upon every detail of the Saxon
marriage scandal. Images of the infant princess Anna Pia Monica, who
was born after her mother's flight from the Saxon court, were a sought-
after commodity. Did the baby look like Prince Friedrich August? The
court did its best to hush up any questions about her paternity. Author's
private collection.

portraying a blend of unpretentious authenticity and fatherly love. The children would later recall an affectionate, strict and 'omnipresent father', who was interested in everything. 'We grew up under an unobtrusive but always-present pressure never to step out of line', Princess Maria Alix wrote in the late 1950s. When they went out, the princes and princesses were to 'sit firmly upright and always look just to the right and left and wave and smile'.[95] Certainly, the Wettin dynasty sought to deal with the scandal by pursuing journalists through the courts and by forbidding Luise-related memorabilia, but these efforts fizzled out. What did bear fruit was the charm offensive by the crown prince as the single father of his large family. As a good Catholic, Friedrich August could not remarry as long as Luise was still alive.

Just how quickly the mood had changed was evident in autumn 1904, when, following the death of his father, Friedrich August ascended the throne. The politically neutral *Dresdner Anzeiger* praised the young king for the 'composure and courage' that he had demonstrated in the wake of the events of December 1902. He had done so 'only through trust in God's succour and consoled by his possession of three sons and two charming daughters, whose mother was ripped from them and to whom he has now dedicated himself with devoted care as an affectionate father with double the love'. Together with his children, 'the prince has undertaken both short and longer travels, for example to the Carpathians last summer. In Dresden and also in [the nearby town of] Wachwitz, the inhabitants have for years had the opportunity to greet Prince Friedrich August on his frequent walks with his happy swarm of children.' The liberal *Dresdner Neueste Nachrichten* praised the prince's geniality and magnanimity, recording that he had borne the pain that Luise had caused him 'with dignity. He did not persecute through hate and repulsion the woman who had been unfaithful to him, but instead it is a conviction generally held that even today he remains attached to the woman who left him. This attractive and very human characteristic and the great love with which he tends to his children has won him the hearts of the Saxon people, even more so than his affability and friendly behaviour towards everyone.'[96]

Two short biographical panegyrics that appeared shortly after Friedrich August ascended the throne similarly testify to the transformation from abandoned prince to model father. 'The king dedicates the greatest attention to the upbringing of his children', reported a booklet by

---

[95] Hans Eggert and Rainer Kubatzki, *Friedrich August III. Lebensbilder, Briefe, Testamente* (Meißen, 2007), pp. 152–153.

[96] *Dresdner Anzeiger* of 16 October 1904; *Dresdner Neueste Nachrichten* of 16 October 1904, 2nd edn.

the Saxon Association of Military Societies, 'He likes to be in the nursery and is often found there.' The author Richard Stecher noted, with reference to the disappearance of the crown princess, 'where up until then he had dedicated himself to his children when and where he could, now he tends to them all the more, and from their merry chatter, from their shining eyes, happiness now looks upon him again'. A more extensive portrait of the king's life provided by Wolf von Metzsch-Schilbach in 1906 emphasised 'how much Crown Prince Friedrich August likes to dedicate to his children the time left to him by his unvaried, ever-returning hour of duty'. Neither excursions to the zoo nor visits to the Dresdner Vogelwiese, a folk festival, were left off the agenda. But 'serious questions of upbringing' were not neglected, either.[97]

Friedrich August's new and happy family life was kept constantly before the eyes of the king's Saxon subjects during the following years of his reign, depicted on numerous postcards and doggedly performed again and again. This contributed to the remarkable popularity acquired by the affable and unassuming king – soon the subject of numerous amusing anecdotes – who discharged his office in a largely depoliticised and sentimentalised fashion. His marriage had collapsed spectacularly before the eyes of the public, but on those ruins he built something new, binding his royal house to values such as love of children and paternal care. After this remarkable comeback, his kingship was precisely where it belonged, according to Walter Bagehot's analysis of the British monarchy: at the 'head of our morality'.[98]

***

The marriages of these heirs to the throne reveal just now difficult it was to fulfil the often-contradictory demands of their position and contemporary circumstances. The marriages of all three future monarchs, of Italy, Württemberg and Saxony, appeared to the public to be happy and aligned with the ideal of the modern family – at least initially. When doubts emerged, or, as in the case of the Wettins, the marriage collapsed spectacularly, the public image of the monarchy was seriously harmed. That damage had to be limited, sometimes in elaborate ways. Umberto, Wilhelm and Friedrich August all found that their choice of bride was restricted by a multiplicity of external pressures. Crown princesses had to come from families that were of a social rank on a par with that of their

---

[97] Richard Stecher, *König Friedrich August III. von Sachsen. Ein Lebensbild* (Dresden, 1905), pp. 22–23; *König Friedrich August III. von Sachsen. Ein Lebensbild zusammengestellt nach dem 'Kameraden'* (Dresden, 1905), p. 27; W. von Metzsch, *Friedrich August III. König von Sachsen. Ein Lebensbild* (Berlin, 1906), pp. 112, 116.

[98] Walter Bagehot, *The English Constitution*, ed. Paul Smith (Cambridge, 2001), p. 46.

husbands and that could help tip the political and dynastic scales, which excluded Rosa Vercellana, Eugenia Litta and Marie Bartling. Nor should we forget that these princesses, married at a very young age, had even less of a chance to secure their personal happiness than was the case for their husbands. In light of these circumstances and the public pressure on princely relationships, it is hardly surprising that many nineteenth-century dynastic marriages were not in fact the bastions of pure and untroubled virtuous happiness that public accounts and panegyric depictions made them out to be. It is all the more remarkable, then, that desperate acts of liberation on the model of the flight of Crown Princess Luise remained relatively rare.[99]

That this should be the case and that the royal houses very largely succeeded in presenting an exemplary marital and family life to the public can be attributed to the confluence of a number of factors. First, the members of the high aristocracy who entered into these marriages, both men and women, generally accepted the life-long task that lay before them. They did so even when accomplishing that duty while appealing to the public would require significant self-discipline and self-denial. Those who broke away, such as Crown Princess Luise, were exceptions that serve to prove the wider rule of monarchical compliance and self-discipline. Princess Margherita wore her pearl necklaces with enviable serenity; Prince Wilhelm and his wife, Charlotte, smiled affably at those they encountered as they walked through Stuttgart; and Prince Friedrich August took his children on excursions in a country that had longed for the return of 'Our Luise'.

The blue-blooded performers in this majestic melodrama also benefited from the compliance of a press which – more or less guided from above – assisted in conveying this delightful tale to the public. Even as the number of illustrated newspapers and journals increased, all but a small number of oppositional newssheets preferred heart-warming scenes of young maidens as brides on the arm of their husband-knights. There is little evidence to suggest that such depictions were rejected by the public who read or viewed them. Additionally, not only was the rule that no criticism of the royal family be expressed within the chambers of the

---

[99] It should be noted, however, that princesses who were weighing up the implications of escaping the life of the highly disciplined court had to reckon on social, financial and personal consequences. The risk that they would be deemed mentally ill, detained and ostracized was entirely real. See Winkelhofer, *Eine feine Gesellschaft*, pp. 200, 209–212, or the memoirs of former Crown Princess Luise: 'To my indescribable dismay I now knew that it was a madhouse. I thought this discovery would kill me. Now I was here in the very place that I feared most in all the world.' (Luise von Toskana, *Mein Lebensweg* (Berlin, 1926), pp. 197–198.)

parliament obeyed almost without exception, but also expressions of profound loyalty echoed extensively.

Monarch and heir might fall out and the heir's marriage might be in difficulties, but the family tensions examined here suggest that the discrepancies between dynastic reality and public image never caused the monarchical system lasting damage. Even a scandal as catastrophic as the Saxon 'marriage perturbation' could be relatively quickly surmounted by a carefully staged politics of emotion. While the sharp contrast between monarch and heir could prove highly advantageous for the system, the royal houses successfully performed idealised marriages for their audiences. In both scenarios, the vital goal of monarchical accommodation and self-assertion was met: the continuation of the simultaneity of the non-simultaneous. The unhappiness of the individuals involved was a tolerable price to pay. The royal families thus affected were, we might say, all alike as unhappy families and, as dynasties, equally successful.

3 'The Affair of His People'
The Education of Royal Heirs in the Nineteenth Century

According to King Umberto I, it did not take much to succeed as a monarch. 'Do not forget', the Italian monarch is said to have instructed his son, 'that to be a king all you need to know is how to write your name, how to read a newspaper and how to mount a horse.'[1] While his advice may sound amusingly self-deprecating, for a prince to combine official business, awareness of the press and athletic–chivalric horsemanship probably was no mean feat. Umberto's sardonic comment certainly seems to suggest, though, that the preparation heirs had to undergo for their royal tasks was not very taxing.

It was not just in Italy that the education and upbringing of future rulers became a topic for discussion. On its publication in 1909, Thomas Mann's satirical novel *Königliche Hoheit* (*Royal Highness*) ran into some controversy. In the journal *Der Kunstwart*, an unnamed German prince reflected critically on Mann's work, refuting above all the idea that any prince could still indulge in 'the luxury of otherworldly Baroque dreams'. After all, princes were 'deposited in a grammar school or the cadet corps', where, in typical boy fashion, they soon found out that the strongest come out on top. After the young prince had 'tested his strength spiritually and physically against others' at school, the author continued, he would join a regiment, where he would not be handled with kid gloves either. A prince who wanted to make his mark, the anonymous reviewer assured the reader, would be 'entirely aware that today he would actually have to achieve something'. In his response, Thomas Mann appeared unimpressed by these observations. 'School boys would not be sycophants?', he asked ironically and added 'Perhaps one has to be a prince to believe that.' In Mann's portrayal, the time Prince Klaus Heinrich, the protagonist of his novel, spent at university amounted to nothing but 'a ceremonial sham-life'.[2]

---

[1] Richard J. Evans, *The Pursuit of Power: Europe, 1815–1914* (London, 2016), p. 601.
[2] Thomas Mann, *Königliche Hoheit* (Berlin, 1909), www.gutenberg.org/files/35328/35328-h/35328-h.htm (accessed 25 November 2016); Ferdinand Avenarius, 'Unsere Fürsten und wir', in *Der Kunstwart* 23, 13 (April 1910), pp. 2–5.

Several years earlier, the *Dresdener Rundschau*, a radical weekly, had already tackled the same subject but had chosen to approach it more robustly. 'Often enough, we hear and read in the willing press that princes who attend a grammar school or university enjoy the same lessons as the other pupils and students. These accounts are riddled with every possible partiality and wordsmithing. Anyone who should happen to have a prince as his classmate will know all too well that for that prince university is about the fencing hall, his feudal fraternity's drinking nights and only occasionally about attending lectures.'[3] By the early twentieth century, the public discussion about how princes were raised had come to focus on how royal schoolboys were treated by their fellow grammar school pupils. Did heirs to the throne work hard at university or did they squander their time in the tavern? Any bourgeois parents might have found themselves asking the same questions of their own offspring, and this illustrates how greatly the public's expectations of monarchical behaviour had changed in the course of more than a century of constitutionalisation. By the beginning of the twentieth century, the training of the future monarch was measured against the standards of a normal course of education. To be raised within an 'otherworldly Baroque dream' was no longer deemed acceptable.

For centuries, great thinkers had pondered how princes could be prepared appropriately and usefully for the high office for which they were predestined. A considerable canon of works existed to guide the adolescent heir to the throne. That collection was launched with the hortatory speech 'How a King Should Reign', which Isocrates dedicated to Nicocles, the future ruler of Cyprus, in the fourth century BCE. Subsequent contributors to the genre included great figures such as Xenophon, Aristotle, Plutarch, Seneca and Marcus Aurelius. Their largely utilitarian considerations, concerned above all with securing power, were supplemented in the medieval period by works that revolved around the ruler's relationship with the church and how monarchs were to answer to God for their actions. Drawing on Augustine's *City of God*, the numerous medieval 'mirrors for princes' were primarily directed at the princely imitation of Christ or the internalisation of the ideal of the Christian knight.[4]

The early modern period produced a flowering of texts on how rulers should be raised. In an early-twentieth-century pedagogical encyclopaedia the educationalist Georg Grunwald came to the conclusion, though,

---

[3] 'Fürstenerziehung', in *Dresdener Rundschau* of 14 March 1903, p. 3.
[4] Hans-Joachim Schmidt, 'Fürstenspiegel', in *Historisches Lexikon Bayerns* (2011), www .historisches-lexikon-bayerns.de/Lexikon/Fürstenspiegel (accessed 6 February 2017).

that the princely ideal generated during the Renaissance had 'arisen more from literary and aesthetic concerns than from serious pedagogical intent'. Alongside a Christian humanist education, future rulers should also be able to demonstrate the virtues Baldassare Castiglione's *Book of the Courtier* celebrated as signs of courtly refinement. They should strive for gracefulness, a quick wit and daring. From the fifteenth to the eighteenth century, treatises by renowned authors – including Enea Silvio Piccolomini, Erasmus of Rotterdam, Jean Bodin, Niccolò Machiavelli, King James VI and I of Scotland and England, Gottfried Leibniz, François Fénelon and Victor de Mirabeau – formed pearls of wisdom that could be strung together to explain how princes might be educated and counselled. Fénelon's *Adventures of Telemachus, the Son of Ulysses*, written by the Archbishop of Cambrai in 1699 for the future king of France, would echo across generations. Repeatedly counselling his young student that problems could be resolved through peaceful agreement with neighbours, reforms and encouragement of agriculture, Fénelon's text contained early Enlightenment impulses.[5]

Notwithstanding this venerable and significant tradition of pedagogical texts for rulers and future rulers, the revolutionary events of the late eighteenth century still marked a caesura. The wise counsel and paternalistic admonitions of mentors, philosophers and theologians were pushed aside by public calls that invoked the nation and the constitution when demanding a say in the formation of the future ruler. The early phase of the French Revolution, during which France became a constitutional monarchy, witnessed a vigorous national debate about this matter. In February 1790, King Louis XVI had had to promise the National Assembly that he and the queen would raise the Dauphin, the four-year-old Louis Charles, in line with the new order and that they would allow the constitution to guide them. The debate in the National Assembly over how the heir to the throne should be groomed for his future role, a discussion fuelled by a flurry of detailed education plans submitted to parliament, was soon dominated by an entirely new understanding. No longer was the state a reflection of the monarch and his virtues; now the reverse was to be true: the values of the constitutional state were to mould the ruler in his formative years. When it came to how the future monarch was to be raised, the interests of the nation now stood alongside – if not even ahead of – the rights of his royal parents. Count Mirabeau proposed that the Dauphin would be brought up according to a plan drawn up by the Académie Française and approved by both crown and parliament.

---

[5] G. Grunwald, 'Fürstenerziehung', in Ernst Roloff (ed.), *Lexikon der Pädagogik*, vol. 2 (Freiburg im Breisgau, 1913), p. 142.

The king would be permitted to select his son's tutors, but only from a list presented to him by parliament. His elementary education complete, the crown prince would attend a public secondary school chosen by parliament. These and other educational plans were moot, however, when France became a republic and after the royal couple had made their way to the scaffold in 1793. Two years later, the Dauphin also died. Imprisoned in the Temple in Paris, the neglected ten-year-old boy succumbed to tuberculosis.[6]

These events did not put an end to the debate that had started in France in 1790 over how the future king of a constitutional monarchy was to be raised and how the public might be part of that process. While nineteenth-century heirs to the throne still grew up in a monarchical century, their world now existed under the shadow of revolution and regicide. Even decades later, the search for the right answer was still ongoing. Crown Prince Vittorio Emanuele would learn that signing his name, reading a newspaper and mounting a horse was not all that was required of him, regardless of what his father's alleged quip had seemed to suggest. The sixteen-year-old was educated according to a carefully thought-out and rigorous programme, whose importance was all too clear to the former Italian prime minister Marco Minghetti. 'Perhaps there has never been a more difficult time for men who are born to sit upon the throne', Minghetti warned the prince's mother in 1885. 'We must be rid of a jealous and resentful democracy, the friend of mediocrity and the vulgar, and we must secure the dynastic pre-eminence.'[7]

The ruling houses of nineteenth-century Europe promised their subjects and the public a particular version of the future. The next generations of monarchs were required to deliver on that promise, on the basis of their appropriate preparation and schooling. As a result, the prospect of a well-trained and capable ruler who represented the political, moral and cultural values of his age turned into a resource on which monarchies could draw to shore up the stability of the system. Redeeming this promise, however, might be anything but plain sailing. Not every scion of an old family was necessarily equipped with the intellect and character required to cope with a demanding education. Additionally, well-established traditions and preferences for other pastimes might need to be abandoned or at least suitably incorporated. Thus, alongside new forms of academic instruction, training in older martial-cum-ceremonial

---

[6] Adrian O'Connor, 'Between Monarch and Monarchy: The Education of the Dauphin and Revolutionary Politics, 1790–1791', in *French History* 27, 2 (2013), pp. 183, 186.

[7] Lilla Lipparini (ed.), *Lettere fra la regina Margherita e Marco Minghetti* (Milan, 1955), p. 183.

skills – such as cutting a fine figure when mounting a cavalry horse – was not to be neglected.

We will first turn to the developing expectations surrounding how the heirs in Europe's constitutional monarchies should be equipped for their future roles, and the solutions conceived in response. The royal houses of Bavaria, Saxony, Württemberg and Italy provide specific examples of what that preparation looked like, and how it was communicated, in the case of monarchies that felt a particular need to justify their existence. How the raising of princes developed across the generations is then illustrated with two examples of monarchical power within different forms of constitutional development: Great Britain and Prussia–Germany. When it came to innovative approaches to preparing future monarchs, no effort was spared in either land.

'Striving Eagerly to Acquire the Necessary Learning for Their Future Life's Calling': Training Princes in Constitutional Monarchies

As constitutionalism gradually advanced throughout Europe in the course of the nineteenth century, the appropriate upbringing of the heir to the throne increasingly attracted attention. Early on, in 1817, Christian von Massenbach, a military officer and member of the assembly of the Württemberg estates, produced a pamphlet entitled *The Education of Princes in Representative Constitutions*. The text, dedicated to the king of Württemberg and the crown prince of Prussia, considered how the monarchical constitutional state could be protected from encroachments by the monarch. 'The strongest guarantee of all representative constitutions', Massenbach explained, 'lies in princes being educated in the spirit expressed by the constitution, that princes grow up, as it were, with the constitution.' Proceeding from this basis, he proposed a detailed educational plan designed to ensure 'that young royals destined for the throne should be infused with the fundamentals of liberty and humanity even while still they are still in their early youth'. This upbringing should take place under the supervision of parliament in an 'educational palace' far from the court, 'in circles composed of several – not princely – good natured and respectable young people of the same age but of different temperaments and abilities'.[8]

In 1843, a pamphlet dedicated to Queen Victoria and bearing the title *Who Should Educate the Prince of Wales?* aroused interest in Great Britain,

---

[8] Christian von Massenbach, *Fürsten-Erziehung in repräsentativen Verfassungen*, 2nd edn (Heidelberg, 1817), pp. 4, 6, 8, 9.

the pioneer liberal and constitutional state. According to its anonymous author, while the 'education of a subject is the affair of his relatives and friends; that of a monarch is the affair of his people'. The author insisted that 'all have the right which I assume, to give their opinions at least upon a matter which so deeply concerns them'. Alongside secondary virtues such as a restrained domesticity, the future ruler was expected to be a patriot and a gentleman, enabling him to embody the national virtues of the British. Additionally, through his internalisation of national culture, he would acquire a reputation as a knowledgeable ruler. The pamphlet ended with a call for public discussion that was answered so vigorously that the renowned magazine *Punch* twice printed the responses of its readers. Startled by the public interest, the royal family quickly consulted a run of experts, who were to draw up an educational programme for the next-in-line, then two years old, with the goal of ensuring that the future king be equipped with the necessary reputation and abilities.[9]

In Spain too, the education of princes made waves. In August 1843, Juan Vincente Ventosa publicly criticised the training of Queen Isabella II, who, at just twelve years of age, had not yet gained her majority. Shortly before, Ventosa had been dismissed for political reasons from his position as the queen's tutor. The newspapers *El Español Independiente* and *La Postdata* reported that he believed Isabella's education to be deficient – it was too feminine and insufficiently academic. She was not, it was argued, being effectively prepared for her future duties as a constitutional monarch. Those at court who were responsible for Isabella's preparation were now under pressure. Internally, the queen's governess (*Aya*) and the queen's senior tutor (*Ayo Instructor*) defended themselves against Ventosa's accusation and, significantly, emphasised that the choice of her tutors had been guided by the views of the public. Above all, however, they pointed out that Isabella was being provided with a new understanding of monarchy, according to which the laws of the country were superior to everything and must be protected in order to secure the independence and freedom of the nation. Eventually, the queen's legal guardian, Agustín Argüelles, who was responsible for Isabella's education as a whole, would have to defend himself before the Spanish parliament.[10]

---

[9] *Who Should Educate the Prince of Wales?* (London, 1843), p. 10; Miriam Schneider, 'Who should educate the Prince of Wales? Eine Debatte im viktorianischen England', BA thesis, Universität Bayreuth 2009, pp. 5, 8, 19–23.

[10] I am grateful to Richard Meyer Forsting for valuable references on the upbringing of the Spanish heirs to the throne in the nineteenth century; see his study *Raising Heirs to the Throne in Nineteenth-Century Spain: The Education of the Constitutional Monarch* (London,

As Richard Meyer Forsting has shown, this pattern was repeated as Spain developed as a constitutional monarchy: over the course of the century, the Spanish public turned eagerly to discussing the intent and content of the training given to their future ruler. In 1894, when King Alfonso XIII, grandson of Isabella II, was only eight years old, the Madrid newspaper *El Imparcial* reflected on 'the education of kings in the constitutional monarchy'. With an unmistakable reference to the situation of the young monarch, the newspaper cited the author of a recently published piece on the education of princes who had advised against an upbringing confined entirely within the walls of the palace. 'If the principal calling is to be a human being and to be a convivial human being, then there is nothing more horrible than isolation founded on the dignity of status and the honours of majesty', declared *El Imparcial*, 'Nothing is as charming as the games of childhood, in which one sees flourish that which is most beautiful about democracies.'[11]

The change to princely education generated by the constitutionalisation of monarchy across almost all of Europe pointed in broadly in the same direction, even though no European royal house went as far as to raise the heir to the throne explicitly as a beautiful democrat. Fundamentally, though, the upbringing of crown princes and crown princesses was no longer purely a family concern; it had become a public and political event. The development that Yvonne Wagner has identified within the Prussian–German Hohenzollern dynasty stood for a general shift: in the second half of the nineteenth century, Europe's ruling houses had to respond to the growing importance assumed by formal qualifications in societies where hierarchy was increasingly based on achievement rather than ancestry. They did so by merging the upbringing of the ruler with aspects of a bourgeois education. And they did this very publicly.[12]

This reorientation was specifically intended to appeal to the bourgeois public. As a result, the programme of education of the next generation was expanded. At German courts or courts influenced by German dynasties, more space was given to neo-humanism, which was revered by the bourgeoisie. According to classical philologist Friedrich August Wolf (1759–1824), a humanist education would awaken in the next generation that 'which by fostering pure human learning and the elevation of all the

2018); Isabel Burdiel, *Isabel II. Una biografía (1830–1904)*, 3rd edn (Madrid, 2011), pp. 112–118.
[11] *El Imparcial* of 22 July 1894.
[12] Yvonne Wagner, *Prinzenerziehung in der 2. Hälfte des 19. Jahrhunderts. Zum Bildungsverhalten des preußisch–deutschen Hofes im gesellschaftlichen Wandel* (Frankfurt am Main, 1995), pp. 57, 313.

forces of the mind and of the spirit produces a beautiful harmony of the inner and external human being'.[13] As the inevitable result of this new focus on the cultural achievements of the ancient world and the engagement with art history, archaeology and ancient languages, public institutions – first universities, then also grammar schools – were soon playing a more important role in princely education. Heirs now encountered a greater variety of people in the course of their upbringing, and they also came into contact with a greater number of individuals of their own age. Additionally, the civilian teacher who acted alongside the military tutor grew in importance. As a basic rule, the impression was to be given that princes would always be held to the same standards and rules as others of the same age. In the second half of the nineteenth century, the upbringing of princes again followed a contemporary trend, with greater emphasis being placed on modern languages, sciences and technical subjects.[14]

The changes to how princes were raised, implemented along the arc of bourgeois preferences and with a keen eye on the public's response, thus formed part of the nineteenth-century transition from absolute to constitutional monarchy. The 'functionalisation' of the monarch within the constitutional system, as Martin Kirsch, has termed it, had considerable consequences for the heirs to the throne, for they now had to demonstrate that they were striving to master a craft.[15] With the success of the crown prince's future rule dependent on his ability to carry out certain tasks – protecting the constitution, non-partisan representation of the state, providing society with a model or embodying a national identity – it was his duty both to attain the necessary skills and to display the assiduous process of their acquisition to his future subjects.

This new attitude towards princes' upbringing, which gradually prevailed in the European monarchies, led to a curious contradiction: the upbringing of future monarchs was to be like that of other mortals, but precisely this fundamentally egalitarian and meritocratic process was intended to prove and signal the pre-eminence of princes anew. A detailed article on the education of princes that appeared in 1867 as part of a four-volume *Encyklopädie des gesammten Erziehungs- und Unterrichtswesens* (*Encyclopaedia of the Entire Field of Education and*

---

[13] Friedrich August Wolf, *Darstellung der Alterthumswissenschaften*, ed. S. F. W. Hoffmann (Leipzig, 1833), p. 45.

[14] See also Jean Meyer, *L'éducation des princes du XVᵉ au XIXᵉ siècle* (Paris, 2004), pp. 205–240, and Peter Gordon and Denis Lawton, *Royal Education: Past, Present and Future*, 2nd edn (London and Portland, OH, 2003), pp. 151–163.

[15] Martin Kirsch, 'Die Funktionalisierung des Monarchen im 19. Jahrhundert im europäischen Vergleich', in Stefan Fisch, Florence Gauzy and Chantal Metzger (eds.), *Machtstrukturen im Staat in Deutschland und Frankreich* (Stuttgart, 2007), pp. 82–98.

Teaching) made plain how excessive these demands were: 'Fear of God, love of others and moral purity, justice and equity, courage and noble-mindedness, strength and endurance, habitualisation of well-ordered work, clarity and acuity in passing judgement, knowledge of human beings and their callings – all these are qualities that are to be acquired through bourgeois education and should be the content of every general upbringing.' This list alone would surely have been sufficient to cause any pupil to break into a cold sweat, and for future monarchs there was yet more: 'A prince requires the same characteristics, but he requires them to a greater degree.'[16]

In the early 1890s, in an extensive memorandum on the upbringing of Emperor Wilhelm II, Georg Hinzpeter, for many years the tutor of the Hohenzollern prince, formulated this additional expectation even more emphatically. In his view, the 'future sovereign's immersing himself in normal school life would certainly not mean the debasement of the monarchy, but rather, in contrast, make his privileged position all the more evident when, having begun the competition from the same starting point, the prince proves able to overtake all others'.[17] The treatise was composed at the request of the Japanese imperial house, which hoped to benefit from the experience of the Hohenzollerns in raising its own princes. In it, Hinzpeter explained almost too candidly that this educational plan and the achievements of its princely participant were seen as a means to defend the established system and were therefore highly political. The path to an updated but enduring monarchy ran via the future ruler's classroom, into which the public might peer.

How the heir's upbringing might help fortify his future subjects' confidence in the ruling house is evident when we look at those monarchies whose position was especially precarious. That description applies to all but one of the twenty-two German monarchical states whose sovereign rights were severely clipped with the founding of the German Empire in 1871, in particular when it came to foreign affairs and defence policy. According to the constitutional historian Hans Boldt, after 1871 Germany was home to only one real 'monarch' in the full sense of the term – the German emperor.[18] The subjects of the kings of Bavaria, Württemberg and Saxony might well have wondered why there was any

---

[16] 'Prinzenerziehung', in *Encyklopädie des gesammten Erziehungs- und Unterrichtswesens*, ed. K. A. Schmid, vol. 6 (Gotha, 1867), p. 357.

[17] Georg Hinzpeter, 'Zusammenstellung der Grundsätze, nach denen die Erziehung S.K. H. des Prinzen Wilhelm von Preußen 1866–77 geleitet worden ist', 21 November 1891 (Geheimes Staatsarchiv Preußischer Kulturbesitz, 1. HA, Rep 76 I, Sektion 1, Nr. 125).

[18] Hans Boldt, 'Der Föderalismus im Deutschen Kaiserreich als Verfassungsproblem', in Helmut Rumpler (ed.), *Innere Staatsbildung und gesellschaftliche Modernisierung in Österreich und Deutschland 1867/71–1914* (Vienna and Munich, 1991), p. 34.

need for a largely disempowered monarchical system beneath the emperor, especially as these subnational monarchies continued to insist upon the 'monarchical principle', whereby the king – and not, for example, parliament – expressed and possessed all the powers of the state. If these princely houses were to maintain the status quo, then they would need to make significant efforts when it came to public relations. The preparation of the heir to the throne for the responsibilities of rule would be vital to this endeavour.[19]

Only twenty years separated the births of the last kings of these small monarchies, Ludwig of Bavaria (1845–1921), Wilhelm of Württemberg (1848–1921) and Friedrich August of Saxony (1865–1932). And yet, a distinct trend can be discerned in their upbringings. Before he attended university, Ludwig was educated on his own, by tutors at the court. The future king of Württemberg was brought up as part of a group of similarly aged boys, with particular attention paid to ensure that the 'prince's lads' of Stuttgart were not all scions of noble families and included the sons of the bourgeoisie. Prince Wilhelm therefore spent his schooldays with a future medical doctor, engineer, judge and forestry official. The young prince was meant to learn, according to a hagiographic biography of the king that appeared just weeks after he ascended the throne, 'to be with others and to influence them as they influenced him'.[20] The evidence does not suggest that Ludwig or Wilhelm took any formal examinations.

For Prince Friedrich August of Saxony the situation was very different. In March 1883, he sat the final examinations that normally concluded the standard nine years of secondary schooling. The official *Dresdner Journal* published a detailed and effusive account of just how punctiliously the examination of the future king had proceeded. 'In the presence of His Majesty the King, and of his Most Honourable Parents, today his Royal Highness Prince Friedrich August underwent the concluding examination at the end of his grammar-school studies, with His Excellence the Minister of Culture and Public Education Dr von Gerber and the Privy School Counsellor Rector Dr Ilberg in attendance. Senior Tutor Dr Jacob conducted the examination in Latin and Greek language and literature, Major Fischer in mathematics, Dr Fritzen in history. His Royal Highness answered all the questions posed in each area of learning with such comprehensive knowledge and performed the tasks he was set with such assuredness in illustration and mastery of form that there could not have

---

[19] For a more extensive analysis of the upbringing of these three heirs to the throne, see Frank Lorenz Müller, *Royal Heirs in Imperial Germany: The Future of Monarchy in Bavaria, Saxony and Württemberg* (London, 2017), pp. 82–93.

[20] Anon. [E. Schweizer], *Wilhelm II. König von Württemberg. Ein Lebensbild* (Ludwigsburg, 1891), pp. 6, 8.

been any doubt that the overall result of the examination was to declare him fully prepared for university study.'[21]

After their school years were over, all three princes attended university. Unlike his father, for whom private lectures had been arranged, Prince Ludwig of Bavaria sat in the lecture halls of his Munich alma mater and followed a broad course of study with great dedication. He developed a life-long interest in economics, technology and agriculture, and became genuinely expert in some areas. Even while still king-in-waiting he received honorary doctorates first from the University of Munich and then also the Technical University in the Bavarian capital. On the occasion of his fiftieth birthday, the *Augsburger Postzeitung* called on everyone who sought to achieve something in life to emulate the future king, attributing his impressive skills to the excellent education he had enjoyed. 'The most outstanding men were responsible for the teaching and upbringing of the prince [...] and on account of his splendid abilities and his tireless application he was the pride of his teachers and a lustrous model for all those who eagerly strive to acquire the necessary learning for their future life's calling.' As was to be expected of a future head of state, the Bavarian heir to the throne was a real expert. The newspaper recalled that the prince had studied 'agriculture, economics and law' and 'in the area of agriculture his knowledge was so extensive and so sound that he was thought a leading authority on all related questions'.[22]

As scholars, the future rulers of Württemberg and Saxony could hardly compete with their Bavarian peer, but they too attended university. In October 1865, Prince Wilhelm matriculated at Württemberg's ancient university in Tübingen and began a broad course of studies, which he had to break off in summer 1866 because of the Austro-Prussian War. In the autumn of the same year, he began four semesters of study at Göttingen, where he became a member of the Corps Bremensia fraternity. In 1868/69, he completed his studies with a final semester in Tübingen, focusing on Württemberg jurisprudence. According to a short biography to which Wilhelm himself contributed, he had thus 'comprehensively prepared himself for his future calling as ruler and statesman and had neglected nothing [...] that might be beneficial for him in this'. And yet, in the 1880s the prince returned to studying. Under the guidance of his former school friend Friedrich von Schmidlin, who had become a judge in Heilbronn, he dedicated himself for six months to learning about legal and administrative issues. The aim of these studies, wrote the recently

[21] *Dresdner Journal* of 18 March 1883.
[22] *Unterhaltungsblatt der Augsburger Postzeitung* of 8 January 1895.

widowed heir to the Kingdom of Württemberg, was 'to ensure that one day I am a useful member of society'.[23]

Friedrich August of Saxony's occasional quirkiness and his strong Saxon dialect led some contemporaries to believe him to be somewhat simple. Emperor Wilhelm II is said to have sneered that Friedrich August was more like a clown than like a heroic king, and the Prussian ambassador Count Dönhoff credited the Saxon monarch with merely a 'not significant intellectual talent'. These mean-spirited evaluations were probably somewhat exaggerated, for the future king of Saxony completed a perfectly respectable programme of study. In 1884, he matriculated at the University at Strasbourg, where he studied law, history and politics. Demonstratively following the prescriptions of a law that required Saxon subjects to graduate from the national university, in 1885 the prince transferred to the University of Leipzig, the first member of his family to matriculate there, and completed his studies in 1886, shortly before his twenty-first birthday. Internal views of the prince's abilities were somewhat mixed. His equerry, Lieutenant-General von Tschirschky, declared that Friedrich August was a quick learner and had a good memory, but he was critical of a 'certain lack of independence'. By contrast, the official *Dresdner Journal* provided the public with an image of flawlessness. The entry into adulthood, noted the paper, 'with each passing year brings to every mortal more mature perceptions, more serious responsibilities and more arduous work, regardless of whether he is a member of the bourgeoisie or comes from a lineage of princely rulers'. The newspaper found Friedrich August superbly well-equipped for the tasks ahead, for 'the whole upbringing of he who now stands before us as a young man fully in possession of the power of his ancestors' had been a bridge between a carefree childhood and 'willing and self-denying application in the great school of real life'. To that end, it was fitting that, having completed his studies, the future monarch acquired practical knowledge of how the state was run from the administration of the districts of Dresden and Dresden-Old Town.[24]

The public staging of the heir's education was certainly far from over when his university education and specialised training were complete. Repeated reference was made to future rulers gaining a significant

---

[23] Karl Biesendahl, *König Wilhelm II. von Württemberg. Ein Fürstenbild. Dem deutschen Volke und Heere zugeeignet* (Rathenow, n.d. (1891)), p. 14; Prince Wilhelm to King Karl, copy, 6 July 1882 (Hauptstaatsarchiv Stuttgart, E14, Bü 85).

[24] Martina Fetting, *Zum Selbstverständnis der letzten deutschen Monarchen. Normverletzung und Legitimationsstrategien zwischen Gottesgnadentum und Medienrevolution* (Frankfurt am Main, 2013), p. 247; *Dresdner Journal* of 25 May 1886; Dönhoff to Bismarck, Nr. 46, 14 March 1886 (Politisches Archiv des Auswärtigen Amtes, R3251).

understanding of state affairs through their valuable work in parliament. That engagement included their longstanding membership of the first chamber of the relevant parliament, which we have already encountered. Even Friedrich August's rather sporadic contributions as a member of the Saxon First Chamber were sufficient to earn him the praise of the *Leipziger Zeitung* in 1904. 'In recent years he has also applied himself to the administration of the state and to parliament', it reported of the new king, 'where, after his illustrious father ascended the throne, the crown prince assumed his position as chairman of the finance committee in the First Chamber.'[25]

There could be no question that all three heirs would also have astoundingly successful military careers. As early as his fortieth birthday Prince Wilhelm of Württemberg was made General of the Cavalry; in 1884, aged thirty-nine, Prince Ludwig of Bavaria was promoted to General of the Infantry, and Prince Friedrich August was also only thirty-nine when, in 1902, also as General of the Infantry, he became commander of the XII (1st Royal Saxon) Army Corps. Of the three princes, Friedrich August certainly had a genuine interest in military matters. Wilhelm, in contrast, tried, unsuccessfully, to avoid taking over as commander of the Württemberg cavalry brigade, and relinquished the position at the first opportunity. Ludwig exchanged the lecture hall for the barracks very unwillingly. After being wounded during the war of 1866, he refused any active form of military service whatsoever. That even this could not stop his promotion to the rank of general illustrates yet again the political need for the heir to be seen to possess the right qualifications. In an age in which military service had become a norm and was understood as a patriotic act, heirs demonstrated their dynasty's devotion to the nation through their involvement with the army. Additionally, with military careers now carrying greater professional prestige, the princes' purported success supported a broader message about the future rulers' honestly acquired capabilities. Alongside their schooling, attendance at university and parliamentary experience, the heirs' military uniforms and decorations bolstered their claim to the highest office in the state.[26]

At least in terms of the public image conveyed, the training received by the future monarchs of Bavaria, Saxony and Württemberg was a success. When the three men ascended the throne in their lands, in 1891, 1904 and 1912, respectively, the public believed them to be not just legal successors but also, and even above all, well-prepared and capable. Ludwig would succeed his father, Luitpold, only in 1912, at the age of

---

[25] *Leipziger Zeitung* of 17 October 1904.
[26] Müller, *Royal Heirs in Imperial Germany*, pp. 93–96.

sixty-seven, but as early as 1895 the *Augsburger Postzeitung* had praised him for being as 'prepared for his high calling as was hardly any other prince in Europe' and for distinguishing himself though his 'education, character and disposition, his theoretical knowledge and practical experience in all aspects of the state'. The mood was similarly sanguine in Württemberg. 'His majesty certainly assumes the government and conduct of the business of state well-prepared', commented the *Schwäbische Merkur* in 1891 on the occasion of King Wilhelm's succession to the throne. He was, the newspaper recorded, familiar with the business of state, into which he had inculcated himself 'with diligent attention and understanding'. King Friedrich August III of Saxony, the *Dresdner Neueste Nachrichten* assured its readers in October 1904, had 'prepared himself for his high office in great seriousness', and, the newspaper continued, 'there is no one who would not be convinced that he is animated by the greatest resolve and is no less dutiful and enthusiastic than was his father'.[27]

Subsequent generations of princes within the smaller German principalities were also educated according to bourgeois standards. Unlike his father, Ludwig's son Rupprecht attended a public grammar school. 'Correctly recognising the dangers of an isolated upbringing for a future ruler', a contemporary biography of Prince Ludwig reported, he and his wife decided 'that their first born should as early as possible come as close as possible to the regular life of the people and should be raised amongst the people for the people. And therefore Prince Rupprecht became a pupil in the sixth grade at the Maximiliansgymnasium in 1882, having successfully passed a regular examination in all subjects that was administered and led by the rector at the time, Linsmeyer. Here, at the express wish of his illustrious parents, the grammar-school pupil was treated entirely as were his fellow pupils.' The situation in Saxony was similar. At the request of Friedrich August, a 'princes' school' was established in the Taschenberg Palace in Dresden in 1904. Following the state's grammar-school curriculum, the sons of the last king of Saxony were educated alongside children of the city's bourgeoisie.[28] Challenged to convey the reassuring message that as future monarchs they had experienced a rigorous and essentially normal upbringing, each new generation of ruler adapted to the trends of his age.

---

[27] *Augsburger Postzeitung* of 6 January 1895; *Schwäbischer Merkur*, cited in *Neue Preußische Zeitung* of 7 October 1891; *Dresdner Neueste Nachrichten* of 16 October 1904, 2nd edn.
[28] Hans Reidelbach, *Ludwig. Prinz von Bayern. Ein Lebens- und Charakterbild* (Munich, 1905), p. 27; Hermann Schindler, *König Friedrich August III. von Sachsen. Ein Lebens- und Charakterbild* (Dresden, 1906/1916), p. 35.

While national unification in Germany had practically cut the ground from under the feet of the Wittelbachs, Wettins and Württembergers, forcing them to secure their position though skilful public relations and accommodation, the creation of the Kingdom of Italy had propelled the House of Savoy to unknown heights. However, while promotion to national dynasty was accompanied by greater prestige and more opportunities, it also came with significant challenges. The new kingdom was splintered and populated by unfamiliar, even hostile, subjects. It had also inherited a revolutionary tradition. Yet elevation to be its ruling dynasty meant that the Savoia had to keep this divided nation united.

Children who might one day determine the future fate of the country – in this instance, the heir to the throne Vittorio Emanuele, born in 1869 – had a vital role to play. For one thing, they were part of the dynasty's efforts to present itself as a likeable royal family and to form a stronger emotional bond with the population. Additionally, a confidence-inspiring message could be sent to the Italian people via a young crown prince and his upbringing. In the case of Vittorio Emanuele III, who succeeded his father on the throne in 1900, that communication appears to have been successful. Even in distant America he was reported to be unusually cultivated. 'The new King's training', declared the *New York Times*, 'is said to have been more rigid than that of any other Prince in Europe. He lived like a Spartan till he came of age, and his studies were of the most extensive character, ranging from military science to literature of his own land. He speaks several languages perfectly, and will be altogether, probably, the most accomplished monarch in existence.'[29]

The publication of such a paean – moreover in a newspaper in the republican USA – was no fluke. It was the product of decades of effort. Queen Margherita had dedicated herself with great energy to the cause of the House of Savoy and its role within the Italian nation-state. Her intervention seems likely to have lain behind the innovation in the upbringing of the princes of this dynasty, for neither Vittorio Emanuele III's grandfather, Vittorio Emanuele II, nor his father, Umberto I, had been raised according to any real plan. It was said of Vittorio Emanuele II that he much preferred hunting to learning, and, throughout his life, his son Umberto was uncomfortable when he had to provide his signature in front of onlookers.[30] As a devoted mother, fierce patriot and sophisticated

---

[29] *New York Times* of 30 July 1900, cited in Valentina Villa, 'An Italian Heir for the New Century: Vittorio Emanuele, Prince of Naples', in Frank Lorenz Müller and Heidi Mehrkens (eds.), *Sons and Heirs: Succession and Political Culture in Nineteenth-Century Europe* (Basingstoke, 2016), p. 166.

[30] Maria-Christina Marchi, 'Morandi's Italian Job: Nationalising Italy's First Heir', AHRC Project *Heirs to the Throne in the Constitutional Monarchies of Nineteenth-Century Europe*

woman, the queen attended to the prudent education of her only son. 'Queen Margherita, herself one of the most cultured ladies in Italy, took charge from the first of his education', a British author reported in 1903, when Vittorio Emanuele had already ascended the throne.[31]

The upbringing of the first actual heir to the Italian throne was very unlike that of his father and grandfather. In 1882, when attending an examination taken by his son, King Umberto was astounded at the breadth of the material covered by the questions and marvelled at the crown prince's evident respect for his teachers. The political reasons for Vittorio Emanuele's attitude were easy to understand. As the future ruler of a land where the majority of the people still had to learn to be Italians and had yet to develop a loyalty to the constitutional rule of the House of Savoy, the future king embodied a dynasty that was itself still learning. The young crown prince thus faced a double undertaking – he had to learn what it was to be a national figurehead and he had to learn how to be a capable ruler.[32]

The nationalising of the heir to the throne had begun with his carefully staged birth in Naples, with his symbolism-laden names and his title as 'Prince of Naples'. The numerous journeys throughout the Italian peninsula, during which the child was repeatedly presented to the public by his parents, helped to acquaint the subjects with their future ruler. When, following the prince's eleventh birthday, his intensive training began, a further element was added: systematic instruction in the Italian language, as the standard language of the nation, and in Italian culture. A cherished hope of the Risorgimento movement was thus realised. In 1881, the court appointed Luigi Morandi, who would serve as the Prince of Naples's instructor for the next five years. In their daily lessons, the renowned philologist, pedagogue and poet sought to ensure the scion of the House of Piedmont's perfect mastery of the Florentine vernacular, which served as received Italian, placing particular emphasis on grammar, spelling and pronunciation. Additionally he made certain that the prince was familiar with the nation's literary classics – from Petrarch, Dante and Boccaccio to contemporary authors such as Manzoni and Collodi. These efforts, bolstered by ruses such as the shrewd appointment of Casimiro Casaglia, who was from Florence, as the prince's valet, ensured that Vittorio Emanuele was the first ruler from the House of Savoy who had a native speaker's command of Italian. In his widely read memoirs,

(1815–1914), 'Heir of the Month' (June 2014), http://heirstothethrone-project.net/?pag e_id=1039 (accessed 17 February 2017).

[31] Sidney Brooks, 'The King of Italy', in *The North American Review* 176, no. 555 (February 1903), p. 247.

[32] Marchi, 'Morandi's Italian Job'.

entitled *Come fu educato Vittorio Emanuele III* (*How Vittorio Emanuele III Was Raised*), published in 1901, Morandi emphasised the linguistic and cultural dimension of the king's training.[33]

Even more formative than Morandi was General Egidio Osio, who from 1881 directed the education of the crown prince for eight years. In addition to drawing on his considerable military career, Osio could also contribute his qualities as an explorer and diplomat. His regime was strict, demanding the greatest discipline and perseverance from his pupil, and closely followed military forms. His curriculum was inspired by the various Italian military academies and by the diplomatic academy under the Foreign Ministry, but it was by no means narrowly conceived. Vittorio Emanuele was taught strategy, logistics, astronomy, economics, applied mathematics, constitutional, criminal and civil law, history, Latin and modern languages. Each year he was tested on the content of his lessons in an oral examination held in the presence of the king, the queen and representatives of the government and the military. Vittorio Emanuele's comprehensive training continued beyond the classroom, where the prince was the sole pupil. He applied himself to learning to drill and ride, to fence and swim. And he hunted, painted and made music. Osio also organised numerous educational tours. Between 1885 and 1889, the prince visited Switzerland, Germany, Malta, Cyprus, Egypt, Palestine, Greece, Spain, Turkey, Russia and Romania.[34]

The highly demanding education of the Italian heir both within and outside the classroom was intended to mould a figure who would embody national integration and a man who would exercise the highest office of state with proficiency. It was also intended to compensate for circumstances that even the most intensive physical training could not offset: to look at, Vittorio Emanuele did not correspond to the image of the powerful ruler so beloved by the media. The masses always seem to think, commented Sydney Brooks in 1903 in his portrait of the king, 'that a prince who is really capable must also be a paladin in externals, an impressive, martial figure'. A delicate prince of small stature could never really be popular, he opined. It mattered little that the heir was healthy and had good stamina, he proposed, for the problem was with his external appearance, as the prince – possibly as a result of the close familiar relationship of his parents – was no more than five feet tall. The varied and cumbersome orthopaedic devices deployed in an attempt to strengthen the boy's limbs proved of little use. His short 'glass-like legs',

---

[33] Villa, 'An Italian Heir for the New Century', p. 165; Marchi, 'Morandi's Italian Job'; Luigi Morandi, *Come fu educato Vittorio Emanuele III* (Turin, 1901).

[34] Villa, 'An Italian Heir for the New Century', pp. 164–165; Denis Mack Smith, *Italy and Its Monarchy* (New Haven, CT and London, 1989), pp. 147–148.

as he himself described them, troubled the young prince greatly for, according to Brooks, the public liked a prince to look like a prince and should he not, they would readily draw the conclusion that he could not act like a prince. The demanding schooling experienced by the future king of Italy was also an attempt to scotch such premature and unflattering conclusions.[35]

The crown prince ended his formal education in 1889 and then spent several years in Naples, in command of a regiment. He also acquired additional experience of international politics during several trips abroad. After his marriage to Princess Elena of Montenegro in 1896, Vittorio Emanuele led a deliberately private and modest married life, which would later earn him a reputation as a 'bourgeois king'. His demonstratively neutral attitude on political questions signalled that – unlike his increasingly interventionist father – he intended his regime to be strictly constitutional. Here too a decisive shift was evident: where his grandfather had been taught that the power of his position came from God alone, Vittorio Emanuele's lessons in constitutional law were based on an understanding that he would one day reign, as explicated by the *Statuto Albertino*, 'by the grace of God and according to the will of the nation'.[36]

For many contemporaries, this thoroughly prepared heir would prove the saviour of the monarchy when, in June 1900, his father was assassinated. His fastidious observation of his duty to respect political neutrality and the emphasis on his happy private and family life had allowed him to keep his distance from the mishaps, poor decisions and scandals in which Italy's elites and his father had become enmeshed in the previous years. A well-educated and unassuming head of state, respectful of the constitution and interested in modern topics in science and technology, accorded with the political demands of the age. Ricciotti Garibaldi, son of the famous hero of the Risorgimento, wrote that the new king would now be able to ensure the Italian monarchy was long lived. He need only use 'the strength of will he is said to possess' to make the crown a true intermediary between the parties. The 'carefully educated level-headed heir to the throne', opines the historian Valentina Villa, 'would be the saviour of the monarchy, which was to exist for another fifty years'.[37]

[35] Villa, 'An Italian Heir for the New Century', p. 164; Mack Smith, *Italy and Its Monarchy*, p. 147; Brooks, 'The King of Italy', p. 247.
[36] Villa, 'An Italian Heir for the New Century', pp. 162, 169.   [37] Ibid., pp. 170–171.

'Famous without Dazzling Exploits': Raising British Heirs, from Victoria to Edward VIII

At the time when Umberto I was assassinated at Monza in 1900, a crisis of the monarchy in Great Britain seemed unimaginable. For sixty-three years the throne had been occupied by the apparently immortal Queen Victoria. In 1897, her Diamond Jubilee had been celebrated with all the pomp a truly imperial monarchy could muster. The crisis of the 1860s, when the invisibility of the reclusive widowed queen had fed the flames of republicanism, was long since forgotten. Even further back in the mists of time lay the era of dissolute monarchy under Victoria's 'wicked uncles', the problematic sons of her grandfather George III. In the meantime, and thanks to Victoria's decades-long experience in performing a dignified and constitutional rule, the perfected execution of public ritual had been combined with an embodiment of national virtues in a successful recipe which the British royal family has continued to follow even up to the present day.

As we would expect, the comprehensive preparation of the heirs for their future task featured amongst the monarchy's successful adaptations to the changing demands and new leanings of the day. Just what form this training took in Britain will be shown here across three generations of rulers: Victoria's first-born son, Edward Albert (1841–1910), his sons Albert Victor (1864–1892) and George (1865–1936) and, finally, George's son Edward (1894–1972).

In 1843, as we have heard, the pamphlet *Who Should Educate the Prince of Wales?* was seized upon by an eager public readership. Even at the beginning of the Victorian era, the 'family on the throne' was already fully conscious of the political relevance of this issue and gave it careful consideration. Their own experiences meant that Victoria and Albert knew full well what a systematic upbringing would entail.

Queen Victoria had come of age less than a month before the death of her uncle and predecessor on the throne, King William IV, who died at Windsor Castle on 20 June 1837. The often-depicted scene, shown here in Figure 9, of the new monarch receiving the news of the death of her uncle is amongst the defining images of the Victorian era: at the centre is a young woman, still in her nightgown in the early morning; before her are kneeling the Archbishop of Canterbury, who is kissing her outstretched hand, and the Lord Chamberlain. All depictions of this historic moment accentuate the youth of the queen, who until so recently had still been viewed as a child. The inexperience and naivety that the depiction suggests were not just

Figure 9. An iconic image in the history of Victorian Britain: suffused in the light of the breaking day, the eighteen-year-old Victoria receives the news of her uncle's death and is paid homage by the Archbishop of Canterbury and the Lord Chamberlain. *Victoria Regina*, 1887 (oil on canvas), Wells, Henry Tanworth (1828–1903)/Royal Collection Trust © Her Majesty Queen Elizabeth II, 2018.

a product of Victoria's age. They also stemmed from the deliberate isolation in which she had both lived and been educated.[38]

After the death of her husband, the Duke of Kent, in January 1820, Victoria's mother, Victoire of Sachsen-Coburg-Saalfeld, had taken sole responsibility for raising her daughter. In surroundings that she perceived as hostile and constantly plagued by financial difficulties, she retreated with her daughter into a resolutely defended private sphere. She thus sought to protect and control the valuable heir to the throne, a security for her own future. The 'Kensington System', designed by Victoire and her comptroller Sir John Conroy, sealed off Victoria almost entirely from the outside world, keeping her away from the royal court and limiting contact

---

[38] Best known is certainly the painting by Henry Tanworth Wells, *Queen Victoria Receiving the News of Her Accession* of 1887, www.rct.uk/collection/406996/victoria-regina-queen-victoria-receiving-the-news-of-her-accession (accessed 22 May 2022).

with other children to her half-sister Feodora and Conroy's own off-spring. Screened off at Kensington, the princess was hot-housed by her demanding mother. She had thirty hours of lessons each week, during which she was taught French, Italian, Latin, history and geography, and also dancing, painting and to play the piano. German was spoken at home, but close attention was paid to ensuring that the future queen learned perfect English. When Victoria was twelve years old, her mother arranged for her to be examined by two bishops, who attested that she possessed a good level of knowledge. In 1830, Victoire and Conroy organised the first of a series of annual journeys by carriage through England and Wales. While these tours served to supplement the young princess's geography lessons, above all they were intended to ensure she was both known and liked. The public acclamation of the heir to the throne was designed to buttress her future claims to power and, under-standably, was met with some misgiving by her uncle, the king. After five demanding trips, the programme, which had at best given Victoria a superficial impression of the land and its people, was halted. Her strict confinement within the Kensington System came to an end only in those early morning hours when the Archbishop and the Lord Chamberlain knelt down before the eighteen-year-old Victoria. Immediately afterwards the young queen resolutely freed herself from the controls applied by her mother and Conroy.[39]

The upbringing of Prince Albert of Sachsen-Coburg and Gotha, Victoria's cousin and future husband, had been no less meticulously planned. As a younger son of Ernest I, the duke of Coburg, and a member of a highly ambitious and extensively networked clan, he had been prepared for the international marriage market from a very young age. The mastermind was his uncle Leopold, who in 1816 had himself married the only daughter of the English king, George IV. Leopold's future as consort of the queen of England was shattered in 1817, when Princess Charlotte died after a stillbirth. Leopold, who in 1830 had become King of the Belgians, succeeded with his second attempt to ensure that the British monarchy acquired a Coburg twist. He paved the way for the marriage between the heir apparent, his niece Victoria, and his nephew Albert. The young man had been carefully educated to this end: initially by home tutors and grammar school teachers in Coburg, then through several months of study at Leopold's court in Brussels, and finally as a student at the University of Bonn and while on several

---

[39] Karina Urbach, *Queen Victoria. Eine Biographie* (Munich, 2011), p. 21; A. N. Wilson, *Victoria: A Life* (New York, 2014), pp. 42–75. For an extensive discussion of the early years and upbringing of Victoria, see Lynne Vallone, *Becoming Victoria* (New Haven, CT and London, 2001).

educational tours. An eager learner, this young man, a lover of culture and music, had been created to be the perfect partner for his cousin, who fortunately fell in love with him right on schedule.[40]

Immediately after their wedding in February 1840, the young couple threw themselves into re-establishing the reputation of the British monarchy, which had been greatly damaged by the apparent mental illness of George III, the scandals surrounding the prince regent, subsequently King George IV, and the less-than-edifying lifestyles of his numerous brothers. All that was now to be remedied by an irreproachable marriage and family life, a modest and dignified lifestyle and an evident neutrality in party politics. The birth of Prince Albert Edward, soon after the marriage, contributed perfectly to this project. The arrival, in 1841, of the desired male heir to the throne also raised the question of how the future monarch was to be prepared for this mission. Prince Albert, with his passion for knowledge and obsession with detail, threw himself into this project. His circle of erudite yet hopelessly convoluted advisors were only too happy to assist. Those responsible for the education of the next-in-line believed their task essential to the future viability of the British monarchy. And their mission – described by Philip Magnus as 'to mould him [the Prince of Wales] in isolation from his contemporaries, into a moral and intellectual paragon' – was correspondingly fraught.[41]

A memorandum on child-rearing composed by Baron Christian von Stockmar, a long-time mentor and confidant of Prince Albert, just a few months after the birth of the Prince of Wales made the existential import of their task very clear to the young prince's parents. The inadequate education of King George III's sons, Stockmar explained, had 'contributed more than any other circumstance to weaken the respect and influence of Royalty in this country'. That disgrace could now be expunged with the help of young Bertie. The challenge was great, Stockmar explained, since the 'first truth by which the Queen and the Prince ought to be thoroughly penetrated is, that their position is a much more difficult one than that of any parents in the kingdom: because the Royal children ought not only to be brought up to be moral characters, but also fitted to discharge successfully the arduous duties which may eventually devolve upon them as future Sovereigns'. It should never be forgotten that more than just the reputation of the monarchy was at stake.

[40] Charles Grey, *The Early Years of His Royal Highness the Prince Consort* (London, 1868), chs. 2, 5, 7 and 9; Hans-Joachim Netzer, *Albert von Sachsen-Coburg und Gotha. Ein deutscher Prinz in England* (Munich, 1988), pp. 63–110; Franz Bosbach (ed.), *Die Studien des Prinzen Albert an der Universität Bonn, 1837–1838* (Berlin and New York, 2010).

[41] Philip Magnus, *King Edward the Seventh* (London, 1964), p. 5.

The admonition would hardly have been necessary, for the young Victoria and her husband did not see the crown as simply a decorative institution. Their goal, the historian David Cannadine has demonstrated, was to secure for the monarchy a constitutive and potent role that for the sake of the nation should expand further. Only an optimally trained monarch would be able to perform the role of royal chief executive that Prince Albert had in mind.[42]

Additionally, Stockmar's plan provided for a systematic exercise of the brain, which could help treat the child's cognitive deficiency which had been diagnosed by the phrenologist Andrew Combe. Bertie was educated on his own, and each of the young boy's school days, which ran from 8 a.m. to 6 p.m., was divided into thirty-minute units, to facilitate his instruction in a range of subjects. This drill failed to produce results. When Bertie was aged seven, Henry Birch, a master from Eton, was appointed to teach the increasingly obstreperous prince according to a curriculum that Prince Albert himself had developed. Bertie was to receive lessons on six days each week, placing him under great pressure and leaving him with less time away from the classroom than any other schoolboy in the land. In terms of both achievement and behaviour, the child, who continued to be taught entirely on his own, still remained far behind the expectations of his parents. Corporal punishment was also tried, but the desired improvement remained elusive.[43]

In 1852, when the Prince of Wales's learning had still not attained the level that Prince Albert had hoped for, Birch was dismissed and replaced by Frederick Gibbs, a lawyer. Birch's final assessment of his pupil was uneven. He attested that the prince showed evidence of a friendly nature, a good memory and sharp powers of observation, but he judged that his mood swings and lack of discipline made systematic and regular instruction impossible. The departing teacher attributed that behaviour in part to 'want of contact with boys of his own age, and from his being continually in the society of older persons'. The prince was always the centre of attention, which also made his healthy development more difficult. Yet Bertie's father was not to be diverted from the path he was taking, and even quickened the pace. On Albert's instructions, Gibbs increased the time allotted to six full hours on six weekdays and arranged for additional lessons in gymnastics and riding. Despite the warnings of Bertie's French

---

[42] Jane Ridley, *Bertie: A Life of Edward VII* (London, 2012), pp. 19–23; Gordon and Lawton, *Royal Education*, p. 152; David Cannadine, 'The Last Hanoverian Sovereign? The Victorian Monarchy in Historical Perspective, 1688–1988', in A. L. Beier, David Cannadine and James M. Rosenheim (eds.), *The First Modern Society: Essays in Honour of Lawrence Stone* (Cambridge, 1989), pp. 127–165, 139–144.

[43] Ridley, *Bertie*, pp. 19–23; Magnus, *King Edward the Seventh*, p. 7.

and German tutors that the constant overloading had left the boy completely exhausted, Gibbs unrelentingly followed through with the programme. Only on the matter of the isolation of the future king was the new tutor able to effect some change, for after 1852 selected playmates were on occasion invited to Windsor Castle or to Buckingham Palace. Prince Albert oversaw every detail of all these endeavours. The tutors were required to provide daily reports. Bertie's father read all the written exercises the heir to the throne produced, organised sightseeing visits in London and arranged for his son to be present at a naval review at Spithead. He invited scholars to give private lectures and arranged for a miniature farm to be built in the park at Osborne House, the seat of the royal family on the Isle of Wight, off the south coast of England.[44]

As all these endeavours and further phrenological attention failed to produce the progress the boy's parents had hoped for, in the summer of 1857 Prince Albert sent his son and four boys of the same age on a longer educational trip to Germany, France and Switzerland. Although Gibbs was still required to provide Bertie's parents with daily updates, the three-month-long journey seems to have been highly enjoyable, especially as the prince succeeded in keeping his first kiss a secret from his parents. As a reward, for his sixteenth birthday in November 1857 Bertie was given permission to select his own clothes, although only as long as his wardrobe was not 'extravagant or casual'. His request to enter the army was denied, but he was permitted to take the entrance examination. Six months later Bertie was confirmed and soon afterwards he was given his own living quarters, White Lodge in Richmond Park. It was Prince Albert's wish that here, isolated 'from the world', Bertie would continue to be taught by Gibbs and by his Latin tutor, Charles Tarver. True to form, Prince Albert drew up a meticulous memorandum for the young lords-in-waiting who were to keep the prince company. They were to ensure that the heir did not keep his hands in his pockets, dress flamboyantly, get up to any highjinks or indulge in pointless pleasures such as playing billiards. After the months in White Lodge had proved similarly unproductive, in November 1858 Gibbs submitted his resignation. He was replaced by a military governor, Major-General Robert Bruce.[45]

Retrospectively, the years that followed, up until the death of the prince consort in December 1861, appear like a frantic rush towards the finish line of Bertie's education. Barely returned from a journey to Germany at the end of 1858, during which Bertie met his older sister Victoria – 'Vicky' – in

---

[44] Magnus, *King Edward the Seventh*, pp. 8, 10–14, 17.
[45] Ridley, *Bertie*, pp. 36–42; Magnus, *King Edward the Seventh*, pp. 20–26; Sir Sidney Lee, *King Edward VII: A Biography*, vol. 1 (London, 1925), pp. 48–56.

Berlin, the heir to the throne embarked on a longer tour to southern Europe in January 1859. Accompanied by Major-General Bruce, his wife, an equerry, a doctor and a chaplain, Bertie visited Rome, Gibraltar, Spain and Portugal. The trip was furnished with the required gravitas – the prince was required to keep a journal, his letters home were corrected and returned, and there was no lack of instruction in history and art history.

When the prince returned to England, first on the agenda was his pomp-filled investiture with the Order of the Garter. Yet even that magnificent ceremony could not console Bertie's critical father for his son's failure to have acquired any appreciable intellectual maturity during the trip. Bertie's travel journal appeared trivial to Albert, and entirely without historical reflection. His son was promptly sent to Edinburgh, where for three months he attended lectures on Roman history, modern history, law and chemistry. At the conclusion of the course of study, Prince Albert made his way to the Scottish capital to hear from his son's teachers at an 'educational conference'. His time in Edinburgh was intended to serve as preparation for Bertie's university studies, which would follow on immediately.[46]

The public was not unaware of the dogged attempts to inculcate the future ruler with learning. In 1859, the renowned satirical magazine *Punch* provided its readership with the poem 'A Prince at High Pressure'. The Prince of Wales's educational ordeal was presented with a concerned irony. In Edinburgh, with his 'poor noddle perplext', he had to 'run the gauntlet' between sundry scholarly endeavours and studying and would then be promptly carted off to the south. There he was to be 'dipped in grey Oxford mixture' before being transferred to Cambridge, 'where dynamics and statics, and pure mathematics/will be piled on his brain's awful cargo of "cram"'. All this together, according to *Punch*, made the story of 'thou dear little Wales' surely 'the saddest of tales'. Sixteen years after a pamphlet had asked *Who Should Educate the Prince of Wales?*, the upbringing of the prince was evidently still a political issue. Nor is that surprising, for with their decision to send Bertie first to Oxford and then to Cambridge, Queen Victoria and Prince Albert were entering uncharted waters. Prior to Bertie, no British monarch had attended university.[47] That may explain why this course was run at only half-throttle. Unusually for Oxford and Cambridge, the Prince of Wales did not live alongside his fellow students in one of the colleges but instead – along with a cadre of companions led by General Bruce – took up

---

[46] Magnus, *King Edward the Seventh*, pp. 27–30; Lee, *King Edward VII*, pp. 57–75; Ridley, *Bertie*, pp. 42–44.
[47] *Punch* of 24 September 1859, p. 126; Gordon and Lawton, *Royal Education*, pp. 159–160.

residence in accommodation specially arranged for him, first in Frewin
Hall in Oxford and subsequently in Maddingly Hall, near Cambridge. An
attractive picture of Frewin Hall, with a portrait of the prince sporting
gown and mortarboard, appeared on 5 November 1859 on the front page
of *The Illustrated London News*, which noted that 'The presence in Oxford
of the heir to the British throne has [...] caused general interest.' At his
residence, Bertie and six specially chosen students enjoyed private lectures by leading Oxford professors, with an emphasis on the liberal arts.
The heir to the throne also attended several public lectures, discussions
and church services. As was the custom, those present stood when the
eighteen-year-old student entered the room.[48]

The press coverage that greeted the start of the prince's studies was
highly favourable. The *Manchester Guardian* noted that the prince had
evidently resolved 'to conform to all the rules of his college, and to
conduct himself in nearly all respects like its ordinary members'. He
was regularly present at lectures, it reported, and attended prayers
promptly each morning. On the occasion of Bertie's eighteenth birthday
two weeks later, the paper praised the whole royal family's attitude
towards work, and added that 'If former Princes of Wales had had such
a training, and such a home as ours of the present day, their worst sins and
most perplexing troubles might have been escaped.'[49]

Even as Bertie's time at Oxford started out so auspiciously, his father's
concerns were not assuaged. He experienced 'terrible anxiety', he wrote
to Bruce, that time might be lost in conviviality and recreation, for the
'only use of Oxford is that it is a place for study'. The importance of the
examinations designed specifically for the prince, which he would sit at
the end of each of the four trimesters, could not be overstated, Prince
Albert averred. Considering his circumstances, Bertie's performance in
these examinations was valiant, and his visit to Canada and the USA
towards the end of his time at Oxford, where he represented the queen,
proved a great success. The prince's self-confidence grew. In
January 1861, just a few weeks after his return from America, when he
began his studies at Trinity College in Cambridge, he complained to the
master of the college that Prince Albert again did not wish him to live with
his fellow students. Instead he resided at Maddingly Hall, a country seat
about five miles outside Cambridge, from which, however, he was able to
organise a more lively social life than he had enjoyed during his time at
Oxford. The prince developed a friendly relationship with Charles

[48] *The Illustrated London News* of 5 November 1859, pp. 431–432.
[49] *The Manchester Guardian* of 26 October 1859 and 10 November 1859.

Kingsley, a history professor, and, alongside Kingsley's teaching, he also attended lectures in chemistry, law and engineering.[50]

As was to be expected, Prince Albert visited Maddingly Hall regularly to keep a watchful eye on his son's academic endeavours. The next step in Bertie's education was already being planned: ten weeks' training with an infantry unit stationed in Ireland. This opportunity fed a desire, long-cherished by the heir to the throne, who to date had had no military experience and had been given the rank of general purely for the sake of form. As usual, an extensive memorandum was composed, signed by the commander-in-chief of the British army, the commanding general of the troops in Ireland and the Prince of Wales. The document provided for Bertie to begin as an ensign, and then, as a result of industrious study, to earn a promotion every two weeks. Within ten weeks, he would then be able to command a brigade in the field. With his trademark pedantry, Prince Albert also laid down how many evenings each week Bertie would dine alone, as a guest, as host and in the officers' mess, and also where – in the barracks – his accommodation should be.[51]

On his arrival in Dublin, the Prince of Wales was met by a large and enthusiastic crowd. Disappointment soon followed, though, for, as was only to be expected, the entirely overambitious plan, designed to catapult an inexperienced civilian into the rank of brigade commander within just a few weeks, foundered. There was no question of his leading a company, his superior, a Colonel Percy, barked at him that August. He was not qualified for that position. By September, the prince still needed assistance if he was even to begin to carry out the responsibilities of military command. It was not all bad news, though. With the help of the charming Nellie Clifden, Bertie did make progress on other fronts. In the autumn of 1861, he returned to Cambridge, where, on 12 December, two days before his father's death, he took his final examination.[52]

The long arm of Albert's educational programme reached out even from beyond the grave. To complete the training of his son, who was now aged twenty, the prince consort had intended that Bertie would undertake a longer trip to the East. Although following his father's death Bertie had not felt disposed to leave the country, his traumatised mother had insisted that her dead husband's plans be carried out. In February 1862 the travellers set out, dressed in mourning as the queen required. Without Bertie's father's active oversight, the tour, which led from Venice to Egypt and then on to the Holy Land, became rather less earnest. Visits to sites of

[50] Magnus, *King Edward the Seventh*, pp. 30–42; Lee, *King Edward VII*, pp. 113–117.
[51] Magnus, *King Edward the Seventh*, pp. 43–44.
[52] Magnus, *King Edward the Seventh*, pp. 46–47; Lee, *King Edward VII*, p. 115.

antiquity and lectures by Professor Arthur Stanley, who was travelling with the party, were neglected; instead Bertie took out several unsuspecting crocodiles from a steamer on the Nile, read the sensational novel *East Lynne*, smoked, drank coffee and while in Jerusalem acquired a tattoo. At the same time, in distant England his mother realised the final step in the programme envisaged by Albert for their son's upbringing: engagement, to Princess Alexandra of Denmark. By the time the heir to the throne returned home in June 1862, all was arranged and he acquiesced. On 9 September, he formally asked for Alexandra's hand in marriage in Brussels; on 10 March 1863 the wedding took place at Windsor Castle. On the day before the ceremony, Victoria led the couple into the mausoleum where the mortal remains of her husband had been laid to rest. '*He gives you his blessing*', the queen pronounced at Albert's grave. The Prince of Wales had now come of age and was a married man. His father's educational experiment was concluded.[53]

Measured against its exorbitant aims, the project had failed. Despite the years of torture for all those involved, the Prince of Wales had not become a moral and intellectual paragon, and the personal relationship between parents and child was in ruins. His mother, who had always been cold towards her son, would never forgive him for supposedly sending her husband, disappointed to the core, to an early grave. In response, Bertie approached his mother, in the apposite words of his biographer, as if he were 'negotiating with a hostile power'. However, in terms of its public impact, the tense and overwrought attempt to create a perfect heir to the throne was successful. The poem in *Punch* was sympathetic and ironic, but it did point out how hard the prince was required to work. The *Times* leader marking the prince's eighteenth birthday even expressed some confidence. Almost reassuringly, the newspaper pointed out that it was the good fortune of the English monarch that he might be 'great even without the possession of extraordinary talents, and famous without dazzling exploits'. If the heir was content to emulate his parents and to endeavour to acquire the affection of the people, then all would be well. The judgement of other papers was even more generous. In February 1863, when the Prince of Wales took his seat in the House of Lords, *The Illustrated London News* lauded him for having 'acquired a store of information rarely to be met with in a man double his age'. He had undertaken a programme of study, the paper noted, that raised him intellectually as far above his fellow men as did his position as heir to the throne and future king. That verdict was closer to the demands of the aspirational Albert than was the rather feeble renunciation of any specific

[53] Ridley, *Bertie*, pp. 67–77.

achievements to which the *Times* was resigned. But the emotional cost of Albert's ambitions had been very high.[54]

How, then, did the Prince of Wales factor his own experiences and the expectations of those around him into the upbringing of his own sons? Bertie and Alexandra's first child, who would be baptised as Albert Victor Christian Edward at the insistence of the queen, was born on 8 January 1864. Although uncertainty surrounds the relevant dates, his birth weight, at just 3 lbs 12 oz, suggests that Eddy, as his family called him, was born about two months premature. A good year later, on 3 June 1865, his brother George followed, with whom Eddy would remain very close throughout his life.

The relationship between parents and children within the Prince of Wales's household was very different from that which Bertie had himself experienced. Unlike Queen Victoria, who could never entirely conceal her abhorrence of small children, Princess Alexandra was practically besotted with her offspring, treating them almost like dolls and showering them all the way into adulthood with an overwhelming affection. Moreover, Bertie had the best of intentions in seeking to avoid repeating the errors of his own upbringing. Excessive strictness, he wrote to his mother, led children to 'get shy and only fear those whom they ought to love'. In the end, however, he also failed at building a close and trusting relationship with his children. As a frequently absent or distracted father, he left the mothering of his children to his wife and their education, as was usual amongst the British upper classes, to tutors engaged for the task.[55]

Under the gentle supervision of their still girlish and playful mother, Eddy, George and their sisters experienced a relatively unburdened, but also unproductive, youth at Sandringham, the country seat of the Prince of Wales. As could only be expected, the queen found the children so 'ill-bred, ill-trained' that she could not 'fancy them at all'. But Benjamin Disraeli too was unsure what to make of it when, during a dinner at Sandringham, the children crawling around under the table pinched at his calves. A tutor was appointed when Eddy was seven years old. The thirty-two-year-old Reverend John Dalton, a curate from the Isle of Wight, had been recommended by Queen Victoria, who liked his warm preaching voice. Thus began a relationship, established as a result of a somewhat chance encounter, that would decisively shape Prince Eddy's and Prince George's development over many years. Initially Dalton's efforts were not particularly successful. Two years after his

---

[54] Ibid., p. 71; *The Times* of 11 November 1859, p. 6; *The Illustrated London News* of 14 February 1863.

[55] Ridley, *Bertie*, pp. 84–85, 93, 164–165; Andrew Cook, *Prince Eddy: The King Britain Never Had* (Stroud, 2006), p. 37.

appointment, Canon Duckworth temporarily substituted for the boys' usual tutor and commented that neither of them could either speak or understand French 'which is a serious drawback for a Prince'. Dalton remained sanguine. Eddy and George were happy and healthy, he reported to Queen Victoria, in January 1874, 'the writing, reading and arithmetic are all progressing favourably: the music, spelling, English History, Latin, Geography and French all occupy a due share of their Royal Highnessess' attention, and the progress in English History and Geography is very marked'.[56]

Only some years later, when the Prince of Wales began to play with the idea of sending his older son to a public school – he was thinking of Wellington College, a boarding school in Berkshire – did Dalton address a subject that had long been a matter of gossip: the supposed mental limitations of the heir to the throne. Eddy was thought to be slow on the uptake and intellectually dull. The extent of his possible learning difficulties is hard to determine. The most important – although certainly not sole – source for these findings was Dalton, who had something to gain from suggesting that the prince was hard to educate and that he alone could save the situation. The sources that document the educational programme now implemented give the impression that the prince's parents allowed themselves to be strongly influenced by a man who knew how to squeeze every last advantage out of an opportunity. On 11 February 1877, Dalton responded to the suggestion that Eddy might attend Wellington College with his extensive 'Memorandum on the Education of Prince Albert Victor and Prince George of Wales'. Learning alongside other children his age would inevitably bring to light Eddy's backwardness, which Dalton deemed a result of the adverse learning conditions in the surroundings of the court. Additionally, he noted, the two boys would then be separated, which would have a catastrophic effect, as 'Prince Albert Victor requires the stimulus of Prince George's company to induce him to work at all'. Without George, educating Eddy would be a very tall order indeed.[57]

Rather than send the future king to a school, the enterprising reverend had a different suggestion, one that would have far-reaching implications: Prince George would, as had always been the plan, go through naval training, and to that end he should transfer to the training ship *HMS Britannia* at Dartmouth. If Eddy – and naturally also Dalton – were to accompany him, this 'would be the very best thing alike for his Royal

[56] Ridley, *Bertie*, p. 164; Dalton to Queen Victoria, 31 January 1874, Royal Archives (henceforth RA), RA VIC/MAIN/Z/450/90.

[57] John Dalton, 'Memorandum on the Education of Prince Albert Victor and Prince George', 11 February 1877 (RA VIC/MAIN/Z/459/90).

Highness's moral, mental and physical development'. The time he spent as a naval cadet would be advantageous in every way, strengthening Eddy's concentration, his attention to detail, his sense of responsibility and his physical conditioning. Naval training, Dalton believed, would help the heir to the throne develop 'those habits of promptitude and method, of manliness and self-reliance, in which he is now somewhat deficient'. On top of that, the tutor added, entrusting the princes to the navy would be 'likely to be exceedingly popular with the nation generally'. The mellifluously voiced and silver-tongued clergyman succeeded not only in convincing the boys' parents of the merits of his plan but also in setting aside the queen's misgivings, and so in October 1878 the two princes became cadets on *HMS Britannia*. This ship, only a hulk, was permanently moored at the mouth of the River Dart, in Devon, where it served the Royal Navy as accommodation and for preparing prospective naval officers.[58]

While George was soon making good progress and proved a competent cadet, Eddy fell short across the board. When, in December 1878, Lord Ramsay, commander of the *Britannia*, wrote to the Prince of Wales he did not mince his words: 'It is painful to be obliged to tell your Royal Highness that Prince Edward is learning nothing or almost nothing [. . .] It seems that he cannot rather than will not learn.' All his instructors, to a man, despaired of him. The following day Dalton also picked up his pen to write to the royal parents about their sons' progress. The picture he sketched was no different: while George was developing well, the contrast with Eddy could not be greater. All Eddy's efforts were calamitous and everyone was of the opinion that the boy's nature was 'almost quite abnormal', with his teacher noting that 'His brain at present is very feeble [. . .] and he has evidently very little conscious regulation over its work-ings.' When, understandably, the parents responded to his report with the greatest concern, Dalton rushed to assure them that all was not doom and gloom when it came to Eddy, who 'has improved and is improving'. He should not quit the *Britannia*, for the influence of the naval officers was preferable to that of schoolteachers, and the cadets were better company than schoolboys. Additionally, the implications of removing Eddy from his naval training would be disastrous, for, Dalton reported, 'Here he has the benefit of Prince George's bright and genial presence; to lose this, by being parted from him, (for the present) would be irreparable.'[59]

---

[58] Ibid.; John Pope-Hennessy, *Queen Mary: The Official Biography*, with an introduction by Hugo Vickers (London, 2019), p. 192.

[59] Lord Ramsay to Prince of Wales, 3 December 1878 (RA VIC/MAIN/Z/473A/1); Dalton to Prince of Wales, 4 December 1878 (RA VIC/MAIN/Z/473A/2); Prince of Wales to

And so both princes remained on board the *Britannia* until, inevitably, the next crisis occurred, in April 1879: Eddy could not possibly graduate from the training course. He was failing not just in one or two subjects, according to Dalton, but in all of them. What was to be done? In another long memorandum, their educator developed a fantastical idea: Eddy should accompany his brother, who was now to go to sea as a naval cadet. There was, he opined, no alternative. The heir's shortcomings – Dalton spoke of 'the abnormally dormant condition of his mental powers' – would be even more evident in the context of a school than on board the *Britannia*, where they could be somewhat masked. Eddy could not keep pace with boys of his age, and it was not desirable for him to be taught along with younger boys. Educating the prince on his own was inconceivable, he insisted, for he needed the company of his brother. Dalton laid out his plan across almost thirty handwritten pages, explaining at the same time why this was the only way forward: the two boys, accompanied by their tutor, should together undertake a world tour as cadets aboard a British naval ship. Despite numerous objections by the queen and the British cabinet to what was, to put it mildly, an eccentric plan, Dalton prevailed. On 17 September 1879, the fifteen-year-old Eddy and his fourteen-year-old brother, shown in Figure 10 in their naval uniforms, put to sea on board the corvette *HMS Bacchante*.[60]

As one might well imagine, the rules for this unusual educational experiment were highly detailed. An especially composed memorandum determined, amongst other things, that Their Highnesses, newly promoted to midshipmen, should be treated as were all others of their rank, that Dalton should give the princes instruction that supplemented the usual training of cadets, that the clergyman should accompany the princes whenever they went ashore, and that Eddy and George should have a servant. Lessons in mathematics and French were subsequently added to the list. On this basis, the future king of England and his younger brother spent a full three years on board the eighty-five-metre *HMS Bacchante*. Their three tours would take them to the Mediterranean, the Caribbean, Ireland, Latin America, Australia, Hong Kong, Singapore and Sri Lanka. The press received extensive reports on their time at sea and on land, especially when the journey turned particularly dramatic, for example when the ship was ordered to sail from the Falkland Islands to the Cape in January 1881 to assist during the First Anglo-Boer War or lost its rudder during a storm in the Indian Ocean and lost its rudder.

Dalton, 8 December 1878 (RA GV/PRIV/AA6/20); Dalton to Prince of Wales, 11 December 1878 (RA GV/PRIV/AA6/211).

[60] Dalton to Prince of Wales, 9 April 1879 (RA VIC/MAIN/Z/453/9).

Figure 10. Educating princes on the high seas: in line with a scheme devised by their resourceful tutor, Princes Eddy and George spent years circumnavigating the globe on board *HMS Bacchante*. The young cadets' adventures were widely reported in the press and formed the basis for a two-volume travelogue. The Print Collector/Alamy Stock Photo.

The need for an appropriately princely upbringing during this period was not overlooked. The Prince of Wales deemed it important that while on board Eddy be instructed in French and history and that, each time they went ashore, Dalton organise an intensive sightseeing programme. But even the healthy sea air could not change Eddy. 'As your Royal Highness is aware Prince Albert Victor has always been to every single teacher he has ever had a most disheartening boy to instruct. He will not exert himself enough', Dalton declared in one of his regular reports to the boys' parents, continuing that he 'is still more fond of animal than of mental gratification; of eating and idling & play than of work & duty'. The accompanying reports from the tutors in mathematics and French painted a similarly gloomy picture. And so Dalton, who, it seemed, would be happy to keep travelling forever, proposed that, at the conclusion of their world tour, he would accompany the two princes on a fairly long trip through French-speaking lands.[61]

The princes' three-year-long cruise on board the *Bacchante* found a significant echo in the press and in 1886 resounded all the more loudly. That year saw the publication of the two-volume work *The Cruise of Her Majesty's Ship Bacchante, 1879–1882*, dedicated to the queen and weighing in at close to 1,500 pages and almost 750,000 words. The tomes were a sumptuous celebration of the learning that Eddy and George had supposedly acquired on board the corvette. The two princes were named as the authors on the title page of the extravagant text, but the work bore all the signs of the authorship of its editor, John Dalton. Even contemporaries used to the most overblown of texts found the lush writing, overloaded with classical citations and mountains of detail, relatively indigestible and would have struggled to believe it was the work of two adolescent boys. Thus, for example, the account of a visit to an ostrich farm in South Africa undertaken in March 1881 covered four pages and left no question unanswered. Topics addressed included the cost of hatching ostrich eggs, the profitability of breeding during the previous year, the price of ostrich feathers, the feeding of the animals and their natural aggressiveness. The diary that Prince George kept at the time has a somewhat more credible ring: 'We then passed an ostridge farm', the sixteen-year-old had written, 'and saw a good many ostridges.'[62]

While composing this wide-ranging work, Dalton continued to see to the education of the princes. In autumn 1882, just a few months after the two young men had returned from their circumnavigation of the globe, he accompanied them to Lausanne, where they were to work on their French for two months. Unfortunately, as the Prince of Wales also complained, progress was slow as too much English was being spoken. When Eddy and George returned to Britain in the summer of 1883, their paths divided for the first time. George received orders to join the corvette *HMS Canada*,

[61] 'Directions for the Guidance of the Revd J. N. Dalton M.A. Governor to HRH Prince Albert Victor & Prince George of Wales', September 1879 (RA VIC/MAIN/L/28); Lord Northbrook to Queen Victoria, 11 November 1880 (RA VIC/MAIN/E/54/27); Dalton to Prince of Wales, 9 January 1882 [with reports from the mathematics and French tutors] (RA MAIN/Z/474/15, 16, 17); Dalton to Prince of Wales, 14 August 1882 (RA VIC/MAIN/Z/474/38).

[62] Kenneth Rose, *King George V* (London, 1983), pp. 14–15.

which was headed for America, as a naval officer, while the heir to the throne was to prepare for the university studies that were now deemed obligatory. Together with a group of select young companions, several teachers and the inevitable Dalton, Eddy was sent to Bachelor's Cottage, a house in the park at Sandringham, where throughout the summer he received intensive tutoring. According to a report by his principal teacher, the historian James Kenneth Stephen, this instruction was hard going. For two months, four hours every day were spent reading books on English history. It had been almost always necessary to read the works out loud, Stephen wrote, for the prince's attempts to read on his own or to provide written responses to questions were largely counterproductive and learning by rote had also not worked. 'Prince Edward's one great difficulty is in keeping his attention fixed', he summarised. 'He hardly knows the meaning of the word to read.'[63]

Notwithstanding such reports, the prince's education moved forward to the next stage – attending university. Unlike his father, Eddy, *The Illustrated London News* reported, would 'not be an outsider, but is to reside within the precincts of Trinity College. There for some time he will, like other students, have to submit to the discipline of college life.' On 3 November, that newspaper even published an entire page filled with drawings illustrating the prince's life as a student: Eddy in chapel, dining, with his mortar board and gown. As was to be expected, the prince was not entirely on his own in Cambridge: his room was immediately along-side that of the everlasting Reverend Dalton, who continued to make himself indispensable and to send regular reports to Eddy's parents. Admittedly, he had now adopted a less critical tone. The prince felt at home in Cambridge, he noted, dedicating four hours each morning to his studies and spending the remainder of his time on tennis, hunting and the cadet corps. A schedule sent by Dalton to the Prince of Wales at the end of October 1883 begins the day with tennis at 6:30 a.m. and breakfast at 8:15 a.m., then three hours of 'reading in rooms', a half-hour break and a further hour of 'reading by self' after 12:30 p.m. The remainder of the day comprised mealtimes, exercise, free time and socialising. In February 1884, Dalton conveyed praise given by the prince's history and German professors, who were pleased with his readiness to learn. Additionally, that March his parents could read that he had drilled with the volunteer corps and was concentrating, as his father had wished, on German texts. In the summer of 1884, the prince spent several weeks in Heidelberg, to work on his German with instruction from Professor Ihne.

---

[63] Prince of Wales to Dalton, 29 October 1882 (RA GV/PRIV/AA6/281); Cook, *Prince Eddy*, pp. 99–104; report by J. K. Stephen, 30 August 1883 (RA VIC/MAIN/Z/474/63).

He made such a good impression in the university town on the River Neckar, the *Pall Mall Gazette* reported, that the Heidelberg choral society serenaded him on his departure. At the end of their performance, the delighted prince had asked to hear *Die Wacht am Rhein* (*The Watch on the Rhine*), a request the patriotic Heidelberg singers had fulfilled with gusto.[64]

A further year at Cambridge was uneventful. Unlike his father, the prince was not required to sit any examinations, and a few years after the end of his studies, he was even rewarded with an honorary doctorate. Eddy's twenty-first birthday fell during this second period at Cambridge. It brought the departure of Dalton, who became a canon at Windsor. Now seemed the moment to test the public's response to all those years invested in the prince's upbringing. The encomia published to mark the occasion struck a tone that was markedly at variance with the insiders' view. Above all, there was the letter from the British Prime Minister, William Gladstone, which was published in many newspapers: 'There has been no period of the world's history', declared the elder statesman, 'at which successors to the Monarchy could more efficaciously contribute to the stability of a great historic system.' The *Pall Mall Gazette* dedicated an illustrated article to 'Prince Edward's Career'. The interested reader could discover that on entering the naval academy the prince and his brother had been tested 'in the same manner as ordinary naval cadets' and had not proved wanting. The tour on the *Bacchante* followed, for which the prince would soon publish his own detailed account. Laudatory reference was also made to his studies in Cambridge, his time spent in Heidelberg to acquire German, and his most recent involvement with the army volunteers.[65]

This article takes us to the final stage of Eddy's education – his time with the army. When, having concluded his university studies in 1885, Eddy joined the 10th Hussars, he proved a proficient horseman but shocked his instructors with the glaring gaps in his knowledge and his complete inability to learn anything from a book. Aurally received information he seemed to absorb far better. Despite his pronounced aversion to effort of any kind and his dislike of military discipline, Eddy stayed with the regiment. In 1887, he even passed the final officer's examination and was promoted to captain. He eventually left the army in 1891 with the

---

[64] *The Illustrated London News* of 27 October 1883 and 3 November 1883; James Edmund Vincent, *His Royal Highness Duke of Clarence and Avondale: A Memoir* (London, 1893), pp. 142–143, 158; Dalton to Prince of Wales, 22 October 1883, 25 October 1883, 20 February 1884 and 25 March 1884 (RA VIC/MAIN/Z/474/67, 69, 72, 74); Cook, *Prince Eddy*, p. 111.

[65] *The Times* of 13 January 1885; *Pall Mall Gazette* of 7 January 1885.

rank of major. By that date, his reputation was already dented, for Eddy was viewed as an ineffectual and pleasure-seeking prince. Thus, in the autumn of 1888, when word was given that he had been granted a relatively long leave of absence to participate in the celebrations marking the king of Denmark's Silver Jubilee, the radical *Reynold's Newspaper* responded with a biting satire:

> Prince Albert Victor goes – deserted is the State.
> Oh, enemies of England! pray Heaven you note it not!
> That we now lose our chiefest strength and shield,
> The military scion of our royal house,
> The lion rampant of the battle-field.[66]

However, before the final stage in the preparation of the heir for his future role could be embarked upon – marriage to a suitable bride, arranged by his family – matters took an unexpected and dramatic turn. The heir to the throne's health had been suffering for some time, probably as the result of alcohol abuse and venereal disease, and in early 1892 he was brought low by influenza that developed into pneumonia. On 12 January 1892, Eddy died at Sandringham, aged just twenty-eight. His early death meant that all that effort and all that careful planning invested for more than a decade in training the king-in-waiting despite his evident lack of fitness had been in vain.

Eddy's place was now taken by his younger brother, George, who had been serving as a naval officer since the return of the *Bacchante* ten years earlier. Again, an amenable press helped smooth over the rupture. In an extensive article on 'The New Heir Presumptive' the *Pall Mall Gazette* attested that Prince George had enjoyed 'a modern and practical education'. He had not shone in Latin and Greek, but he had studied the natural sciences, history and navigation, the newspaper reported, had led the healthy and unassuming life of a naval cadet, and had sailed the world on the *Bacchante* as a 'budding Nelson'. He had earned his demanding lieutenant's commission under entirely normal conditions and had then made his career as an officer at sea. Further measures were quickly taken to prepare the former 'Sailor Prince' for his role as heir to the throne. A final attempt was made to improve George's facility with foreign languages, although a longer stay in Heidelberg did not produce the desired results. In May 1892, George became engaged to Princess Mary of Teck, who had previously been Eddy's fiancée. A month later, the heir to the throne, recently made Duke of York by the queen, took his seat in the House of Lords.

[66] Cook, *Prince Eddy*, p. 135; Ridley, *Bertie*, p. 272; *Reynold's Newspaper* of 11 November 1888.

George was deeply affected by Eddy's death and found his new duties a great burden, but he took his responsibilities as heir, husband and father very seriously. He continued to be taught history and constitutional law by John Robson Tanner, a historian from Cambridge until 1894. The future king even crafted a summary of Bagehot's famous study of the English constitution. His training as a naval officer would remain, however, with Prince George throughout his life, as was evident when it came to the upbringing of oldest son, the future King Edward VIII.[67]

On 23 June 1894, just less than a year after her wedding to Prince George, Princess Mary gave birth to their first child. Unlike his father, young Prince Edward Albert Christian George Andrew Patrick David, called David by his family, was heir apparent from birth. The memoirs of the later King Edward VIII certainly give the impression that home life under his parents' regime was strict. His father in particular, meticulous when it came to appearances, a strict disciplinarian and with a tendency to be brusque, is reputed to have contributed little to ensuring his children developed happily. 'My parents first materialize on the threshold of memory as Olympian figures who would enter the nursery briefly to note, with gravely hopeful interest, the progress of their first-born', the Prince of Wales later recalled. By 1905, George and Mary had four more sons and one daughter. As was usual, care for the children when they were younger was in the hands of nursery maids and governesses. Prince Edward received little systematic instruction in his early years. He was taught to read and write and learned a small amount of history; German and French were on his schedule, but mathematics, the sciences and Latin were absent. For religious instruction – probably the result of a mix of nostalgia and a jaw-dropping lack of imagination – the Reverend Dalton was reactivated, but all in all Edward's early schooling remained somewhat piecemeal, or, as he himself described it later, 'more or less spasmodic'.[68]

That would change in spring 1902, when Prince George stomped up the stairs to the nursery in York House, threw open the door and announced 'This is Mr Hansell', as he explained, 'your new tutor'. He then exited, leaving the children alone with the 'tall, gaunt, solemn stranger'. An embarrassing silence followed for everyone present. Much like the Reverend John Dalton before him, Henry Hansell would have an abiding impact on his pupil's upbringing. And also much like Dalton, the thirty-nine-year-old Hansell was selected for an important task for which

---

[67] *Pall Mall Gazette* of 15 January 1892; Rose, *King George V*, p. 25; Harold Nicolson, *King George the Fifth: His Life and Reign* (New York, 1953), pp. 61–62.

[68] *A King's Story: The Memoirs of the Duke of Windsor* (New York, 1951), pp. 8, 21; Philip Ziegler, *King Edward VIII: The Official Biography* (London, 1990), p. 12.

he was ultimately not equipped and which he somehow managed to retain across the years.[69]

Hansell, the son of a Norfolk landowner, had studied history at Oxford and had proved himself a good football player. Before being appointed as Edward's tutor, he had taught the son of Edward's great uncle. Looking back, his princely pupil would recall his tutor with a mild scorn. Hansell was the product of an age when English schoolmasters knew only the Classics and Protestant doctrine and had to be decent athletes, he recorded in his memoirs. His teacher 'combined a mild scholarship with a muscular Christianity, accentuated by tweeds and an ever-present pipe'. The diligent and honest Hansell threw himself into his task and held on fast, as it were, right up to the end of Edward's university studies, but the results of his efforts were disappointing. Under the aegis of an unimaginative and complacent tutor, his pupil developed limited work discipline and even less intellectual curiosity. In conversation with the historian Harold Nicolson in the 1950s, Edward described his teacher as 'melancholy and inefficient'. Hansell had not taught him or his brother anything: 'I am completely self-educated.'[70]

That verdict was doubtless an exaggeration, for Hansell provided methodical and carefully planned instruction. His meticulous diary for 1904 records three to four-and-a-half hours of instruction each day. The schedule covered arithmetic, history, German, French, poetry and dictation, and also riding lessons and hiking trips. As the princes' father had rejected Hansell's suggestion that the boys attend school, their teacher was determined to recreate the atmosphere of an English school for the two older princes – Edward and his eighteen-months-younger brother, Albert Frederick. Two desks, a blackboard and wall maps were installed and a timetable adopted. Unfortunately, these efforts did not pay off, as Prince George discovered in 1906, when his sons failed to solve a problem he set them – to calculate the average weight of all the stags he had shot the previous year. His concern about such shortcomings, for which he blamed not the teacher but the stupidity of his children, grew all the greater as the naval academy entrance examination approached in 1907. Prince George had decided that his son should follow in his footsteps: 'The Navy will teach David all that he needs to know.'[71]

This decision can be attributed to the preferences of an ingrained naval officer, but it was by no means eccentric, for the prince would have the opportunity to learn in the company of other boys of his age and within a recognised and standardised educational system. The hope was that the

[69] *A King's Story*, p. 20.   [70] Ibid., p. 21; Ziegler, *King Edward VIII*, pp. 14–15.
[71] *A King's Story*, pp. 25–26, 57–59.

navy would teach Edward qualities such as punctuality, discipline and independence. Additionally, in this era the Royal Navy was regarded as a charismatic institution, the proud embodiment of national and imperial greatness. As early as 1877, Dalton had been able to describe a naval education for princes as a popular choice, and three decades later, this was even more the case.[72]

Careful preparations were made for the prince's entrance examination. Between December 1906 and April 1907 letters went back and forth between Hansell and Vincent Baddeley, private secretary to the First Lord of the Admiralty. They discussed the subjects in which the prince would be tested, the medical examination and the composition of the examining board, but they also returned frequently to how the press might be handled. By the middle of April 1907, the procedure had been determined. Sitting in a large hall alongside dozens of other boys, the prince spent three days sweating over his test papers. The relief at Edward's sound performance was great: 'We propose to publish the result in Friday morning's papers', wrote Baddeley on 10 April. In fact, his results were rather mediocre – the prince had proved weak in arithmetic and geometry in particular – but that would not spoil the delight. Edward's mother recorded of his passing the examination, 'This has pleased us immensely.'[73]

At the time, the apprenticeship of a British naval cadet lasted four years, with the first two spent at the Royal Naval College in Osborne on the Isle of Wight and the final two at Dartmouth, in Devon. Edward began his training in May 1907 and performed not at all badly. His achievement suffered from a marked weakness in mathematical subjects and stage fright during exams, but, to his father's joy, with perseverance he succeeded in developing into an undistinguished naval cadet. Shortly before his arrival in Dartmouth, the curriculum had been supplemented by a course in civics, in which rising naval officers and future monarchs were to learn the foundations of British constitutional law, study the political system in the mother country and the colonies and gain some understanding of social and economic issues. In late summer 1911, as was usual for a naval cadet, Edward, now promoted to midshipman, ended his training with a tour at sea lasting several months. He served on the battleship *HMS Hindustan* during a routine voyage in British waters.

[72] Cynthia Behrman, *Victorian Myths of the Sea* (Athens, OH, 1977), pp. 77–152; W. Mark Hamilton, *The Nation and the Navy: Methods and Organization of British Navalist Propaganda, 1889–1914* (London, 1986).

[73] Ziegler, *King Edward VIII*, pp. 19–20; letters exchanged between Hansell and Baddeley, December 1906–April 1907 (RA VIC/ADDF/155, RA PS/PSO/GV/C/O/2574/2–8, 14); Baddeley to Hansell, 10 April 1907 (RA PS/PSO/GV/C/O/2574/23); *A King's Story*, p. 60.

When he left the ship, the crew sang *Auld Lang Syne* for him, to mark his departure. The choir of journalists was equally upbeat. *The Manchester Guardian* devoted a very friendly article to Edward when he completed his naval training. In an interview with the captain of the *Hindustan*, the heir to the throne was praised as a 'hard worker', who 'always appeared to get an intelligent grip of what was set him to learn', and particular emphasis was placed on the prince's having received no special treatment and having served like every other midshipman.[74]

Although Edward's father, who ascended the throne as George V after the death of Edward VII in 1910, had nurtured a desire for his son to serve in the Royal Navy, an institution he loved, that path was barred to an heir to the throne as 'too specialised'. If he was to fulfil the demands of his future office, the next-in-line would need to undergo a more broadly conceived training. Prince Edward would therefore, his father informed him personally, have to first, give up the navy, secondly, travel to France and Germany to work on his languages and learn more about those countries, and thirdly, study at Oxford.[75]

In his memoirs, Edward would describe his father's decision to send him to university as surprising. As a naval man George V supposedly had little time for professors and the unfamiliar world they inhabited. Advice from Lord Derby, a friend of the king's, who planned to send his own son to Oxford, to Magdalen College, had evidently been the decisive factor. Hansell too played a role, for he championed the idea that the prince might join his old college, with Hansell himself accompanying him. A flood of letters sent by Edward's tutor to Herbert Warren, President of Magdalen College, in the winter of 1911/12 make evident how doggedly, even obsessively, he worked to extract a decision in favour of Oxford from the king. The correspondents kept a noticeably close eye on press reports on plans for Edward's university studies. 'I think the accounts in the papers have been quite good', Hansell wrote to Warren on 17 February 1912, adding 'I do not quite like the leading article in today's "Times".' His reference was to a comment by the newspaper that Edward Gibbon had described his time at Magdalen College in 1751 as 'the most idle and unprofitable of my whole life'. Although the *Times* acknowledged that 'the Oxford of today abounds in intellectual vigour and aspiration', the sensitive Hansell baulked at even the slightest hint of criticism.[76]

---

[74] Ziegler, *King Edward VIII*, pp. 20–32; 'A Year's Course of "Civics"' (RA PS/PSO/GV/C/O/2574/40); *The Manchester Guardian* of 26 October 1911.
[75] *A King's Story*, p. 82.
[76] Ibid., p. 83; Ziegler, *King Edward VIII*, p. 35; Hansell to Warren, 15 December 1911 to 17 February 1912 (archives of Magdalen College, Oxford, Warren Papers); *The Times* of 17 February 1912.

After spending several months in France, the heir to the throne began his time at Oxford in October 1912. In the meantime, Hansell, Warren and the king's private secretary had arranged everything down to the smallest detail. His rooms in college had been specially prepared, an equerry had been selected for the prince and the first decisions about his course of study had been made. 'There is one thing that I fear and one only: that is the "Press"', Hansell wrote to Warren in early October, 'Will they give us a chance?' The president of the college certainly had his hands full dealing with these representatives of the public. 'I am bombarded with reporters, interviewers & photographers', he groaned on 8 October 1912. As far as we can see, however, there was little reason to complain about the attitude of the British press. The reports on the start of Edward's studies were both extensive and friendly. *The Illustrated London News* printed a large-format portrait photograph of the prince dressed in a dark suit and carrying several books, and followed it up with a scene depicting the young heir to the throne in gown and mortar board in the picturesque quadrangle of Magdalen College. Although Edward lived with servants, his equerry, his own bathroom and without the pressure of examinations, the usual references were made to the prince's being an entirely normal student. The press hailed this incorrect claim, Edward wrote self-critically in his memoirs, 'as fresh evidence of the innate democracy of the British Monarchical system'. Additionally, the newspaper reported on the subjects he would study and the furnishing of his rooms in college. An almost identically worded report in *The Manchester Guardian* on the same theme suggests that the press had received a communique from the royal household which it now conveyed to the public as authoritative. Because of the extensive reporting, Oxford was soon teeming with tourists who had come to gawk at the Student Prince.[77]

The press interest did not wane during the two years that Edward spent at Oxford as a student. Lovingly pasted into the extensive scrapbooks kept by President Warren are newspaper reports on the royal heir's studies. As early as February 1912 *Country Life* was already reporting on the 'general satisfaction' with which news of Edward's plans to study had been received, and declared that Magdalen College was at the head of all Oxford colleges. According to a report in the *Times* of 12 October 1912, Edward had received a very warm welcome. 'Privileged persons' permitted onto the railway platform had hailed his arrival in Oxford and, as he

[77] Hansell to Warren, 2 October 1912 (archives of Magdalen College, Warren Papers); Warren to Hansell, 8 October 1912 (RA PS/PSO/GV/C/O/2575/522); *The Illustrated London News* of 12 October 1912 and 19 October 1912; *The Manchester Guardian* of 8 October 1912; *A King's Story*, pp. 94–95.

drove through the town, he had been cheered by an enthusiastic crowd. 'This reception', according to the newspaper, 'was spontaneous and altogether unexpected.' At the college, it continued, he had been greeted by President Warren and accompanied to his rooms – which had already been extensively described in the previous Tuesday's paper.[78]

Subsequent articles found in the president's collection depict the prince hunting with hounds kept by Magdalen College and New College, enthusiastically cheering on his college's rowers or behind the wheel of a car. Warren also carefully archived press reports on Edward's longer trip to Germany in the summer of 1913. After the prince ended his studies in 1914, the president had the opportunity to reflect on Edward's experiences in Oxford in an extensive article in the *Times*. Warren drew a picture of a broadly engaged, teachable, sporty and modest young man who had developed his intellectual abilities without becoming a bookworm. When he left Oxford, Edward had become what England expected of him, wrote Warren in November 1914, 'a force and a factor in national life', comprehensively prepared for the real role of a prince within a constitutional system, namely, 'to guide rather than to dominate, to persuade rather than to compel, to influence by the attraction of character and personality, and the example of the chivalry of modern days, and of duty, steadfastly and eagerly if unostentatiously pursued'.[79]

Hidden behind this bombastic hymn of praise was Edward's very average achievement as a student. Certainly, he did not embarrass himself during his almost two years in Oxford, where his studies concentrated on history, modern languages, politics and economics, and his results were on the whole pleasing. But his engagement with the material tended to be superficial and limited by his unwillingness to read deeply and independently as well as by a readiness to be diverted into sporting activities, socialising and driving. During his second year, his enjoyment of riding to hounds and his engagement with the university cadet corps also swallowed up a great deal of time. Edward's teachers lamented a certain lack of maturity, both in his character and in his intellect, which was underlined by his youthful appearance. 'The Prince of Wales is still young', Warren wrote sympathetically in March 1913 about his pupil, who would shortly turn nineteen, 'and cannot be expected to show the mature work of a practiced student of say twenty or twenty one.' Although outstanding teachers were mobilised and a curriculum was carefully designed around

---

[78] *Country Life* of 24 February 1912, c272; archives of Magdalen College, P233/2/MS2/1; The President's Notebooks, 1910, f. 386 (archives of Magdalen College).
[79] The President's Notebooks, 1910, f. 473, f. 478, f. 496 (archives of Magdalen College); archives of Magdalen College, P233/2/MS2/1 and GPD/66/9/2; *The Times* of 18 November 1914.

the heir's current deficits and future tasks, the academic sparks would not fly. 'Oxford failed to make me really studious', Edward conceded in his memoirs.[80]

In the spring of 1914, his second year of university was coming to an end and Edward trusted that he might soon leave his constrained Oxford life, which he found dreary. When Warren asked whether he might not want to stay for one more term and receive an academic degree, the young man gave his feelings free rein in his diary: 'The answer to the 1st is NO and the second doesn't interest me at all!' He found the programme his father had planned more appealing – beginning in summer 1914, he would undertake several trips and then, in 1915, join a Guards regiment. But matters turned out differently. In late June 1914, Edward partici-pated with the cadet corps in a week-long military exercise. 'When in camp I make it a rule *never* to open a newspaper', he wrote from there to a friend, 'so I am completely ignorant of all happenings in the outer World, except that the Austrian Archduke and his wife have been assas-sinated. I expect it has caused a stir in Germany.'[81]

Only a short time later Britain was at war with the country at whose princely courts Edward had spent such carefree days just the previous summer. The parameters of what was expected of a crown prince and of his upbringing would shift very quickly. There could be no surprise that, by November 1914, in his appraisal of his princely student President Warren only briefly noted that Edward would certainly never become a man of books, and then heaped praise on his sense of duty, his chivalry and his ability to march like every other soldier.

Influenced by a variety of forces, the raising of four generations of British heirs to the throne had repeatedly adapted to the circumstances of the moment. Victoria, born in 1819, had been prepared in almost monastic seclusion and entirely in England. She was exposed to the public only during a few carefully choreographed tours. Her son Prince Albert Edward was the subject of a Coburg–British educational experiment that, alongside its highly ambitious curriculum, involved several trips abroad, time spent at two public universities and the basics of military training. The princes of the subsequent generation – Victor Albert and George – were educated away from the court and alongside boys of their own age at a recognised public institution, the Royal Naval Academy. For the heir to the throne there then followed further studies at the University of Cambridge and training with the cavalry. Prince Edward, the last

---

[80] Warren to King George V, 10 March 1913 (RA PS/PSO/GV/C/O/2575/528); *A King's Story*, p. 97; Ziegler, *King Edward VIII*, pp. 35–42.

[81] Ziegler, *King Edward VIII*, pp. 42, 47.

British heir to the throne before the First World War, underwent training with the British navy, which had acquired the status of a national icon, and then completed the now obligatory university studies.

This progression was characterised by several continuities: since the 1840s, there had been a lively public interest, channelled through the press, in the preparation of the future ruler. The royal household and its staff responded, for they were fully aware of the importance of press reporting. It is therefore hardly surprising that the formation of the future ruler increasingly conformed with the preferences of the middle classes that underpinned the state: it evolved towards recognised examinations, the British navy and venerable universities – where the princes at first resided at a certain distance while eventually living in the midst of their fellow students. A second, more perplexing continuity is to be found in the role of the princes' tutors, who were selected somewhat randomly, formed part of the broader court family, and were not especially competent. Birch, Gibbs, Dalton and Hansell succeeded in gaining the trust of their pupils' royal parents and over many years left their mark on the education of the heirs as they grew into adulthood. Failures as princely educators across the board, these men were all products of institutions that were without exception highly esteemed by the public – Eton, Cambridge, the Anglican Church and Oxford – and they all embodied a uniformly respected style, namely that combination of 'mild scholarship and muscular Christianity'. Thus, even these court mediocrities helped generate the British public's confidence in the preparation of their future rulers.

'In Order That He Acquire a Clear and Lively Awareness of His Own Time': Raising Prussian Heirs during the Nineteenth Century

Looking back on his time at Oxford, the former King Edward VIII adopted a markedly ironic tone as he wrote about the democracy that supposedly suffused the British monarchy. Where the Hohenzollern dynasty, whose close family ties to the British royal family dated back to 1858, when Princess Victoria married Friedrich Wilhelm, the heir to the Prussian throne, is concerned, talk of democracy is generally far more limited. The highly traditional Prussian royal family is rarely associated with a progressive mind-set or a readiness to align with bourgeois values and practices. Yet when the dynasty is examined through the lens of princely upbringing, such sweeping judgements must be revised, at least in certain respects. The three heirs to the Prussian throne born in the nineteenth century – Emperor Friedrich III (1831–1888), Emperor

Wilhelm II (1859–1941) and Crown Prince Wilhelm (1882–1951) – illustrate that even highly traditional dynasties could not but adopt innovative approaches to this task.

A clear break with tradition can already be observed in the upbringing of Prince Friedrich Wilhelm, the future Emperor Friedrich III. The preparation of his father, Wilhelm (1797–1888), later Emperor Wilhelm I, and of Wilhelm's older brother, King Friedrich Wilhelm IV (1795–1861), had rested entirely in the hands of private tutors such as Johann Friedrich Delbrück, Jean Pierre Ancillon and Carl August Zeller. Delbrück had rigorously followed a wide-ranging curriculum, deploying a progressive pedagogical approach. Neither brother was expected to go to school or subsequently attend university, probably because of a family tradition whereby each Hohenzollern prince was placed in the hands of a military tutor at age ten or eleven. The turmoil of the Napoleonic wars may also have played a role. For Wilhelm, the younger son, in particular, literary and historical material had taken a back seat by the time he was twelve, in favour of the science of war.[82]

The approach to the upbringing of Wilhelm's son Friedrich Wilhelm was very different. This shift that can principally be traced back to Friedrich Wilhelm's mother, Princess Augusta. She hailed from the Duchy of Sachsen-Weimar-Eisenach, which had become a constitutional monarchy as early as 1816, and she was an intellectually ambitious woman. Living in the Hohenzollern court at the side of her wooden and military-minded husband, she yearned for the cultural and intellectual flair of Goethe's Weimar, where she had grown up. Augusta was resolved to bring about change at the rather austere Prussian court. The vehicle for this transformation was to be her son, born in 1831 as heir presumptive to the Prussian throne. She therefore kept a weather eye on his upbringing. According to Ernst Curtius, who became the prince's tutor, 'The subject of her constant thoughts was that he should grow up strong in spirit and body so that he could meet the colossal tasks of his time.' Augusta was aware that her neo-humanist educational ideals, which she sought to realise with Curtius's assistance, ran counter to the privileging of the military favoured by her husband and at Potsdam generally. The princess's letters make evident how greatly she was influenced by the political developments of her time. Her son belonged to 'the present and the future', she wrote in October of the revolutionary year of 1848 to Albrecht von Roon, a military officer, 'He must absorb the new ideas and process them within himself in order that he

---

[82] Guntram Schulze-Wegener, *Wilhelm I. Deutscher Kaiser – König von Preußen – Nationaler Mythos* (Hamburg and Bonn, 2015), pp. 20–25, 34, 54–55; *Im Dienste Preußens. Wer erzog Prinzen zu Königen?* (Berlin, 2001), pp. 129–139, 153–164.

acquire a clear and lively awareness of his own time and lives not external to it, but rather within and with it.' Augusta, whom her husband called a 'hothead', demonstrated considerable forcefulness in the pursuit of this goal. In the face of tough resistance, she succeeded in ensuring that the unavoidable military component of her son's training was accompanied by a non-military education of a new quality and intensity. According to Andreas Bernhard, the later Emperor Friedrich III would be the first Prussian heir to be educated in line with bourgeois educational principles.[83]

Upon his appointment in 1838, Frédéric Louis Godet, a young theologian from Neuchâtel, became the prince's first tutor without a military background. At the same time, the prince was given a schoolmate and playmate of his own age. Rudolf von Zastrow would be raised as an equal alongside the future monarch for almost a decade, becoming in effect a surrogate brother. The boys were taught by Godet and a run of civilian teachers. Their lessons encompassed a broad spectrum of subjects, and occasionally Friedrich Wilhelm's vigilant mother sat in on them to monitor her son's progress. According to a schedule approved by General Karl Georg von Unruh, the prince's military governor, during Friedrich Wilhelm's fifth year of schooling forty-nine hours were to be dedicated every week to the 'occupation' of the boys. These hours were divided across seventeen hours of 'homework' and thirty-two hours of instruction, of which ten were allocated to languages, eight to the sciences, seven to the arts, five to physical education and two to religion. In 1844 Godet was replaced by Ernst Curtius, a celebrated scholar of the ancient world. As an authority on the history and culture of the classical age and a proponent of the constitutional development of the state, Curtius, the scion of a well-known bourgeois family in the city-republic of Lübeck, conformed to Augusta's characteristically bourgeois educational values and political ideals. Curtius took on the direction of the education of the prince, who was now thirteen years old, and would stay with him up until he began his university studies six years later.[84]

Curtius soon recognised that too much had been expected of his pupil, a boy of only average talent, and that he had been assessed rather harshly. He relaxed the educational programme by adding in museum visits and by having military cadets and Berlin grammar-school pupils join the lessons, ensuring that the prince had more opportunity to spend time with boys of his own age. The majority of these playmates were from

---

[83] Wagner, *Prinzenerziehung*, pp. 74, 77; *Im Dienste Preußens*, p. 173; Karin Feuerstein-Praßer, *Augusta. Kaiserin und Preußin*, 2nd edn (Munich and Zurich, 2011), p. 82.
[84] *Im Dienste Preußens*, pp. 181–182, 185–186; Wagner, *Prinzenerziehung*, pp. 90–92.

a middle-class background, ideally the sons of civil servants and professors. Augusta's handwritten notes make evident how much it mattered to her that her son had access to the world beyond the court. The princess also insisted – unlike Curtius but in agreement with von Unruh – on an ambitious workload that certainly placed excessive demands on Friedrich Wilhelm. In 1844 the thirteen-year-old prince was receiving thirty-five hours of instruction a week in fourteen different subjects, including Latin and modern languages, mathematics, geography and history. He was also instructed in riding, gymnastics and dancing. Established experts and pedagogues were brought in for some of the teaching, for example the mathematician Karl Schellbach. Additionally, Curtius took his pupil on trips to the Harz mountains, to Silesia and to his own homeland of Holstein and Lübeck, where in 1845 the prince met his teacher's family. That visit too did not happen without ulterior political motives or an eye to how it would play out with the public. Curtius was delighted that Friedrich Wilhelm acquired a 'love for the bourgeoisie of Lübeck and respect for the farmers of Holstein'. The tutor expected much of the 'two to three days spent living with our family', in which the 'young princely son', an expression used by the *Allgemeine Preußische Zeitung,* encountered 'the image of a decent bourgeois family for the first time'.[85]

With the help of powers at court that reflected a more progressive and less military mind-set, Queen Augusta succeeded in delaying the intensive phrase of her son's military education. Within the Prussian royal family, proper training with the armed forces usually began at age fourteen, but in Friedrich Wilhelm's case it was delayed until the prince had concluded his school education. 'I have deferred this requirement until my son's sixteenth year', declared Prince Wilhelm with palpable reluctance in 1847, 'because he is presumably destined for a call other than that of the purely military, and I do not want to reproach myself for having instilled in him an all-round preference for the military; and all my behaviour in this matter of his instruction and upbringing is evidence of this intention, whose realisation has often burdened me.' When these additional two years were over, however, he insisted that his son now at last dedicate himself to the army, so central to the Hohenzollerns. In doing so, he thwarted Augusta and Curtius's plan that would have had the young prince start his studies at the University of Bonn as early as the winter of 1848. In Augusta's eyes, however, it was imperative that the heir to the throne experience a university education. 'Today no one is allowed to be uneducated', she wrote that same year, after her son had been surprisingly successful in an examination, 'and only if one has reached

[85] Wagner, *Prinzenerziehung,* pp. 94, 106; *Im Dienste Preußens,* pp. 187–188.

a certain level of education will one strive for impartiality and for the life of the mind in general, which I cannot image a diligent man not having.'[86]

This time Wilhelm would not relent and so in May 1849 their son joined the First Foot Guards. His mother's progressive educational programme was already bearing fruit, however, for at a dinner that same month, the prince contradicted General Leopold von Gerlach's anti-constitution comments with the proposition that a parliament was in fact necessary. Only a few months later, in October 1849, the liberal *Deutsche Zeitung* praised Friedrich Wilhelm on the occasion of his eighteenth birthday as gentle, caring and well intentioned. Above all, the newspaper reported that his inclinations had developed 'more in harmony with those of his mother than with those of his father'. Since this was the case, the future king was given a leave from the army as early as the autumn of 1849 to allow him to matriculate at the University at Bonn, far from the Berlin court.[87]

Accompanied by his tutor Curtius and his new military governor, General Friedrich Leopold Fischer, the prince relocated to the Rhine, where he spent four enjoyable and productive semesters. In the course of his studies in law, philosophy and political science, he was taught by renowned scholars such as the philosopher Christian August Brandis and the jurist Clemens Theodor Perthes, but also by such liberal–national luminaries as the historians Ernst Moritz Arndt and Friedrich Christoph Dahlmann. It was his mother's hope that these figures and his fellow students would offer the heir to the throne 'instructive discussions with able men of all estates', enabling him to assemble knowledge for himself and form an independent judgement. Princess Augusta would surely have welcomed that these discussions revolved in large part around the development of the monarchy of Prussia, which, following a royal decree issued in December 1848, had become a constitutional state. As much as his position allowed, Prince Friedrich Wilhelm also participated informally in the social life of this university town. In the spring of 1852, he looked back on his years of education with palpable satisfaction.[88]

Augusta was less satisfied. Friedrich Wilhelm's intellectual development consistently failed to meet his impatient mother's unrealistically high expectations. It could also not have pleased her that, during the rapid military career that followed, the prince demonstrated a typically Prussian enthusiasm for all things military. As early as 1851, shortly before he completed his university studies, Friedrich Wilhelm had been promoted

---

[86] Wagner, *Prinzenerziehung*, pp. 107–108; *Im Dienste Preußens*, p. 193.
[87] Frank Lorenz Müller, *Our Fritz: Emperor Frederick III and the Political Culture of Imperial Germany* (Cambridge, MA, 2011), pp. 65–66.
[88] Wagner, *Prinzenerziehung*, pp. 118–119.

to captain. Four years later, he had already held several commands – including in the First Guards Regiment and with the Dragoons – had attended the War Academy in Berlin and had been promoted to colonel. In 1858, he was named a brigadier-general.

This rather more traditional military career did not take anything away from Augusta's earlier efforts to ensure the efficacy and public appeal of her son's preparation as a future monarch. Alongside his schooling in the humanities, the future ruler's training as a capable military officer was understood to form a part of the broad competency that was expected of a monarch. In the nineteenth century, such appreciation of the military was not just a Prussian phenomenon and it applied to bourgeois circles as well as to the traditional elites.

Fredrick Wilhelm's civilian education had been characterised by significant innovations: his years of schooling according to bourgeois and neo-humanistic ideals, his upbringing in the company of middle-class boys of his own age and finally his studies at a university. The public had followed the prince's education with interest and were aware of how it might have shaped Friedrich Wilhelm's political views. Soon hopes were being pinned on him and the bourgeois values and national outlook that would have resulted from a neo-humanistic education. In 1879, for example, it was reported that his wife had given him an old edition of Livy's *History of Rome* for his birthday. 'As a good German', a contemporary pamphlet swiftly recorded, he naturally 'took pleasure in such learned matters.'[89]

The process of modernising the upbringing of princes in Prussia was by no means complete with the young Prince Friedrich Wilhelm. The raising of his oldest son, Prince Wilhelm, born in 1859, would give scope for further innovation, and again a modern-minded mother played a decisive role.

The birth of the future Emperor Wilhelm II, in January 1859, had been perilous for both mother and child. Although the gynaecologist Eduard Martin, called late to the bedside, had been able to deliver the eighteen-year-old mother of her infant, the baby had experienced significant trauma during the breech birth. The damage to his left arm could not be reversed. Throughout his life Wilhelm would have one arm distinctly shorter than the other and the limb was largely paralysed. Additionally, it seems likely that the baby was deprived of oxygen during the birth, which affected the future monarch's physical development and behaviour. These health-related problems would bear heavily on the future emperor's childhood and on the relationship between mother and son.

---

[89] Müller, *Our Fritz*, pp. 125–126, 129–131.

Much like her own mother, Princess Victoria was obsessed with the idea that her son's upbringing should produce a replica of the almost deified Prince Consort Albert, Victoria's father. This endeavour would fail as spectacularly for Prince Wilhelm as it had done for his uncle, the later King Edward VII. Her admiration for the unattainable perfection of her Coburg–British model father, who had died in 1861, only heightened Vicky's awareness of her own child's weaknesses, adding to the struggle the Hohenzollern prince faced. To correct the boy's physical afflictions – the paralysed small arm, the sloping of his body, his problems with balance – a protracted and sometimes bizarre programme of traumatising quackery was pursued. Stretching machines, electro-shock therapy and his slathering with supposedly stimulating tinctures were deployed along-side surgery, gymnastics and 'animal baths', during which the child's arm was bound up within a freshly slaughtered hare. The failure of these measures to yield results or to encourage calmer behaviour by the child thus abused only served to irritate the young mother even more.[90]

It was all the more important, then, that the future monarch's intellectual upbringing satisfy the highest demands. Here the crown prince and crown princess had very clear ideas, which they tenaciously pressed home in the face of considerable resistance at court. To some extent, patterns that had determined the upbringing of Crown Prince Friedrich Wilhelm himself were now repeated: a progressively minded mother – this time the energetic British–Prussian Crown Princess Vicky – had to wrest conces-sions from Wilhelm I, who was now the ruler. In her efforts, she was, however, consistently and prudently supported by her husband, who as a rule shared his wife's views.

The central figure in the upbringing of the future emperor was the stern and strong-minded Dr Georg Hinzpeter. The classical philologist and pedagogue, a strict Calvinist, took up his position as the prince's civilian educator in autumn 1866. He had been chosen for the post, after a careful selection process, at the suggestion of a British diplomat who was a friend of the crown prince and crown princess, and he would enjoy their com-plete trust. The seven-year-old Prince Wilhelm had previously been cared for by nursery maids and governesses such as the resolute Fräulein von Dobeneck. An experienced teacher from Potsdam had equipped him with the basics of reading and writing, and in 1864 he had begun early instruc-tion in French. Looking back in 1888, Hinzpeter would declare that his efforts had certainly had a political thrust. 'In line with the parents'

---

[90] On Wilhelm II's birth and health issues and his relationship with his mother, see John C. G. Röhl, *Young Wilhelm: The Kaiser's Early Life, 1859–1888* (Cambridge, 1998), pp. 1–53, 62–81, and Thomas A. Kohut, *Wilhelm II and the Germans: A Study in Leadership* (Oxford, 1991), pp. 19–224.

requirements, the upbringing was intended to ensure that, counter to tradition, the adolescent prince's interest in bourgeois life came before his interest in the military life.' He had previously formulated the intended purpose in a memorandum dated 1876: 'The rank and tasks of princes in the modern age are essentially different from those in earlier centuries. [. . .] For even while the individuality of the prince no longer gives the life of the people a specific character that changes with the person, the most complete development of his powers is not for that reason any less important for the wellbeing of the whole. The prince was certainly never so reliant on his own powers as he will be amidst the upcoming struggles between the great popular parties; on account of his rank he alone will be capable of impartiality.'[91]

The crown prince and crown princess believed that in Hinzpeter they had found the man to prepare their first born for this Herculean task. In contrast, the various historians who have directed considerable attention to the formative years of the last German emperor are in agreement – allowing for some nuances – that the gaunt, joyless, pious and consistently demanding Hinzpeter was entirely unsuitable for providing the loving encouragement and steady support needed by this unsettled and probably traumatised boy, who forever oscillated between uncertainty and over-confidence. Whether one categorises Hinzpeter's regime as virtually sad-istic, as does John Röhl, or judges the pedagogue's actions more leniently, as does Yvonne Wagner, the fact remains that, as a result of his parents' liberal approach, Prince Wilhelm's upbringing was very different from that of his predecessors.

Initially, Wilhelm's parents and Hinzpeter succeeded in curtailing the formerly dominant influence of the military governor, an established role in Prussia, in favour of the civilian tutor. The first passage in a document written in 1866 and signed by both the prince's parents laid down that Hinzpeter was 'independently responsible to us, the parents, not only for the *instruction* but also for the complete upbringing, and therefore in those connections not *subordinate* to Captain von Schrötter'. Thus demoted, the military governor Gustav von Schrötter requested his discharge. After the crown princess had rejected all the influential and assertive replace-ment candidates proposed by the military cabinet as an 'outrageous imposition', the entirely unknown Lieutenant August O'Danne was appointed to the position at the request of the crown prince. The young officer was just as unable to prevail against Hinzpeter as was his successor

---

[91] *Im Dienste Preußens*, p. 205; Wagner, *Prinzenerziehung*, pp. 154–155, 156; Kaiser Wilhelm II., *Aus meinem Leben, 1859–1888*, 4th edn (Berlin and Leipzig, 1927), pp. 22–23.

Walter von Gottberg, who from his very first day was concerned about Hinzpeter's 'autocracy'.[92]

The clipping of the military governor's wings was accompanied by a marked delay in the military training of the prince. It began – aside from a number of decorative components – as late as January 1877, after the future emperor had completed his school education and shortly before his eighteenth birthday, and even then it amounted to little more than a whistle-stop visit. In early February 1877, Wilhelm began his military service as a lieutenant with the Sixth Company of the First Foot Guards Regiment and simultaneously attended the War Academy in Potsdam. By July that same year, he had already passed his officer's examination – naturally exhibiting 'outstanding knowledge'. Only three months later, however, he was given leave to study at the University of Bonn. The primacy of a civilian upbringing thus continued, and not without consequences. Christopher Clark suggests that Wilhelm never succeeded in internalising the commitment to self-discipline and appreciation of obedience that were the core lessons of a Prussian military education. For all his later enthusiasm for gleaming weapons and martial words, Emperor Wilhelm II – unlike his father and grandfather, who had both seen active service – remained a uniformed civilian.[93]

One further modern facet of Prince Wilhelm's education was Hinzpeter's plan for his pupil to 'practise personal sympathy'; in other words he was to be made aware of the conditions in which the lowest classes lived, thus ensuring that the future ruler developed a sensitivity and 'learnt to comprehend the social question'. During a trip to Thuringia, the tutor had the prince confront a 'blackened bricklayer decked out in rags, his lamenting wife and illegitimate grandson'. Visits to mines, steelworks, foundries, workers' accommodation and a glass-blowing workshop were also on his schedule. Attention was thus paid to ensuring that Wilhelm II was acquainted with a world that was not that of the nobility. Such had also been the case for his father, but now the barriers that separated the upper and lower classes were to be broken much more clearly. As a result, Hinzpeter believed, Wilhelm II was more justified in presenting himself as himself as 'the personification of his people'.[94]

---

[92] Röhl, *Young Wilhelm*, pp. 147–151, 180–182; Wagner, *Prinzenerziehung*, pp. 170–171.

[93] Wagner, *Prinzenerziehung*, pp. 200–201, 264; Christopher Clark, 'Fathers and Sons in the History of the Hohenzollern Dynasty', in Frank Lorenz Müller and Heidi Mehrkens (eds.), *Sons and Heirs: Succession and Political Culture in Nineteenth-Century Europe* (Basingstoke, 2016), p. 29.

[94] Wagner, *Prinzenerziehung*, pp. 172–176.

The most remarkable innovation in the upbringing of the last German emperor was, however, his attendance at a public school – a step that Hinzpeter regarded as an 'experiment without precedent'. He had been pursuing this plan since 1870, but it required several years of scheming to ensure the emperor gave his permission. Even before Wilhelm eventually joined the Friedrichsgymnasium in Kassel in the autumn of 1874, the tutor had already attempted to get him used to lessons in a classroom context within the bounds of what was permitted. In the later 1860s Wilhelm and his younger brother, Heinrich, had been taught alongside several village children in the school at Bornstedt near Potsdam, where the crown prince and crown princess possessed a country estate. In April 1873, in the presence of Hinzpeter and teachers from Berlin's Joachimsthalsches Gymnasium, the heir to the throne passed examinations in Latin, Greek and mathematics, thus demonstrating that he was fit to be admitted to the equivalent of the fifth form of a state grammar school. Even then his transfer to Kassel – to attend school far from the court – had remained in doubt, as Emperor Wilhelm I continued to have great misgivings.[95]

Notwithstanding all of Hinzpeter's enthusiastic efforts since 1866, Prince Wilhelm would still need weeks of intensive coaching by the teachers at the grammar school in Kassel before finally, in October 1874, he was able to enter the equivalent of sixth-form classes (*Obersekunda*). In a letter written by the fifteen-year-old to his mother while he was cramming, the prince complained, 'I am squeezed like a sponge left and right and morning to night by the Latin, Greek and mathematics teachers, such that I hardly have time to breathe.' Hinzpeter knew that Wilhelm would enter the class as one of the youngest and least well-prepared pupils, but he placed great hopes in the pedagogical impact of the rivalry that would ensue. 'With its competitive atmosphere, the school should really force the prince to set his intellectual powers in motion.' And indeed, in the two-and-a-half years until he sat the *Abitur*, the grammar-school leaving examination, the heir to the throne succeeded in rising to a middle position in his class. This success was hard won. Even before lessons began at 7 a.m., Wilhelm would already have completed an hour of study with Hinzpeter, and on many days he would also be coached by individual teachers in the evenings. It was not unusual for the schoolboy to work from 5:30 a.m. until 10 p.m. without significant breaks. Aside from Sundays and mealtimes, only eleven hours each week were categorised as free time, during which the boy was afforded such

---

[95] Röhl, *Young Wilhelm*, pp. 201–206; *Im Dienste Preußens*, p. 207; Wagner, *Prinzenerziehung*, p. 104.

dubious pleasures as walking or riding with Hinzpeter. Wilhelm's time-table was dominated by the study of ancient languages, which occupied him for a full nineteen hours each week – excluding additional tutoring. Only very little time was allocated to the sciences and modern languages, and as a result Wilhelm had to acquire the latter during additional private lessons.[96]

The prince, shown in Figure 11 in his grammar-school garb, settled well into his school, where – as Hinzpeter had strongly insisted – he was not to be given any special treatment. The nit-picking corrections and harsh marking that can be seen in a recently edited exercise book that Wilhelm completed in 1875 suggest that such was indeed the case. Nevertheless, he came tenth in his class of seventeen students in the *Abitur* examination. Additionally, Wilhelm established friendships with several of his fellow pupils, some of whom remained in contact with him for decades, and the broader public impact of the 'experiment' was also heartening. Overall, his classmates spoke in friendly terms about their famous fellow pupil, and press reporting was laudatory. In 1874, the London *Times* specifically noted that the crown prince and crown princess had presented their child to the headmaster 'and, like ordinary citizens, had him examined in their presence'. Additionally, the newspaper noted, his father had stipulated that Prince Wilhelm be 'treated in all respects as were the other boys'. The renowned British paper did not lose sight of the story, reporting in January 1877 that Prince Wilhelm 'has passed with credit the final examination at Cassel'. Years later, splendid postcards depicting the emperor as a grammar-school pupil in Kassel could still be purchased. And yet his schooldays under the thumb of his ever-present and chronically dissatisfied tutor left Wilhelm highly embittered. As an adult, he repeatedly gave voice to his resentment at the obsessive philological dissection of endless ancient texts, the antiquated and alien subject matter, as well as the joyless and dry atmosphere, which lacked any youthful energy. It was very clear that he would not impose this 'fossilised and most soul-destroying of all systems' on his own sons.[97]

Sitting the *Abitur* by no means marked the end of the training of the heir to the throne, even though he had come of age by this stage. After a short and predictably successful time with the First Guards Regiment in the autumn of 1877, he enrolled at the university in Bonn. Like his father before him, the future emperor would remember his four semesters in the town on the Rhine, interrupted by several trips, as an idyllic time.

---

[96] Röhl, *Young Wilhelm*, pp. 206–208, 226–227; Wagner, *Prinzenerziehung*, p. 211.
[97] Röhl, *Young Wilhelm*, pp. 210–217; Ulf Morgenstern, *Lehrjahre eines neo-absoluten Monarchen. Kaiser Wilhelm II. als Kasseler Abiturient im Spiegel eines unbekannten Aufsatzheftes* (Friedrichsruh, 2011); *The Times* of 1 October 1874 and 26 January 1877.

Figure 11. In 1874, Prince Wilhelm of Prussia joined the Friedrichsgymnasium grammar school in Kassel, where his passed his final exams three years later. No Hohenzollern prince before him had ever attended a public school. Wilhelm did not enjoy his time in Kassel and later remembered his schooling as 'ossified' and 'mind-numbing'. Kaiser Wilhelm II., *Aus meinem Leben, 1859–1888* (Berlin and Leipzig, 1927), p. 128.

Accompanied only by two officers, Wilhelm moved into a villa on the Koblenzerstraße. Freed from Hinzpeter's strict tutelage, the prince was relatively relaxed about his studies and enjoyed what the Rhineland had to offer, as well as the distance from his parents back at home in Berlin. Without investing particularly great effort, he dipped his toe into various subjects: history, law, philosophy, physics, German, literary history, economics, art history, finance and archaeology. He sometimes attended public lectures, but most of his instruction was in private classes. His social world was very much that of his fraternity, the exclusive Corps Borussia, dominated by East Elbian nobility, with which his father had also had ties. Under the influence of the assertive, militaristic and masculine atmosphere it fostered, and which had already appealed to Wilhelm as a soldier in Potsdam, his personality changed in a way that increasingly alienated him from his more bourgeois-oriented parents.[98] As all the omens predicted, when his grandfather demanded that the prince end his studies and continue his military career, Wilhelm did not resist. In October 1879, the twenty-year-old prince returned to the army in Potsdam, much to the regret of the crown princess, who sharply criticised his most recent development. 'Willy is chauvinistic and *ultra* Prussian to a degree & with a violence wh[ich] is often very painful to me', she wrote to her mother a few months later.[99]

The enthusiasm with which Wilhelm embraced the world of the army did not release the prince from all non-military instruction. The future ruler's induction in the apparatus of the state, begun in Bonn with his study of finance and administration, continued during the 1880s. Here the crown prince and crown princess were for once in agreement with the emperor. An order of the cabinet, given on 2 October 1882, mandated the prince's six-month instruction in taxation and economic issues, to be provided by Heinrich von Achenbach, the provincial governor of Brandenburg. Additionally Wilhelm attended meetings of the district council in Teltow and the provincial council in Potsdam. In 1886, the future ruler was also introduced to the work of the Foreign Office, directed by Otto von Bismarck's son Herbert, and given access to official documents. This final initiative triggered a bitter conflict between the liberal crown prince and crown princess, who had opposed the measure, and their reactionary opponents, with whom Prince Wilhelm had sided vigorously.[100]

The parents had hoped that their progressive educational model, carefully envisioned and steadfastly applied, would guide Prince Wilhelm in an emphatically bourgeois, constitution-friendly and open-minded direction. Their plan had utterly failed. His father had developed a worldview that was relatively liberal for Prussia, not least as a result of his upbringing and the influence of his mother. Wilhelm took off in the opposite direction, partly in defiance of his demanding and never-satisfied mother, whose liberalism he demonstratively rejected. The development of the future emperor into a superficial, erratic and autocratically minded figure, whom even supporters of the monarchical system soon regarded as a problematic miscasting, unfolded in stark contrast with his liberal upbringing.

[98] Röhl, *Young Wilhelm*, pp. 274–305; Wagner, *Prinzenerziehung*, pp. 265–266.
[99] Röhl, *Young Wilhelm*, p. 409; Roger Fulford (ed.), *Beloved Mama: Private Correspondence of Queen Victoria and the German Crown Princess, 1878–1885* (London, 1981), p. 85.
[100] Wagner, *Prinzenerziehung*, pp. 268, 273–279; Clark, 'Fathers and Sons in the History of the Hohenzollern Dynasty', pp. 30–33; Röhl, *Young Wilhelm*, pp. 584–598.

The heir to the throne became emperor far sooner than could have been expected, when his father died in June 1888. He had received what appeared to be an entirely modern and extremely thorough preparation for his role as ruler: grammar school, *Abitur*, officer's examinations, university studies and also instruction in the administration of the state. That, despite all of this, Wilhelm presented as brash and self-satisfied, that he loved the grandiose and militaristic can be explained in part by his personality and the challenging family constellations surrounding the crown prince. Structural factors also played a role, though, in particular the traditional power of the military establishment in Prussia and the contemporary and Europe-wide popularity of the militarisation of public life. Yet, notwithstanding all that was backward in his political thinking, when it came to how his own sons were to be raised, Emperor Wilhelm II was not resolutely reactionary, for he made a remarkable attempt to learn from his own experience.

On 6 May 1882, Princess Auguste Victoria, Prince Wilhelm's wife, gave birth to their first son, named Wilhelm after his ruling great-grandfather. As was usual, the birth was marked with a 101-gun salute. Soon after, a famous photograph of the four emperors was taken, with the new-born boy on the lap of Emperor Wilhelm I, flanked by Crown Prince Friedrich Wilhelm, who would become Emperor Friedrich III, and Prince Wilhelm, who would reign as Emperor Wilhelm II from 1888. Following the early death of his grandfather Friedrich, young Wilhelm became crown prince when he was aged just six. Having inherited the throne while still a young man, unlike his father and grandfather, Wilhelm II did not have to ask for the approval of the head of the family when it came to the education of his own children – between 1882 and 1893 he became father to six sons and one daughter. He could do as he wanted, following his own whims.

Initially the education of the young crown prince was entirely conventional, not least because his not very family-oriented and frequently absent young father rarely entered the children's rooms. 'For all questions of upbringing, I am not responsible, but rather the empress is', he is said to have told his sons' first tutor on his appointment. By the time he began his actual education, at the age of six, Prince Wilhelm had already learnt English from his nursery maid, a Miss Atkinson. A young theologian, Johannes Kessler, was engaged as his tutor, but additional instruction was given by Heinrich Fechner, an experienced teacher from Berlin, Charles Girardin, who taught languages, and, later, Dr Paul Esternaux, a historian and philologist. A military senior governor, Eugen von Falkenhayn, was appointed for the crown prince only in 1887; he was also to be responsible for the boy's riding instruction. On his tenth birthday, in keeping with Prussian tradition, the young prince joined the First Company of the First Foot Guards and received the star of the Order of the Black Eagle. The emperor greeted the appointment in typical manner: 'While the crown prince is not yet of an age to be able to serve in the military, it is still of the greatest importance that through the regiment he becomes familiar with those laws of discipline and obedience that have forever been a bedrock.'[101]

Wilhelm II may have publicly insisted on discipline, but the provision of a regimented education for his two oldest sons, Wilhelm and Eitel Friedrich, was made challenging by the restless travels of the imperial family and all the diversions of the imperial court. The switching of location and entertainment on offer contributed to the two princes' progress being deemed unsatisfactory. The boys' instruction also suffered, the crown prince would later recall in his memoirs, because they had no classmates and therefore lacked the 'competition that spurs one on'. The conspicuous deficiencies were immediately evident to Johann Georg von Deines on his appointment as military governor, and he insisted on a radical reworking of the princes' education. This general staff officer, who had himself attended university, had demanding goals which he formulated clearly. 'A crown prince is not by nature a higher human being, he is only more highly placed within this world', he declared in a memorandum on how a prince should be raised. 'To make a capable man out of him, in general the same path must be followed as for other sons of the educated and cultured estates.' The fifty-year-old von Deines then listed a dozen virtues that made up an 'entirely proficient and manly man' and must therefore be taught. The spectrum ranged from godliness, truthfulness and self-confidence to a good memory and 'love for the people'. A 'healthy and hardened body' was also required.[102]

Von Deines was in agreement with the princes' principal teacher, Dr Paul Esternaux, that their instruction must take place in peaceful surroundings and at a distance from the many distractions of life at court. Only in such a location would it be possible to realise what he had in mind. Von Deines had probably come to this conclusion as a result

---

[101] Johannes Keßler, *Ich schwöre mir ewige Jugend* (Leipzig, 1935), pp. 121–122; Klaus W. Jonas, *Der Kronprinz Wilhelm* (Frankfurt am Main, 1962), pp. 18–19; *Im Dienste Preußens*, pp. 220–221; Frank Lorenz Müller, '"Distant from the Court and All of Its Influences": The German Crown Prince at the *Prinzenschule* in Plön', AHRC Project *Heirs to the Throne in the Constitutional Monarchies of Nineteenth-Century Europe (1815–1914)*, 'Heir of the Month' (January 2015), http://heirstothethrone-project.net/?page_id=1349 (accessed 24 February 2017).

[102] Karl Rosner (ed.), *Erinnerungen des Kronprinzen Wilhelm. Aus den Aufzeichnungen, Dokumenten, Tagebüchern und Gesprächen* (Stuttgart, 1922), pp. 28–29; E. von Witzleben, *Adolf von Deines. Lebensbild, 1845–1911* (Berlin, 1913), pp. 217–219.

of reading the recently published memoirs of the legendary Prussian minister of war and field marshal Albrecht von Roon. The work contained a description of how, in the autumn of 1848, von Roon had been approached about taking on responsibility for the education of the future Emperor Friedrich III. When, however, Princess Augusta had rejected Roon's condition that Prince Friedrich Wilhelm, as he then was, be educated 'at a distance from the court and all its influences', he had refused the offer. Von Deines succeeded where von Roon had failed: despite bitter opposition from the empress, who did not want to be separated from her sons, Emperor Wilhelm II agreed to the plan to establish what would be termed the 'Princes' School' in Plön.[103]

The small town of Plön is located in Holstein, around 200 miles from Berlin. It was not selected simply because it was the location of a renowned officer training school. The decision was also intended as a consolation for the empress, who was a Holstein princess, and even more significantly it was intended to generate a greater allegiance to the ruling dynasty amongst the population of a province that had been annexed by Prussia as recently as 1867. The school-for-princes project involved the creation of a small boarding school in which the emperor's sons would live and learn, each accompanied by three boys of similar age. The renovation of the *Lusthaus* building within the park at Plön Castle progressed swiftly and the school was quickly up and running. Crown Prince Wilhelm and Eitel Friedrich, who was one year younger, arrived in Plön in April 1896, accompanied by the sorrowful empress. Two years later, they were joined by Adalbert, the emperor's third son. Sons four, five and six – August Wilhelm, Oskar and Joachim – and their fellow pupils moved to the school at Plön in 1901 and 1904. Instruction at the Princes' School, where Senior Governor von Deines was in charge, was delivered by a small staff of civilian teachers, who lived either in the school itself or in nearby Plön.

The Princes' School was neither part of the officer training school at Plön nor tied to the Plön grammar school. Indeed, instructions were issued that contact with the pupils at those two institutions be kept to a minimum. A game of football, a rowing regatta or a snowball fight was possible only by breaking through 'this barrier', as the crown prince revealed in his memoirs. All the more important, then, were the three fellow pupils selected for each prince. The heir to the throne was taught alongside Hans Count von Hochberg, Konstantin von Sommerfeld and Gustav Steinbömer. The latter was a member of a bourgeois family from

[103] Albrecht von Roon, *Denkwürdigkeiten aus dem Leben des Generalfeldmarschalls Kriegsminister Grafen von Roon*, vol. 1, 4th edn (Breslau, 1897 [1892]), pp. 212–232.

Lübeck and would become a life-long friend of the crown prince. The curriculum at the Princes' School was in line with that of a Prussian *Realgymnasium*, a type of grammar school in which ancient languages were deemed less significant and greater emphasis was placed on modern languages and the sciences. This shift had been very important to the emperor, much influenced by his own experiences. He also arranged for the creation of a chemistry laboratory in the basement of the school building and required that additional hours be allocated to instruction in English and French.[104]

Beyond the curriculum, Plön itself offered numerous stimuli, which at least in part were in accord with the emerging reform pedagogy of the age. Ernst von Dryander, who was responsible for the princes' religious education, recalled an absolute idyll, 'Everything was available that might delight the heart of a lively and healthy boy. There were proper gymnastics, there was rowing, initially in larger navy boats and later in small and narrow sports boats, there was swimming, drill and riding – all with youthful pleasure, on occasion fruit was harvested or potatoes dug up.' The boys had their own garden and a small farmhouse. The crown prince even received a couple of lessons from the local wood turner. All this fun was weighed down by great expectation, though. Dryander observed that a 'Prussian prince should and must learn more than others. Not only must our princes take the regular examinations of a Secondary School of the First Order [*Realschule 1. Ordnung*], they must speak fluent English and French, command their horses like cavalrymen and be able to ride through the land with a map in hand.'[105]

While this depiction of princely achievement certainly contains a good dose of monarchical advertising, there can be no doubt that their training in Plön placed significant demands on the emperor's sons. As had been the case for their father before them, comparison with classmates only highlighted their shortcomings. Crown Prince Wilhelm and his brother Eitel Friedrich received additional tutoring for months in order to reach the same level as their fellow students and, even then, their performance was, at best, average. That they were never entirely removed from the court was a contributing factor. Their lessons were repeatedly interrupted by ceremonial events in Potsdam, at the naval base in nearby Kiel, at the castle of Wilhelmshöhe in Kassel or by the arrival of important visitors, who kept them from their studies. The emperor dropped by only occasionally and usually did not stay long. Sometimes, when His Majesty was

---

[104] Müller, 'Distant from the Court and All of Its Influences'; *Hundert Jahre Erziehung der Jugend auf Schloß Plön. Eine Festschrift* (Plön, 1968), pp. 47–53; Rosner (ed.), *Erinnerungen des Kronprinzen Wilhelm*, p. 30.
[105] *Im Dienste Preußens*, p. 224.

on his way to a regatta in Kiel, the encounter was limited to a brief greeting of his sons and their teachers on the platform of the newly constructed 'Princes' Station' in Plön. His few longer visits certainly left a lasting mark on the other pupils. Years later Crown Prince Wilhelm's classmate Steinbömer still recalled a genial emperor who joked with the boys and attempted in vain to catch them out with rather lame humorous trick questions. But he impressed his young public with improvised short discourses on obscure themes, such as the electromagnetic Hall effect. While Empress Victoria, the princes' grandmother, visited only once, their mother, Empress Auguste Viktoria, was a regular guest. She sat quietly at the back of the classroom, occupied with her needlework, and in the afternoon invited the pupils to join her for cake and hot chocolate.[106]

The lessons themselves were hardly a source of joy for the crown prince. Although he was certainly quick-witted, he lacked concentration and genuine interest. His somewhat blasé superficiality and flightiness were reflected in his marks. His report for 1896/97 stated that 'Prince Wilhelm must continue to make an effort to master his volatility and to apply himself commendably also to those subjects that interest him less'; he received an overall mark of 'satisfactory to adequate'. Over the course of the following years, however, Wilhelm's performance – supported by constant additional tutoring – would improve to the extent that he could face the *Abitur* without panic.[107]

The examination was carried out by Privy Senior Governmental Councillor Dr Reinhold Köpke, who had previously inspected the school on behalf of the Prussian Ministry of Culture and who had advised governor von Deines for several years. In February 1900, he arrived in Plön to examine the four members of the senior class, of which the crown prince was a member. Unlike the marks of his stellar classmate Steinbömer, Wilhelm's results were only average. Yet the emperor was enthusiastic, probably because he recognised another opportunity to demonstrate the capabilities of his royal house. Court photographer Ottomar Anschütz was sent to Plön to make a record of the examination. The carefully staged event, with the crown prince sitting attentively at a desk at its centre, was subsequently displayed prominently in the Hohenzollern Museum in Berlin. The deserving Dr Köpke was presented with the Royal House Order (Second Class), while the crown prince's most important teachers – Dr Paul Esternaux, Dr Karl Sachse and Charles Girardin – received

---

[106] Gustav Hillard [Gustav Steinbömer], *Herren und Narren der Welt* (Munich, 1954), pp. 108–111.

[107] Jonas, *Der Kronprinz Wilhelm*, pp. 23–24; Helmut Ries, *Kronprinz Wilhelm* (Hamburg, Berlin and Bonn, 2001), pp. 56–57.

financial gifts of 1,000 Marks apiece. The emperor felt a responsibility to thank Senior Governor von Deines in particular. 'I wish to congratulate you for having brought the oldest one so far', His Majesty telegraphed when news of his son's having passed the examination reached him. 'Looking back on the time at Plön that for him is now coming to an end, I wish to express to you my thanks for all the sacrifices you have made on his account. May he continue to develop so well!'[108]

His hope would not be fulfilled, for the stages in his son's education that now followed lacked the discipline fostered by the seclusion and rigour of Plön. 'From now on he no longer had diligent, conscientious and responsible pedagogues at his side', a biography of the crown prince regretted, and instead was 'without achieving anything, surrounded by flatterers and yea-sayers. Awestruck, everyone looked up to him, the future ruler.'[109] That sycophancy doubtless fed Wilhelm's natural inclinations for superficiality, arrogance and recklessness, but he still continued, or at least appeared to continue, a substantial programme of education. He completed officer training intended to take nine months in just nine weeks, having already passed the cadet examination in 1898, while still at Plön. The conclusion of his service as a lieutenant in the spring of 1901, the crown prince later recalled, was followed by two 'beautiful and rich years' at the university at Bonn, 'filled with serious study and the happy experiences of a student, surrounded by all the magic of Rhenish magnificence and love of life'. Philipp Zorn, professor of constitutional law and Wilhelm's most significant teacher in Bonn, described the crown prince's four semesters, interrupted by several trips, in similar terms. The crown prince, depicted in Figure 12 wearing the colours of his student fraternity, Zorn recalled, had been attentive to the lectures, although without any particular engagement, and otherwise had felt at home in Bonn. He played the violin, danced 'with pretty young girls, even if they were of bourgeois origins' and engaged in sporting activities. 'Certainly the crown prince could have been more eager in his studies', Zorn admitted, 'but judged against our students on the whole, the crown prince was hard-working.' The university did not have a decisive influence on the development of the future ruler, he added. 'His contact with learning remained simply contact.' Nor would matters be different when the crown prince later attended the occasional science lecture at the Technical University at Charlottenburg.[110]

---

[108] *Im Dienste Preußens*, pp. 225, 229; Geheimes Staatsarchiv Preußischer Kulturbesitz, 1. HA, Rep. 89, Nr. 3101 and Nr. 3274; Witzleben, *Adolf von Deines*, p. 244.

[109] Jonas, *Der Kronprinz Wilhelm*, pp. 24–25.

[110] Rosner (ed.), *Erinnerungen des Kronprinzen Wilhelm*, pp. 41–42; Philipp Zorn, 'Erinnerungen an den deutschen Kronprinzen', in *Deutsche Revue* 46, 4 (1921),

Figure 12. Like his father and grandfather before him, Crown Prince Wilhelm studied at the University of Bonn, and just like them he also had close ties with the exclusive and aristocratic 'Corps Borussia'. This photograph shows Wilhelm wearing the colours of this fraternity. Jean Baptiste Feilner, 'Crown Prince Wilhelm as a Bonn Borussian' ['Kronprinz Wilhelm als Bonner Preuße'], 1901.

After February 1903, Wilhelm's university studies were followed by several years with the army, interrupted by numerous trips, during which his career advanced smoothly. As early as September of the same year he was promoted to captain. In 1905, the year of his marriage to Cecilie von Mecklenburg-Schwerin, he progressed to captain in the cavalry and two years later was promoted to major. He recalled that, as a young father, he had sensed an intense need 'to work on advancing my still very patchy

pp. 207–210; *Bei Kronprinzens. Aus dem Familienleben des Kronprinzenhauses* (Berlin, c. 1914), p. 13.

knowledge in the areas of statesmanship and the national economy'. The emperor responded to this need in October 1907 with an instruction that allowed the heir to the throne to sit in at the Provincial Governor's Office in Potsdam, the Ministry of the Interior, the Ministry of Finance, the Ministry of Agriculture and the Imperial Naval Office. The elegantly uniformed trainee attended the ministries every day to learn about their remit, although he made a rather underwhelming impression. The department head to whom it fell in 1908–1909 to ensure the crown prince had a grasp of administrative law would describe him as a likeable and sincere young man, but also noted that 'He could not be induced to do the actual work.' The official was not entirely surprised, however, as 'such was also the case for his father in his own time'.[111]

Friedrich III, Wilhelm II and Crown Prince Wilhelm all lacked powers of concentration and, despite the best-laid plans for their upbringing and education, their achievements were never more than middling. Perhaps the explanation lies in chance, or genes, or in Kant's 'crooked timber of humanity'. Certainly, the persistently strong influence of the military ethos and of elites and institutions bound in with military traditions and structures had an unmistakable Prussian character, but its sway was hardly unusual in nineteenth-century Europe. The military training of the future ruler united traditional elements, such as ceremony and the image of the noble–knightly soldier, with modern aspects, such as instruction in the science of war, the passing of qualifying examinations, and military displays as public spectacle. Beyond this, though, the influence of bourgeois and meritocratic ideals around education and culture was also unmistakeable. For all three of the generations examined here, these ideals led to a programme that gave a civilian academic education a prominent place alongside strict military training. While Frederick III had been taught in private and largely on his own, Wilhelm II attended a humanist public grammar school. Like his son after him, Wilhelm II took his final school exams in a formal setting away from the court. For Crown Prince Wilhelm the curriculum of the more progressive *Realgymnasium* was selected, while, under the influence of reform pedagogy, his schooldays were communal and semi-public. All three princes attended a public university. Wilhelm II and his son also completed internships with different branches of the Prussian government.

---

[111] Rosner (ed.), *Erinnerungen des Kronprinzen Wilhelm*, pp. 66–67; Jonas, *Der Kronprinz Wilhelm*, pp. 64–65. For Jes Fabricius Møller 'meritocratisation' is only one of the five key elements of monarchical survival in the nineteenth century, see Jes Fabricius Møller, 'Die Domestizierung der Monarchien', in Benjamin Hasselhorn und Marc von Knorring (eds.), *Vom Olymp zum Boulevard. Die europäischen Monarchien von 1815 bis heute – Verlierer der Geschichte?* (Berlin, 2018), pp. 35–45.

Their education programmes were carefully conceived and doggedly pursued, but they were not always blessed with success. None of the three heirs to the throne internalised a bourgeois identity or vindicated his claims to monarchical authority with outstanding achievements on a level playing field. Even though it was repeatedly emphasised that the royal pupils were not to receive any special treatment, there could be no doubt about their vast privilege. Nevertheless, the changes in the nature of princely upbringing in Prussia seem to have been successfully embedded within the changes in the nature of monarchy in nineteenth-century Europe. Without losing the magic associated with royal exceptionalism, the heirs to the throne integrated themselves into precisely the structures within which the bourgeois public hoped their own children could profitably be raised. For the monarchy, it could only be a welcome development if the student prince in Bonn danced with a young bourgeois woman whose parents, on their most recent trip to Berlin, had gazed in wonder at the photograph of his successful *Abitur* examination, proudly displayed in the Hohenzollern Museum.

***

Everywhere in nineteenth-century Europe, the raising of future rulers was a source of excellent publicity, both in images and in stories. Numerous photographs depicted heirs to the throne as eager schoolboys, assiduous grammar-school pupils, smart university students or capable soldiers. Examination results were proudly presented to the public. University towns spruced themselves up to welcome royal scholars. The press reported the good marks received by the Spanish Prince Alfonso at the Theresianum in Vienna and by Prince Wilhelm in Kassel, just as they recorded Prince Edward's new skills as a naval officer or the linguistic gifts of Crown Prince Vittorio Emanuele. Increasingly, these reports were accompanied by pictures that left their mark on their future subjects. The royal houses deployed this widespread staging of the monarchy both to illustrate and to reinforce a message about their own membership of bourgeois society, which, over the course of the century, increasingly defined itself in terms of culture, education and ability. They also used it to document the changing conception of the monarchical office. Previously, Grand Duke Ernst Ludwig of Hessen wrote in July 1907 in his work *Fundamental Ideas of a Constitutional Prince* (*Grundideen eines konstitutionellen Fürsten*), the grace of God had been sufficient, 'now, however, the prince must provide evidence of his ability to rule a country'. A call to the monarch therefore ran, 'demonstrate through your work that it justifies the position you hold, just like any other person in their own sphere of life!' Here, using an argument about ability, the grand duke connected, on the one hand, the right of every member of society to status associated with their work with, on the other hand, the right of the prince to rule.[112]

If this correlation were accepted, then the monarchy would remain on a sound footing for as long as the prince performed his demanding task competently. Like any honest trade, princely rule could be learned. The constitutional royal houses of Europe therefore made significant efforts to convey to their subjects the impression that precisely this was happening. Just how successful they were is hard to determine, with that judgement dependent on the perspective of the onlooker. Responses ranged from scepticism, as expressed by Thomas Mann or the *Dresdener Rundschau*, all the way to agreement with an elderly woman who, according to a popular anecdote, fell into conversation with former King Wilhelm of Württemberg near Bebenhausen in autumn 1920. As she talked of the misery of the post-war period, she sighed, 'If only we again had a king trained for the task.'[113]

---

[112] Eckart G. Franz (ed.), *Erinnertes. Aufzeichnungen des letzten Großherzogs Ernst Ludwig von Hessen und bei Rhein* (Darmstadt, 1983), p. 165.

[113] Anni Willman, *Der gelernte König. Wilhelm II. von Württemberg. Ein Porträt in Geschichten* (Stuttgart, 2007), p. 21.

4   'Making the Princess Known and Securing Friends for After Times'

Royal Heirs in Politics, Press and the Public Sphere

Few nineteenth-century heirs bewailed their ostensible political irrelevance as dolefully or for as long as did Friedrich Wilhelm, the Prussian crown prince. He eventually succeeded to the throne at the age of fifty-seven, in March 1888, only to die ninety-nine days later. Emperor Wilhelm I's son had railed against his fate long before he was diagnosed with terminal cancer: 'Fifty years, so my life is behind me', he wrote gloomily in his diary in October 1881, on reaching his half-century. 'An idle spectator, exercising self-discipline day after day. Accustomed to a lifetime of self-denial, condemned to pass the final years in inactivity.' The crown prince no longer made any effort to hide the despair he experienced on account of his isolation and lack of influence from his small circle of close friends. His endless moaning reminded the former chief of the admiralty, Albrecht von Stosch, of the Good Friday lamentations one could witness in a Catholic church. 'And here I had exactly the same feeling', he wrote after a meeting with Friedrich Wilhelm in 1886, 'the endless lamentation of a soul.'[1]

The crown prince's depressive mood had causes that were not directly related to his position as next-in-line to the throne, in particular his grief at the death of two sons and an especially profound midlife crisis. Notwithstanding these other factors, though, his low emotional state was fundamentally associated with his role as heir. His lack of access to the crown's instruments of political power that he was to inherit one day, condemning him the role of 'idle spectator', left him embittered. His experience is indicative of a characteristic and seemingly paradoxical phenomenon: while heirs were of tremendous significance for the future of the dynastic regime, they usually enjoyed only limited direct political participation before the death of their predecessor. It was a particular tragedy of many nineteenth-century royal heirs that the painful contrast between their prominence and their constrained situation was so evident. This was no accident either, for the public portrayal of the future ruler,

---

[1] Frank Lorenz Müller, *Our Fritz: Emperor Frederick III and the Political Culture of Imperial Germany* (Cambridge, MA, 2011), pp. 28, 149.

depicted so vividly to the people, was just as much part of the logic of constitutional monarchy as were the ruling monarch's jealous efforts to preserve all the remaining rights and power of the crown. The latter included a heightened awareness of the monarch's privileges within the family and the strict application of the rigid house rules that governed the sovereign's immediate family.

The foundational texts and practices of the constitutional monarchies of Europe in the nineteenth century contained little about the future sovereign's role in state and society, especially when it came to the heir's political functions. While individual passages addressed the line of succession, the heir's membership of the parliamentary upper chamber and sometimes the apanage the heir was to receive, constitutional documents were largely silent on the heir's political rights and responsibilities. How a crown prince was initiated into his future tasks as ruler and how he positioned himself in relation to the political issues of his time was dependent on decisions made by the ruler, on the particular circumstances of the day and on the personality of the heir. The inherently knotty negotiations about the future monarch's role were also frequently burdened by bitter generational conflicts within the family. On occasion, personal or political differences rendered the relationship between monarch and heir completely dysfunctional. The development of the heir's political functions was thus fraught with difficulty. It was further complicated by political factions and the media, factors that lay beyond the control of the monarch and were sometimes perceived as a potential threat to the crown. Another significant force was public opinion, which both monarch and heir sought to shape.

For heirs to the throne, this tightly woven net of power, rules and influences could produce utterly perplexing contrasts. On the very day the despairing German crown prince turned fifty and complained so bitterly about his infantilisation by his father, the press celebrated him in glowing terms. 'Our crown prince, who after the glorious days of the Battle of Wörth became "Our Fritz" wherever the German language rings out', the *Berliner Tageblatt* gushed on 18 October 1881, 'is thought by the whole nation to be the worthy erstwhile successor of his exalted imperial father, and the reassurance of our having him gives our circumstances an especially reassuring stability for which we are envied by many of those less favoured.' The *Norddeutsche Allgemeine Zeitung* expressed itself in similarly enraptured terms: 'In Crown Prince Friedrich Wilhelm Germany loves and reveres a bastion of exemplary family life, the ideal of a deferential son, the shining example of untiring, self-denying performance of duty, a character formed in the struggles of life, under the thunder of cannons.'[2]

---

[2] *Berliner Tageblatt* and *Norddeutsche Allgemeine Zeitung* of 18 October 1881.

The next-in-line was caught between the opposing poles of parental control and media acclaim – a contrast that many heirs to the throne struggled to reconcile. Crown princes might seek to develop their own political profile, even diverging from the line adopted by the monarch. That course was not unproblematic, and generally led to struggles from which they would often emerge defeated and thus as the wounded party. Yet, even if the future monarch did prevail against the current ruler, he risked damaging the hegemony of the crown, which required loyal obedience. This involved the risk of destabilising the monarchical system. As a result, many royal heirs steered a course of loyal conformity or abstained from political engagement altogether.

Notwithstanding these limitations, nineteenth-century heirs to the throne – including those defeated in the royal power struggle and disciplined by the head of the dynasty – also had access to an increasingly significant instrument of power: the public stage. Here, future rulers were able – in fact, obliged – to present themselves as laudable and lovable figures characterised by admirable qualities. As the media age dawned, they turned into celebrities. This process was not apolitical. It influenced the role of the heir to the throne and the monarchical system as a whole, for the future ruler thus gained access to a power base largely independent of permission or direction from the monarch. In cultivating and consolidating the affections of the public, the royal heir increased not only his own popularity but also that of the monarchy as a whole, whose future he embodied. In this respect, the future of the monarchy was dependent on the talents of the heir to the throne.

With the heirs to the throne excluded from exercising direct political power, their efforts to win the affections of their future subjects were ultimately about acquiring another form of power, one that was crucial for the constitutional monarchies of Europe in the nineteenth century – and has been ever since. This 'soft power', a term coined by the American political scientist Joseph S. Nye in the 1990s, concerns the ability to ensure that others buy into one's own aims, but that outcome is achieved not through the application of 'hard power', by means of coercion, brute force or payment, but rather by directing the preferences and predilections of others through inclusion, persuasion, allurement, enticement or model behaviour. 'If I am persuaded to go along with your purposes without any explicit threat or exchange taking place – in short, if my behavior is determined by an observable but intangible attraction – soft power is at work', Nye explains.[3]

---

[3] Joseph S. Nye, Jr, *Soft Power: The Means to Success in World Politics* (New York, 2004), p. 7.

For monarchies, constitutionalisation was tantamount to a progressive loss of the instruments of hard power. The making of law, the administration of government, a monopoly over the use of force within the state, the levying of taxes: all of these were no longer in the hands of the monarch alone, but instead required the involvement of constitutionally guaranteed institutions. Even military affairs, a realm particularly prized by crowned heads, were no longer their personal playground. As their access to hard power diminished, the acquisition of soft power increased in importance. As a result, everywhere in Europe in the course of the nineteenth century rulers threw themselves into nurturing the frequently invoked affection of their subjects.[4]

Nineteenth-century monarchs no longer limited themselves to defending and exercising the instruments of hard power that remained to them, for now, more than ever before, kings also had to perform the part of the benevolent father of the nation. Their wives had to embrace the role of nurturing mother of the people. It fell to the entire royal family to awaken and tend that affection, and doing so involved more than just a public display of the monarch's marital virtue and family idyll. The heirs to the throne and their families were also central to kindling that affection. Young, underemployed, frequently impatient and increasingly at the centre of public attention, they were under pressure to justify their privileges and their destiny. In October 1904, on the occasion of the accession of Friedrich August III as king of Saxony, the *Dresdner Rundschau* spelt out this reality. 'It has often been said that the loyalty of the Saxon people to their hereditary ruling house is so unshakeable that not even August the Strong [1670–1733] managed to destroy it. There is a deep truth to this claim; the people are indeed loyal, but we live in a different time, not that of the reign of August the Strong', recorded the newspaper, giving the new monarch pause for thought. 'The love of the people', it insisted, 'is no longer inherited; it must be won!'[5]

In order to ensure their own future, as well as that of the idea of monarchy, royal heirs laboured day in, day out to acquire that affection. Reading the signs of a new media society, they were ready to take up the reins of soft power and thereby win the approval, regard or even love of their future subjects. They rewrote their own role, but they also changed the overall character and development of constitutional monarchy, whose instruments of power and self-representation became increasingly 'soft'.

[4] Hubertus Büschel, *Untertanenliebe. Der Kult um deutsche Monarchen 1770–1830* (Göttingen, 2007).
[5] Jean Quataert, *Staging Philanthropy: Patriotic Women and the National Imagination in Dynastic Germany 1813–1916* (Ann Arbor, MI, 2001), pp. 21–53; *Dresdner Rundschau* of 22 October 1904, p. 2.

In 1885, in a congratulatory epistle addressed to Prince Albert Victor, the heir to the British throne, the Liberal Prime Minister William Gladstone described the monarchy as a 'great historic system dependent even more upon love than upon strength'. The principal political task of the monarch-to-be was to ensure this love survived into the future.[6]

Europe's royal heirs approached this task in various ways. Here, we look first at the experiences of heirs who were politically engaged in a narrow sense or were linked to political initiatives that were not consonant with the course adopted by the reigning monarch. Then we turn to the new parameters dictated by the 'political mass market', within which the monarchies of the nineteenth century had to claim their place through their political actions and their representation in the media. Finally, we explore the heirs' relationship with the media and the broader public in the nineteenth century, focusing on their attempts to acquire and employ instruments of soft power.

'Every Prince Is Somewhat More Liberal Than His Predecessor': Royal Heirs as Agents of Opposition

In dynastic systems, the power that can be exercised by the next-in-line is a fundamental problem. Often that power is perceived as hostile. In Shakespeare's *King Lear*, the classic tale of an ageing monarch's loss of authority and dignity, the arch-schemer Edmund succinctly conveys the generational power game: 'The younger rises when the old doth fall.' The power of elderly rulers was hollowed out when 'everything smiles towards the future', as the German diplomat Friedrich von Holstein put it in 1884, referring to the son of the eighty-four-year-old Emperor Wilhelm. It is therefore not surprising that there was often a severe backlash when heirs advocated political positions that were not in accord with the views of the reigning monarch and threatened to undermine his supremacy.[7] In eighteenth-century Britain, the pioneer constitutional state, the creation of opposing political fronts between ruling fathers and their oldest sons had been practically de rigueur: King George I and his son clashed, as did King George II and his son, Prince Frederick Louis, and also King George III and the future King George IV. According to Andrew Hanham, 'Under the Hanoverian monarchs it became almost the norm for princes of Wales and their households to provide a focus of opposition to the king and his ministers.' These family conflicts often mirrored the

---

[6] *The Times* of 13 January 1885.
[7] William Shakespeare, *King Lear*, Act III, Scene 3; Friedrich von Holstein, *Die geheimen Papiere Friedrich von Holsteins*, ed. Norman Rich and M. H. Fisher, German edition by Werner Frauendienst, vol. 2 (Göttingen, 1957), pp. 73–74.

conflicts between contemporary parliamentary factions, with which the royal adversaries were intertwined. The tradition of tension between the court of the king and that of his successor was so strong that it stretched even into the time of Princess Victoria while she was a minor. Much to the displeasure of King William IV (1765–1837), Victoria's mother, the Duchess of Kent, and her confidant Sir John Convoy deliberately kept the young heir at a distance from her uncle and sought to carve out a position of her own for the future queen.[8]

The political differences between monarch and heir were one of the dubious Hanoverian traditions brought to an end under Victoria. Neither Prince Albert nor Queen Victoria was inclined to permit a son of whom they thought so little to have any political role. Occasional attempts by third parties to provide the largely idle heir with an office, or at least a task, foundered either on the unyielding attitude of the monarch or on Bertie's pronounced preference for an easy life. Prime Minister Gladstone encountered the problem for himself in the summer of 1872, when he composed a thirty-four-page letter urging the queen to send the Prince of Wales to Ireland as representative of the crown. Neither this letter, to which Victoria simply responded 'The Queen has so much to write and to do', nor Gladstone's subsequent efforts on this matter met with any success. 'Any preparation of this kind is quite useless', Victoria informed her private secretary, who consequently wrote to Gladstone roundly rejecting the political deployment of the heir in the name of the queen. The relationship between Bertie and his mother was always tense, but not for political reasons. After Victoria's death, the new king, Edward VII, and his own son George similarly did not clash over politics.[9]

Abstinence from political opposition was widespread amongst heirs to the throne. This pattern was followed in the case of the Italian crown princes Umberto and Vittorio Emanuele, in Saxony amongst the Wettin heirs, in Württemberg and in the Kingdom of Belgium. On some occasions, though, this self-restraint was breached, as happened in the Netherlands, France, Sweden and Denmark. The political opposition of Crown Prince Friedrich Wilhelm of Prussia, Prince Ludwig of Bavaria and Archduke Franz Ferdinand of Austria carried on for years and drew

---

[8] Christopher Clark, 'Fathers and Sons in the History of the Hohenzollern Dynasty', in Frank Lorenz Müller and Heidi Mehrkens (eds.), *Sons and Heirs: Succession and Political Culture in Nineteenth-Century Europe* (Basingstoke, 2016), pp. 33–34; Andrew Hanham, 'The Leicester House Faction', www.historyofparliamentonline.org/periods/hanoverians/leicester-house-faction (accessed 10 May 2017); Andrew Thompson, 'Fathers and Sons: Intergenerational Conflict in the Early Hanoverian Monarchy', lecture given at Hampton Court in 2013, unpublished manuscript (with my thanks to the author).

[9] Jane Ridley, *Bertie: A Life of Edward VII* (London, 2012), pp. 160–162; Philip Magnus, *King Edward the Seventh* (London, 1964), pp. 98–117.

particular attention. Irrespective of whether their efforts were successful, the political activities of the next-in-line could actually benefit the dynasty as a whole if the future wearer of the crown appeared to herald a new direction that was favoured by large parts of the population. The system could thus demonstrate its ability to regenerate.

*

For the Dutch king Willem I (1772–1843) and his son Prince Willem of Orange, just as for Victoria and her son Bertie, the relationship between monarch and heir suffered as a result of the many sexual affairs of the latter. In the Dutch case, the situation was not only embarrassing but also damaging for the moral reputation of a royal family that had only been reinstalled as recently as 1814. The prince's philandering was also expensive: the king found himself repeatedly required to pay significant sums to silence blackmailers. In addition, the friction between Willem I and his son had a significant political dimension. Dominated by his austere and authoritarian father, the heir developed what Jeroen Koch has described as 'dynastic claustrophobia'. Willem struggled with his role as heir, blamed his father for every setback and threw himself into foolhardy enterprises, including plots against the rulers of foreign states. When his entanglements became known, a severe conflict erupted. Dramatic scenes played out between these two members of the House of Orange, who were, in the words of the liberal-conservative statesman Gijsbert van Hogendorp, as different as water and fire.

Where the father was strict and guided by reason, his son followed the radical ideas of Rousseau when determining how his own sons would be raised. While representing the dynasty in Brussels, the capital of the newly acquired Belgian provinces, the Dutch crown prince was in contact with liberal jurists such as Alexandre Gendebien, who conveyed to him the thinking of French politicians such as François Guizot and Pierre Royer-Collard. The romantic and radical plans the crown prince developed as a result aimed at linking princely rule and popular freedom.[10]

Only in late 1821, after several years of conflict, did father and son reconcile. The prince, now married and the father of several children, had sailed into calmer waters, concentrating on his family and concerning himself with cultural matters. He also travelled, and eventually he developed political views that were sufficiently conservative for his father to appoint him to the Council of Ministers in the late 1820s. In 1830, the

---

[10] Jeroen Koch, 'The King as Father, Orangism and the Uses of a Hero: King William I of the Netherlands and the Prince of Orange, 1815–1840', in Frank Lorenz Müller and Heidi Mehrkens (eds.), *Royal Heirs and the Uses of Soft Power in Nineteenth-Century Europe* (London, 2016), pp. 275–276.

revolutionary year in which the southern provinces broke away from the Kingdom of the United Netherlands to form an independent Belgium, the Prince of Orange acted as his father's emissary. He twice sought to prevent the division of the kingdom, but his efforts were unsuccessful. Subsequently, King Willem I and his heir found their views diverging again. This time they quarrelled over the strategy to be adopted at the negotiations over Belgian independence and over the failed attempt to win back the southern provinces by force of arms in 1831. Their relationship remained tense. In 1839, just before the king's abdication, the crown prince strongly leant on his stubborn father, who took the moniker 'Willem the Obstinate' as a badge of honour, to agree to the changes to the constitution demanded by the parliament. While the crown prince considered it right for the elected chamber to be able to call the government to account and believed that ministers should be answerable to parliament, his father was strongly opposed. On 4 September 1840, King Willem I nevertheless did sign the relevant decree. Only a month later, though, he abdicated in favour of his son, 'out of unwillingness to be burdened any longer with the government after the changes made to the constitution'.[11]

Similar conflicts erupted between the French king Louis Philippe (1773–1850) and his oldest son, Ferdinand Philippe, duke of Orléans (1810–1842). The conservative course of the July Monarchy and its cautious foreign policy did not appeal to the prince. Eager for action, he was particularly keen to see the purportedly anti-French border that had been agreed at the Congress of Vienna in 1814–1815 redrawn to the benefit of France. The hot-blooded crown prince with his connections to the left-wing Movement Party (*Parti du Mouvement*), was causing a stir in other respects too. King Louis Philippe regarded his throne, created by the Revolution of July 1830, as far too vulnerable to allow his son to play the part of an oppositional Prince of Wales. In 1837, he sharply rebuked his heir, 'You are accused, or at least suspected, of having a belligerent attitude that is less inclined than mine to put prudence and the needs of peace before glory on the battlefield and the dangerous allure of victory. That is what our enemies seek to allege; that is where they attack and thus try to prove that peace and prudence one day will be buried with me.' Thus criticised, the prince, whom Prime Minister Casimir Périer had

---

[11] Hans A. Bornewasser, 'König Wilhelm II.', in Coenraad A. Tamse (ed.), *Nassau und Oranien. Statthalter und Könige der Niederlande* (Göttingen and Zurich, 1985), pp. 260–274; Hans A. Bornewasser, 'König Wilhelm I.', in Coenraad A. Tamse (ed.), *Nassau und Oranien. Statthalter und Könige der Niederlande* (Göttingen and Zurich, 1985), pp. 250–251; Jeroen van Zanten, *Koning Willem II, 1792–1849* (Amsterdam, 2013), pp. 252, 257, 259–260.

already excluded from meetings of the Council of Ministers in 1831, backed down. From then on, and up until his early death in 1842, he kept a low profile in political matters.[12]

The convictions of Crown Prince Oscar (1799–1859), who would ascend the Swedish throne in 1844, were also less conservative than those of his father, King Carl XIV Johann (1763–1844). Opposition voices occasionally referred to the heir to the throne as 'Sweden's future', for Oscar, who looked to France and England, championed liberal domestic reforms in areas such as education and local government. King Carl XIV Johann was as aware of the crown prince's liberal attitudes as of his numerous affairs and disapproved of both. He therefore sought to limit his son's political influence. While the situation was tense, father and son did not fall out. They were able to maintain a close relationship above all because of the evident loyalty of the heir to the throne, who never publicly threw his weight behind the demands of the radical liberals.[13]

Somewhat further south and a generation later, Crown Prince Frederik of Denmark, the later King Frederik VIII (1843–1912), chafed under the rigid conservative politics championed by his father. The son of the long-lived King Christian IX (1818–1906) was crown prince for a full forty-three years. During this time, the firmly liberal Frederik's support for oppositional politics became increasingly blatant. The heir showed sympathy for the left-liberal Venstre party and participated – although anonymously – in newspaper debates. Contemporaries attributed King Christian's decision in 1901 to introduce a parliamentary system that required the government to be backed by a parliamentary majority to the influence of the crown prince.[14]

*

---

[12] Munro Price, *The Perilous Crown: France between Revolutions, 1814–1848* (Basingstoke and Oxford, 2007), pp. 227, 270–271; H. A. C. Collingham, *The July Monarchy: A Political History of France 1830–1848* (London and New York, 1988), p. 104; Heidi Mehrkens, 'The Impossible Task of Replacing a Model Heir: The Death of Ferdinand-Philippe d'Orléans and the "New France"', in Frank Lorenz Müller and Heidi Mehrkens (eds.), *Sons and Heirs: Succession and Political Culture in Nineteenth-Century Europe* (Basingstoke, 2016), pp. 196–197; Guy Antonetti, *Louis-Philippe* (Paris, 1994), pp. 838–839.

[13] Jörg-Peter Findeisen, *Die schwedische Monarchie. Von den Vikingerherrschern zu den modernen Monarchen*, vol. 2 (Kiel, 2010), pp. 311–312; Jörg-Peter Findeisen, *Jean Baptiste Bernadotte. Revolutionsgeneral, Marschall Napoleons, König von Schweden und Norwegen* (Gernsbach, 2010), pp. 343–346, 353.

[14] Jes Fabricius Møller, 'Domesticating a German Heir to the Danish Throne', in Frank Lorenz Müller and Heidi Mehrkens (eds.), *Sons and Heirs: Succession and Political Culture in Nineteenth-Century Europe* (Basingstoke, 2016), pp. 139–140; Olaf Jensen and Winfried Steffani, 'Königreich Dänemark', in Winfried Steffani (ed.), *Regierungsmehrheit und Opposition in den Staaten der EG* (Opladen, 1991), p. 95.

The future German emperor Friedrich III would never enjoy as much influence on the actions of his father and the political development of the nation as Prince Willem of Orange or the Danish crown prince Frederik. Yet, for years, he was reputed to nurture liberal convictions and to be in cahoots with organised political forces. Even as a young man, Friedrich Wilhelm of Prussia was thought comparatively liberal and constitution-friendly, not least because of the presumed influence of his mother, Princess Augusta of Saxony–Weimar. This assumption – along with public interest in his political stance – was heightened by his engagement to the British princess Victoria in 1855 and by their wedding three years later. At the time Great Britain was widely seen as the leading light of political and social constitutionalism. The Prussian heir's young wife and his father-in-law, Albert, the British–Coburg consort of the English queen, sought to mould Friedrich Wilhelm accordingly – and thereby shape the future character of the Hohenzollern monarchy. The possibility that they might succeed had been a concern in conservative circles even as early as the announcement of the prince's engagement. In 1856, having learned of the match, Bismarck had prophesied that the marriage would only be a blessing for the country if the princess succeeded 'in leaving the English woman at home and becoming a Prussian woman'. Otherwise, he noted, it was always problematic when an outsider married into a family, for this allowed the bride's family to wield influence. As the resolute Vicky had no thoughts of leaving the English woman at home and Prince Albert was determined to see his son-in-law flourish under his tutelage, conflict with the conservative forces within Prussia seemed all but inevitable.[15]

In the summer of 1863, in the midst of the dispute between the crown and Bismarck on the one hand and the liberal parliamentary majority on the other, that quarrel erupted. The so-called 'constitutional conflict' revolved around the question of whether the king had the right to push through a decree when parliament was using its authority over the budget to refuse to finance the royal bill. In the final analysis, the conflict was over where within the state ultimate power lay. When Bismarck resorted to questionable methods to move against the oppositional press, the crown prince, who was concerned for the constitution, used a speech he gave in Danzig in June 1863 to distance himself from the course adopted by the government. While the heir's rather muted protest had no influence on

---

[15] Frank Lorenz Müller, '"Frau Deines Mannes, Tochter Deiner Mutter". Victoria und das Scheitern einer Mission', in Jürgen Luh and Julia Klein (eds.), *Perspektivweitung – Frauen und Männer machen Geschichte. Beiträge des zweiten Colloquiums in der Reihe 'Kulturgeschichte Preußens – Colloquien' vom 10. und 11. Oktober 2014*, https://perspectivia.net//publikatio nen/kultgep-colloquien/2/mueller_scheitern (2016) (accessed 23 May 2017); Otto von Bismarck, *Werke in Auswahl*, ed. Gustav Adolf Rein, vol. 2 (Darmstadt, 1963), pp. 96–98.

the outcome of the conflict, it permanently shattered the mutual trust between father and son in political matters. Having received a sharp rebuke from the king, the crown prince would forever refrain from adopting an independent political position. He nevertheless continued to be seen – by both liberal and conservative forces – as representing the liberal course. This alignment seemed to be confirmed by his closeness to his decidedly liberal wife, Vicky, and by his occasional meetings with liberal politicians such as Berlin mayor Maximilian Forckenbeck. His progressive reputation also appeared substantiated by his unconditional support for national unification during the founding phase of the German Empire. At times, he would still send discrete signals, for example, by visiting a synagogue at a time of antisemitic agitation or by praising the Berlin city administration when it was in liberal hands. Although he was certainly a moderate liberal, the heir to the throne was no longer able or willing to take a stronger stance. He did not have the stomach for another fight with his father or with Bismarck, the powerful imperial chancellor.[16]

As long as the majority of the national-liberal forces in the new German Empire continued to collaborate with Bismarck – the 'founder of the empire' – the crown prince's political orientation could in any case have little impact. The situation became explosive only in the late 1870s, when the imperial chancellor turned away from the once-dominant National Liberal Party after it had fractured. Now the left-liberal groupings opposed to Bismarck looked to make political capital out of their supposed closeness to the crown prince. In the early 1880s, the chancellor found himself facing a hostile majority within the imperial parliament and supported only by a monarch well advanced in years. No one could know then that Emperor Wilhelm I would die only in 1888 at the age of almost ninety-one, so Bismarck's authority appeared precarious. It seemed that time was not on his side; according to one insider, everyone looked to the future, which would soon see a new ruler on the throne. The Social Democrats also took the intensified courting of the royal heir to be a carefully calculated 'liberal policy for the future'. According to an article in *Der Sozialdemokrat* in July 1883, this policy rested 'on the hypothesis that Emperor Wilhelm, now in his eighty-seventh year, would soon have to pay the ferryman and on the myth of the "liberal crown prince"'.[17]

All eyes were on Friedrich Wilhelm, while rumours circulated of a left-liberal 'crown prince faction', whose members intended to see off Bismarck after the throne had changed hands. Their aim, it was said, was to alter the character of the empire in line with their convictions. The

---

[16] Müller, *Our Fritz*, pp. 19–25, 71–73, 155–158.
[17] *Der Sozialdemokrat* (Zurich) of 24 July 1883.

imperial chancellor raged against these 'ministers of the future' and accused them of wanting to form a cabinet on the model of British Prime Minister Gladstone, so hated by Bismarck – but so admired by the crown princess. Bismarck spoke disparagingly of the crown prince faction, which was initially associated with a new left-liberal splinter group, created in 1880. When, in 1884, this group merged with the Progress Party, the supposed crown prince faction grew still further, now under their new name of the German Free-Thinking Party. The imperial chancellor could not ignore this threat to his power. While the crown prince was still marginalised by his father he remained very hesitant, but the death of the aged emperor would create an entirely new situation. Bismarck therefore moved heaven and earth to limit the potential for a political about-turn after the succession: his colonial policy, foreign policy and armament policy all weakened the left-liberals in the elections held in 1884 and 1887; personal political intrigues removed supposedly dangerous advisers from around the crown prince; and the chancellor's ensnaring of the emperor's son ensured that his future position under Emperor Friedrich III would be safe. The few concessions that Bismarck had been required to make – for example, the promise to bring moderate liberals such as Rudolf von Bennigsen or Johannes Miquel into the government – had been a small price to pay. The terminal cancer that would carry off the new emperor in June 1888, only three months after the death of his father, spared the imperial chancellor from having to honour even this limited political promise. 'All is easy and pleasant where it concerns the exalted gentleman', Bismarck smirked shortly after the accession of the terminally ill emperor, 'like a game of roulette.'[18]

In the light of the crown prince's years of political timidity, which were followed first by his long-drawn-out public demise and then by the nation's mourning of the much-loved late emperor, all that remained for the liberal party and its hope for change was to mobilise the public. Via their press, the Free-Thinking Party sought to build up Friedrich as the standard-bearer of a liberal turn. In his name – and then to honour his memory – they sought to push through at least part of their programme. Notwithstanding the public sympathy enjoyed by Crown Prince, and later Emperor, Friedrich, the attempt to commandeer him for partisan political purposes failed to produce results. Even as early as 1883 *Der Sozialdemokrat* had been pessimistic. The weak crown prince, the Socialist paper noted, had not the least influence on the business of government, and even his supposed liberal antipathy to the chancellor

[18] Müller, *Our Fritz*, pp. 149–190, 219.

was 'fundamentally of a harmless nature, for otherwise, in the course of twenty years, it would have been expressed or have exploded in some action or other. There has been no lack of opportunity. In short, the future-oriented politics of the liberals, for which they rely on the "liberal crown prince", rest on very, very shaky foundations.' Despite all the popularity and prominence of the crown prince, who was celebrated as a benevolent friend of the people and a glorious military commander, he did not prove a vehicle for political change – his personality was too weak, the conservative, dynastic opposing forces were too strong, and his death occurred too soon.[19]

*

If we turn to Bavaria, we see that it could have been different. In contrast to the Prussian–German heir to the throne, whose political impact was a product of public imputation and perceptions rather than of his own actions, Prince Ludwig of Bavaria (1845–1921) feistily intervened in political affairs and left his mark in multiple ways. The prospect of Prince Ludwig, the future King Ludwig III, actually inheriting the throne was a late development. On 13 June 1886 his cousin King Ludwig II (1845–1886), who was roughly of an age with the prince, drowned in Lake Starnberg, shortly after he had been declared legally incompetent on grounds of mental instability. The crown passed to Prince Otto (1848–1916), the late king's younger brother, who was incapable of ruling and remained detained as a psychiatric patient at the castle of Fürstenried until his death in 1916. Having been appointed regent in 1886, Prince Luitpold (1821–1912), the uncle of the two royal brothers, now ruled in Bavaria. For Luitpold's son Ludwig – cousin of his late royal namesake and the mentally unstable Otto – that changed everything. 'So much, however, is certain', rejoiced the *Münchener Tageblatt* only a few days after Ludwig II's watery death, 'that sooner or later the oldest son of Prince Luitpold – Prince Ludwig – will ascend the throne of Bavaria as King Ludwig III, and we believe that even now we can already claim that then again a blessed era will dawn for our poor and tested Bavarian fatherland.'[20]

Suddenly courted by the media and in politics as the future king, Prince Ludwig did not hesitate to make his mark and set his own agenda. Despite wholeheartedly affirming that in a monarchical state 'always only one person is master', so only one person has the decision-making power, he clearly did not follow the course set by his father. While the elderly prince regent preferred to keep away from routine political business and

---

[19] Ibid., pp. 207–219, 233–258.   [20] *Münchener Tageblatt* of 28 June 1886.

presented himself as the worthy and caring father of his people, the prince was eager for the crown to have an active role in government. Luitpold owed his office as regent to his nephews' being declared legally incompetent, an event that had been followed almost immediately by Ludwig II's mysterious death. Luitpold therefore used his markedly modest demeanour to defuse any accusations that he had seized the sceptre out of a thirst for power. He staunchly rejected all efforts to end the regency and have himself or his son declared king in place of the incapacitated Otto. That was precisely the step advocated by Prince Ludwig, though. He rued the decline in royal power during the regency and would also have benefitted financially from formally becoming crown prince. Indeed, the longer the situation lasted, the more unsettling it became. In 1907 the writer Ludwig Thoma excoriated the undignified spectacle; 'Ah yes, right! A poor soul vegetates in Fürstenried and even his attendants pay no attention to his babbling', he wrote on the occasion of the annual celebration of the ailing king's name day. 'Having a madman supposedly as the highest power', Thoma claimed, 'leads to ridicule that is irreconcilable with the gravity of the business of state.' Ludwig's participation in several attempts to bring this situation to an end was well known to those who kept a close eye on the political scene. While his father, who also disapproved of other aspects of his son's political activities, was still alive, Ludwig was unable to assert his own position. By 1913, though, within a year of the venerable regent's death, Ludwig was king.[21]

The Bavarian royal heir's concerns were not just for the status of the crown in Bavaria, but also for the independence of the Bavarian kingdom within the German Empire, which had been created in 1871. King Ludwig II had been traumatised by the decimation of Bavarian sovereignty and experienced Bavaria's incorporation within an empire led by Prussia as an affront to his royal dignity. This pain certainly contributed to his flight into a romantically transfigured sham world of dreamy castles and neo-absolutist reveries. While Luitpold calmly accepted Bavaria's role within the German Empire and did nothing to hinder the empire-friendly politics of the Bavarian ministers, his son smarted under the imperial yoke. 'There lives within Prince Ludwig all the pride and defiance of the House of Wittelsbach', commented the Prussian envoy Count Monts in 1896, 'but at the same time his reason tells him that, for the foreseeable future, Germany cannot offer his house a position other than that of second place.' The heir to the throne faced a dilemma: his dynastic

---

[21] Stefan März, *Ludwig III. Bayerns letzter König* (Regensburg, 2014), p. 65; Ludwig Thoma, 'Ein kranker König' (1907), in Ludwig Thoma, *Gesammelte Werke*, vol. 1 (Munich, 1968), pp. 449, 451; Frank Lorenz Müller, *Royal Heirs in Imperial Germany: The Future of Monarchy in Nineteenth-Century Bavaria, Saxony and Württemberg* (London, 2017), pp. 24–29.

confidence and his aspirations for the Bavarian kingdom had to wrestle with the reality that for Bavaria there was no alternative to membership of the German Empire.[22]

Trapped in this impasse, Ludwig was limited to rattling the imperial German cage loudly and somewhat crabbily in his role as the intrepid banner-waver of Bavarian particularism. A frequent speechmaker in parliament and at public events throughout the country, he had plenty of opportunity to do so. He caused full-blown scandals when he spoke in Moscow in 1896 and in the town of Straubing in 1900. When the princes of the German Empire gathered in Moscow on the occasion of the coronation of Tsar Nicholas II, the heir to the Bavarian throne did not hold back. A somewhat inept official speaker had welcomed Prince Heinrich, brother and representative of the German emperor, and the German princes who had come to Russia as part of Prince Heinrich's 'retinue'. We are not the vassals of the Hohenzollerns, the Wittelsbach prince had barked, we are their allies. The other German princes had been equal players in the creation of the empire, he insisted, and Germans would do well not to neglect their loyalty to their respective ruling houses. An awkward silence followed. Prince Heinrich pointedly left the event, and soon after a storm broke in the national and international press. Catholic and particularist circles celebrated the prince's prickly response. Figure 13 even shows him as a hero slaying the mighty Prussian dragon. Yet, the opposing political faction – and above all Emperor Wilhelm II – were appalled at the prince's behaviour, which struck them as dangerously anti-empire. With the help of the mortified Bavarian government, the waters could be calmed when Ludwig and the emperor met in Kiel. The Bavarian heir to the throne had not yet shot all his powder, though. 'For His Royal Highness Prince Ludwig the humiliation of Kiel does not seem to have been sufficient', groaned Friedrich Krafft von Crailsheim, head of the Bavarian ministry, in May 1900. Shortly before, while speaking in Straubing, Ludwig had declared that it had not been a 'gracious gift' for Bavaria to be part of the empire, which 'had been joined together with the Bavarian blood just as with the blood of other peoples'. Bavaria should therefore not be seen 'as a lesser brother but rather as a full brother' within the Reich. An animated public debate ensued, and, supported by the Bavarian government, the prince regent again attempted to soothe tempers in Berlin.[23]

---

[22] Monts to Hohenlohe, no. 20, 28 January 1896 (Politisches Archiv des Auswärtigen Amtes, R2802).

[23] Monts to Hohenlohe, no. 20, 28.1.1896 (Politisches Archiv des Auswärtigen Amtes, R2802) and no. 74, 24.5.1900 (R2805); Müller, *Royal Heirs in Imperial Germany*, pp. 172–184.

Figure 13. Munich's *Volkszeitung* celebrated Prince Ludwig's public insistence that he was not Prussia's vassal as 'golden, truly Bavarian words'. A few days later, the same newspaper printed this cartoon, showing Ludwig as the slayer of the Prussian dragon. 'Prince Ludwig as the victorious knight fighting the dragon of Prussian particularism' [Prinz Ludwig als siegreicher Ritter im Kampf gegen den Drachen des preußischen Partikularismus], *Münchner Volkszeitung* 15./16. Juni 1896, Bayerisches Hauptstaatsarchiv, GHA, PrASlg Königin Marie Therese XIII, www.gda.bayern.de/muenchen.

In establishing himself as the strong man of Bavarian autonomy within the empire, Prince Ludwig won the support of the Catholic-clerical Bavarian Centre Party. He maintained close ties to this grouping even though it was the declared opponent of the national-liberal government, which Prince Regent Luitpold supported. Another political initiative brought the prince the goodwill even of forces further to the left, for Ludwig took a stand on reforming the franchise in Bavaria. In early 1906, after every attempt to modernise the kingdom's distorting electoral system had failed, the prince voiced his support for the reform proposed by the Centre Party. He thus contributed decisively to the introduction of the equal, secret and direct vote in Bavaria, which was largely in line with the progressive suffrage for the all-German parliament. During an earlier parliamentary speech, Ludwig had criticised other states 'which had artificial electoral systems that ran counter to the great majority of the population's sense of what was fair'. His stance had won him a positive reception from those fighting for the abolition of the three-class franchise in Saxony and Prussia. And indeed, on 21 January 1906 he was praised by the leader of the Social Democrats, August Bebel: 'If we had an imperial constitution, according to which the emperor was elected by the people and which required the emperor to be elected from one of the ruling princely houses – I guarantee you that Prince Ludwig would be most likely to become the German emperor.' His party colleagues, claimed Bebel, would to a man vote for the Wittelsbach prince.[24]

As the new Bavarian suffrage favoured the Centre Party, the heir to the throne also received much affirmation from this quarter. The prince's advocacy for the Centre Party politician Georg von Hertling was so effective that in February 1912, only months before Luitpold would die at the age of ninety-one, the prince regent conferred the office of minister president on Hertling. With him, the government was now headed by a representative of the party that had won a majority in January's elections. Although it was evident that Ludwig had promoted the political forces that he himself favoured, many contemporaries saw Hertling's appointment as a decisive step towards a parliamentary system. 'There can be no doubt that in the resolution of the recent Bavarian ministerial crisis, the wishes and opinions of Prince Ludwig tipped the balance', the *Berliner Tageblatt* commented. 'It is a fact that the first ministry formed in line with the directives of the heir to the throne took account of parliamentary circumstances. One can only hope that the second-largest federal state will be a model on this point for an empire whose princes otherwise see it as something of their life's task to exert an artificial pressure on the given circumstances rather than deal with them pragmatically.'[25]

---

[24] Müller, *Royal Heirs in Imperial Germany*, pp. 205–207.

[25] Ibid., pp. 207–209; 'Von Prinzregent Ludwig zu König Ludwig III.', www.hdbg.eu/koe nigreich/index.php/themen/index/herrscher_id/4/id/51 (accessed 13 May 2017); *Berliner Tageblatt* of 29 February 1912.

The efforts he made over a period of decades had enabled the future Bavarian king to develop a distinct political profile. He was seen as an upholder of Bavarian particularism and a champion of dynasty, committed to the executive role of the crown and not averse to a cautious modernisation of the constitutional institutions. To that end, Ludwig had invested in his public role as member of the first chamber of the Bavarian parliament and as a frequent speechmaker, and he was regarded as well-informed and very able. Additionally, he had supporters in the press and within the political parties, above all amongst the ranks of the Centre Party, with which he was affiliated. He was thus able to develop a considerable impact even as his father and the elites in the Bavaria government attempted to neutralise him politically.

*

In the late Habsburg Empire, the bifurcation of royal power, with one faction supporting the monarch and another grouping championing the heir to the throne, was much more extreme than in the Kingdom of Bavaria. In a speech given before the Austrian parliament in 1910, Karl Renner, leader of the Social Democrats, proposed that for the Habsburgs one could speak no longer of a *mon*archy, only of a *dy*archie, of rule by two potentates. He pointed to the intense discord within the monarchy's state and government apparatus that emanated from the palaces of Schönbrunn and Belvedere, the Viennese residences of Emperor Franz Joseph and his designated successor, Archduke Franz Ferdinand (1863–1914), respectively. The ageing emperor, who entered his ninth decade in 1910, baulked at making significant concessions to his heir. Unlike the German Crown Prince Friedrich Wilhelm, however, Franz Ferdinand was not content to remain inactive and bide his time; instead, he deployed his power and pursued his ends with a certain ruthlessness.[26]

Like Crown Prince Rudolf, the emperor's son who had died in 1889, Franz Ferdinand believed the politics pursued by Franz Joseph were ill-omened, and he opposed them just as tenaciously as his predecessor had done. The two men's aims and the means they employed to achieve those ends were entirely different, though. Rudolf was caught in a web of contradictory feelings. On the one hand, he believed he had to criticise what he regarded as the emperor's misguided and outdated politics and seek to ensure they were redirected towards liberal solutions; on the other hand, he could only capitulate to his father, surrendering dispiritedly. His

---

[26] Günter Kronenbitter, 'The Opposition of the Archdukes: Rudolf, Franz Ferdinand and the Late Habsburg Monarchy', in Frank Lorenz Müller and Heidi Mehrkens (eds.), *Sons and Heirs: Succession and Political Culture in Nineteenth-Century Europe* (Basingstoke, 2016), p. 211.

opposition was limited to largely anonymous newspaper articles and pamphlets and to contacts with oppositional journalists. By the end, the crown prince's tone had become more strident, 'But pay heed, your majesty!', a pamphlet from the spring of 1888 declared, 'You are not treading this path unwarned.' Rudolf cautioned his father against 'politics which are absurd in the present and destructive for the future'. It is likely, though, that neither the emperor nor the members of the Austrian government ever took any notice of this text, which was published anonymously in Paris. The pamphlet, Brigitte Hamann has written, found no audience and made no enemies. After its publication, the heir to the throne made his first plans to commit suicide. Eight months later, he died at Mayerling.[27]

Rudolf's successor as heir to the throne, Archduke Franz Ferdinand of Austria–Este, was cut from a very different cloth. Originally, the chance of the emperor's nephew inheriting the throne seemed rather remote and attention turned to him only after Crown Prince Rudolf had died without leaving a son. Franz Ferdinand's father, Archduke Karl Ludwig (1833–1896), a younger brother of the emperor, had no ambition to occupy the imperial throne, and when the emperor's only son took his own life in January 1889, Karl Ludwig's son Franz Ferdinand effectively became heir presumptive. The archduke, whose public profile had been negligible until this date, had undergone purely military training and was almost entirely unprepared for his new role. Rather than make his way to Vienna, he initially remained with his military units in Prague and then at Sopron, in Hungary. Thereafter, he undertook a ten-month world tour, returning only in the autumn of 1893. Initially his political influence was minor, which could in part be ascribed to his precarious health. In 1885, he had been granted leave to recuperate in northern Italy, but his medical problems had not disappeared. In 1894, he was diagnosed with pulmonary tuberculosis. During the two years of his convalescence, the talk in Vienna was that he was little more than a walking corpse, his death seeming imminent. But he did survive.[28]

The archduke demonstrated a similar tenacity when it came to the woman who was to be his partner in life. Strict Habsburg family law seemed to rule out a relationship with Countess Sophie Chotek, with

[27] Ibid., pp. 212, 217; Brigitte Hamann, *Kronprinz Rudolf. Ein Leben* (Vienna, 2006), pp. 101–106, 146–151, 178–215, 340–351; Julius Felix [Kronprinz Rudolf], 'Oesterreich-Ungarn und seine Alliancen. Offener Brief an S. M. Kaiser Franz Joseph I.', in Kronprinz Rudolf, *'Majestät, ich warne Sie ...'. Geheime und private Schriften*, ed. Brigitte Hamann (Vienna, 1979), pp. 191, 226.

[28] Alma Hannig, *Franz Ferdinand. Die Biografie* (Vienna, 2013), pp. 49–54; Friedrich Weissensteiner, *Franz Ferdinand. Der verhinderte Herrscher* (Vienna, 2007), pp. 72–112.

whom he had fallen in love in the late 1890s, for although she was descended from an ancient Bohemian noble family, she was not considered his social equal. Franz Ferdinand's decision that he would relinquish neither Sophie nor the throne caused a public scandal and a deep rift in his relationship with Franz Joseph. The monarch, supported by many representatives of the court and the government establishment, believed that such a misalliance would jeopardise the very foundations of the imperial house. After robust discussions, during which the heir to the throne apparently threatened 'a second Mayerling', the emperor eventually capitulated and permitted the morganatic marriage. In return, Franz Ferdinand had to agree that neither his wife nor their future children would be considered members of the imperial family or enjoy the related rights of inheritance. The countess was snubbed at the Viennese court, where she was not permitted to appear at her husband's side. That attitude certainly helped ensure that the heir to the throne largely kept his distance from the court and regarded Schönbrunn with hostile detachment.

The wedding was celebrated on 1 July 1900 at the castle of Reichstadt in Bohemia – far from Vienna and as a purely private event. For the heir to the throne, his marriage and, later, his family formed the 'epitome of happiness'. As he wrote to the German ambassador, he was at last being allowed this pleasure, after 'years of struggle, after hard battles, after tolerating many bitter hours'. His wife, Franz Ferdinand informed his mother, was a treasure: 'She looks after me, I am doing splendidly, I am healthy and much less tense. I feel reborn.'[29]

Only in 1898, two years after the death of his father and with the archduke considered completely recovered from his illness, was Franz Ferdinand declared to be 'at the disposal of the Supreme Command (*zur Disposition des Allerhöchsten Oberbefehls*), the language that officially identified him as heir to the throne. The position came with a responsibility to inspect larger units of the armed forces, put him in change of training the troops and transferred to him the command function in war. Over the following years, Franz Ferdinand would use his position to build up a considerable and dependable staff. The heir to the throne's military chancellery, which was located in the Belvedere Palace, his official residence in Vienna, almost became a second centre of government and a powerful weapon that the recently married and reinvigorated archduke wielded to considerable effect. He used his influence within the military apparatus to ensure the appointment of personnel who suited his own intentions: supporters were promoted and the careers of officers,

[29] Hannig, *Franz Ferdinand*, pp. 54–77; Weissensteiner, *Franz Ferdinand*, pp. 113–149.

diplomats and officials thought hostile were wrecked. For a number of reasons, Franz Ferdinand was able to advance his plans much further than had Rudolf before him. The archduke was distinctly more ruthless and stronger-willed than Rudolf. Additionally, the elderly emperor was now frail and the apparently inevitable transfer of power to his heir was being anticipated within government. Rudolf's efforts to exercise his influence had also foundered because Archduke Albrecht, a highly respected field marshal and general inspector, had dominated military affairs. The death in 1895 of this aged war hero had cleared the path for the new heir to the throne. Even then, the influence that Franz Ferdinand's military chancellery was able to exert in the years before the First World War was remarkable: the archduke arranged for the dismissal of Austrian Minister President Vladimir von Beck, brought down two ministers of war and one chief of staff, and promoted Leopold Count Berchtold into office as Foreign Minister over Alois Lexa von Aehrenthal, his predecessor. Numerous officers, officials and diplomats were nurtured or dismissed on the initiative of the Belvedere.[30]

The influence of the group around the heir to the throne was not limited to the internal apparatus of the military and the administration. Franz Ferdinand found favour with journalists and publicists from the Catholic and conservative camp. Moreover, he enjoyed support from representatives of the clerical and antisemitic Christian Social Party. Even though the archduke made little effort to present a likeable image to the public, the military chancellery was alive to the political influence of the press and knew how to use it to good effect. Articles – a number written by Franz Ferdinand himself – were carefully targeted. The *Reichspost* in particular, whose chief editor met Friedrich Funder, head of the military chancellery, several times a week, developed into an important organ of the Belvedere. As a result, the Christian Social newspaper experienced a marked upturn in its distribution. Whereas at its inception in 1895 some 5,000 copies had been printed, by 1914 it managed a circulation of 36,000, making it one of the most influential voices in the German-speaking part of the monarchy. Other newspapers, for example the *Österreichische Rundschau*, *Danzer's Armee-Zeitung* or the *Vaterland*, were also won over to the Belvedere's cause, as was evident in 1913, when on the occasion of the heir to the throne's fiftieth birthday, several newspapers published especially well-disposed articles. According to *Danzer's Armee-Zeitung*, Franz Ferdinand stood for 'a new Austria' and

[30] Hannig, *Franz Ferdinand*, pp. 53–54, 85–86; Kronenbitter, 'The Opposition of the Archdukes', pp. 212, 221–223; Samuel R. Williamson Jr, 'Influence, Power, and the Policy Process: The Case of Franz Ferdinand, 1906–1914', in *The Historical Journal* 17 (1974), pp. 417–434.

he was, the *Reichspost* stated, a man who as 'adviser to an elderly monarch on important matters is today already helping shape the future of the empire'.[31]

What – other than a naturally antagonistic personality – led the heir to the throne to position himself counter to the emperor? His disagreement with the emperor's politics was not as sharp as in the case of Crown Prince Rudolf. The archduke did not challenge the conservative monarch as a result of the standard 'crown prince liberalism'. Franz Joseph's attitudes and his nephew's views often even coincided – although their personal relationship was anything but warm and the emperor was bent on limiting the archduke's political influence. Both men sought a strong role for the crown and the maintenance of the power and prestige of the monarchy. To that end, they both banked on conservative and Catholic forces, and when it came to foreign policy, they both endorsed the alliance with the German Empire. They both rejected liberalism and socialism. The emperor and his heir did not coincide, however, in their methods or on their priorities. Franz Josef favoured compromise and tended to support existing structures, particularly in terms of the German–Hungarian dualism introduced as part of the constitutional 'Compromise' of 1867. Franz Ferdinand, in contrast, preferred a more resolute approach, expressed through a political vocabulary that was frequently rabid. He spoke, according to Alma Hannig, of 'crushing, cleansing and shooting', language that made evident a hate-filled aversion to those he considered enemies of the monarchy: Socialists, Liberals, Protestants, Jews, journalists and – above all – the Hungarian elites. He accused his uncle of an excessive forbearance in the treatment of the supposedly insubordinate Magyars and demanded far-reaching reforms. He was concerned to strengthen the forces that bound the empire together and to see power centralised and secured for the crown. The Sudeten-German publicist Emil Franzel even termed Franz Ferdinand a 'conservative revolutionary'. While that designation went further than the facts warrant, it is certainly the case that the heir's essential goals met with approval right across the conservative spectrum. Some welcomed in the archduke the leader of a new politics, which, according to Robert A. Kann, basically held fast to the conservative goals of Habsburg tradition.[32]

---

[31] Hannig, *Franz Ferdinand*, pp. 115–121.

[32] Ibid., pp. 96–97; Michaela Vocelka and Karl Vocelka, *Die private Welt der Habsburger. Leben und Alltag einer Familie* (Graz, 2015), pp. 330–332; Emil Franzel, *Franz Ferdinand d'Este. Leitbild einer konservativen Revolution* (Vienna and Munich, 1964), p. 83; Kronenbitter, 'The Opposition of the Archdukes', pp. 217–218; Robert A. Kann, 'Groß-Österreich', in Robert A. Kann, *Erzherzog Franz Ferdinand Studien* (Munich, 1976), pp. 34, 36.

That Franz Ferdinand's power base was largely a product of his institutional status, as heir to the throne, was evident in the moment of his death. In Viennese governmental circles and certainly also in Budapest the news of his assassination in Sarajevo in June 1914 was met with undisguised relief. His military chancellery in the Belvedere Palace was immediately closed down. Franz Ferdinand's marked unpopularity at all levels of public life made it easy to erase all the tracks left by his activities. The press initially reacted with shock to the death of the heir to the throne, but attention was quickly directed instead to the much more loveable young Archduke Karl, who would now inherit the crown. The memory of the assassinated archduke that would prevail found its best-known expression in Stefan Zweig's memoirs, *The World of Yesterday*: 'Franz Ferdinand lacked everything that counts for real popularity in Austria: amiability, personal charm and easygoingness. [...] He was never seen to smile, and no photographs showed him relaxed. He had no sense for music, and no sense of humour, and his wife was equally unfriendly. They both were surrounded by an icy air; one knew that they had no friends, and also that the old Emperor hated him with all his heart because he did not have sufficient tact to hide his impatience to succeed to the throne. [...] The news of his murder therefore aroused no profound sympathy.'[33]

***

Amongst the oppositional heirs to the throne considered here, Archduke Franz Ferdinand was in many respects an exception, and not only in that his murder triggered the war that would bring a bloody end to Europe's monarchical century. He was alone amongst them in creating an unusually strong and institutionally secured power base, upon which he was able to erect, against the will of the ruling monarch, a veritable counter-government. Referring to this constellation, which made governing the institutionally already highly complex Austro-Hungarian Dual Monarchy all the more challenging, Minister President Ernest von Koeber tersely commented that the land had not just two parliaments but also two emperors. Additionally, the archduke did not follow the usual model of crown princely opposition, for he did not counter the conservative attitude of the ruling monarch with a critique that could be

---

[33] Kann, 'Groß-Österreich', p. 31; Stefan Zweig, *The World of Yesterday*, trans. Benjamin W. Huebsch and Helmut Rippinger (Lincoln, NE and London, 1964), p. 216; Alma Hannig, 'Archduke Ferdinand: An Uncharming Prince?', in Frank Lorenz Müller and Heidi Mehrkens (eds.), *Royal Heirs and the Uses of Soft Power in Nineteenth-Century Europe* (London, 2016), pp. 139–160.

interpreted as liberal and progressive. He departed abruptly from the 'myth of the liberal crown prince', in which even the sceptical journalists of *Der Sozialdemokrat* believed. This idea was not just a matter of 'political comedy and calculation', the weekly newspaper declared in 1883, 'no, every prince is somewhat more liberal than his predecessor – and here is the grain of truth in the myth of the liberal crown prince.' With his decidedly conservative views, Franz Ferdinand consciously broke ranks with this 'ancient myth' that 'for centuries has ensured that patient peoples remain calm'.[34]

The Austro-Hungarian heir was able to set aside the norms of political behaviour exhibited by his peers not least because he was indifferent to whether he was liked by the general public. In fact, he was downright averse to investing in his reputation. 'What does popularity even mean? I care nothing for it. It is my opinion that the duty of the ruler is to do in every case what he deems right, without considering whether it will be well received or not', he told the Hungarian statesman Gyula Andrássy in 1906. Franz Ferdinand faithfully reflected this attitude, and he projected a deeply unattractive image of himself – leading to comments like that by Stefan Zweig. While so many royal figures assiduously presented themselves to the public as affable, charming and loveable, Franz Ferdinand made no effort to make political capital from being a happily married man and a loving father. Private photographs portraying him in civilian clothes, laughing and at ease did not find their way to the public. Instead, he created the image that Viennese author Karl Kraus observed: 'Not for him the graceful greeting. He had nothing of that "winning way" that calms a people of spectators about what they have lost. He never had in his sights the uncharted land that the Viennese calls his heart.'[35]

Franz Ferdinand's refusal to reach out 'winningly' disconcerted his contemporaries. By then, the rule proved by this prominent exception was evidently well established. Even monarchs with designs on hard power were wise to invest in generating soft power too, for their own sake and for the sake of the crown.

---

[34] Friedrich Weissensteiner, *Große Herrscher des Hauses Habsburg. 700 Jahre europäische Geschichte* (Munich, 1997), p. 337; *Der Sozialdemokrat* of 2 August 1883.

[35] Hannig, 'Archduke Ferdinand', pp. 139–140, 145–152, 160; Georg Franz, *Erzherzog Franz Ferdinand und die Pläne zur Reform der Habsburger Monarchie* (Brünn [Brno], Munich and Vienna, 1943), p. 59; Karl Kraus, 'Franz Ferdinand und die Talente', in *Die Fackel* 400–403 (10 July 1914), pp. 3–4, www.textlog.de/39154.html (accessed 29 May 2022).

'Then Even the Most Ancient of Hereditary Rights Means Nothing': Monarchy, the Politics of the Media and the Political Mass Market

In a satirical essay from 1907, the author and journalist Ludwig Thoma mused on the affection that the Bavarian people felt for their ruler. He wondered whether 'all the respect that has been accrued might disappear down the drain' if the king had to be kept under lock and key on account of mental illness, as was indeed the case for King Otto. After all, according to Thoma, so much was now missing in Bavaria 'that serves as an important educational tool elsewhere. For example, the object lesson given by photographic depictions of a prince's soldierly handsomeness and family bliss.' In 'lands that are blessed', he noted, 'only Odol, Rayseife and Henkell Trocken [brands of mouthwash, soap and sparkling wine] appear as frequently before the eyes of the people as does the intimacy of the ruling house.' Thoma's sarcastic equation of scenes from royal life with everyday household items was in line with Karl Kraus's characterisation of a monarch's subjects as 'a nation of spectators'. These early twentieth-century comments indicate that the relationship between ruler and ruled had changed profoundly: subjects now constituted the very audience without which any performance is pointless; those who had previously been recipients of royal commands were now much-courted consumers of the royal product. As spectators always have the option to look away and consumers can select a different product, the actors and producers of that monarchical performance had to invest in advertising.[36]

Political behaviour in nineteenth-century Europe was increasingly conditioned by the evolution of what the historian Hans Rosenberg, writing as early as the 1940s, has characterised as a 'political mass market'. In different places at different times, and not absolutely everywhere, the traditional 'politics of notables', which had been executed by and within a small elite, was gradually supplanted. New political forms were now directed at and engaged with the majority of the population. The result was a mass market within which various political actors – governments, those running for elected office, parties, interest groups and also royal figures – competed for the attention, favour and support of an ever-expanding public. This market was the product of constitutional developments, political shifts and the looming media age. It stemmed from a multiplicity of factors: the constitutional guarantee of citizens' political rights and, as censorship was gradually dismantled, of their political freedom; the introduction of elected parliaments; the expansion of the

---

[36] Thoma, 'Ein kranker König', p. 451.

franchise to cover larger sections of the population; the creation of political parties and advocacy groups; increased literacy; greater participation in elections; and the vast distribution of print media, which – increasingly affordable and attractively illustrated – soon reached a vast readership.

The changes in the media landscape proceeded at breathtaking pace, not least on account of revolutionary technological advances such as the rotary printing press. In the first half of the nineteenth century, the most important German newspaper, the *Augsburger Allgemeine*, had a maximum circulation of barely 10,000 copies. Soon after its founding in 1883 the *Berliner Lokal-Anzeiger* had a circulation of 100,000 copies, even though it was up against distinctly keener competition. The small newssheets of the beginning of the century, designed for a limited readership, were replaced a few decades later by extensive daily papers, which offered numerous supplements targeting specific and substantial political and social subsets. These newspapers were accompanied by magazines, almanacs, calendars and the massive book market. Beyond the printed words themselves, the vigorous and ever-growing demand from readers was satisfied by photographs, lithographic prints, postcards, public panoramas, exhibitions, museums and eventually also moving images. The first two-thirds of the century had already seen an astonishing growth in the media public, and yet this development accelerated in the 1880s. This period has been identified as the beginning of a 'mass media saddle period', an age of accelerating change, during which the relationship between media, politics and society was formed anew. Significant contributions came from new forms of communication (telegraph, telephone), duplication (illustrated print) and reproduction (photography, phonography).[37]

Additionally, the development of a modern consumer society and a modern economy, full of technological achievements and new advertising practices, influenced the political contest. 'It's just like the publicity, advertising, and travel for any business', explained Friedrich Engels in the spring of 1883 as he sought to spur on the Social Democratic politician August Bebel, who was finding all the effort associated with the elections for the imperial parliament rather too much. 'Success comes only slowly

---

[37] Jörg Requate, 'Einleitung', in Jörg Requate (ed.), *Das 19. Jahrhundert als Mediengesellschaft* (Munich, 2009), pp. 10–11; see also Jörg Requate, 'Kennzeichen der deutschen Mediengesellschaft des 19. Jahrhunderts', in Jörg Requate (ed.), *Das 19. Jahrhundert als Mediengesellschaft* (Munich, 2009), pp. 30–42, and Jörg Requate, 'Politischer Massenmarkt und nationale Öffentlichkeiten – Die Entstehung einer "vierten Gewalt"? Deutschland, England und Frankreich im Vergleich', in Martin Kirsch, Anne G. Kosfeld and Pierangelo Schiera (eds.), *Der Verfassungsstaat vor der Herausforderung der Massengesellschaft. Konstitutionalismus um 1900 im europäischen Vergleich* (Berlin, 2002), pp. 145–168; Frank Bösch, *Mediengeschichte. Vom asiatischen Buchdruck zum Fernsehen* (Frankfurt am Main and New York, 2011), pp. 109–128.

and in some instances not at all. But there is no alternative.' Even at the very top, efforts were made to keep up with marketing innovations. In September 1910 a report from the German diplomat Richard von Kühlmann, who was posted to London, piqued the interest of the emperor. Kühlmann explained that, during the most recent election campaign, Conservative Party representatives had toured the country with removal vans. Equipped with loudspeakers and projectors and decorated with election posters, he reported, the vehicles had been used at some 10,000 events as mobile stages. Emperor Wilhelm was evidently impressed by this innovation and wrote in the margin of the report, 'something that might be employed in our election campaigns'. A transcript of the report from London was therefore sent to the Ministry of the Interior.[38]

The historian James Retallack has written of ruthless competition in the election arena. Deregulation, he proposes, meant that the government gradually ceased to police the political marketplace and could no longer control what wares were on offer. Like all other actors, monarchs had to assert their presence within the political mass market and follow the rules of that market, where they traded in the highly desired commodity that was political influence. They needed to advertise, to be visible and present, to appeal to the 'buyer' and to give the consumer a plausible reason for engaging in the political transaction, for, explained the writer and politician Friedrich Naumann in 1912, when it came down to it, monarchs lived 'on being regarded as necessary. If that belief is gone, then even the most ancient of hereditary rights means nothing.' The emergence of the political mass market therefore compelled Europe's current and future monarchs to preserve and when possible bolster the belief that they were indispensable. As their power shrank, it was imperative, according to the historian Frank Bösch, that their presence in everyday life grew. While this reality offered new opportunities, it also made new demands.[39]

The emerging media age provided the crowns with new channels to showcase their dynamism and efficacy, to portray the tasks that fell to monarchs and their dynasties, and to highlight the characteristics that supposedly distinguished them. Those features included the ability and willingness to carry out the duties of a constitutional monarch laudably

---

[38] James Retallack, 'Obrigkeitsstaat und politischer Massenmarkt', in Sven Oliver Müller and Cornelius Torp (eds.), *Das Deutsche Kaiserreich in der Kontroverse* (Göttingen, 2009), p. 131; Richard von Kühlmann to Theobald von Bethmann-Hollweg, no. 733, 15 September 1910 (Politisches Archiv des Auswärtigen Amtes, R6053).

[39] Friedrich Naumann, 'Monarchie und Demokratie' (1912), in Friedrich Naumann, *Werke*, vol. 2 (Cologne and Opladen, 1964), p. 443; Retallack, 'Obrigkeitsstaat und politischer Massenmarkt', p. 130; Bösch, *Mediengeschichte*, p. 121.

and appropriately, an exemplary marriage and happy family and a commitment to raising children according to bourgeois and meritocratic ideals, as a guarantee of their future competence. Additionally it might be helpful, or even necessary, to evoke military prowess.

The Faustian pact with the media had a dark side. Via newspaper articles and photograph albums, the members of the royal family could become a presence in the everyday and private lives of millions of subjects, but they were exposed warts and all. Even crowned heads and future monarchs were not spared in the columns of the deregulated and not infrequently critical press. The gaze of the media reached – as Bertie, Prince of Wales, and Crown Prince Friedrich August were to discover – even into the bedroom. Staged royal events, dashing military figures and happy princely families were seen in a new, brighter light, but that illumination also revealed everything essentially human, all that was lacking, all that was repellent. Europe's political mass market of the nineteenth century knew not just the monarchical celebrity but also the royal scandal. A diary entry made by the Bavarian king Maximilian II (1811–1864) in middle of the century reveals how exhausting this life in plain view could be and the vulnerability that accompanied it. 'It struck 2 o'clock, sitting alone in a glass carriage, I leave the residence surrounded by all the celebratory pomp of kingship. The glass carriage, exposed to all eyes, is the image of the modern throne, no purple covers shroud it from the suspiciously curious crowds; those who wish to ascend it must never forget to act in such a way that they do not need to shy away from that gaze.'[40]

Even though involvement with the medial mass market was not without its risks, hardly any royal could avoid participating. There was no alternative. What may have helped was that royal public relations were not an invention by the constitutional monarchies that came into being after 1815. In antiquity and during the Middle Ages, the available media had already been skilfully employed to increase the ruler's prestige, and in the era of absolutism their deployment had reached new heights. The splendid and carefully staged multimedia displays of Louis XIV (1638–1715) had a single purpose – to direct attention to the French 'Sun King' as the dazzling centre of his state. As Jürgen Luh has recently shown, the Prussian king Friedrich II (1712–1786), 'Frederick the Great', was no

---

[40] King Maximilian's memoirs cited in Anja Schöbel, *Monarchie und Öffentlichkeit. Zur Inszenierung der deutschen Bundesfürsten 1848–1918* (Cologne, Weimar and Vienna, 2017), p. 11; Martin Kohlrausch, *Der Monarch im Skandal. Die Logik der Massenmedien und die Transformation der wilhelminischen Monarchie* (Berlin, 2005); Frank Bösch, *Öffentliche Geheimnisse. Skandale, Politik und Medien im Kaiserreich und Großbritannien, 1880–1914* (Munich, 2009).

less concerned to appear magnificent to both contemporaries and posterity. His style was less opulent than that of the Sun King, but Friedrich demonstrated extraordinary aptitude in his engagement with the media of the eighteenth century. In the nineteenth century, though, a distinct shift occurred: the power in the relationship between monarch, media and public now no longer lay so clearly with the crown. The 'media monarchy' of the post-revolutionary period had to handle its public image far more deliberately.[41]

In the case of Queen Victoria, whom a leading study calls the 'first media monarch', even contemporaries were aware of the challenges of dealing appropriately with the media. A humorous article from 1845 has the queen ponder whether she would one day be remembered in the same manner as the legendary 'Queen Bess', the Tudor Queen Elizabeth I (1533–1603). 'There is one thing sure enough', Victoria declares, 'that posterity will know far more about us than about Bess; for all of our movements are recorded in the papers – our balls, our dinners, our visits to the Opera, the French plays, or the legitimate – all are in print, to last as long as England herself.' The very fact that the satirical press gave column inches to what the queen might think of the press's invasion of her private life suggests how multi-layered the relationship of media and monarchy had become even by the first half of the century. In John Plunkett's judgement, Victoria was already no longer in a position to control the political and commercial forces that formed the 'public character' of the monarchy. For Victoria's grandson Emperor Wilhelm II two generations later, the situation was even more complex. The Hohenzollern monarch, labelled the 'media emperor', was concerned about the manipulation of his likeness in photographs, preferred to be photographed only during 'emperor weather', and grappled with the ownership of the rights to photographs taken of him during his public appearances.[42]

Despite all the changes, however, the emperor abided by the basic rules of engagement with the media that his grandmother and her husband, Prince Albert, had introduced after 1840 and that had then been adopted

---

[41] Peter Burke, *Die Inszenierung des Sonnenkönigs* (Berlin, 1993); Jürgen Luh, *Der Große. Friedrich II. von Preußen*, 2nd edn (Munich, 2011). On the relationship between media and monarchy, see also Martin Kohlrausch, 'Die höfische Gesellschaft und ihre Feinde. Monarchie und Massengesellschaft in England und Deutschland um 1900', in *Neue Politische Literatur* 47 (2002), pp. 450–466; Torsten Riotte, 'Nach "Pomp und Politik". Neue Ansätze in der Historiographie zum regierenden Hochadel im 19. Jahrhundert', in *Neue Politische Literatur* 59 (2014), pp. 209–228.

[42] John Plunkett, *Queen Victoria: First Media Monarch* (Oxford, 2003), pp. 1–2; Gaby Huch, *Zwischen Ehrenpforte und Inkognito. Preußische Könige auf Reisen. Quellen zur Repräsentation der Monarchie zwischen 1797 und 1871*, vol. 1 (Berlin, 2016), p. 4; Eva Giloi, 'Copyrighting the Kaiser: Publicity, Piracy and the Right to Wilhelm II's Image', in *Central European History* 45 (2012), pp. 407–451.

in turn by almost all the ruling houses of Europe, in what Karina Urbach has identified as a franchise-like process.[43] According to John Plunkett's analysis of Queen Victoria's media politics, her interactions with the media focused on three core features: mobility, visibility and 'civic publicness'.

First – mobility. The monarchs of the nineteenth century spent a remarkable amount of time on the road. The itinerancy of the ruler within his or her own lands that had been a typical feature of the Middle Ages and the early modern period had eventually been curtailed by the extravagance of court life during the eighteenth century. In the nineteenth century, the practice was revived, although it now served different ends. As Gaby Huch has noted, during this restive age, their travels allowed monarchs to re-anchor royal rule within the public consciousness. As the bond between monarch and subject became more personal and more emotional, it also became closer. These carefully managed moments ensured that the monarchy was both near at hand and visible even in the provinces. Populations far away from the court and from the elites of the capital city were deliberately targeted, for it was always possible that their ties of traditional loyalty to the crown might be loosening. Victoria and Albert, Plunkett writes, 'undertook an unprecedented number of regional tours, foreign visits, and civic engagements, forging a role that would be successfully followed by future British monarchs'.[44]

In the light of this royal propensity for travel, Johannes Paulmann has explored forms of peripatetic rule, a practice to which rulers returned from the middle of the nineteenth century. With the ruling elite now travelling by train or steamship, and later also by automobile, the journeys undertaken by crowned heads acquired an entirely new quality. Rapid transportation allowed monarchs to become virtually omnipresent as they openly embraced a modern age characterised by mobility, speed and technological progress. Prince Ludwig of Bavaria probably went farthest, for in autumn 1910 he accompanied Count Zeppelin onboard the dirigible *Parseval VI* for a scenic flight above Munich. Under the heading 'A Modern Prince in the Best Sense', the *Allgemeine Rundschau* declared that

---

[43] Karina Urbach, 'Die inszenierte Idylle. Legitimationsstrategien Queen Victorias und Prinz Alberts', in Frank-Lothar Kroll and Dieter J. Weiß (eds.), *Inszenierung oder Legitimität. Die Monarchie in Europa im 19. und 20. Jahrhundert. Ein deutsch–englischer Vergleich* (Berlin, 2015), p. 23.

[44] Plunkett, *Queen Victoria*, pp. 13, 38–54; Johannes Paulmann, 'Peripatetische Herrschaft, Deutungskontrolle und Konsum. Zur Theatralität in der europäischen Politik vor 1914', in *Geschichte in Wissenschaft und Unterricht* 53 (2002), pp. 452–453; Schöbel, *Monarchie und Öffentlichkeit*, pp. 149–194.

this episode was evidence of the 'progressive spirit' that animated the Bavarian heir.[45]

Even when royal visitors kept their feet firmly on the ground, theatrical occasions, accompanied by all the ritual of cheering crowds and red carpets, provided rich material for favourable press reports. Foreign travels and royal gatherings were particularly well-suited to conveying to a newspaper-reading public back home that their mobile monarch was 'the personification of the prestige of the nation'. The symbiosis of monarchy and nationalism so characteristic of the second half of the nineteenth century was graphically evident in such moments. Frank-Lothar Kroll has proposed that the search for a comprehensive and integrative ideology that could provide a durable bond between the participation-seeking masses and the royal elites led to the nationalisation of the monarchy and thus also of the European royal families. The gradual process of identifying the monarchy with the nation built on the prior constitutionalisation of monarchical rule. Both projects unfolded within the public sphere.[46]

The visibility of the monarch – the second weapon in Victoria's media arsenal – was achieved through royal travels and at public appearances. It reached even further, though, since this immediate visibility was supplemented by a mediated visibility, conveyed especially by reports in newspapers and journals. This conspicuousness was greatly enhanced by the deliberate embrace of visual media such as photographs and other pictorial images. Here too Victoria's monarchy was a pioneer. As early as 1857, a photograph of the prince consort had been displayed at a public exhibition; the following year the London Photographic Society exhibited a group portrait that included the queen. Then, in August 1860, photographer John Edwin Mayall published his *Royal Album*, which comprised fourteen carte-de-visite photographs depicting Victoria, Albert and their three children. The album was an overwhelming commercial success. Within only a few days, more than 60,000 orders were placed. Sales of such images now boomed in Britain, with some 400 million cartes-de-visite bearing the image of famous individuals estimated to have been sold in the course of the 1860s. Photographs of the members of royal families were soon ubiquitous and highly cherished. A frequently related anecdote about Emperor Wilhelm I told of how, during a walk in Bad Ems, the elderly

---

[45] Paulmann, 'Peripatetische Herrschaft, Deutungskontrolle und Konsum', pp. 452–453; *Allgemeine Rundschau* of 15 October 1910, p. 738.
[46] Frank-Lothar Kroll, 'Zwischen europäischem Bewußtsein und nationaler Identität. Legitimationsstrategien monarchischer Eliten des 19. und frühen 20. Jahrhunderts', in Hans-Christof Kraus and Thomas Nicklas (eds.), *Geschichte der Politik. Alte und neue Wege* (Munich, 2007), pp. 359–361.

monarch encountered several young boys standing in front of a shop window, fighting over which photograph they should purchase with their meagre funds. At last the decision was made: 'Yes, yes, we will buy ourselves an emperor!' Thereupon the emperor insisted on treating each of the boys to his own 'emperor'. Soon, everyday items were carrying the royal countenance to mark special occasions, such as Queen Victoria's Golden Jubilee in 1887. It was a win–win situation for everyone involved: manufacturers could transfer the charisma of the monarch onto their products, while the crown reaped the benefits of a vast advertising campaign.[47]

The Victorian monarchy used its mobility and media-enabled visibility to occupy a much-coveted position in the limelight of public attention. It thus positioned itself exactly where, according to Walter Bagehot's famous analysis, it belonged: 'at the head of our morality'. 'We have come to believe', the British commentator observed in the 1860s 'that it is natural to have a virtuous sovereign, and that the domestic virtues are as likely to be found on thrones as they are eminent when there.' In Great Britain, where elections and parliamentary majorities greatly enhanced the significance of public opinion for the government, the means used by the crown to exert its influence necessarily had to change. The establishment of the monarchy as a moral force marked, as constitutional historian Vernon Bogdanor has noted, 'the transformation from power to influence'. With its authority thus enhanced, 'the sovereign came to be seen as head of the nation as well as head of state'.[48]

The British monarchy under Victoria and Albert threw itself into the task of ensuring that it was perceived and respected as a moral beacon for the nation. John Plunkett has described their method as 'civic publicness'; the historian Frank Prochaska writes of the highly visible construction of a 'welfare monarchy'. In line with this precept, Prince Albert regarded it as the duty of the monarchy to act as 'the headship of philanthropy'. Consequently, the crown publicly committed itself to a multitude of charitable, praiseworthy and honourable endeavours. With royal benevolence and Christian devotion, it dedicated itself assiduously and conspicuously to caring for the poor and the socially disadvantaged and

---

[47] Plunkett, *Queen Victoria*, pp. 144–198; Franziska Windt, 'Majestätische Bilderflut. Die Kaiser in der Photographie', in Generaldirektion der Stiftung Preußische Schlösser und Gärten Berlin-Brandenburg (ed.), *Die Kaiser und die Macht der Medien* (Berlin, 2005), pp. 67–77; Eva Giloi, *Monarchy, Myth, and Material Culture in Germany 1750–1950* (Cambridge, 2011), p. 242; Paulmann, 'Peripatetische Herrschaft, Deutungskontrolle und Konsum', pp. 455–456; Thomas Richards, *The Commodity Culture of Victorian England: Advertising and Spectacle, 1851–1914* (London, 1990), pp. 73–117.

[48] Walter Bagehot, *The English Constitution*, ed. Paul Smith (Cambridge, 2001), p. 46; Vernon Bogdanor, *The Monarchy and the Constitution* (Oxford, 1995), pp. 27, 36–37.

other worthy causes. Sanitation and economic improvements became areas of interest; visits were made to hospitals, universities and museums. With time, these efforts would bear fruit. 'Every clergyman, philanthropist and social reformer has had, these sixty-three years past, an ally and sympathiser on the throne of this country', preached Canon Herbert Henson on 27 January 1901 in Westminster Abbey on the death of the queen, 'We thank Almighty God for the gift of that gracious and serviceable life, we add to our national treasures the priceless jewel of a pure and lofty tradition bound about the ancient and famous English crown, and henceforth we connect *our civic duty* with a dear and honoured name.'[49]

A funeral sermon does not amount to evidence of how the institution of monarchy was perceived by the country at large, and we must recognise that the concept of the socially engaged monarchy could also be found elsewhere in Europe – for example in Prussia or France. Britain provides an outstanding example, though, of how a monarchy that realised it had been divested of the instruments of hard power could instead equip itself with a considerable measure of soft power, using a carefully crafted programme of public promotion. For, Plunkett summarised, even as the power of the Crown dwindled, Victoria's deft and dogged maintenance of her public image enabled the British queen to remain an 'overarching yet intimate figure' for all the nation.[50]

***

Hoping for similar results, numerous other European rulers followed in Queen Victoria's wake. They too set about securing their position with the tools of soft power, even in countries where the constitution still allowed the crown access to a broader range of instruments of hard power than was the case in Great Britain. In the autocratic Russian empire, where even a hesitant constitutionalisation emerged only in 1905, individual tsars in the nineteenth century sought to display 'an affectionate bond, based on benevolence and gratitude' and to connect the ruler to the people. The survival of the monarchical system was not

---

[49] Plunkett, *Queen Victoria*, pp. 13–67; Frank Prochaska, *Royal Bounty: The Making of a Welfare Monarchy* (New Haven, CT and London, 1995), pp. 67–135, quotations pp. 80, 135 (italics in the original); Frank Prochaska, 'The Crowned Republic and the Rise of the Welfare Monarchy', in Frank-Lothar Kroll and Dieter J. Weiß (eds.), *Inszenierung oder Legitimität. Die Monarchie in Europa im 19. und 20. Jahrhundert. Ein deutsch–englischer Vergleich* (Berlin, 2015), pp. 144–146; Volker Sellin, *Gewalt und Legitimität. Die europäische Monarchie im Zeitalter der Revolutionen* (Munich, 2011), pp. 241–261.

[50] Frank-Lothar Kroll, 'Die Idee eines sozialen Königtums im 19. Jahrhundert', in Frank-Lothar Kroll and Dieter J. Weiß (eds.), *Inszenierung oder Legitimität. Die Monarchie in Europa im 19. und 20. Jahrhundert. Ein deutsch–englischer Vergleich* (Berlin, 2015), pp. 111–140; Plunkett, *Queen Victoria*, p. 11.

simply a matter of defending what remained of monarchical power against the signs of the time. In 1895, Friedrich von Holstein warned that, if it were carelessly squandered, 'royal capital' would one day be painfully missed. It therefore fell to the monarchy, he noted, to increase this capital, which meant amplifying, popularising and utilising new political resources.[51]

To do so, royal dynasties needed to ride the strongest cultural and moral currents. If they did so successfully, the royal family could set the tone on significant issues and would make the most of their personal and institutional charisma. That leading role would then enhance their authority. That authority could be deployed to ensure that others wanted what they themselves wanted. Here was soft power in action.

'The King's Son Wins Their Trust and Their Devotion': Royal Heirs and the Instruments of Soft Power

When it comes to the monarchies' efforts to acquire soft power, heirs to the throne were of particular significance. For soft power, writes Joseph Nye, 'depends more than hard power on the existence of willing interpreters'. The crown sought to narrate a compelling story, which the next generation almost inevitably embodied. Royal heirs inherently directed attention to the future. As a rule, they were not included in the immediate exercise of royal power, and, as a result, these often still-young figures on whom future hopes were pinned could use the media of the political mass market to popularise monarchical rule, to demonstrate new relevance for an old institution and to supplement the ruler's instruments of power. The theatricalisation of politics in the nineteenth century might bring a romanticised twist to this tale. Such, at least, was the take of the Copenhagen newspaper *Illustreret Tidende* when in 1885 it described the tasks of a crown prince to its readers in the language of the fairy-tale: 'The king's son walks around amongst us in disguise; he slays the dragon of envy and of narrowmindedness; he shares the fate and circumstances of the people and wins their trust and their devotion.'[52]

---

[51] Richard S. Wortman, *Scenarios of Power: Myth and Ceremony in Russian Monarchy*, vol. 2 (Princeton, NJ, 2000), p. 13 (referring to 'Scenario of Love' by Tsar Alexander II); John C. G. Röhl (ed.), *Philipp Eulenburgs politische Korrespondenz*, vol. 2 (Boppard am Rhein, 1979), pp. 1440–1441.

[52] Nye, *Soft Power*, p. 16; Joseph S. Nye, 'The Infant Prince George Is a Source of Real-World Power', in *The Financial Times* of 24 July 2013, www.ft.com/content/0bd55672-f482-11e2-a62e-00144feabdc0 (accessed 1 June 2017); *Illustreret Tidende* of 6 September 1885. I am grateful to Miriam Schneider for directing me to the article in *Illustreret Tidende*. On the theme of royal heir and 'soft' power, see also Frank Lorenz Müller, '"Winning Their Trust and Affection": Royal Heirs and the Uses of Soft Power in

Such words may sound syrupy and somewhat fantastical, but they also indicate just how demanding and multifaceted the part was which future rulers would play in the constitutional monarchies of Europe during the nineteenth century, a role in which they had to shine. Those three central facets of the royal public image – visibility, mobility and 'civic publicness' – were also of decisive importance for heirs to the throne as they sought to acquire soft power and secure the future of the dynasty.

*

The need for heirs to be visible to their future subjects – as early as possible – was nothing new. In 1194, Constance of Hauteville, who was already aged forty, supposedly agreed to give birth to the future Emperor Friedrich II of Hohenstaufen (1194–1250) publicly – in a tent in the market square in the central Italian town of Jesi. It was her intention to dispel any doubts about her motherhood and the legitimacy of her son. While Princess Margherita of Savoy did not have to permit the public such intrusive access to her private sphere, parallels did exist. The Italian crown princess's decision to present her new-born son proudly to the market women of Naples makes evident that ensuring the visibility of the future heir was still thought politically astute. In the case of the later king of Italy, it was less a matter of avoiding doubts about his legitimacy than about fostering, via the natural appeal of a new-born child and his mother, an emotional bond with the House of Savoy, which was still an alien presence in southern Italy. Crown Prince Umberto and his wife, Margherita, were by no means the only heirs who presented their first-born so directly to the people. In the spring of 1859, several grenadier guardsmen were on their way from Potsdam to the village of Eiche when they encountered the Prussian crown prince, Friedrich Wilhelm, and his wife, Victoria, out for a walk with their four-month-old son, Wilhelm. On seeing the soldiers, the crown prince was said to have commanded them to halt and then to have taken the infant out of the pram and introduced him to the grenadiers, insisting that each man shake the tiny hand of the little boy. Friedrich Wilhelm then wished the delighted soldiers a good morning and sent them on their way.[53]

In both instances, future heirs to the throne – Vittorio Emanuele and Wilhelm – were displayed to the public while they were still infants, with the current heirs – Umberto and Margherita, Friedrich and Victoria – presenting

Nineteenth-Century Europe', in Frank Lorenz Müller and Heidi Mehrkens (eds.), *Royal Heirs and the Uses of Soft Power in Nineteenth-Century Europe* (London, 2016), pp. 1–19.

[53] Although the rumours that Constance had given birth in public seem likely to have been anti-Staufen propaganda: Hubert Houben, *Kaiser Friedrich II. (1194–1250). Herrscher, Mensch und Mythos* (Stuttgart, 2008), pp. 26–27; Maria Christina Marchi, 'Margherita'; B. Richter, *Kleine Episoden und Charakterzüge aus dem Leben unseres Kaisers Friedrich III.* (Reudnitz and Leipzig, 1888), p. 32.

themselves as proud, loving and genial parents eager to share their private happiness. This behaviour created the emotional connection on two levels still used by media-oriented monarchies today: even if the visibility of the infant heir could not be produced through direct contact – for example by shaking His Highness's tiny hand – the same effect could be communicated via images instead. In the nineteenth century, the childhood of heirs to the throne was richly pictured and displayed to the public even before the invention of photography.

The visual representation of the next generation was rarely pursued with such evident partisan political intent as in the case of Isabella II (1830–1904), who became queen of Spain aged just three, on the death of her father, Ferdinand VII (1784–1833). The right of the child queen to inherit the throne was challenged by her ultraconservative uncle Carlos de Borbón (1788–1853) and his supporters, eventually even with military means. The Carlists' liberal opponents responded by turning Isabella into a constitutional icon. Numerous carefully composed paintings, like the one shown in Figure 14, and printed images were distributed throughout the country as propaganda: they portrayed her as the 'girl of freedom' (*niña de la libertad*). As the angelic, peace-bringing patron of the constitution of 1837, the young Isabella appeared to be safeguarding the freedom of the nation, but the image also appealed to a natural instinct to protect this delicate creature and the dynastic future for which she stood from the wrongs being perpetrated by the Carlists.[54]

Before Isabella, another future constitutional queen had also been frequently depicted while still a child, and here too the context was political. Following the early death of Princess Charlotte (1796–1817), heiress to the English throne, the sons of George III, no longer in the first flush of youth themselves, took up the challenge of providing a legitimate heir. Duke Edward of Kent (1767–1820), little esteemed by his own family, emerged the victor from this eleventh-hour dynastic and procreational panic. In 1819 his wife, Victoire, whom he had married less than a year before, bore him a healthy daughter, Princess Victoria. Yet the Kents' relationship with the royal court remained tense and grew only worse after 1820, the year the duke died and his oldest brother ascended the throne after the death of their father, George III. Soon an unconcealed enmity raged between the new king, George IV (1762–1830), and the widowed duchess, who jealously watched over her daughter. The situation

---

[54] Richard Meyer Forsting, 'Isabel II: Niña de la libertad', AHRC Project *Heirs to the Throne in the Constitutional Monarchies of Nineteenth-Century Europe (1815–1914)*, 'Heir of the Month' (March 2014), http://heirstothethrone-project.net/?page_id=900 (accessed 22 June 2017).

Figure 14. Queen Isabella II, the fairy-like 'girl of liberty', promising Spain progress and a constitution, is at the centre of this painting by José Ribelles y Helip (1833). Alamy Images.

was little different under King William IV (1765–1837), who succeeded his brother in 1830. The duchess and her adviser, Sir John Conroy, kept Victoria away from the ill-reputed court, but did seek to ensure that the future monarch was known to the general public. The many portraits of the princess played their part, including paintings by Johann Georg Paul Fischer (1819), Sir William Beechey (1821), Stephen Poyntz Denning (1823), Henry Bone (1824), Thomas Williamson (c. 1825–1832), William James Ward (1825 – shown here as Figure 15), Alexandre-Jean Dubois Drahonet (1833) and Sir George Hayter (1833). 'Victoria's childhood face and figure', the historian Lynne Vallone has concluded, 'were not a mystery to her future subjects.' The princess's diaries make evident just how many hours she spent sitting for her portrait. To satisfy the curiosity of the public, the resulting images were then often reproduced as engravings. This wide dissemination served the intentions of the Duchess of Kent, for the many variations on the theme of youthful innocence

Figure 15. Sticking to a clever public relations policy, the Duchess of Kent succeeded in making the image of her daughter Victoria well known across Britain. The pure, young girl provided a pleasing contrast to the rule of her aged uncle. The princess's diary reveal how much time she spent sitting to have her portrait painted. Royal Collection Trust, www.royalcollection.org.uk/collection/search#/28/col lection/605587/queen-victoria-as-princess.

distinguished her daughter from her elderly and scandal-ridden ruler-uncles and held out hope of a better future.[55]

Prince Ferdinand Philippe, the oldest son of the French king Louis Philippe, died in 1842 as the result of an accident, aged just thirty-two. While he therefore did not live to see the dawn of the age of photography, his likeness was still disseminated and immortalised, in magnificent portraits by painters such as Louis-Joseph Noyal, Louis

---

[55] Karina Urbach, *Queen Victoria. Eine Biographie* (Munich, 2011), pp. 22–23; Lynne Vallone, *Becoming Victoria* (New Haven, CT and London, 2001), pp. 109–121.

Hersent, Jean-Auguste-Dominique Ingres and Horace Vernet. He was depicted as a child holding his mother's hand, as a young and dashing mounted officer or in the company of his father and his brother. Photography would not replace this older visual medium entirely, and indeed the painting of royal portraits experienced a late flourishing in the nineteenth century. The most sought-after painters of the era repeatedly reached for their palettes to capture the heirs to the throne. Franz Xaver Winterhalter painted Edward Albert, Prince of Wales, in 1846 as a sweet four-year-old; in 1849 along with his brother Alfred, when the boys were dressed in tartan and kilts; in 1859 when his subject sported the uniform of a Lieutenant-Colonel of the Guards; and in 1864 as colonel of the 10th Royal Hussars. Like the French and British heirs, the later German emperor Friedrich III tended to appear more traditional and more martial in his portraits than on photographs: thus a painting by Heinrich von Angeli from 1874 depicts the Hohenzollern prince wearing the gleaming breast plate of the Pasewalk Cuirassiers. In another work from that year, by Franz von Lenbach, Friedrich Wilhelm is sporting the same uniform but with the addition of a marshal's baton, which he is also holding in Gottlieb Biermann's portrait from 1888. In Anton von Werner's renowned painting *Emperor Friedrich as Crown Prince at the Court Ball 1878*, notable figures from the worlds of art, scholarship and politics surround the future ruler, who is wearing the dress uniform of his Cuirassiers regiment, with his left hand resting on the pommel of his ceremonial sword.[56]

Surveying royal group portraits from the period from the seventeenth to the nineteenth century, the historian Simon Schama has argued that members of the ruling dynasty were transformed 'from a clan of deities to a domestic parlour group'. He writes of a 'domestication of majesty', which emerged from greater convergence with the ideals of the bourgeois family.[57] While this tendency may be observable in group portraits, it is not uniformly present in individual portraits of royal heirs. When depicted as adults, future rulers continued to appear as royal figures, in stiff and feudal poses and bedecked in uniformed splendour. They clung to this old magic and used it alongside the technological innovation offered to them by photography. Its invention was a quantum leap for the visibility of heirs in the media and presented them with new and previously unimagined possibilities. Photographs could bring the marketplace in Naples and

---

[56] Müller, *Our Fritz*, pp. 113–114, 126–127.
[57] Simon Schama, 'The Domestication of Majesty: Royal Family Portraiture, 1650–1850', in *The Journal of Interdisciplinary History* 17 (1986), p. 155.

footpaths through the fields of Brandenburg, where the new-born ruler-to-be might be presented directly to the public, into millions of sitting rooms, picture frames and photograph albums. Generated by methods old and new, a 'flood of royal images' rained down in the nineteenth century and made the childhood and adolescence of the future monarchs visible to everyone everywhere.[58]

A certain haste was warranted when a recent birth provided the final piece of a four-generation portrait, a particularly popular image-type in which an ancient crowned head looks benevolently on three generations of direct successors. The first photograph of the future Crown Prince Wilhelm of Prussia and Germany (1882–1951) was taken on 7 May 1882, just one day after his birth. 'What a blessing and I an old man', the eighty-five-year-old Emperor Wilhelm I is said to have uttered as he sat in the park at the palace of Babelsberg and held his great-grandson on his lap, his son Crown Prince Friedrich Wilhelm on his right and Friedrich Wilhelm's son Prince Wilhelm on his left. All three eminent figures were dressed, of course, in military uniform. The future King Edward VIII (1894–1973) of Great Britain was already three weeks old when, on 16 July 1894, he was photographed at White Lodge in Richmond along with his great-grandmother Victoria, his grandfather Edward, Prince of Wales, and his father, Prince George. In Bavaria, Prince Regent Luitpold's seemingly indestructible health made it possible for the taking of the photograph entitled 'Four Generations of the Bavarian Ruling House' to be delayed until 1905, by which date Luitpold, the great-grandson of the eighty-four-year-old regent was already four. In Figure 16, the young boy, clad in white and wearing shorts, stands in front of his uniformed father, Prince Rupprecht, and his grandfather Prince Ludwig, while his hands rest on the knee of his seated great-grandfather Luitpold.[59]

These multi-generational images were particularly suited for generating goodwill towards the depicted dynasty. They provided evidence of the fecundity and continuity of the ruling house while also depicting the various generations in their obligatory roles: as a delightful child, as a proud father, grandfather, or great-grandfather or great-grandmother, and as a loyal son or grandson. The public visibility of heirs to the throne, carefully staged in photographs capturing each phase of their life, was characteristic of the age, while photography itself became a 'royal

[58] Windt, 'Majestätische Bilderflut'.

[59] Jörg Kirschstein, *KaiserKinder. Die Familie Wilhelms II. in Fotografien* (Göttingen, 2011), p. 38; www.rct.uk/collection/2105900/the-four-generations-white-lodge-richmond (accessed 23 June 2017); www.br.de/radio/bayern2/sendungen/bayerisches-feuilleton/vom-maerchenkoenig-zur-prinzregentenzeit-foerg100.html (accessed 23 June 2017).

Orig.-Aufn., Eigent. u.Verlag v. Fr. Müller, Hofphotograph, München 1905

VIER GENERATIONEN IM BAYRISCHEN HERRSCHERHAUSE

Figure 16. 'Four Generations of the Bavarian Royal House': like many other photographs of the genre, this postcard of 1905 was designed to illustrate the steady continuity of the Wittelsbach dynasty. The venerable Prince Regent Luitpold is genially looking down on his name-sake great-grandson, who was born eighty years after him. Author's private collection.

passion'. Members of the royal families of Europe were a sought-after motif, especially the heirs to the throne. They were photographed in all possible roles, garb and circumstances, as children, school pupils, students, bridegrooms, fathers, soldiers, speech-givers and sportsmen; with a hobbyhorse, mounted on horseback, at the wheel of an automobile; sometimes with stately bearing, sometimes relaxed and *en famille*. Otto May's investigation of the postcard as a medium in Wilhelmine Germany identified over 640 different depictions of the emperor, while a collection analysed by Anja Schöbel contains more than 2,400 postcards of the imperial family, 762 of the Bavarian royal family and almost 500 of Saxon royalty. Even the more manageable collection for the duchy of Saxe-Coburg and Gotha contains 187 different motifs. For Britain, John Plunkett has established the number of photographs for which the subject held a personal copyright. For the period 1862 to 1901, the heir to the throne and his wife, Alexandra, led the field, with over 600 different photographs each. With more than 400 photographs, Queen Victoria is only in fourth place – behind the actress Ellen Terry. Prince Albert Victor and Prince George, the sons of the heir to the throne, together have more than 400 images. Eight members of the royal family are amongst the top twenty. Even today thousands of contemporary picture postcards are still for sale online, evidence of just how common this medium became.[60]

Photographs, lithographs and engravings of future rulers, carefully composed and designed to engender affection for the dynasty, were everywhere. In November 1905, the newly elected but not yet inaugurated king of Norway, King Haakon VII (1872–1957), sailed to his new kingdom onboard the battleship *Heimdal*. When he was received on the quayside by Minister of State Christian Michelsen, the young king was carrying his two-year-old son, the future King Olav V (1903–1991), highly visible in a long white shawl. 'It was an affecting image', the press reported the scene depicted in Figure 17. 'The king stood with the small, bright crown prince in his arms looking like a little Norwegian boy.'[61]

The Prussian heir Friedrich Wilhelm had himself photographed not just in a similar mode – as a loving father surrounded by his many children – but also, somewhat surprisingly for a Prussian, as a hearty Alpine mountaineer, dressed in traditional Bavarian costume, including lederhosen and tufted hat, against a painted mountain panorama. While still young, the future King Vittorio Emanuele III of Italy often appeared in photographs along with this mother, Queen Margherita, in a pose that echoed the traditional depiction of the Virgin and child; subsequently he was usually dressed in the uniform of one of his various military ranks. Court photographer Ludwig Angerer

---

[60] Anne M. Lyden, *A Royal Passion: Queen Victoria and Photography* (Los Angeles, CA, 2014); Otto May, *Deutsch sein heißt treu sein. Ansichtskarten als Spiegel von Mentalität und Untertanenerziehung in der Wilhelminischen Ära (1888–1918)* (Hildesheim, 1998); Schöbel, *Monarchie und Öffentlichkeit*, pp. 261–290; Plunkett, *Queen Victoria*, p. 157.
[61] Odd Holaas, *Norge under Haakon VII, 1905–1945* (Oslo, 1976), p. 10.

Figure 17. When the newly elected King Haakon VII stepped onto Norwegian soil to be welcomed by ministers in 1905, he carried – visible to all – his son in his arms. Photo: Jens C. F. Hilfling Rasmussen. The Royal Collection, Oslo.

captured the five-year-old Crown Prince Rudolf sitting on a chair with his cat Tomi; the crown prince is wearing the cap of his regiment, the 19th Infantry. Two years later, while the young boy was on a hunting trip with his father, Emperor Franz Joseph, Angerer photographed the crown prince against the backdrop of the Dachstein mountains. In March 1880, the Brothers Géruzet's studio in Brussels published Rudolf's engagement photograph in cabinet-card format. The young prince, wearing uniform, appears alongside his bride, Princess Stephanie of Belgium, who is dressed entirely in white. A similar engagement photograph taken in 1868 had conveyed the Danish Crown Prince Frederik's intention to wed Princess Lovisa of Sweden.[62]

The British royal family, and especially the heir to the throne, Bertie, and his wife, Alexandra (1844–1925), proved remarkably skilful when it came to visual media. The Princess of Wales's command of style and knowledge of fashion left a particular mark that was first evident on the numerous photographs taken by the renowned Belgian photographer

[62] Müller, *Our Fritz*, pp. 148–149; over 800 carefully catalogued images of Crown Prince Rudolf can be found at https://onb.wg.picturemaxx.com (accessed 23 June 2017).

Louis Ghémar on the occasion of the couple's engagement in 1862. It subsequently shone through the wedding photographs by the British photographer John Mayall. As a true media celebrity, Princess Alexandra was able to launch a good number of fashion trends, but depictions of her irreproachable behaviour and loving motherliness also made up for her husband's tendency for scandalous faux-pas. The wife of the heir to the throne was at the top of the list composed by John Plunkett, ahead of even her husband. Figure 18, her most successful *carte*

Figure 18. The dawning of the media age turned royal heirs into celebrities. More than 300,000 copies were sold of this photograph of Princess Alexandra carrying one of her children on her back. Royal Collection Trust/© Her Majesty Queen Elizabeth II 2018.

photograph, an apparently informal picture in which she is carrying one of her children on her back, sold more than 300,000 copies.[63]

*

The intimacy and approachability conveyed by the ostensibly authentic, unmediated photographs were reinforced by the camera's ability to depict and document royal mobility. In effect, everyone could now accompany royalty at close quarters. In July 1862, interested members of the public could visit an exhibition in London's Bond Street to view more than 170 images that the photographer Francis Bedford had taken several months earlier while accompanying the Prince of Wales during a trip to the Middle East. They included a number of carefully staged pictures of the heir to the throne: sitting on a camel next to the Pyramids, standing with tour guides in front of a ruined temple in Karnak, resting under a fig tree on the shores of the Sea of Galilee and sporting a fez. The images were sold individually, but especially eager subjects might buy the complete 172-part set. Pictures of Albert Edward's visit to India in 1875–1876 were also available for purchase, including one entitled 'The Prince's First Tiger' – complete with hunting party, rifles and a very dead big cat.[64]

Extensive travels, with an intensive media presence, were entirely standard for European heirs in the second half of the nineteenth century, and not just for those who, like the future king of Great Britain and emperor of India, would one day rule over a colonial empire. Aristocratic travels were an extension of the tradition of the grand tour and other educational excursions of the Ancien Régime. During these trips, young noblemen had gathered impressions, experiences and know-ledge that they were to put to use in their future careers as military officers, officials or diplomats. While there was a continued emphasis on the educational character of such travels, the weight had now shifted: as a tourist, the heir to the throne was now a highly effective advertisement and his travels had become 'an official act' (*Staatsakt*), as cultural soci-ologist Justin Stagl has observed. The arresting images and exciting accounts that appeared in the press not only served as evidence of the royal heir's cosmopolitanism, physical prowess and international

[63] More than 1,500 images of Princess/Queen Alexandra can be found at www.rct.uk (accessed 23 June 2017); Plunkett, *Queen Victoria*, p. 157; Imke Polland, 'How to Fashion the Popularity of the British Monarchy: Alexandra, Princess of Wales and the Attraction of Attire', in Frank Lorenz Müller and Heidi Mehrkens (eds.), *Royal Heirs and the Uses of Soft Power in Nineteenth-Century Europe* (London, 2016), pp. 201–221.

[64] Sophie Gordon, 'Travels with a Camera: The Prince of Wales, Photography and the Mobile Court', in Frank Lorenz Müller and Heidi Mehrkens (eds.), *Sons and Heirs: Succession and Political Culture in Nineteenth-Century Europe* (Basingstoke, 2016), pp. 92–108.

reputation but also satisfied the reading public's growing fascination with other worlds and its desire for entertaining tales of adventure. In this respect, the heirs to the throne were similar to their younger brothers and cousins who delivered a worldwide presence when deployed in the service of the dynasty as 'sailor princes'. Hardly a single European ruling house in nineteenth-century Europe failed to provide a carefully scripted part for a princely naval officer whose professional competence, patriotic fearlessness and global mobility portrayed the relevant monarchy in a highly advantageous light.[65]

With the exception of Princes Eddy and George, whose widely publicised tour on board the corvette *HMS Bacchante* took them around the world, crown princes did not go to sea, for they were considered too indispensable to be allowed to sail the oceans for months at a time. However, long-distance journeys undertaken by heirs to the throne were a tried-and-tested tool of monarchical image-making. As an army officer, the French heir to the throne Ferdinand Philippe had been involved in lengthy campaigns in North Africa as early as the 1830s. Between 1854 and 1865 the future Belgian king Leopold II (1835–1909) travelled to India, China, Egypt and the Near East, and he subsequently gave numerous speeches before the Belgian senate on the trading opportunities and possibilities for colonial policies that he had identified on the ground. The first time Bertie represented his mother in the affairs of state on a significant scale was in summer 1860, when the British heir travelled to North America; public interest in his visit to Canada and the USA ran extremely high. Subsequently he visited the Middle East and journeyed as far as India. The Prince of Wales set new standards with his visit to the subcontinent in 1875–1876, when he was accompanied by the renowned journalist W. H. Russell of the London *Times*. He performed royalty against an Oriental backdrop and turned his visit into a magnificent historical event. In 1905–1906 and 1921–1922, respectively, his son George and his grandson Edward would each follow in his father's footsteps and undertake equally splendid trips to India.[66]

[65] Justin Stagl, 'Einleitung', in Justin Stagl (ed.), *Ein Erzherzog reist. Beiträge zur Weltreise Franz Ferdinands* (Salzburg, 2001), p. 3; Miriam Schneider, *The 'Sailor Prince' in the Age of Empire: Creating a Monarchical Brand in Nineteenth-Century Europe* (London, 2017).

[66] Georges-Henri Dumont, *Léopold II* (Paris, 1990), pp. 64–90; Ian Radforth, *Royal Spectacle: The 1860 Visit of the Prince of Wales to Canada and the United States* (Toronto, 2004); Ridley, *Bertie*, pp. 174–180; Milinda Banerjee, 'Ocular Sovereignty, Acclamatory Rulership and Political Communication: Visits of Princes of Wales to Bengal', in Frank Lorenz Müller and Heidi Mehrkens (eds.), *Royal Heirs and the Uses of Soft Power in Nineteenth-Century Europe* (London, 2016), pp. 81–100; Chandrika Kaul, 'Monarchical Display and the Politics of Empire: Princes of Wales and India 1870–1920s', in *Twentieth Century British History* 17, 4 (2006), pp. 464–488.

The Prussian crown prince Friedrich Wilhelm represented his father in 1869 at the pomp-filled opening of the Suez Canal. The royal heir used the occasion for an elaborate tour through Italy, Greece, the Levant and the Holy Land and then on to Egypt. His festive entry into Jerusalem formed a highpoint of his journey: with gleaming medals on his chest and mounted on a magnificent white charger, the Hohenzollern prince rode through the Damascus Gate and on to the Church of the Holy Sepulchre. The moment left such a lasting impression on him that in the 1870s he commissioned Wilhelm Gentz to paint a monumental depiction of the scene. The huge canvas was exhibited in the National Gallery in Berlin in December 1876, attracting widespread acclaim. Later travels by the German crown prince also generated commemoration-worthy moments. His visit to the new Italian royal couple Umberto and Margherita in 1878 yielded a scene described extensively in the *Volksblatt*, a German weekly: 'The king appeared on the balcony with his wife to the cheers of the many thousand voices of those present. After a while the two withdrew. Once more calls could be heard for them to appear again. Now the German crown prince also came out, took the young son of the king in his arms, embraced him, kissed him and showed him to the people. Who can possibly describe the rejoicing that now broke out amongst the Roman people? It was such an entrancing appearance that it was long talked about and reported in newspapers. The successor to the German imperial throne, who is so at ease amongst his own flourishing swarm of children, hugs Italy's crown prince and shows him to the people! Truly a beautiful picture to paint.'[67]

Ten years later the boy on the balcony had become a young man who undertook his own extensive travels each summer, with the future King Vittorio Emanuele III visiting Russia, Syria, Egypt, the Ottoman Empire and Palestine. The Saxon royal heir, who would rule as King Friedrich August III from 1904, proved similarly eager to travel. Having already visited the Habsburg Monarchy, Germany and Great Britain, the Wettin prince set off in October 1889 on a journey lasting several months. His travels would take him via Venice, Palermo, Barcelona, Cadiz, Madrid, Tangiers, Malta, Cairo, Jerusalem, Damascus, Smyrna and Athens to Istanbul and Bucharest. In 1906, a sympathetic biographer of the new king rhapsodised that the fruits of this journey 'one day will redound to the well-being and blessing of the Saxon people'.[68]

---

[67] Müller, *Our Fritz*, pp. 111–112; *Volksblatt*, no. 8, 1878, pp. 57–58, https://de .wikisource.org/wiki/K%C3%B6nig_Humbert_von_Italien_und_seine_Gemahlin (accessed 29 June 2017).

[68] Valentina Villa, 'An Italian Heir for the New Century: Vittorio Emanuele, Prince of Naples', in Frank Lorenz Müller and Heidi Mehrkens (eds.), *Sons and Heirs: Succession and Political Culture in Nineteenth-Century Europe* (Basingstoke, 2016), p. 165; W. von

Even the least winsome of European royal heirs travelled, accompanied by a virtual public. The world tour undertaken in 1892–1893 by Archduke Franz Ferdinand of Austria covered 33,000 kilometres and took him to India, Java, Australia, Japan, Canada and the USA. As the enterprise had been declared a scientific expedition, Franz Ferdinand was accompanied not just by members of his official household, several cooks and the photographer Eduard Hodek, but also by several natural scientists. During his travels, the royal heir threw himself into killing, with characteristic accuracy of shot, a great number of exotic creatures. In India alone, he bagged seven tigers (one of them is shown in Figure 19),

Figure 19. The press kept the public well informed about Archduke Franz Ferdinand's tour around the world in 1893. The heir to the throne was sometimes presented as a champion big-game hunter, whose marksmanship was such that his personal taxidermist had his hands full. In his travel diary, Franz Ferdinand always made sure to refer to his deep love for his Austrian homeland. Bildarchiv Austria.

Metzsch, *Friedrich August III. König von Sachsen. Ein Lebensbild* (Berlin, 1906), pp. 64–81; Hauptstaatsarchiv Dresden, MfÄ, 9295.

five panthers, three elephants and more than 1,300 other animals. The taxidermist, who had been included in the party for good reason, must have had his hands full.

During the ten-month journey, the wider public was kept well informed about the imperial heir's exploits by the *Neue Freie Presse* in Vienna, and also by other news outlets. An even more extensive account was provided by the two-volume, richly illustrated travel diary based on the archduke's personal notes that was published in 1895–1896. It contained information about the countries visited and endless descriptions of the archduke's hunting feats, but its pages also contained numerous affecting references to his homesickness and his attachment to the beautiful landscape of his homeland.[69]

The overseas travels of the European heirs provided spectacular evidence of the mobility of the monarchies and also produced a wealth of pictures and stories from distant lands to delight the public. During their travels, future rulers could actively engage in what might be termed public diplomacy. They supported efforts to improve the image of the home country, not just as viewed by the government of the host country but also in the eyes of its people. Erik Goldstein identifies such visits by 'royal ambassadors' as a classic example of how soft power might be exercised. They offered, he proposes, an opportunity to improve relations via the attention and publicity that they generated. Additional diplomatic work also fell to royal heirs when they represented ageing monarchs who could no longer be expected to undertake arduous journeys. In 1887, for example, Crown Prince Friedrich Wilhelm travelled to London to represent Emperor Wilhelm I at the celebrations marking Queen Victoria's Golden Jubilee, while for her Diamond Jubilee ten years later, Prince Friedrich August represented the Kingdom of Saxony and Archduke Franz Ferdinand the Austrian imperial house, as neither King Albert nor Emperor Franz Joseph wished to embark on a journey to faraway London. At the coronation of Tsar Nicolaus II in 1896, the heirs to the thrones of Great Britain, Italy and Bavaria each represented the relevant sovereign.[70]

The mobile younger generation thus made a significant contribution to the theatrical diplomatic culture of nineteenth-century Europe, which the historian Johannes Paulman has examined through the lens of the many

[69] Jean-Paul Bled, *Franz Ferdinand. Der eigensinnige Thronfolger* (Vienna, 2013), pp. 58–64; Hannig, *Franz Ferdinand*, pp. 33–49.

[70] Nancy Snow and Philip Taylor (eds.), *Routledge Handbook of Public Diplomacy* (London, 2009); Erik Goldstein, 'Royal Ambassadors: Monarchical Public Diplomacy and the United States', in Frank Lorenz Müller and Heidi Mehrkens (eds.), *Royal Heirs and the Uses of Soft Power in Nineteenth-Century Europe* (London, 2016), p. 64.

instances when Europe's crowned heads came together. For the period from 1814 to 1914, he identified more than 220 increasingly grandiose gatherings and demonstrated that the involvement of the broader public was not only desired by the official authorities but also expected by the bourgeoisie. A diary entry by the American journalist R. D. Blumenfeld, who was present in London to witness the jubilee celebrations of 1887, illustrated that even actors on this stage who were not ruling monarchs could catch the audience's eye: 'I thought the German Crown Prince [Emperor Friedrich], in his silver helmet and shining cuirass, the most striking figure in the procession.'[71]

World tours, jubilees and coronations were exceptional moments showcasing monarchical mobility and visibility. They took place alongside less extraordinary opportunities for royal heirs to demonstrate their accessibility to the people in their own country. While their common touch and amiability were on display at these more routine events, the monarchical aura that surrounded them created a mystical soft power that secured the trust and devotion of the people. The young Princess Victoria stands as an example. In her efforts to render the young girl the 'hope of the nation', her mother did not stop at the distribution of her daughter's image but also purposefully deployed her mobility, by arranging for Victoria to travel systematically throughout her future kingdom. Between 1830 and 1835, the young princess undertook carefully planned annual trips through England and Wales and was greeted enthusiastically everywhere. She would receive the veneration of local dignitaries and listen to recitations of previously commissioned attestations of loyalty. The political impetus behind the enterprise was all too evident to King William IV, who sought to have these tours halted. Lady Elizabeth Belgrave, a friend of Victoria's mother, was unequivocal when it came to their purpose: 'under the semblance of a quiet journey, making the Princess known and securing friends for after times'. As these friends were to come from all levels of society, her travels took Victoria not just to the landed estates of the nobility, but also to factories (such as the cotton mill in Belper in Derbyshire), slate mines, prisons and folk festivals. Over the course of several years, Victoria criss-crossed the country. Flowers were strewn in her path; local versifiers composed poems in her honour: 'Victoria comes – our Britain's hope, / To view the ancient Towers', ran the text in Oxford; spectators thronged the streets. No one was to leave unsatisfied. When the crowds in Leamington were unable to make out the

---

[71] Johannes Paulmann, *Pomp und Politik. Monarchenbegegnungen in Europa zwischen Ancien Régime und Erstem Weltkrieg* (Paderborn, 2000), pp. 413, 421; R. D. Blumenfeld, *R. D. B.'s Diary 1887–1914* (London, 1930), p. 2.

petite princess at her hotel window, her mother promptly placed Victoria on a footstool and Sir John Conroy lit the scene with two candles.[72]

The charm of royal children was similarly capitalised upon to advertise the monarchy throughout Italy. In autumn 1861, Crown Prince Umberto, aged seventeen, and his younger brothers Amedeo and Oddone, the sons of King Vittorio Emanuele II, travelled through the northern provinces. This territory had only shortly before been annexed by Piedmont-Sardinia and incorporated into the united Kingdom of Italy. Their presence had two purposes: the princes should become acquainted with lands still foreign to them but now ruled by their family, and the populations of those lands should be transformed into loyal subjects of the Savoyard dynasty. Travelling by train, the royal party visited forty towns within a month, including Pisa, Florence, Rimini, Brescia, La Spezia and Pavia. They met provincial dignitaries, listened to music performed by local bands, waved to enthusiastic crowds and took the salute at parades. Expert guides led them through historic buildings. Then, in the spring of 1862, it was the turn of the south of Italy. This time the party travelled by steamship to Sardinia and Sicily as well as to the area around Naples. The experiment of the previous year was now expanded to include the bestowing of cash prizes and alms. According to contemporary newspaper reports, this second trip was a great success. Wherever they went, the princes were greeted along the bedecked streets with great shouts of *Evviva*. Seven years later, Prince Umberto would provide further evidence of the mobility of his royal house, when, freshly married, he and his wife, Margherita, returned to Naples. The future ruler of united Italy took up residence in the former capital of the Bourbon Kingdom of the Two Sicilies, where in 1869 their son, the future King Vittorio Emanuele III, was born.[73]

The Swedish–Norwegian Bernadottes also dispatched mobile royal heirs in an effort to win over potentially reticent sections of the population. The union of the kingdoms of Sweden and Norway, formed in 1814, involved little more than both countries being ruled by a single royal house, that of the former French marshal Jean Baptiste Bernadotte. He had been elected heir-presumptive of Sweden in 1810 and, from 1818, ruled as King Carl XIV Johan of Sweden and King Carl III Johan of Norway. Although this foreign dynasty focused on its Swedish kingdom, there was no doubt in Stockholm about the urgent need to develop

---

[72] Urbach, *Queen Victoria*, pp. 24–25; Kate Williams, *Becoming Queen* (London, 2009), pp. 162, 213; Vallone, *Becoming Victoria*, pp. 76, 90–91.

[73] Maria-Christina Marchi, 'Princes on the Road', AHRC Project *Heirs to the Throne in the Constitutional Monarchies of Nineteenth-Century Europe (1815–1914)*, 'Heir of the Month' (May 2015), http://heirstothethrone-project.net/?page_id=1548 (accessed 30 June 2017).

a Norwegian identity too. Successive generations of the royal family would spend time in Norway in order to become familiar with the land and its people and with its language and culture. Crown Prince Oscar (1799–1859) was followed by his sons Carl (1826–1872) and Oscar (1829–1907), his grandson Gustaf (1858–1950) and finally his great-grandson Gustaf Adolf (1882–1973). The goal was to acquire what the historian Trond Norén Isaksen identified as 'the power of presence', whose potency was such that the extremely fragile union of the two lands held until 1905.[74]

Crown Prince Oscar, who learned Norwegian as soon as his father had come to power, first resided as viceroy in Christiania (Kristiania from 1877; Oslo since 1925) in 1824 and then again for several months seven years later. He also travelled to Bergen and along the west coast of Norway. When his oldest son, Prince Carl, held office as viceroy for thirteen months in the mid 1850s, he brought his family with him to the Norwegian capital and travelled through the south of the country. Carl, who succeeded King Oscar I in 1859 as Carl XV, remained childless after the death of his son. His younger brother, Prince Oscar, therefore took on the task of representing the dynasty in Norway and of acquiring soft power. Oscar travelled to remote areas in western Norway such as Romsdal and Sogn, served on Norwegian ships, gave speeches in Norwegian and ensured that his son Gustaf had a Norwegian education. When, in 1872, he succeeded his brother on the throne as Oscar II, it seemed, he recorded in his memoirs, as if he were more beloved in Norway than in Sweden. In order to secure his position further, he travelled to the North Cape in the summer of 1873 before his coronation in Trondheim. Through these journeys, reported the *Aftenposten* newspaper in July 1873, the king had won the hearts of his subjects.

In hindsight, however, this moment was evidently the swansong of the Swedish–Norwegian union. Although Oscar's oldest son, Crown Prince Gustaf, and grandson Gustaf Adolf both studied in the Norwegian capital, the disputes between the two countries continued to grow. Finally, Oscar's descendants' much censured reluctance to reside in Norway was the catalyst for the dissolution of the shared dynastic ties that had bound the two kingdoms together for more than ninety years. Yet the Norwegian people had not lost their faith in the idea of monarchy. While Norway went the way of independence, it did so under its own king, Haakon VII, a Danish prince, sanctioned by a plebiscite and a vote in parliament. As

---

[74] This passage is based on analysis of Trond Norén Isaksen, 'The Power of Presence: Crafting a Norwegian Identity for the Bernadotte Heirs', in Frank Lorenz Müller and Heidi Mehrkens (eds.), *Royal Heirs and the Uses of Soft Power in Nineteenth-Century Europe* (London, 2016), pp. 103–121.

we would expect, this new monarch immediately set about being mobile, visible and present. For the coronation, the royal couple travelled to Trondheim by train, carriage and ship, making numerous stops along the way to meet their subjects. The following year, King Haakon and Queen Maud continued their coronation tour, travelling through the northern regions of their kingdom.[75]

Strategic travels within one's own sphere of influence – young Victoria's journeys by carriage, the Savoy princes' tours by train and boat, the Bernadotte heirs' stays in Norway – were significant steps on the path to building up soft power. Below the level of these staged trips, monarchical mobility and visibility were conveyed in a multiplicity of seemingly humdrum ways, intended to awaken a sense of inevitability. As pupils, students, soldiers, parliamentarians or patrons, but also on 'private' occasions, royal heirs in nineteenth-century Europe presented themselves to their future subjects publicly and seemingly routinely. In repeatedly mingling with their subjects, the future monarchs demonstrated a trust-inspiring relatability.

This happened in a variety of ways. Beginning with Prince Ferdinand Philippe d'Orléans, who attended the Collège Henri IV secondary school in Paris as early as 1819, and continuing on to Crown Prince Rupprecht of Bavaria, who attended the Maximiliansgymnasium in Munich from 1882, increasing numbers of royal heirs left the sheltered world of the court to receive instruction at public schools, universities and military academies. The later King Ludwig III of Bavaria could be spotted on the Marienplatz, the central square in Munich, not only as a young guardsman but also as a student making his way on foot to the Ludwig-Maximilian University. During his time as a student at Oxford, Edward, Prince of Wales, was photographed by the paparazzi cheering on his college's rowers. Crown Prince Wilhelm of Prussia visited the Berlin Christmas market with his wife to buy presents for their children, and Prince Wilhelm of Württemberg demonstratively strolled through the shops of Stuttgart with his second wife in order to dispel rumours of a crisis in their marriage. Crown Prince Friedrich August of Saxony hiked with his children in the countryside around Dresden and often called in on cafés frequented by fellow ramblers. The future King Vittorio Emanuele III of Italy accompanied his father, Umberto, throughout the land when he visited the troops or attended manoeuvres. During the Olympic Games in Athens in 1896, Crown Prince Konstantínos of Greece (1868–1923) found it impossible to remain seated when the

---

[75] www.royalcourt.no/artikkel.html?tid=28678&sek=28571 (accessed 2 July 2017); Tim Greve, *Haakon VII. Menneske og monark* (Oslo, 1980), pp. 104–126.

Greek shepherd Spyridon Louis approached the finish line in the marathon in first place; with his brother Prince Geórgios he stormed onto the home straight, ran the final metres alongside the exhausted athlete and then hoisted him up onto his shoulders.

Virtually omnipresent and set on convincing a broader public that they cut a fine figure abroad and were benevolent and friendly towards future subjects at home, royal heirs supplied plentiful material for exhilarating newspaper reports, vivid images and numerous oft-repeated anecdotes. They thus fulfilled what Walter Bagehot had defined as the central function of the royal family at the head of a monarchical system; they brought 'down the pride of sovereignty to the level of petty life'. In doing so, they acquired soft power and contributed to the peripatetic rule that was typical of the age.[76]

*

No heir to the throne provided his land with a more luminous model of virtuous conduct than did the Prussian–German Crown Prince Friedrich Wilhelm. Such was certainly the view of the *Berliner Tageblatt*, expressed in a paean composed in October 1881 to celebrate the crown prince's fiftieth birthday: 'Always in the vanguard in providing a home amongst us for what is true, good and beautiful for the sake of the wellbeing of our common community, the crown prince is for us all a symbol of that humble and yet so assiduous activity that always puts one's self last.' The fact that the *Berliner Tageblatt* – and many other newspapers too – used this significant birthday as an opportunity to report extensively on the great virtue of the heir suggests that, however pronounced Friedrich Wilhelm's humility, he was not one to hide the light of his accomplishments under a bushel. Through skilful engagement of the press and well-judged public appearances, the prince had acquired an image that ensured he appeared to the public at the 'head of our morality'. In seeking to serve nation and society as a beacon of moral behaviour that cast its light forward, into the future, the royal heirs helped mould the relationship between monarch and people, 'The prince closest to the throne', commented the *Allgemeine Zeitung* in January 1905, with an eye to the Bavarian heir, bears the responsibility 'above all, to lead his fellow citizens, lighting the way in fulfilling all the particular duties that make up the citizen, and thus multiply within the best people within the land, who along with its rulers look conscientiously beyond the present and into the future, the joy of dedicating oneself to one's country'.[77]

---

[76] Bagehot, *The English Constitution*, p. 37.
[77] *Berliner Tageblatt* of 18 October 1881; *Allgemeine Zeitung* of 7 January 1905.

Royal heirs had to prove themselves in five areas: promotion of a national identity, culture and learning, philanthropy, military prowess and familial virtues. To play the role of father or mother of the nation convincingly, they, along with their spouses and their offspring, had to appear as the model family, composed of a devoted husband and dedicated wife who were the loving parents of well-brought-up children. Skilful public relations and showmanship ensured that such was the impression – even if it did not match the reality – received by the public. King Haakon VII of Norway and the German Crown Prince Friedrich Wilhelm, Princess Margherita of Italy and Prince Wilhelm of Württemberg, Princess Alexandra of Wales and even Crown Prince Friedrich August of Saxony, whose wife had left him, they all, and many others besides, understood how to present their familial virtues to the public and thus justify the exalted position of their monarchy's first family. A prince who served as a model for the people added to the lustre of his country. Prince Ludwig, praised the *Bayern-Kurier* in January 1895, had created a family life 'that has been blessed by heaven for more than twenty-five years, that appears transfigured by the extraordinary enchantment of true German domesticity and is widely praised as a luminous model for every German home, for every German hearth'.[78]

King Ludwig III, as the prince would become, would be married for almost fifty-one years and have twelve surviving children. In addition to his familial role, Ludwig also took on the part of the impeccable patriot, the epitome of a dynasty whose roots in the land and its people reached back through the centuries, the embodiment of their values and traditions. He deftly embraced the strategy whereby the monarchy became the nation. 'I and my people feel ourselves to be as one', he stated in 1897 at a gathering of Bavarian farmers, quoting the late King Ludwig II to explain why in Bavaria there was no need for the close bond between prince and people to be specially fêted. 'If a people and its princely house have stood together without interruption for 700 years and the princely house itself was a product of the people, and if the people have on occasion spilled their blood in that cause and the dynasty also acknowledges that it must defend the people when necessary, then, I say, one does not need such celebrations.' Land and ruler were inseparable; it could not be otherwise. In 1891, after he had given a speech in Nuremberg, Prince Ludwig proposed a toast 'to the land with which I am bound together with every fibre of all my life, to our much-loved Bavaria!' This self-representation was warmly echoed in the well-disposed press. 'As this honourable royal dynasty that is firmly rooted in

[78] *Bayern-Kurier* of 7 January 1895.

the Bavarian land and people has grown so intimate and close to its subjects', declared the *Bayern-Kurier* on the prince's fiftieth birthday, the 'longstanding Bavarian love for the House of Wittelsbach' would 'send forth new blooms'.[79]

Prince Ludwig was not alone amongst his peers in serving as a figurehead of the patriotic and loyalist movement within his country. As the standard bearer of 'Orangism', Prince Willem of Orange (1792–1849), the later King Willem II, upheld the traditions and interests of his dynasty but also promoted an all-Netherlands patriotism. At stake was the cohesion of the United Kingdom of the Netherlands, founded in 1814. The charismatic Prince Willem, a decorated soldier who seemed tolerant of Catholicism yet was also liberally inclined, managed to preserve the support of his subjects in the ancestral northern provinces while also acquiring the sympathies of the citizens of the southern Belgian territory within the kingdom. Prince Alfonso (1857–1885), the Bourbon heir to the Spanish crown who would rule as King Alfonso XII from 1875, also claimed to speak for the values and aspirations of the whole nation. In December 1874, he published his 'Sandhurst Manifesto', in which he addressed his fellow Spaniards ahead of his return from exile to lay the ground for the restoration of his dynasty. Alfonso declared himself ready to take on 'the difficult task of re-introducing lawful order and political freedom into our honourable nation' and termed himself the 'sole representative of monarchical rights in Spain'. He ended with the promise that he would never cease to be 'a good Spaniard or – as were all my forebears – a good Catholic, or – as a man of my own age – truly liberal'.[80]

By cloaking themselves in the supposedly ancient traditions of their dynasties that bound people and ruler to one another, Prince Ludwig of Bavaria, Prince Wilhelm of Orange and Prince Alfonso of Bourbon were donning the garb of the patriot. Crown Prince Konstantínos of Greece had to reach far more deeply into the public relations box of tricks. For one thing, the Danish–German dynasty of Schleswig-Holstein-Sonderburg-Glücksburg had ascended the Greek throne only as recently as 1863. Elected by the Greek national assembly and backed by the European Great Powers, Konstantínos's father, Geórgios I, King of the Hellenes (1845–1913), was primarily concerned with foreign policy

---

[79] J. M. Forster, *Prinz Ludwig von Bayern. Biographie und Reden Sr. Königl. Hoheit des Prinzen Ludwigs von Bayern* (Munich, 1897), pp. 112–113; *Münchner Neueste Nachrichten* of 13 March 1891; *Bayern-Kurier* of 7 January 1895.

[80] Koch, 'The King as Father, Orangism and the Uses of a Hero', pp. 270–274; *La America* (Madrid) of 28 December 1874, pp. 3–4, http://heirstothethrone-project.net/wp-content /uploads/2014/05/Manifesto-in-print.pdf (accessed 5 July 2017).

issues, and it fell to his son to make the imported ruling house popular within Greece. Konstantínos had been prepared for this task since earliest childhood: he had been instructed in the Greek Orthodox faith, his teachers were Greek and he had mastered the national language. Thus armed, the crown prince sought to deploy a mix of cultural politics and public diplomacy in an attempt to shape the general discourse about the national identity of the Greek kingdom. He looked deliberately to the ancient world, building on the definition provided by those classical foundations. He campaigned to stage the Olympic Games in Athens in 1896, and their success was in large part his achievement. In 1905, on his initiative, an international archaeological congress was held in the Greek capital, opened on 25 May, Greek independence day. In his welcome address, given at the foot of the restored Parthenon, Konstantínos emphasised that Greece had succeeded in 'preserving and rescuing, discovering and unearthing the monuments of its national past'. The entire world therefore now had access to 'a treasure shared by all civilised peoples'. The following year, intercalated Olympic Games were brought to Athens to mark the tenth anniversary of the modern games, and this celebration too proved a great success, not least for the crown prince as its advocate and organiser. In 1906, the Greek daily newspaper *Asty* celebrated Konstantínos, who had built on the 'living pillars of antiquity', as Greece's 'Sporting Hermes'. The prince, the newspaper recorded, was not only a national savant, but also well-nigh the 'sum and incarnation of the most noble ideals of his race'.[81]

In the nineteenth century, patriotic expression and the promotion of a nation's culture frequently went hand in hand. Scholarship and knowledge came to be greatly valued, and culture also became an arena in which members of the royal house could win the affections of the public through their exemplary behaviour. Royal heirs readily adopted the persona of the cultivated man of letters. This process began with the prince's upbringing but became increasingly significant for the adult royal heir, too. Prince Johann, the later King Johann I of Saxony (1801–1873), led the field when it came to a scholarly reputation. His contributions as a philologist, patron of research on the ancient world and translator of Dante earned him the respect of experts, but many of his fellow heirs

---

[81] Miriam Schneider, 'A "Sporting Hermes": Crown Prince Constantine and the Ancient Heritage of Modern Greece', in Frank Lorenz Müller and Heidi Mehrkens (eds.), *Royal Heirs and the Uses of Soft Power in Nineteenth-Century Europe* (London, 2016), pp. 243–261; Miriam Schneider, 'The Prussian Duke of Sparta', AHRC Project *Heirs to the Throne in the Constitutional Monarchies of Nineteenth-Century Europe (1815–1914)*, 'Heir of the Month' (March 2015), http://heirstothethrone-project.net/?page_id=1467 (accessed 5 July 2017).

could also impress the wider public with an interest in culture and learning to the wider public. Ferdinand Philippe d'Orléans was reputed to be culturally involved, as a significant collector and a patron of art and learning. He maintained close ties to leading lights of France's intellectual and artistic life. In 1842, Alexandre Dumas travelled from Florence to Paris specifically to attend the prince's funeral; Victor Hugo sent condolences to the bereaved king on behalf of the Institut de France; and the romantic poet Alfred de Musset composed thirty-one verses on the prince's death, in a poem entitled *Le treize juillet*.[82]

Two other royal heirs who died prematurely were also conspicuously involved with culture and education. The German crown prince Friedrich Wilhelm was known for his diverse educational interests. He maintained the village school at his estate in Bornstedt and inspected it personally, was a benefactor of a training school for educators, the Pestalozzi-Fröbel-Haus in Berlin, and a patron of the Crown Prince Friedrich Wilhelm Foundation (*Kronprinz-Friedrich-Wilhelm-Stiftung*), which made grants to destitute artisans and draftsmen. From the mid 1880s, he was also an examiner at the Berlin vocational training school. Even more sensational was his appointment in 1871, as 'protector' of the Prussian royal museums. During the period the crown prince held this office, the institutions' budget increased five-fold. In 1878, the royal protector oversaw a reform of the museums' organisational structure. His achievements were not only appreciated by the various museum directors but also praised by the public. 'Gifted by nature with a discriminating taste and artistic appreciation', assessed the *Vossische Zeitung* in January 1883, 'the crown prince instigated the manifold enrichments lately experienced by our art collections and thus by the art of the nation altogether.'[83]

The scholarly engagement of Crown Prince Rudolf, heir to the Austro-Hungarian throne, was even more pronounced than that of his Hohenzollern contemporary. Since childhood, he had been an enthusiastic

---

[82] Frank-Lothar Kroll, 'Monarchen als Gelehrte. Zum Typus des "homme de lettres" in den deutschen Fürstenstaaten des 19. Jahrhunderts', in Sächsische Schlösserverwaltung and Staatlicher Schlossbetrieb Schloss Weesenstein (eds.), *König Johann von Sachsen. Zwischen zwei Welten* (Halle an der Saale, 2001), pp. 135–140. On Johann of Saxony, see Katharina Weigand, 'Der gelehrte Monarch und die Kulturpolitik. Johann von Sachsen und Maximilian II. von Bayern im Vergleich', in Winfried Müller and Martina Schattkowsky (eds.), *Zwischen Tradition und Modernität. König Johann von Sachsen 1801–1873* (Leipzig, 2004), pp. 189–202; Sebastian Neumeister, 'Philalethes – König Johann als Dante-Übersetzer', in Winfried Müller and Martina Schattkowsky (eds.), *Zwischen Tradition und Modernität. König Johann von Sachsen 1801–1873* (Leipzig, 2004), pp. 203–216; Mehrkens, 'The Impossible Task of Replacing a Model Heir', pp. 203–204.

[83] Müller, *Our Fritz*, pp. 125–126.

naturalist, particularly drawn to ornithology. Rudolf had close ties to leading zoologists of his time such as Alfred Brehm, and he undertook numerous expeditions, including to Hungary, Spain and Morocco. The learned articles he published in ornithological journals would eventually fill three volumes. In 1878, his book entitled *Fünfzehn Tage auf der Donau* (*Fifteen Days on the Danube*) provided a detailed picture of the flora and fauna of the Hungarian Danube wetlands. The press praised the prince's work as a masterful literary and scholarly achievement. The young archduke was made an honorary member of the Academy of Sciences in Vienna and was presented with an honorary doctorate by the University of Budapest. Rudolf's two-volume work *Eine Orientreise* (*A Journey in the Orient*), containing his impressions of Egypt and the Holy Land, followed in 1881. The crown prince was also interested in advances in technology, as his widely reported speech to mark the opening of the International Electrical Exhibition in Vienna in summer 1883 demonstrated. He also promoted improvements in general sanitation and in medical treatment for soldiers. From the mid 1880s, Rudolf threw himself into preparations for the monumental national encyclopaedia entitled *Die österreichisch-ungarische Monarchie in Wort und Bild* (*The Austro-Hungarian Monarchy in Word and Image*), whose first volume he respectfully presented to his father in 1886. By the time of his death three years later, five volumes had already been published, but it would be another thirteen years before the appearance of the final, twenty-fourth, volume.[84]

This list of culturally and intellectually engaged royal heirs is far from exhaustive. We could add Prince Ludwig of Bavaria, holder of several honorary doctorates, who was one of the founding fathers of the German Museum in Munich, or Prince Vittorio Emanuele of Italy, who became an acknowledged expert on Italian numismatics and, from 1910 on, personally edited the twenty volumes of the *Corpus Nummorum Italicorum*.

Shining brightly alongside learning and culture in the 'firmament of bourgeois values' was another star – the princely undertaking identified in *Pierer's Universal-Lexikon* of 1857 as 'involvement in the promotion of the common good'. Here monarchies excelled, for philanthropy, the historian Jean Quataert has proposed with an eye on dynastic behaviour, 'was a stage on which to enact wider state identities around issues of community obligations and responsibilities'. Philanthropic activities – patronage, official visits, financial donations – were especially mighty instruments within the dynastic toolbox.[85]

---

[84] Hamann, *Kronprinz Rudolf*, pp. 118–141, 216–244.
[85] Matthias Röschner, 'Förderer und Protektor. Die Rolle Ludwigs III. in der Gründungs- und Aufbauphase des Deutschen Museums', in Ulrike Leutheusser and Hermann Rumschöttel (eds.), *König Ludwig III. und das Ende der Monarchie in Bayern*

In earlier eras, miraculous healing powers had been attributed to individuals with royal blood. In the nineteenth century, the numbers of those who still held this belief had dwindled. The 121 desperate scrofula sufferers who made their way to the cathedral at Rheims in 1825 to be touched, and cured, by the newly crowned King Charles X (1757–1836) were members of a rapidly disappearing group. Visiting the sick and the suffering remained a vital element of monarchical image-making, though. King Umberto I of Italy and Emperor Franz Joseph of Austria rushed to be with the victims of natural disasters such as floods, earthquakes and epidemics. In 1855, Queen Victoria came in person to the Brompton Hospital to share words of courage with soldiers who had been injured during the Crimean War. Royal heirs participated in these rituals: in 1832, Ferdinand Philippe d'Orléans caused a furore by visiting Parisian hospitals during a cholera epidemic despite the risk of infection. A painting by Alfred Johannot that captured the scene shows the uniformed prince moving as a Christ-like figure through a group of sufferers, to whom he is bringing solace. The Prince of Wales accompanied his mother on a visit to the sick in 1855, and, in wartime, crown princes made regular appearances in hospitals – Crown Prince Friedrich Wilhelm of Prussia and Prince Wilhelm of Württemberg in the war of 1870–1871, and the British heir Prince Edward in the First World War.[86]

The monarchy's reputation as a pillar of philanthropy rested not just on such occasional visits but also, and above all, on patronage of specific causes. In 1883, for example, the German crown prince assumed the mantle of patron when donations were sought for the victims of the earthquake on the Italian island of Ischia. Sincere, systematic and consistent advocacy on social issues was indispensable if the concept of 'social kingship' was to be used to justify monarchy as a form of government. The principal concern of government by the 'mothers of the nation' and 'fathers of the nation', Frank-Lothar Kroll has proposed, was necessarily the wellbeing of the subjects entrusted to them, and the poverty of so

(Munich, 2014), pp. 127–144; Lucia Travaini, *Storia di una passione. Vittorio Emanuele III e le monete*, 2nd edn (Rome, 2005); Manfred Hettling and Stefan-Ludwig Hoffmann (eds.), *Der bürgerliche Wertehimmel. Innenansichten des 19. Jahrhunderts* (Göttingen, 2000); www.zeno.org/Pierer-1857/K/pierer-1857-003-0474 (accessed 6 July 2017); Quataert, *Staging Philanthropy*, pp. 3–4.

[86] Giorgio Bordin and Laura Polo D'Ambrosio, *Medicine in Art* (Los Angeles, CA, 2010), p. 99; Werner Telesko, *Geschichtsraum Österreich. Die Habsburger und ihre Geschichte in der bildenden Kunst des 19. Jahrhunderts* (Vienna, 2006), p. 226; www.npg.org.uk/collections/se arch/portraitExtended/mw08509/Queen-Victorias-First-Visit-to-her-Wounded-Soldiers (accessed 7 July 2017); Heidi Mehrkens, 'The Prince, the President and the Cholera', AHRC Project *Heirs to the Throne in the Constitutional Monarchies of Nineteenth-Century Europe (1815–1914)*, 'Heir of the Month' (January 2014), http://heirstothethrone-project.net/?page_id=768 (accessed 7 July 2017).

many during the early industrial age provided them with much opportunity to minister. Even though no established concept or constitutional arrangement dictated so, the expansive system of princely benefaction identified by Kroll continued to grow, involving the ruling houses of nineteenth-century Europe across the board in Christian and socially responsible welfare initiatives. The monarchy made charitable donations, served as patrons, and gave their names to schools, hospitals, all kinds of educational facilities, institutions for the needy and orphanages.[87]

All these efforts were highly praiseworthy – and they also appealed strongly to the public. Little wonder that royal heirs who were well-known for their conscientiousness, such as Prince Ludwig of Bavaria, made sure to do their bit. Yet even the less committed princes had good reason to make an appearance on the philanthropic stage. From 1892, Prince Ludwig was involved with the Simonshof, a charitable foundation in Bastheim in Lower Franconia that provided accommodation for itinerant labourers, and subsequently he pushed for legal protections for those who worked in their own homes, often carrying out low-paid piecework. As early as the 1830s, Ferdinand Philippe d'Orléans had addressed social inequality, and, in 1888, the Central Association for the Wellbeing of the Working Classes felt called to publish a pamphlet honouring Crown Prince Friedrich Wilhelm of Prussia's 'services for the welfare of the people'. From improvements in healthcare stemming from the cooperative movement all the way to the elimination of vagrancy, no philanthropic venture by the future German emperor went unmentioned.[88]

Even the otherwise hedonistically inclined British royal heir, Albert Edward, was provided with a philanthropic role. By the time he turned ten, his mother had already given funds in his name to fifteen charitable organisations. By the time of his wedding in 1863, he was associated with 130 such institutions, and, in the 1860s, he devoted between twenty-five and thirty days each year to philanthropic activities. After recovering from a serious bout of typhus in the early 1870s, the Prince of Wales intensified his involvement, committing himself in particular to support for the sick and the poor, and not just in Great Britain but in other parts of the British Empire, too. In 1884, he became a member of a commission assembled by Prime Minister Gladstone to examine housing for the poor. In February 1884, he made an incognito visit to the slums of London that brought home to him the shocking living conditions of many in the capital. Afterwards, the prince gave his only significant speech in the

---

[87] Kroll, 'Die Idee eines sozialen Königtums im 19. Jahrhundert', pp. 113, 137.

[88] Müller, *Our Fritz*, pp. 123–124; Müller, *Royal Heirs in Imperial Germany*, pp. 204–205; Mehrkens, 'The Impossible Task of Replacing a Model Heir', p. 204.

House of Lords, in which he called for legal measures to improve the slums. Although in the end the uninspired report produced by the commission would have no impact, the enterprise, writes Frank Prochaska, provided 'excellent publicity for the Prince'. In 1892, Bertie unhesitatingly declared that he was willing to serve as a member of a new commission that would address poverty amongst the elderly. This initiative similarly delivered very little, not least because the prince did not wish to align himself with a minority within the commission who called for the introduction of a state pension. Each year in the decade before he became king, the Prince of Wales carried out on average forty-five charitable engagements, and he donated tens of thousands of pounds to almost a thousand institutions – including seventy-five hospitals nationwide. Bertie's involvement was surpassed by that of his wife, Princess Alexandra, who undertook hundreds of charitable visits and whose philanthropic bounty bordered on the irresponsible. On one occasion, it was said, she drew out 2,000 pounds in cash from under a couch cushion and presented the money to the head of a London hospital.[89]

***

According to the pre-eminent scholar of the British monarchy's charitable work and social engagement, Victoria's subjects never doubted that their 'dear and honoured' queen played a role beyond political ritual that was both practical and symbolic.[90] Their conviction is evidence that the crown's efforts to acquire soft power bore fruit. The monarchy had made itself appealing to the British people, whom the crown had convinced to desire precisely the values and order that the ruling house modelled for them. The integration into this project of the next generations of rulers – the Prince of Wales and his sons Albert Victor (Eddy) and George – ensured its continuation.

Here lies the essential political import of the heir to the throne in the nineteenth century – through incremental changes and by enlarging the available resources for exercising soft power, the heir guaranteed that the system had a future. If they were narrowly politically engaged or even more broadly opposed to the ruling monarch, they represented the political renewal and innovation that would come when the next generation took up the reins. Whatever their direct political involvement, almost all heirs helped to make their dynasty a more effective agent within the political mass market. Legal, political and media limitations may have left crowns little room to deploy their remaining hard power, but royal heirs proved especially suited to obtaining and exercising soft power. To

---

[89] Prochaska, *Royal Bounty*, pp. 109–126 (quote: p. 122).   [90] Ibid., p. 135.

do so, they stepped on board airships, charmed all those they greeted, appeared exemplary in many respects, and made themselves as photo-genic as possible.

Monarchy needed to adapt to survive. With ruling, and often ageing, monarchs inherently creatures of habit, it fell to succeeding generation of heirs to accompany, and even determine, monarchical innovations. Visible, mobile, present, affable and exemplary, or at least apparently so, the royal heirs were living proof that monarchy was indeed still needed – and would still be needed in future.

5 'From My Earliest Youth the Army Has Been My Absolute Love'

Royal Heirs and the Militarisation of the Monarchy

Prince Edward, the future King Edward VIII of England, spent the summer of 1913 visiting his extensive network of royal relatives in Germany. At the wheel of his car, he toured from palace to palace: from Stuttgart all the way to Neustrelitz in Mecklenburg, from Reinhardsbrunn near Gotha to the Royal Palace in Berlin. There, his journey reached its official climax when he met his father's cousin, the German emperor. Entering Wilhelm II's study, the young prince found the emperor at his desk, wearing a uniform. As a nonplussed Edward recorded in his memoirs, Wilhelm was sitting astride a saddle fitted on a wooden block. He was so used to being mounted on a horse, the emperor explained to his disconcerted visitor with a smile, that he preferred working in a saddle to sitting on an office chair. At dinner, the emperor sported a uniform even more impressive than that which he had worn in his study, and after dessert, Wilhelm excused himself briefly because before he and the English heir went to the opera he had to change into the 'most dazzling of all uniforms'.[1]

This almost grotesque overemphasis on things military, which can also be gleaned from Figure 20, was a product of both the moment and the man. Just before the outbreak of the First World War, the whole of Europe revelled in an explosive and demonstrative militarism, made up of a poisonous mix of nationalist hubris, armaments races, Great Power rivalry, mutual distrust and Social Darwinist pseudoscience – all relayed through a blaze of aggressive media and sabre-rattling boasts. Additionally, from his earliest years, the Hohenzollern prince had learned to compensate for his physical disability and his emotional instability by adopting a brash and exaggerated military habitus. The macho swaggering and martial strutting encountered by Prince Edward in Berlin was by no means unusual. Even an *enfant terrible* is a child of its time, though, and the last German emperor was no exception. This flamboyantly militaristic monarch, who donned one uniform after another and charged at

[1] *A King's Story: The Memoirs of the Duke of Windsor* (New York, 1951), pp. 98–103.

Figure 20. In 1890, the painter Max Koner portrayed Emperor Wilhelm II in this almost comically overblown pose. 'This is not a portrait', a French contemporary is said to have commented, 'but a declaration of war.' *Kaiser Wilhelm II*, oil on canvas, 1890, Max Koner: https://commons.wikimedia.org/wiki/File:Kohner_-_Kaiser_Wilhelm_II.jpg.

paperwork as if he were leading a cavalry attack, was the product of a decades-long process. It lasted throughout the nineteenth century and resulted in the militarisation of Europe's monarchies and of the ways in which they performed. It is a bitter fact of history that a development that had created a gaudily uniformed emperor mounted on a wooden horse would end in a world war that brought a bloody end to Europe's monarchical century.

The association of monarchy and military was far from unusual in the nineteenth century. As the historian Volker Sellin reminds us, the principal tasks of the ruler from time immemorial had been to protect the weak, defend the people against their enemies and win victory in battle. Alexander the Great, Emperor Constantine, the English king Henry V and, more recently, Frederick the Great had sought to justify and assert their power through military prowess. 'It is seen that when princes have thought more of ease than of arms, they have lost their states. And the first cause of your losing it is to neglect this art', Machiavelli had trenchantly warned.[2] In order to engender obedience and loyalty amongst their subjects, monarchs needed to be successful military commanders, or at least be perceived as such. The establishment of standing armies throughout Europe's monarchies in the seventeenth century made that role all the more important, for this new instrument of power was theirs to wield. Rulers therefore had to master the art of performing a heroic monarchy, which explains their eagerness to be immortalised in paintings in martial poses. Even in the early modern period, though, writes Martin Wrede, royal military leadership thus portrayed would frequently have consisted of little more than the occasional visit to the battlefield, and the monarchs' heroic deeds would have been carefully stage-managed.[3]

In Frederick the Great (1712–1786), the unity of king and commander reached a late apotheosis in the middle of the eighteenth century. More commonly, Ancien Régime monarchs were happy to crown themselves with laurels for victories won by military professionals – by generals and admirals such as Prince Eugene, the Duke of Marlborough, Lord Hawke, the Prince of Conde or Viscount Turenne. By the nineteenth century, almost all monarchs would cease to lead their troops on the battlefield. This trend had been intensified by Europe's experience of the usurper Napoleon, whose empire was created on the battlefield, where it also perished. For the political thinker Benjamin Constant, it was characteristic of a real monarch that he was *not* to be found on the frontlines: 'A king

---

[2] Niccolò Machiavelli, *The Prince*, trans. W. K. Marriott, ch. 14, www.gutenberg.org/files/1232/1232-h/1232-h.htm (accessed 9 May 2022).

[3] Volker Sellin, *Gewalt und Legitimität. Die europäische Monarchie im Zeitalter der Revolutionen* (Munich, 2011), p. 105; Martin Wrede, 'Einleitung. Die Inszenierung der mehr oder weniger heroischen Monarchie. Zu Rittern und Feldherren, Kriegsherren und Schauspielern', in Martin Wrede (ed.), *Die Inszenierung der heroischen Monarchie. Frühneuzeitliches Königtum zwischen ritterlichem Erbe und militärischer Herausforderung* (Munich, 2014), p. 11; Michael Epkenhans, 'Das Ende eines Zeitalters. Europäische Monarchen und ihre Armeen im Ersten Weltkrieg', in Winfried Heinemann und Markus Pöhlmann (eds.), *Monarchen und ihr Militär* (Potsdam, 2010), p. 61.

does not need to lead his armies. Others can fight on his behalf, while through his disposition for peace he acquires the love and respect of his people', he wrote in 1814. 'The usurper, by contrast, must constantly stand at the head of his praetorians.'[4] It was rare indeed for monarchs to have command of their own forces in the conflicts of the ensuing century. When they did so – and such instances were in any case largely symbolic – the outcomes were not good: in 1859, Emperor Franz Joseph experienced a bitter defeat, as did Emperor Napoleon III eleven years later. Even the militarily experienced King Wilhelm I left the actual command of his forces to his chief of general staff, Helmuth von Moltke, in the successful campaigns of 1866 and 1870–1871.

Constant had differentiated between the inherited legitimacy of the traditional monarch and the regime of the adventurer, which was dependent on the capricious goddess of victory. The defeat of Napoleon and the separation of the roles of ruling monarch and battlefield commander did not mean, though, that the process Heinz Dollinger identified as 'the militarisation of the monarchy' would come to an end. Instead, the pressures of the post-revolutionary age, which played out within the context of the constitutionalisation of royal power, provided new impulses that led to the continuation and elaboration of the bond between the crown and the military. While constitutional developments restricted the monarch's access to central elements of state power, retaining supreme military command formed a significant exception everywhere. This command could often even be exercised without any parliamentary involvement. Soldiers declared their allegiance to the ruler, not the constitution. Those who enlisted in Britain spoke of taking 'the king's shilling', in Prussia they wore 'the king's coat' (*des Königs Rock*) and in Denmark they donned 'the king's clothes' (*i kongens klæder*). Rulers were thus closely bound to an institution of great domestic and international significance, and they resolutely defended their military leadership against demands for parliamentary oversight. Their attitude was welcomed by the military elites, who were thus able to seal off their 'state within a state' from external influences. As mass armies and conscription gradually became the standard almost everywhere in Europe in the course of the nineteenth century, monarchies could deploy their special relationship with the military to emphasise their ties to the people. In the German Empire, membership of the *Kyffhäuserbund* eventually peaked at 2.8 million, making this association of former soldiers the largest organisation in the country by membership. According to its

---

[4] Sellin, *Gewalt und Legitimität*, p. 105.

statutes, the association championed 'love and loyalty for emperor and empire, ruler and fatherland'.[5]

Monarchies' efforts to use the role of commander-in-chief to garner the affection of the people were successful largely because they were embedded in a broader process. As the nineteenth century proceeded and the bloodshed of the Napoleonic Wars increasingly morphed into a romanticised and nostalgic memory, states were able to set increasing store by the use of military force to defend their territories and advance their interests. Victorious battles were celebrated and became the focus of national commemorations of a glorious past and of hopes for a dazzling future. In many places the state's armaments policy intertwined with a vocal militarism amongst the people, often organised into associations, to produce a pro-military dynamic. At the same time, the status of the soldier, and in particular of the officer, rose. A man in uniform was not simply a patriotic hero; he was esteemed as a skilled practitioner of the science of war, a knowledgeable expert in a highly regarded area of modern technology.[6]

This development provided royal families with the opportunity to adopt an additional strategy for justifying and consolidating their authority: they could portray the military training of their sons – and of future rulers in particular – as thorough and fully modern. The advantages were all the greater if the heir to the throne could actually demonstrate valorous military conduct. If he had even done so on the battlefield, the crown's military leadership could be celebrated in great style. As the craft of war became increasingly complex, however, and as the other demands on the heir to the throne expanded, this aspiration became harder to fulfil convincingly and consistently.

For most monarchs and their sons, a real military role was simply unthinkable. Crowned heads had to make do with the wooden mock-up of a horse in their private home, while in public their supreme command of their country's military forces was diluted to the point where it amounted to little more than a representative notion.[7] They had to

[5] Heinz Dollinger, 'Das Leitbild des Bürgerkönigtums in der europäischen Monarchie des 19. Jahrhunderts', in Karl F. Werner (ed.), *Hof, Kultur und Politik im 19. Jahrhundert* (Bonn, 1985), p. 340; Dieter Fricke und Kurt Finker, 'Kyffhäuser-Bund der Deutschen Landeskriegerverbände (KB) 1900–1943', in Dieter Fricke (ed.), *Die bürgerlichen Parteien in Deutschland. Handbuch der Geschichte der bürgerlichen Parteien und anderer bürgerlicher Interessenorganisationen vom Vormärz bis zum Jahre 1945*, vol. 2 (Leipzig, 1970), pp. 296–312.

[6] Johannes Paulmann, *Pomp und Politik. Monarchenbegegnungen in Europa zwischen Ancien Régime und Erstem Weltkrieg* (Paderborn, 2000), pp. 160–164; Stig Förster, *Der doppelte Militarismus. Die deutsche Heeresrüstungspolitik zwischen Status-Quo-Sicherung und Aggression, 1890–1913* (Stuttgart, 1985), p. 300.

[7] Dollinger, 'Das Leitbild des Bürgerkönigtums', p. 341.

write a part for themselves that would dazzle their audience. Since they were unable to command highly complex armed forces, the rulers' public performances needed to become all the more arresting, their costumes all the more colourful. This eye-catching militarisation of the monarchy was displayed to the broader public at parades and investitures, at ship launches, monument unveilings, royal jubilees and wreath-layings. The militaristic poses, the magnificent uniforms and the patriotic speeches took the place of actual military command and the clamour of battle. Such events functioned as an expression of the nation's military might, conveyed in great magnificence both to potential enemies beyond the borders and to the ruler's own subjects at home. This military spectacle found particularly extravagant expression in the French Second Empire. Napoleon III, who had absolutely no military experience, had the starring role. 'As he paraded around, wearing a uniform he had not earned and sword he had never used, he assumed a role he had inherited from his uncle, the military leader. But what had come naturally to the First Emperor was playacting for his heir', Matthew Truesdell has commented.[8]

European monarchies were able to sustain this vibrant performance for long periods during the nineteenth century above all because after 1815 the continent enjoyed an age of relative peace. The few military conflicts either took place on the periphery, as in the case of the Crimean War (1854–1856) and the Russo-Turkish War (1877–1878), or were short, localised and one-sided, like the campaigns in northern Italy (1859), Schleswig (1864), Bohemia (1866) and France (1870–1871). Spurred on by growing nationalism, a 'folkloric militarism', as the historian Jakob Vogel termed it, took root across much of the continent. The expression captures the good-natured and unencumbered public display of colourful military spectacle in which much of the population participated with genuine delight: when serving in the military, as veterans of the forces, as spectators, on excursions, as marching-band enthusiasts, as newspaper readers and even as monarchs. Rituals such as the daily appearance of Emperor Wilhelm I at the 'historical corner window' of his palace opposite the *Neue Wache* guardhouse in Berlin belong in this category. Emerging on schedule, like a wooden figure on a glockenspiel, to watch the noon-time changing of the guard, the ageing emperor was gaped at by the crowd and became a tourist attraction himself.[9]

[8] Matthew Truesdell, *Spectacular Politics: Louis-Napoleon Bonaparte and the 'Fête Imperiale'*, *1849–1870* (New York and Oxford, 1997), p. 138.

[9] Jakob Vogel, '"En revenant de la revue". Militärfolklore und Folkloremilitarismus in Deutschland und Frankreich 1871–1914', in *Österreichische Zeitschrift für Geschicht*

In the course of the nineteenth century, Europe's monarchies successfully steered a course that allowed the crown's real and enduring privileged ties to the military to be merged with an idealised popular conception of military culture in the people's mind. The dynasty's dual role would have weighty political consequences. The impulses behind the militarisation of the continent were heightened when the European state system capsized in summer 1914. As the ostensibly martial raison d'être of Europe's monarchies was tested by the outbreak of the war, some royal houses found themselves facing an existential crisis, challenged precisely by the claims to military leadership that had been asserted so brightly and bombastically to the *oompapahs* of endless military bands. Now the very same monarchs had to dismount from the wooden horses in their studies or the magnificent beasts they rode on parade and actually assume military responsibility under the most difficult circumstances imaginable. Monarchs and heirs needed to justify through military action the inherited rights that they had claimed and proclaimed, the same military action that their (future) subjects had to perform as a duty to the fatherland. Yet in monarchic panegyric over preceding decades, the expectations of heirs to the throne had been blithely raised to entirely unrealistic heights. Living up to those expectations under conditions of what would soon be total war and in the glare of propaganda proved almost impossible for royal heirs who had rarely been sufficiently prepared for the task.

This chapter addresses the part played by Europe's royal heirs in the militarisation of the monarchy in the nineteenth century. It considers first the relatively peaceable century that began with the victory over Napoleon and ended in summer 1914 and the militarisation of the monarchy that happened during these years. Here we will look at the part played more broadly by crown princes in that popular militarism, before turning an eye to heirs who between 1815 and 1914 were celebrated as soldierly heroes, whether or not that acclaim was justified. Finally, we shall accompany the royal heirs into the catastrophe that was the First World War, the dreadful conclusion to Europe's monarchical century.

---

swissenschaft 9 (1998), pp. 9–30; Alexa Geisthövel, 'Wilhelm I. am "historischen Eckfenster". Zur Sichtbarkeit des Monarchen in der zweiten Hälfte des 19. Jahrhunderts', in Jan Andres, Alexa Geisthövel und Matthias Schwengelbeck (eds.), *Die Sinnlichkeit der Macht. Herrschaft und Repräsentation seit der Frühen Neuzeit* (Frankfurt am Main, 2005), pp. 163–185.

'There Rose to Heaven Military Music, Military Music!': Heirs to the Throne on the Military Stage in the Nineteenth Century

In 2008, the historian James Sheehan published a study entitled *Where Have All the Soldiers Gone?* It addressed 'the transformation of Europe' that resulted in a gradual departure from the earlier universal willingness to regard war as a legitimate and appropriate instrument of politics. On the eve of the First World War, the starting point of Sheehan's investigation, soldiers had been numerous, omnipresent and visible. A century later, they seemed to have disappeared. Before 1914, the military had been an unquestioned and prized presence in public spaces. Soldiers were everywhere – on squares and at train stations, in parks and outside barracks, in large cities and in small garrison towns. 'Prussia's capital city was unimaginable without soldiers and military music', recorded Emperor Wilhelm II as he recalled his childhood. For the emperor, as for most monarchs who reigned on the continent, military uniform was what one wore to work. The army – the festive regimental ball just as much as onerous life in the barracks – was part of everyday life. With conscription almost universal, male citizens performed this duty to the state in their millions, which meant that the army not only influenced family life but often also shaped it.[10]

Sheehan's reflections on the disappearance of the military from the minds of Europeans and the spaces they inhabited were undertaken in full awareness of the horrors of the twentieth century. His work is therefore launched with that modern song of lament, made famous by Marlene Dietrich, about lost flowers, girls, young men and soldiers. In the nineteenth century contemporaries sang a very different tune. One can hardly imagine a sharper contrast than with the ironically dashing soundscape painted by Detlev von Liliencron to depict the rush of the march-past of a military band.

> Ting-a-ling, boom-boom and oom-papah,
> Is this the din of Persia's shah?
> Oh no, there sounds the thund'rous bray
> Of tuba calls on judgement day,
> Led by the Turkish Crescent.
>
> Boom-boom, the massive bombardon,
> The cymbals' clash, the helicon,
> The piccolo, the cornettist,

---

[10] James J. Sheehan, *Where Have All the Soldiers Gone? The Transformation of Modern Europe* (New York, 2008); Epkenhans, 'Das Ende eines Zeitalters', p. 63; Kaiser Wilhelm II., *Aus meinem Leben, 1859–1888*, 4th edn (Berlin and Leipzig, 1927), p. 4.

The Turkish drum and the flautist,
And then there comes the captain.

The captain, full of pluck and pride,
A gleaming sabre by his side,
A sash adorns his manly chest,
By Jove! This business is no jest,
And then come the two lieutenants.

Two lieutenants, pink and brown,
They guard the flag with watchful frown,
Here comes the flag, quick! bow your head,
For we must love it till we're dead.
And then all the grenadiers come.

The grenadiers march like the clock,
Their boots go tick and step and tock,
A stamp, a snap, a clash, a thwack
Make window panes and glasses crack.
And then all the little lasses.

The lasses all stand side by side
Their hair so fair, their eyes so wide
From every house along the street
Jane, Jill and Katie catch a peek,
But now the music's over.

Ting-a-ling, ching-ching and crack of drum,
From far away a distant hum
Quite faintly now the trumpets' cry;
Was that a dazzling butterfly
Ching-ching floating round the corner?[11]

For all the unmistakable scoffing at the pomp of the parade, the self-satisfaction of the captain and the exaggerated reverence for the colours, we also find here an expression of the contemporary reaction to the military. It was this response to which the monarchy's public image could connect: the rousing music, the sense of community, the men marching in step, the smart uniforms, the colourful interruption of the everyday, also so appealing to children, and the apparent harmlessness of the 'colourful butterfly' passing by. What Liliencron captured in this vignette was later identified by Jakob Vogel as 'folkloric militarism': the unusually high status granted to the military and to representations of the military within the popular culture of the nineteenth century. Men, women and children throughout Europe rallied to military ceremonial

---

[11] Detlev von Liliencron, *Die Musik kommt* (1883), www.projekt-gutenberg.org/liliencr/ge dichte/chap028.html (accessed 10 May 2022); translation by Frank Lorenz Müller.

and commemorations; children grew up surrounded by toy soldiers and uniforms, and – as in Joseph Roth's novel *Radetzky March* – military music was the refrain of social life in the community. Even a left-wing satirist like Kurt Tucholsky, who looked back at his schooldays disenchanted by his experience of the First World War, found that the intoxicating effect of this performance still lingered: 'And when the drums and fifes / tuned into the Prussian March / I almost fell to the ground from joy – / eyes shone – there rose to heaven / military music, military music!' Other critical contemporaries, recorded the *Frankfurter Zeitung* in May 1913, could not escape the magic of the military parade either: 'Now under the linden trees, in the sunshine, with joyful eyes they marvelled at this military guard, they know every regiment and its history, they are proud, feel a sense of ownership, and join in with the "hurrah!" whenever the cry is started by anyone caught up in the emotion or who likes to have fun.'[12]

There is a tendency to describe such moments as characteristically Prussian or German, but a similar mood and similar performances could be found throughout Europe – and not just in monarchical states. Vogel's analysis demonstrates that a comparable popular enthusiasm for the military existed in the France of the Third Republic. In the Kingdom of Italy, the national holiday – nominally in honour of the constitution but in practice above all a memorialisation of the wars of unification, the army and its royal commanders – provided another opportunity to celebrate this folkloric militarism. The great military parade held to mark the *Festa dello Statuto Albertino* brought soldiers and schoolboys together, as nation and state seemed to be as one. A particularly exciting passage in Edmondo De Amici's well-known work *Cuore*, written in 1886 and intended for a younger readership, describes how a father and son are swept up in the patriotic mood during the parade. The father explains to his son the various units that make up the troops, he recounts heroic tales, and praises the splendour of the companies that pass. At the end, his son calls out in great joy, 'How beautiful this is!'[13]

---

[12] Vogel, 'En revenant de la revue', pp. 9–10; Jakob Vogel, *Nationen im Gleichschritt. Der Kult der 'Nation in Waffen' in Deutschland und Frankreich, 1871–1914* (Göttingen, 1997); Kaspar Hauser [Kurt Tucholsky], *Unser Militär!*, (1919), www.textlog.de/tucholsky-unser-militaer.html (accessed 20 March 2017); Daniel Schönpflug, *Die Heiraten der Hohenzollern. Verwandtschaft, Politik und Ritual in Europa 1640–1918* (Göttingen, 2013), pp. 224–225.

[13] Ilaria Porciani, 'Der Krieg als ambivalenter italienischer Gründungsmythos – Siege und Niederlagen', in Nikolaus Buschmann und Dieter Langewiesche (eds.), *Der Krieg in den Gründungsmythen europäischer Nationen und den USA* (Frankfurt am Main and New York, 2003), p. 194; Catherine Brice, *Monarchie et identité nationale en Italie (1861–1900)* (Paris, 2010), pp. 119–127.

Within the Austro-Hungarian Empire, the army had a particularly prominent role in the public representation of the state. On 18 August, the birthday of Emperor Franz Joseph, military bands played throughout the land. In great cities, small towns and villages alike, patriotic tunes rang out – even at 4:30 a.m., for the edification of the early risers amongst the emperor's loyal subjects. In a partly autobiographical story (*Esti Kornél*, 1934), the Hungarian writer Desző Kosztolányi (1885–1936) described a scene from Budapest that fits seamlessly with the portrayal of the military during the Belle Époque: 'Reveille had sounded in the barracks. A column prepared to move out of a courtyard. At the head was the captain, on a high-stepping horse, sword drawn, rapping out German words of command', recalls Kornél Esti, the hero of the novel. 'Young subalterns, redolent of eau de cologne, were at their posts. The morning sun gleamed on their swords, their black and yellow sword knots. King and Emperor Franz Josef I ruled, up there on his high throne in Vienna.' Britain too knew how to stage a military parade in grand style – we need think only of the almost endless parades to mark the funeral of the Duke of Wellington in 1852 or in celebration of Queen Victoria's Jubilees in 1887 and 1897. In this island nation, though, a different form of military display was more typical. Naval theatre was a powerful demonstration of Britain's might at sea. Thus on Saturday, 17 July 1909, more than 150 warships, almost the entire Home Fleet, sailed up the Thames and anchored for a week within the British capital, where they were admired and visited by an estimated 4 million Londoners. The spectators were entertained with fireworks, exhibition battles, searchlight displays and troop parades. 'Sensation followed sensation', one enthusiastic visitor recalled.[14]

Public performances by the military were common long before the First World War, with the general populace as eager spectators. In time, military symbols were adopted by gun clubs and music bands, and the rhythm of military service assumed the pattern of a popular tradition. The cavalrymen of the 6th Brandenburg Cuirassiers are not the main subject of Franz Krüger's famous 1829 painting *Parade auf dem Opernplatz* (*Parade on Opera Square*); its focus is rather the people of Berlin – men and women, a cobbler's boy and also dogs – who do not want to miss out on the military spectacle and have come in great numbers and full of excitement to watch the event. The public presence of the army was greatly intensified in the second half of the nineteenth century, mirroring the growing importance of all things military. Military texts, paintings and prints composed

---

[14] Daniel Unowsky, *The Pomp and Politics of Patriotism: Imperial Celebrations in Habsburg Austria, 1848–1916* (West Lafayette, IN, 2005), p. 98; Desző Kosztolányi, *Kornél Esti: A Novel*, trans. Bernard Adams (New York, 2011), pp. 83–84; Jan Rüger, *The Great Naval Game: Britain and Germany in the Age of Empire* (Cambridge, 2007), pp. 12–13.

a genre now distributed on a massive scale, and associations for soldiers and former soldiers were founded everywhere. Public military events drew ever greater audiences and developed into lively public celebrations, accompanied by much eating and drinking. When the Berlin police wanted to throw a wide cordon of barriers around the imperial parades, the city's innkeepers complained about the loss of trade, 'because the spectators returning from the parade have always called in at our inns'. The atmosphere in the Parisian Bois de Boulogne, not far from the military's great parade field, was similar. 'Groups sit around a "tablecloth" made from an unfolded newspaper, stuff themselves full of meat pastries, open tins of sardines, consume inexpensive sandwiches of liver pâté. The white wine flows freely and allows a somewhat coarse merriment to take hold of their minds', ran the *Petit Parisien*'s description of the scene in July 1906. 'From time to time a regiment parades past, enveloped in resounding brass and lustily supported by the clashing sound of the drummers, which brings a heroic note to this picture of insatiable gluttony.'[15]

The public celebration of the military was not simply about meeting the emerging consumer society's need for entertainment or about the bourgeois and sub-bourgeois grasping at somewhat spontaneous recreational opportunities. The carefree consumption of a liver-pâté sandwich was not unpolitical if it took place in the context of folkloric militarism organised or at least supported by the state. Such public celebrations were part of the popular support for the prevailing system of rule and above all for the royal presence at its apex. This was both recognised and condemned by contemporary critics. For Karl Liebknecht, a radical socialist member of the German parliament, the exaltation of the armed forces, ingrained in the functions of the state and constantly present in the media, represented nothing more than a 'system devised to drench the public and private life of the people in a militaristic spirit'. The army, the historian Ute Frevert noted with reference to the German Empire, was a powerful engine of internal nation-building, with conservative and authoritarian portent. It is hardly surprising that Europe's monarchical regimes, with their traditionally close relationship to the military, were well aware of the possibilities afforded by this tool and used it to stabilise their own power.[16]

---

[15] Jakob Vogel, 'Der "Folkloremilitärismus" und seine zeitgenössische Kritik – Deutschland und Frankreich 1871–1914', in Wolfram Wette (ed.), *Militarismus in Deutschland 1871 bis 1945* (Münster, 1999), pp. 280–281; Gerd Bartoschek (ed.), *Preußisch korrekt – berlinisch gewitzt. Der Maler Franz Krüger 1797–1857* (exhibition catalogue) (Berlin, 2007), pp. 147–149; Vogel, 'En revanant de la revue', pp. 15–16.

[16] Vogel, 'En revanant de la revue', p. 10; Ute Frevert, 'Das jakobinische Modell. Allgemeine Wehrpflicht und Nationsbildung in Preußen-Deutschland', in Ute Frevert (ed.), *Militär und Gesellschaft im 19. und 20. Jahrhundert* (Stuttgart, 1997), p. 45.

Throughout Europe, crowned actors in uniform were soon giving consummate performances that fed the popular enthusiasm for all things military. Kings and emperors took the salute at parades, inspected troops and fleets, promoted each other to be honorary colonels of tradition-steeped regiments and launched national commemorations of heroic moments. Thus on 2 July 1871 the Italian king Vittorio Emanuele II participated in a triumphant entry into Rome, the new capital of his kingdom. The following day he attended the opening of a gun club's firing range and shortly after watched another military parade, on the Piazza del Popolo. Three days later, he was present when 100 conscripts born in 1850 and therefore now liable for military service were enlisted in a ceremony on the Capitoline Hill: each name was read out and the new recruits were presented individually to the king. While officially this public occasion had a military purpose, the Bavarian ambassador recognised it was above all 'a celebration of the monarchy'. On his arrival at Rome's Termini train station, Vittorio Emanuele would have been greeted by several busts of himself, setting the tone for the king-focused festivities to follow. The goal was to transfer some of the glory of the struggle for unification onto the royal dynasty. Historian Lucy Riall has written of how Giuseppe Garibaldi (1807–1882), the hero of the Risorgimento, and his fellow soldiers had caused the old picture of an effeminate and effete Italy to be supplanted by an image of a 're-virilised' nation, well able to defend itself. The monarchy was naturally very keen to be part of this heroic, masculine narrative. The king, who was celebrated for his military achievements, used his demonstrative role at the head of his troops to assert a 'military legitimisation' of his rule in this new kingdom and to create national consensus.[17]

When Queen Victoria celebrated her Diamond Jubilee in the summer of 1897, she had no need for such legitimisation. But the opportunity was not to be squandered. Troops from all corners of the empire came to pay homage to the queen and to display the power of this island nation. On a double-page spread, the *Illustrated London News* provided its readers with portraits of all these exotic-seeming soldiers: the field artillery from Trinidad, the Haussas from the African Gold Coast, the Victoria

[17] Manuel Borutta, 'Repräsentation, Subversion und Spiel. Die kulturelle Praxis nationaler Feste in Berlin und Rom, 1870/71 und 1895', in Ulrike von Hirschhausen und Jörn Leonhard (eds.), *Nationalismen in Europa. West- und Osteuropa im Vergleich* (Göttingen, 2007), pp. 250, 253; Lucy Riall, 'Men at War: Masculinity and Military Ideals in the Risorgimento', in Silvana Patriarca and Lucy Riall (eds.), *The Risorgimento Revisited: Nationalism and Culture in Nineteenth-Century Italy* (Basingstoke, 2012), pp. 152–170; Paolo Colombo, 'In consenso spezzato. La legittimazione militare die Vittorio Emanuele II', in Elena Fontanella (ed.), *Vittorio Emanuele II. Il Re Galantuomo* (Turin, 2010), pp. 66–73.

Mounted Rifles from Canada, the lancers from Australian New South Wales, the police force from British New Guinea, the Dyaks from Borneo and many more besides. Even the drummer boys of the Royal Niger Constabulary were not forgotten. Equally celebratory – although less international – were the events held in Germany in 1913, when the various German states commemorated the victory over Napoleon 100 years earlier. At two great gatherings – in August at the Hall of Liberation in Kelheim, whose foundation stone had been laid by the Bavarian king Ludwig I in 1841, and in October at the dedication of the Monument to the Battle of the Nations in Leipzig – they identified themselves and their dynasties with the run of victories from the Battle of Leipzig in 1813 to the Battle of Paris in 1814. 'Where could we grasp more profoundly than here the nature and continuing effect of the wars of liberation', declared Emperor Wilhelm II in Kelheim, 'where one of the German princes has erected in bronze and marble a remembrance of the heroic acts of our fathers.' The Leipzig celebrations were dedicated to the German people, but the princes of the empire still pushed themselves to the fore: 'As I greet you, the German princes and representatives of the Free Cities, with the German emperor at your head, you, the representatives of those who rule beyond Germany, whose forefathers participated in the great battle of the nations that took place 100 years ago', declared King Friedrich August III of Saxony, 'I commemorate the glorious feats accomplished 100 years ago by German, Austrian, Hungarian, Russian and Swedish troops upon this battlefield.'[18]

The militarisation of monarchy and society provided the ruler-to-be with numerous opportunities to herald the auspicious potential of the monarchical system. Soldiering was to be learnt by starting at the bottom, and that undertaking seemed almost made for a youthful heir. While embodying the monarchical dimension to the military, the heir to the throne could benefit from the army's role in teaching the values of the nation. The army, and especially an army composed of conscripts, was tasked with functioning as the nation's school. It was not just to toughen the body but also to convey patriotic virtues and an aggressive manliness. Military socialisation began at elementary school. In his book *Léon Gambetta and His Armies* of 1877, the Prussian general and military theoretician Colmar von der Goltz argued that it was here that 'discipline, order, obedience, community spirit' were to be fostered and 'space for

---

[18] 'Colonial Troops in England for the Queen's Diamond Jubilee', in *The Illustrated London News* of 19 June 1897; Jeffrey R. Smith, 'The Monarchy versus the Nation: The Festive Year 1913 in Wilhelmine Germany', in *German Studies Review* 23 (2000), pp. 257–274; *Deutscher Geschichtskalender*, founded by Karl Wippermann, vol. 2 (Leipzig, 1913), pp. 68, 178–179.

a military education of young people' should be created. This would by no means turn Germany into 'one large drill ground, but rather promote the moral standards of the masses, their discipline and their obedience'. Similar goals were pursued beyond the walls of the school – conveyed through toy soldiers, uniforms for dressing-up, sailor suits and wooden rifles, practised at the gymnastics club or with the Scouts.[19]

As the numerous photographs and postcards that depict a future ruler as a soldier-child indicate, the offspring of the ruling house were much-loved poster children of this process of education and representation. They were just as awestruck by the military as had been the young Tucholsky. Numerous contemporary accounts tell of the great pride of the Prussian prince Wilhelm – later Emperor Wilhelm I – when his seven-year-old son Friedrich Wilhelm, sporting the uniform of the Stettin Militia Guards Regiment and with full military bearing, provided him with a status report for the palace guard. Their mutual fascination with the military was a bond for father and son through the years. In June 1860, on his appointment as colonel of the 1st Prussian Infantry Regiment, the future emperor Friedrich III experienced such a 'daze of joy' that he became 'actually rather jittery', as he excitedly wrote to his wife. The twenty-eight-year-old prince added with a youthful pride that his regiment was the oldest in the army and that he had even been permitted to retain the uniform of the 1st Guards Regiment. Friedrich's grandson Crown Prince Wilhelm (1882–1951) felt very similarly: 'Now at last I have something decent to put on!', the ten-year-old called out on the morning of 6 May 1892, when he was given the uniform of a lieutenant of the 1st Foot Guards.[20]

In Ferdinand Georg Waldmüller's portrait of the three-year-old Archduke Franz Joseph (Figure 21), the future emperor was depicted next to a drum and a flag, wearing a grenadier's cap, holding a rifle and playing with his wooden soldiers. When he was two years older, the heir to

---

[19] Ute Frevert, 'Das Militär als "Schule der Männlichkeit". Erwartungen, Angebote, Erfahrungen im 19. Jahrhundert', in Ute Frevert (ed.), *Militär und Gesellschaft im 19. und 20. Jahrhundert* (Stuttgart, 1997), pp. 145–173; Colmar von der Goltz, *Léon Gambetta und seine Armeen* (Berlin, 1877), pp. 294–295; *Handbuch der deutschen Bildungsgeschichte*, vol. 3, ed. Karl-Ernst Jeismann and Peter Lundgreen (Munich, 1987), pp. 362–377; *Handbuch der deutschen Bildungsgeschichte*, vol. 4, ed. Christa Berg (Munich, 1991), pp. 127–129, 136–137, 501–527; Sonja Levsen, 'Gemeinschaft, Männlichkeit und Krieg. Militarismus in englischen Colleges und deutschen Studentenverbindungen am Vorabend des Ersten Weltkrieges', in Christian Jansen (ed.), *Der Bürger als Soldat. Die Militarisierung europäischer Gesellschaften im langen 19. Jahrhundert. Ein internationaler Vergleich* (Essen, 2004), pp. 230–246.

[20] Frank Lorenz Müller, *Our Fritz: Emperor Frederick III and the Political Culture of Imperial Germany* (Cambridge, MA, 2011), pp. 16–17, 83; Jörg Kirschstein, *KaiserKinder. Die Familie Wilhelms II. in Fotografien* (Göttingen, 2011), p. 38.

Figure 21. The militarisation of the future monarch began in the nursery. Ferdinand Georg Waldmüller's painting shows the three-year-old Franz Joseph, who would become the Austrian emperor in 1848, wearing a busby and holding a rifle, surrounded by a flag, wooden soldiers and a drum. Alamy Images.

the throne received the uniform of a cuirassier as a Christmas present. All this was trumped on 18 August 1843 by a much more wonderful gift. 'Today is my thirteenth birthday. A surprise had been prepared for me', Franz Joseph recorded in his diary. 'When the doors to the room where my presents lay were opened and Mama and Papa led me in and I saw the dragoon uniform lying on the table, my first thought was that the uniform was just a toy, but soon I divined to my greatest joy that it was real. [. . .] I was proud now to be counted one of the officers of the Austrian army. I am already looking forward to appearing in uniform and mounted on a horse at the parades. Throughout the day I undertook that in my fourteenth year and as an officer I would never again show any fear and would never again tell a lie.' While not every family could present a son with a regiment of dragoons for his birthday, the young prince's reaction – his pride, his eagerness to be part of military parades, his decision that in future he would ensure his character befitted his new status – was entirely in accord with what the military 'school of manliness' sought to teach the population at large.[21]

Here lay the central goal: to present to the public a royal heir who had proved himself through his military training and demonstrated soldierly and manly virtues to the nation that one day he was to lead and embody. As the civilian education of heirs to the throne was intensified, their military schooling was not forgotten. For many royal families that training began with the symbolic enrolment of princes in the army at a very young age and their outfitting with uniforms. In Prussia, this step took place when the boy was nine years old. The later King Oscar II of Sweden was eleven when he entered the navy and thus the same age as Prince Leopold, who as Leopold II would later be King of the Belgians, when he was named a lieutenant in 1846. The last king of Saxony, Friedrich August III, became a second lieutenant in the 1st Grenadiers at the age of twelve. The future Emperor Franz Joseph became a colonel at thirteen; his son, Rudolf, did not have to wait so long: he was given the same rank on the day he was born. Such symbolic appointments marked only the start of heirs' service in the cause of raising the military prestige of their dynasty. There followed a mix of soldierly training, rapid military advancement and a public display of military prowess, both the heir's own and that of the dynasty as a whole.

For all male heirs in the nineteenth century, service with a branch of the army or – as was the case for Britain and Sweden – with the navy was an unavoidable stage on the path to the throne. A nation that counted on its ability to defend itself militarily and understood the bearing of arms as the duty of the patriotic citizen required that its leaders be demonstrably skilled and successful precisely in these respects. Even heirs who were not cut out for the military, for example the future King Wilhelm II of Württemberg or Ludwig III of Bavaria, could not avoid a minimum of military service and ultimately promotion to general. It was important to demonstrate their military and manly habitus, which they did by wearing uniforms, becoming military commanders, attending manoeuvres and celebrating their years of service.

[21] Jean-Paul Bled, *Franz Joseph. 'Der letzte Monarch der alten Schule'* (Vienna, 1988), p. 14; Heimo Cerny (ed.), *Die Jugend-Tagebücher Franz Josephs (1843–1848). Ungekürzte kommentierte Textedition* (Vienna, 2003), p. 33.

The trend towards a demonstrative militarisation of the dynasty was particularly pronounced in the case of the Saxon Wettins. King Albert I and his brother and successor Georg were reputed to have performed impressively during the wars of 1866 and 1870–1871, while they were both still princes. Albert had participated in the German victories at Gravelotte, Beaumont and Sedan in 1870, while Georg had commanded a Saxon division at St Privat. Both were later awarded the rank of field marshal. The military reputation of the Wettin family was the object of a carefully staged festive culture, which culminated in 1893 with a great celebration to mark the king's fifty years of military service, which Albert I described as his 'golden wedding with the army'. The young Emperor Wilhelm II travelled to Dresden to present the venerable Saxon king with a precious field marshal's baton and did so in the presence of numerous other princes who had been close to the honouree during his military service during the campaigns of 1849, 1866 and 1870–1871. Alongside these august figures and the members of the army command, thousands of representatives of military and civilian associations also paid homage to Albert.[22]

The next Saxon heir to the throne, Prince Friedrich August, made every effort to contribute to this intensification of the dynasty's militaristic self-image. Born in 1865, the prince could not draw on his own experience of war, but he was highly engaged in the culture of remembrance, and every effort was made to prove his love of those who served in the military. As part of the festivities laid on in Dresden in July 1871 to greet the victorious Saxon troops returning from France, the six-year-old prince welcomed back his father and the soldiers on Dresden's Neumarkt square. In June 1878, he marched as a thirteen-year-old lieutenant in the parade to mark the king and queen's silver wedding anniversary. Four years later he participated in the great manoeuvres attended by Emperor Wilhelm I and, in recognition of this feat, was decorated with the Order of the Black Eagle, Prussia's highest medal. In July 1883 the prince was the first member of his dynastic family to take the soldier's oath of allegiance in public and a lightning career followed: he became first lieutenant in 1883, captain in 1887, major in 1889, and then raced through the ranks of lieutenant-colonel and colonel in the early 1890s to emerge as a general in 1898, when aged just thirty-three. According to reports, during his rapid ascent the prince showed himself to be good-natured and sociable, which made him popular with the troops. 'One had only to hear the "long

---

[22] Simone Mergen, *Monarchiejubiläen im 19. Jahrhundert. Die Entdeckung des historischen Jubiläums für den monarchischen Kult in Sachsen und Bayern* (Leipzig, 2005), pp. 249–253; Frank Lorenz Müller, *Royal Heirs in Imperial Germany: The Future of Monarchy in Nineteenth-Century Bavaria, Saxony and Württemberg* (London, 2017), p. 100.

fellows" talk about their prince as they bivouacked in the evening to recognise how much they all liked him', a pamphlet declared. In October 1904, Saxony's new king could announce to his soldiers that, 'From my earliest youth the army has been my absolute love', for the groundwork for his statement had been carefully laid over decades.[23]

In monarchies such as Saxony and Bavaria, where the military merits of the Wittelsbachs were also publicly celebrated, it was evidently deemed advantageous in the nineteenth century to highlight the soldierly traditions of the royal house and in particular the prowess of the future ruler. Should the very existence of the monarchy be at risk, the prospect of a future ruler who seemed to embody all the virtues of the soldier had even greater significance. Such was the case, as Richard Meyer Forsting has shown, for Spain, where the rule of the Bourbon dynasty was interrupted repeatedly throughout the course of the nineteenth century by civil wars, revolutions, republican intermezzi and enforced exile.

After what was termed the 'Glorious Revolution' in 1868, for instance, Queen Isabella II had to leave Spain with her eleven-year-old son, Alfonso. She abdicated in exile in 1870. Meanwhile, a new king had been chosen in her place and later a republic was proclaimed. Yet, not long after the Bourbons had found themselves forced out of the country, pictures were circulating in Spain of Alfonso as a pupil at the Theresianum, the elite school in Vienna at which he was being educated. The great hope of those who supported the restoration of the former royal dynasty was depicted wearing the uniform of an Austrian cadet, including a sword. He appears on photographs from 1873 and 1874 clad in a Spanish uniform, with moustache to match. From his 'Sandhurst Manifesto', the Spanish learned of Alfonso's time as a cadet at the English military academy at Sandhurst. Subsequently, in 1875, he returned as king and promptly joined successful campaigns against rebels in northern Spain. His involvement earned him the honorary title of *El Pacificador* and provided material for numerous further images, in which the young monarch, now sporting a full beard, was usually depicted on horseback and in uniform. Alfonso XII retained this strongly militaristic image until his sudden death ten years later. The martial element was also to the fore in the case of his posthumous son, King Alfonso XIII. As shown in Figure 22, when the king came closer to taking up the reins of government on his sixteenth birthday in 1901, he was more frequently depicted in uniform and in the company of soldiers. In the two years

---

[23] Müller, *Royal Heirs in Imperial Germany*, pp. 98–100; Walter Fellmann, *Sachsens letzter König. Friedrich August III.* (Berlin and Leipzig, 1992), pp. 39–40; Richard Stecher, *König Friedrich August III. von Sachsen. Ein Lebensbild* (Dresden, 1905), p. 11; *Dresdner Journal*, special edition of 16 October 1904.

Figure 22. Given that Alfonso XIII, who was born after his father's early death, was an underage king until his sixteenth birthday in 1902, his presentation as a martial young man was of particular importance. Hi-Story/Alamy Stock Photo.

before his reign began, the illustrated press showed him visiting weapons factories, warships and manoeuvres accompanied by military officers. The captions praised the fifteen-year-old for his horsemanship, his knowledge of military affairs and his proficiency on the battlefield.[24]

Great value was also placed on ensuring that the upbringing of the Prince of Naples, the future king Vittorio Emanuele III of Italy, had a military flavour. The somewhat delicate prince was educated on his

---

[24] Richard Meyer Forsting, 'The Importance of Looking the Part: Heirs and Male Aesthetics in Nineteenth-Century Spain', in Frank Lorenz Müller and Heidi Mehrkens (eds.), *Royal Heirs and the Uses of Soft Power in Nineteenth-Century Europe* (London, 2016), pp. 181–200.

own, but his instruction followed the curricula of various military academies. In the majority of the surviving photographs, the young heir appears in uniform, probably as a counterweight to his less than impressive stature, for, as King Umberto's adjutant observed, 'It is to be regretted that his short legs diminish the militaristic impression that is so desirable for a crown prince.' Yet his lack of physical stature did not hold the heir back from active engagement with militarily matters, an involvement displayed to the public. As a youth, he accompanied the king to large-scale manoeuvres, as, for example, in August 1888, when he travelled to Forli in the region of Emilia-Romagna. During a state visit to Germany two years later, Vittorio Emanuele inspected a Guard Uhlans cavalry brigade and observed infantry exercises. In the same year – on the occasion of his twenty-first birthday – his father appointed him commander of a regiment in Naples, where Vittorio Emanuele would then serve for several years. In March 1895, one year after he had been promoted to lieutenant general, the crown prince accompanied an Italian naval squadron on a fleet visit to England.[25]

At Portsmouth, the home of the Royal Navy, Vittorio Emanuele had arrived on the very stage where in the second half of the nineteenth century the British royal family displayed the military capabilities of future generations of rulers. Queen Victoria exhibited a remarkably lively interest in military matters and could embrace her official role as supreme commander, for her performance was largely limited to inspecting the troops and making the occasional rousing statement. To her distress, while her oldest son, Bertie, later King Edward VII, had shown an early interest in serving with the armed forces, he demonstrated only limited talent as a soldier. In a conversation with her younger son Arthur, the queen once regretted that Arthur, the successful commander-in-chief of the British Army in Ireland, was not her successor. Bertie, whose girth and lifestyle suggested a lack of soldierly discipline, subsequently insisted on a far more military upbringing for his own sons Albert Victor (Eddy) and George than his father had deemed necessary for Bertie himself. His brother Alfred's popularity with the British public as a 'sailor prince' and serving naval officer may have encouraged the Prince of Wales to approve John Dalton's suggestion that his two oldest sons undergo, in the glare of publicity, the many years of training to be naval officers, both at the naval academy and on board the corvette *HMS Bacchante*. For Eddy, the heir apparent, several years with a Hussars regiment followed, which

---

[25] Paolo Paulucci, *Alla corte di Re Umberto. Diario segreto* (Milan, 1986), p. 59 (I am grateful to Maria-Christina Marchi for this reference); *The Times* of 29 August 1888, 3 September 1888, 10 June 1890, 13 November 1890 and 18 March 1895; Alexander Robertson, *Victor Emmanuel III: King of Italy* (London, 1925), pp. 112–113.

prompted his commander-in-chief, Viscount Wolseley, to describe the prince's 'brain & thinking powers, as maturing slowly'. The next royal heir, Prince Edward, continued the naval tradition and completed the regular four-year training of an officer-cadet.[26]

The royal family was fully aware of how well its sailor princes were received by the British public and was not going to squander this opportunity. In June 1885, shortly after ending his studies at Cambridge, Prince Albert Victor presented prizes to boys on board the training ship *HMS Warspite*. In his speech, which was reproduced in *The Standard*, the heir to the throne recalled his own time as a naval cadet and his travels across the oceans. He praised the discipline and energy of the young mariners on board the *Warspite* and called on them 'in whatever part of the world your duty may call you to act always worthily of the English name and race'. When his nephew Prince Edward completed his training on board the warship *HMS Hindustan* in the summer of 1911, the press fell into line, with the *Illustrated London News* providing a large format photograph of the prince in naval uniform and reporting that he 'is thoroughly enjoying the experience, is keen on his work, and very popular with his comrades in the gun-room'.[27]

'The Resplendent Hero Returning Home from Warring in Foreign Lands Tanned by the Sun': Staging Crown Princes as War Heroes

Following the sudden death of his older brother in 1892, Prince George, who had already embarked on a career as a naval officer, unexpectedly found himself heir to the throne. Just one day after Albert Victor's death, the *Pall Mall Gazette* welcomed George as the future ruler and addressed the question of whether he should continue to expose himself to the dangers of a life at sea. The British public would certainly be saddened to see him forced back onto dry land, commented the newspaper, adding, 'His cousins of the Imperial House of Hohenzollern have never shrunk from perilous duty merely because they stood near the throne – indeed, the late German Emperor Friedrich, when Crown Prince of Prussia, fought like a Trojan and quitted himself like a man on many a stricken

---

[26] Walter Arnstein, 'The Warrior Queen: Reflections on Queen Victoria and Her World', in *Albion* 30 (1998), pp. 1–28; Miriam Schneider, *The 'Sailor Prince' in the Age of Empire: Creating a Monarchical Brand in Nineteenth-Century Europe* (London, 2017); James Pope-Hennessy, *Queen Mary: The Official Biography*, with an introduction by Hugo Vickers (London, 2019), p. 193.

[27] *The Standard* (London) of 26 June 1885; *The Illustrated London News* of 9 September 1911.

and bloody field of battle.'[28] With a note of envy, the newspaper had highlighted a reality that somewhat undermined the great military claims of most of the highly decorated royal heirs: having engaged in little more than shadow boxing, princes rarely had any first-hand experience of war. Much was therefore made of the rare cases where a future ruler had actually won some battle honours.

The United Kingdom of the Netherlands, created at the Congress of Vienna in 1814–1815, not only had a venerable dynasty – the House of Orange – and a brand-new constitution, but also possessed a resplendent war hero: Prince Willem of Orange, the future King Willem II. The prince's fame as victorious warrior and saviour of the nation was not just impressive but also advantageous, for it could be deployed to tackle a central challenge facing the new kingdom: how to ease the tensions between the Dutch provinces in the north and the Belgian lands in the south. The ultimate goal was to create a patriotism embraced by the new nation as a whole. The prince was born in The Hague in 1792, but, after the French occupation of the Netherlands, he spent the majority of his youth in exile. He attended the Prussian military academy in Berlin before being sent to study at Oxford. Then, on his father's orders, he accompanied the English general Arthur Wellesley, the later Duke of Wellington, to Spain, where he distinguished himself fighting Napoleon's troops. His performance at the battles of El Bodón (1811), Badajoz (1812) and Salamanca (1812) had earned him the respect of his troops and his superiors. Once he was back in England, his father appointed him General Inspector of the yet-to-be-created Dutch forces. After Napoleon had been driven out of the Netherlands, the House of Orange returned in 1813. Prince Willem, now a general in the British army, became commander of the troops in the southern Netherlands and took up residence in Brussels. His reputation as a successful military officer and his actual experience of war would prove extremely useful to the House of Orange.[29]

The first test came in June 1815. Napoleon had returned from his exile in Elba and again seized power in France. The war was thus reignited. Prince Willem led the Dutch forces and, like his younger brother Frederik, was on the battlefield when the anti-French coalition prevailed

[28] *Pall Mall Gazette* of 15 January 1892.
[29] Hans A. Bornewasser, 'König Wilhelm II.', in Coenraad A. Tamse (ed.), *Nassau und Oranien. Statthalter und Könige der Niederlande* (Göttingen and Zurich, 1985), pp. 256–267; Jeroen Koch, 'The King as Father, Orangism and the Uses of a Hero: King William I of the Netherlands and the Prince of Orange, 1815–1840', in Frank Lorenz Müller and Heidi Mehrkens (eds.), *Royal Heirs and the Uses of Soft Power in Nineteenth-Century Europe* (London, 2016), pp. 263–280.

first at Quatre Bras and then only a few days later at Waterloo. Wounded at Waterloo, the crown prince became a national hero as the saviour of his father's crown and a conqueror of Napoleon. For the Dutch, the true hero of Waterloo was – and is – the Prince of Orange, not Wellington or Marshal Blücher, writes the historian Jeroen Koch. That status derived less from the prince's actual performance at Quatre Bras and Waterloo, which for good reason came in for sharp criticism from experts, than from the intensive myth-making that followed.[30]

Prince Willem eagerly prepared the ground himself. 'We had a magnificent affair against Napoleon today', he wrote to his parents after the battle, 'it was my corps which principally gave battle and to which we owe the victory.' His family readily adopted this version. 'The heroic part played by my grandson really established the Royal House and gave it firm ground' was the assessment of Wilhelmine, mother of King Willem I, just a few weeks after the battle. The House of Orange never tired of exploiting the propagandistic potential of the role Prince Willem had played. Between 1823 and 1826, the king had a forty-metre-high mound raised up on the battlefield at Waterloo, on which was placed a twenty-eight-ton statue of a lion. This new hill marked the very spot where the prince had been wounded. Equally enormous in scale was Jan Willem Pieneman's 1824 painting, acquired by the crown, entitled *De slag bij Waterloo* (*The Battle of Waterloo*). It features the wounded prince in the foreground. At almost forty-seven square metres, the canvas remains the largest painting in the Amsterdam Rijksmuseum. Quatre Bras and Waterloo were the foundations on which the new Dutch state would rest, the king declared in parliament in August 1815, and then called out, 'Happy is the father whose sons had the honour of erecting these pillars and of anointing them with their blood.' The public took up this cult enthusiastically: ballad-singers and storytellers recounted Prince Willem's act of heroism; at the theatre the audience rose from their seats to show their reverence for the prince; and the parliament decided immediately to assign him three palaces.[31]

In 1831, the poet Willem Hendrik Warnsinck was still celebrating the 'hero of Waterloo, / The crown prince, the hope of the Dutch, / He avenges us; he saves our honour, / And gives us peace at heart.'[32] Even the carefully cultivated reputation of the crown prince, who was also popular in the southern provinces, was not sufficient, however, to stop the forces that were tearing the United Kingdom of the Netherlands apart. During the

---

[30] Koch, 'The King as Father', p. 273.

[31] Bernard Cornwell, *Waterloo: The History of Four Days, Three Armies and Three Battles* (London, 2014), p. 323; Koch, 'The King as Father', pp. 273–274.

[32] Koch, 'The King as Father', p. 274.

Belgian Revolution of 1830 the southern provinces seceded and claimed their independence, with the Belgian throne subsequently offered to Leopold, a prince of Coburg. As the King of the Netherlands, the title inherited by the 'hero of Waterloo' after his father's abdication in 1840, Willem therefore did not rule over the 'Lion's Mound', which stood not far from Brussels and had been created in his honour.

Far more tragic is the story of another future monarch whose military successes made him the great hope of his dynasty. The French July Monarchy had a similarly promising heir to the throne. The portraits of Prince Ferdinand Philippe d'Orléans, duke of Chartres, painted by Ary Scheffer and Horace Vernet (Figure 23) in the early 1830s, depict the

Figure 23. Every inch a future ruler: Horace Vernet's painting of 1832 depicts Prince Ferdinand Philippe, King Louis Philippe's oldest son, as a glamorous military hero. ART Collection/Alamy Stock Photo.

resplendent young officer in heroic pose, wearing the uniform of a Hussar or mounted on his charger. The oldest son of King Louis Philippe was in many respects the perfect heir. He had attended a public school – the famous College Henri IV in Paris – and subsequently maintained numerous friendships with members of the bourgeoisie; his politics were liberal and he was known for his artistic and cultural interests. His visits to plague hospitals had advertised his humanity to the broader public. After his marriage to Helene of Mecklenburg-Schwerin, he proved himself to be a caring father to his two sons. Ultimately, though, his star shone so uncommonly bright because of his impressive military career.[33]

Having commanded the 1st Hussars since 1828, in 1831–1832 the heir to the throne participated in the campaign in Belgium, where the French troops advanced against Dutch forces that had moved into Belgium in an effort to overturn that country's newly won independence. As there was no actual fighting, the prince – who in the meantime had been promoted to brigadier-general and received the cross of the Legion of Honour – could only prove his courage and prowess at the siege of the citadel of Antwerp in November and December 1832. There he insisted – much to the consternation of his aunt Adélaide, who would have preferred him to have stayed as far away from the front as possible – on being allowed to carry out the most dangerous tasks. He thus proved, according to a contemporary account, that 'the blood of stronger races never degenerates and that he is a worthy successor of Henry IV'. The supreme commander Marshal Gérard was also full of praise: 'His example electrified our young soldiers', he reported on 30 November 1832. Prince Ferdinand's heroic deeds at Antwerp would also become the subject of great historical paintings, including the panorama of the battle by Horace Vernet of 1840.[34]

In 1835, the prince went to Algeria, where he fought with the army of Marshal Bertrand Clauzel in the colonial wars against Amir Abdelkader. He was present at the battles of Habrah and Tlemcen, where he was wounded, and participated in the capture of Mascara. In 1836, he returned in triumph to Paris. Four years later, he was back in North Africa, where, in May 1840, he supposedly played a decisive role in the fighting at Col de Mouzaia. With the opposition carefully defending its position, the cautious Marshal Sylvain-Charles Valée is said to have

[33] Heidi Mehrkens, 'The Impossible Task of Replacing a Model Heir: The Death of Ferdinand-Philippe d'Orléans and the "New France"', in Frank Lorenz Müller and Heidi Mehrkens (eds.), *Sons and Heirs: Succession and Political Culture in Nineteenth-Century Europe* (Basingstoke, 2016), p. 204.

[34] Adrien Pascal, *Vie militaire, privée et politique de Son Altesse Royale monseigneur le duc d'Orléans* (Paris, 1842), pp. 8–9, 15–16; Joëlle Hureau, *L'espoir brisé. Le duc d'Orléans 1810–1842* (Paris, 1995), pp. 187–208; Munro Price, *The Perilous Crown: France between Revolutions, 1814–1848* (Basingstoke and Oxford, 2007), p. 241.

turned to the prince for advice. 'Always attack', came the response, 'with French soldiers everything can be attempted.' No one dared challenge such élan, and so the order to attack was immediately given. The advance of the three columns was said to have been so well coordinated that it climaxed just as the battle cry rang out: 'Long live France! Long live the Duke of Orleans!' A contemporary account suggests an almost religious scene: 'The bugles sounded, the drummers pounded their drums, the colours were lowered to the ground as the duke passed in review, and from all throats rose the same frenetic cry of adulation: "Long live the crown prince!"'[35]

Had the prince fallen at this victory, in the midst of his solders, according to the author of a posthumous panegyric, then France would have been able to bear her pain at his loss all the better. For only two years after the triumph at Col de Mouzaia, Crown Prince Ferdinand died after an accident near Neuilly. He had jumped out of his carriage when the horses bolted, hit his head on the ground and within a few hours he was dead. The demise of their great hope, glorified as a shining example, threw the French into deep mourning. The royal family, the political and social elites, and the broader population responded with profound shock to his loss, identified by some historians as the beginning of the end for the July Monarchy, which collapsed six years later. The obituary in the London *Times* left no doubt about the prince's status as a war hero at the time of his death. 'He always entertained a marked predilection for military employment, and a strong love of military glory, and was understood to be much beloved by the soldiers under his command, many of whom – sturdy veterans of the Napoleon armies – shed tears as his lifeless body was carried from the fatal spot', the newspaper reported.[36]

Ferdinand Philippe continued to watch over the nation even after his death. On 26 July 1845, a bronze statue of the prince on horseback was erected in front of the Louvre. A crowd of thousands accompanied the statue on its journey from the foundry where it had been cast, strewing flowers in its path. A few months later, a copy of the Parisian statue was unveiled on the Place Royale in Algiers. Two reliefs on the pedestal recalled the Battles of Antwerp and Col de Mouzaia. The third monument erected in honour of the deceased heir to the throne was also distinctly martial in tone. The residents of the northern French city of Saint-Omer had become very fond of Ferdinand during winter manoeuvres in 1840/41 and, immediately after his death, they took up

---

[35] Pascal, *Vie militaire, privée et politique*, pp. 59, 64.
[36] Mehrkens, 'The Impossible Task of Replacing a Model Heir', pp. 196–210; Hureau, *L'espoir brisé*, pp. 313–318; Price, *The Perilous Crown*, pp. 309–312; *The Times* of 16 July 1842.

a collection for a monument in his honour. The necessary sum was raised relatively quickly for a design in which the prince was standing, dressed in uniform and cape, his sword at his side, a scroll in his right hand and his left hand raised imperiously. After some delay, the monument was unveiled in 1847, but it had to be removed again only a few months later, in the spring of 1848. In the interim the July Monarchy had fallen. The royal hero in bronze had been unable to prevent its replacement by a short-lived republic.[37]

Even if the military contributions of an heir to the throne were hard to determine or of questionable merit, much could still be made of them. Such was the case, for example, for Prince Umberto of Piedmont, who succeeded his father as king of Italy in 1878. He had commanded the 16th Division at the Battle of Custoza in 1866. Although the Italian army had been defeated, his performance and bravery in commanding his infantry square, the *quadrato*, when it was attacked by Austrian cavalry were deemed so exemplary that they could form the basis of his reputation as a true soldier. Edmondo De Amicis's phenomenally successful children's novel *Cuore* mentioned the *quadrato di principe Umberto* and his command of the '16' several times. The historian Giuseppe Guerzoni, a contemporary, wrote with great passion of the courage displayed by the heir to the throne during the fighting. If during the battle the prince had forgotten the noble blood that ran through his veins or had been afraid, then all would have been lost, he insisted. Fortunately, that had not been the case: 'Umberto of Savoy suddenly proved himself to be a soldier and turned to face the enemy. His example served for everyone to emulate and thus the enemy crashed into a wall of breasts filled with courage, ready to defend in the son of Vittorio Emanuele the whole of Italy.'[38]

While Umberto would demonstrate a life-long passion for all things military and carefully tended his own image as a soldier, the last king of Bavaria was a profoundly non-military man. He ended his active military service at the earliest possible moment and subsequently concerned himself very little with soldierly matters beyond otherwise unavoidable routine demands. Bespectacled, corpulent and notoriously lackadaisical when it came to matters sartorial, the Wittelsbach prince, born in 1845,

---

[37] https://statuesmonumentsnpdc.pagesperso-orange.fr/duc_orleans.htm (accessed 4 June 2022).
[38] Edmondo De Amicis, *The Heart of a Boy (Cuore)*, trans. G. Mantellini (New York, 1895), pp. 8, 21–22, 104, www.google.co.uk/books/edition/The_Heart_of_a_Boy/e21KAAAA IAAJ?hl=en&gbpv=1 (accessed 1 June 2022); Guerzoni cited in *Dizionario del Risorgimento Nazionale*, vol. IV: *Le persone* (Milan, 1937), pp. 506–507; Geoffrey Wawro, *The Austro-Prussian War: Austria's War with Prussia and Italy 1866* (Cambridge, 1996), pp. 104–107.

hardly met the ideal of the princely warrior. In 1909, a famous caricature entitled 'Imperial Manoeuvre' that appeared in the satirical Munich journal *Simplicissimus* (Figure 24) depicted the contrast between the hyperactive über-briskness of the German emperor, Wilhelm II, and the

Figure 24. In 1911, the satirical magazine *Simplicissimus* poked fun at the military self-staging of some rulers: the excessively brisk Emperor Wilhelm II stands in marked contrast to the slovenly corpulence of Prince Ludwig, the future king of Bavaria. O. Gulbransson, 'Imperial Manoeuvres' ['Kaisermanöver'], 1911 (*Simplicissimus*) bpk | Bayerische Staatsgemäldesammlungen © VG Bild-Kunst 2018.

somewhat bumbling ponderousness of the Wittelsbach prince, in his poorly fitting uniform. The Bavarian heir could afford to adopt a civilian persona, because other members of his family – above all his father Luitpold, but also his brothers Leopold and Arnulf – were viewed as established military professionals who could look back on impressive army careers and thus vouch for the dynasty's military credentials. When it came to the monarchy's public image, however, the unsoldierly Ludwig had an additional ace up his sleeve, or, more accurately, a piece of lead in his thigh. Whereas Emperor Wilhelm II was eager to appear battle-ready, Ludwig had actually experienced combat. In 1866, as a young lieutenant he had taken up arms against Prussia, and on 25 July had been wounded in a militarily insignificant skirmish at Helmstadt in Lower Franconia. Not realising who this officer actually was, his comrades had brought him to a field hospital, where he was finally recognised. It proved possible to halt the bleeding, but the bullet could not be removed, and from then on Prince Ludwig walked with a slight limp.[39]

Although Helmstadt ended the prince's actual military activities once and for all, it was there that his career as a war hero really began. In 1886, it became evident that Ludwig was likely to be king one day and the patriotic press made assiduous efforts to ensure that the heroic actions of the future ruler would not be forgotten. Twenty-five years after the war, the *Neue Freie Volkszeitung* published a narrative of the campaign in Franconia that was accompanied by a poignant drawing with the title 'Wounding of His Royal Highness Prince Ludwig at the battle of Helmstadt, 25 July'. In 1895, to mark the prince's fiftieth birthday, the *Bayerische Kurier* printed a picture entitled 'Prince Ludwig as Soldier and Hero (Wounded at Helmstadt 1866)'. Ten years later the same newspaper reminded its readers, 'Prince Ludwig has also been in the thick of battle alongside the sons of the people.' The climax of this adulation was reached in 1909: over forty years after the battle, the inhabitants of the village of Helmstadt erected a monument to commemorate the wounding of the future king of Bavaria. The honouree, dressed in a dark suit and wearing a bowler hat, personally attended the unveiling, which elicited a substantial response in the press. The monument in Helmstadt recalled words supposedly spoken by Prince Luitpold, Ludwig's father and at the time his commander, as he stood by the bed of his wounded son: 'In this moment my responsibilities as a father retreat to make way for the higher

---

[39] Frank Lorenz Müller, 'Ludwig of Bavaria and Helmstadt: The Heroic Memory of an Unmilitary Prince', AHRC Project *Heirs to the Throne in the Constitutional Monarchies of Nineteenth-Century Europe (1815–1914)*, 'Heir of the Month' (July 2016), http://heirsto thethrone-project.net/?page_id=2512 (accessed 28 March 2017); Müller, *Royal Heirs in Imperial Germany*, pp. 100–105.

responsibilities to the fatherland that I must fulfil.' The military honouring of the unmilitary Ludwig could thus also serve a pedagogical purpose for the people more broadly.[40]

For Prince Wilhelm of Prussia, the future King and Emperor Wilhelm I, public recognition of his military successes also came later, although in his case significantly later. As the younger brother of the crown prince and later Prussian king Friedrich Wilhelm IV (1795–1861), the prince was not initially considered a likely heir to the throne. He therefore concentrated on his military career. Once the wars against Napoleon, in which he participated as a youth, were over, though, this Hohenzollern prince had little opportunity to win military laurels. When, shortly before his sixtieth birthday, Wilhelm started to pay attention to how he might be remembered by posterity, the only military achievement to which he could point was his command of the Prussian troops who had extinguished the last flames of the revolution first in the Palatinate and subsequently in Baden in 1849. In 1856, he commissioned a flattering biographical sketch to be published in the journal *Der Soldatenfreund* (*The Soldier's Friend*). The text celebrated his military career by emphasising the counter-revolutionary campaign. The prince, it recounted, moved into his headquarters at Rastatt, 'where he was always close-by his troops, each day inspected their positions, visited their bivouacs and gave all the orders that at last brought resistance throughout Baden to an end'. The success, the journal noted, was complete: 'Within only a few weeks and almost entirely as laid out in the first plan for the operation, the prince of Prussia freed the Palatinate and Baden of the tyranny they were under, sharing all the dangers with his soldiers and increasing their respect and allegiance to the highest degree.'[41]

Wilhelm was a military hero, and he looked the part. Louis Schneider, the author of his biography, quoted with relish from a description of the prince during the campaign. He was, it noted, 'a handsome and tall figure, with a friendly, cheerful and extremely winning countenance, lively eyes and spoke with a deep melodious voice'. It continued, 'The prince bears a large, blond moustache, its ends twisted up somewhat and precisely the same beard on chin and cheek as has now been introduced in the Prussian army. He wears the simple uniform of a general, with the *Pour le Mérite*

---

[40] *Neue Freie Volkszeitung* of 2 August 1891; *Bayrischer Kurier* of 7 January 1895 and 7 January 1905.

[41] Frederik Frank Sterkenburgh, 'Narrating Prince Wilhelm of Prussia: Commemorative Biography as Monarchical Politics of Memory', in Frank Lorenz Müller and Heidi Mehrkens (eds.), *Royal Heirs and the Uses of Soft Power in Nineteenth-Century Europe* (London, 2016), pp. 281–301; Louis Schneider, 'Der Prinz von Preußen. Zum 1. Januar 1857', in *Der Soldatenfreund* 24 (December 1856), pp. 119–121, 126.

order and in his buttonhole the Iron Cross won in the Wars of Liberation.' This self-advertisement presented the heir to the throne, who was no longer a young man, as a virile military officer with battlefield experience, a refreshing change from his older brother, King Friedrich Wilhelm IV, who did not exactly cut a dashing figure, had no beard and was somewhat rotund. It thus foreshadowed a different monarchical role, although in the mid 1850s Prince Wilhelm could not have suspected that in the years and decades after his sixtieth birthday he would have opportunity to succeed his brother and win military glory. The 'German Wars of Unification', as they would come to be known, with campaigns against Denmark (1864), Austria (1866) and France (1870–1871), raised the elderly Prussian king into the Valhalla of venerated military figures, but the status of heroic wartime commander was granted, above all, to his son.[42]

In 1892, London's *Pall Mall Gazette* struck an unmistakeably reproachful tone when it pointed out to the heir to the British throne that elsewhere crown princes did not shrink from the dangers of war. The example it referenced was Crown Prince Friedrich Wilhelm. The newspaper had set the bar high, for 'Our Fritz', as the Prussian heir to the throne was lovingly called, was a military celebrity amongst the royal heirs of the nineteenth century. In the eyes of the German public, the prince – the victor at the Battles of Königgrätz (1866), Wissembourg (1870) and Wörth (1870) – was a charismatic and brave military commander, whose contribution to the triumphs over the Austrians and French had been heroic and decisive. He had thus earned enormous prestige and popularity, but, additionally, his exceptional abilities appeared to predestine him for his future office as ruler and even to legitimise the monarchical system. The crown prince's military fame formed the core of his later popularity as heir and as emperor. 'We would never have seen the indifferent figure of Crown Prince Friedrich Wilhelm of Prussia become the imposing and engaging type that was "Our Fritz", the idol of the first German army', Georg Hinzpeter wrote as early as 1883, 'if the external circumstances had not forced upon him the opportunity in which his great talent, his strong will, and his full heart had had to manifest themselves.'[43]

The Prussian heir was certainly a competent officer, but he was definitely not a military genius. The successes of the armies that he had commanded in 1866 and 1870–1871 were primarily owed to his chief of staff, the later Field Marshal Leonhard von Blumenthal, but that reality was of little consequence to the broader public. Crucially, the heir to the

---

[42] Schneider, 'Der Prinz von Preußen', p. 126.
[43] The discussion of Crown Prince Friedrich Wilhelm that follows draws on Müller, *Our Fritz*, pp. 127–139.

throne was able to relate to his soldiers, personally courageous and physically fit. He exuded energy and decisiveness. A victorious prince who smoked and swam with his soldiers, could sit in the saddle for fourteen hours at a stretch, and had a chivalrous reputation even amongst his opponents was a walking advertisement for a militarised monarchy. The image was consummately conveyed: after the victory at Königgrätz, King Wilhelm I and his son met on the battlefield; the crown prince kissed his father's hand, the two embraced – crying with emotion – and then the king hung his own *Pour le Mérite* order around his son's neck. No patriotic account of Prussian history would fail to include this tear-jerking scene or omit to remind its readers that Friedrich Wilhelm was the first Prussian heir ever to attain the rank of field marshal.

A mix of media soon contributed to the carefully constructed image of military perfection. Simple rhyming soldiers' songs recounted tales of our 'crown prince, who's called Fritz, and he strikes, just like a blitz, / right amongst the Frenchmen's mob'. In newspapers ranging from the left-liberal *Vossische Zeitung* all the way to the conservative *Neue Preußische Zeitung*, Friedrich Wilhelm was credited with an outstanding contribution to the origins of the German Empire in combat and mention was made of the 'eternal renown' that he had acquired on the battlefield. Parallels were readily drawn between, on the one hand, the 'old Fritz', Frederick the Great, who constituted the central myth of the monarchy and, on the other, the 'young Fritz', with the beguiling masculine attractiveness of the heir – his tall stature, his blue eyes – a frequent theme. 'Like a warrior from the North from long since forgotten times, his appearance radiates amongst the group of paladins who surround the honourable figure of Emperor William the White Beard', rhapsodised the *Berliner Tageblatt* in 1881, on the occasion of the heir's fiftieth birthday. The *Freisinnige Zeitung* recalled the crown prince's arriving back from France, as the 'archetype of manly strength and beauty, the resplendent hero returning home from warring in foreign lands tanned by the sun'.[44]

The shadow of that heroic narrative fell across Crown Prince Friedrich Wilhelm's son, later Emperor Wilhelm II, who, unlike his father and grandfather, could produce no actual experience of war and had to make do with rousing speeches and eccentric office furniture. Moreover, in the summer of 1914, the moment when the *oompah, oom-pahs* of folkloric militarism acquired a life-or-death seriousness, an over-whelming weight descended on the heir to the throne, and on the whole system of militarised monarchy that during the nineteenth century had paraded so colourfully to the sounds of the brass bands and had

[44] Ibid., pp. 135–138.

celebrated its supposedly heroic royal heirs so exuberantly. As military officers, bearers of hope for the future, men and patriots, the heirs to the throne found themselves tested as never before by the outbreak of war.

'This Was My 1st Real Sight of War, & It Moved and Impressed Me Most Enormously': Royal Heirs as Soldiers in the First World War

On 29 September 1915, Edward, Prince of Wales, the heir to the British throne, penned a diary entry about what he considered 'probably the 4 most interesting hrs of my life'. Together with Lord Cavan, the commander of the Guards Division, the young officer had visited the front near the northern French town of Loos after a British attack. 'Of course the dead lie out unburied & in the postures & on the spots as they fell, & one got some idea of the horror & the ghastliness of it all!! ... Those dead bodies offered a most pathetic & gruesome sight; too cruel to be killed within a few yds. of yr. objective after a 300 yds. sprint of death!! This was my 1st real sight of war, & it moved and impressed me most enormously. [. . .] I have seen & learnt a lot about war today.' Edward's description was written while he was suffering from shock – while waiting at the car during the prince's visit to the front, his driver had been killed by an exploding shell. This diary entry illustrated one dimension of the heirs' experience of the Great War: where they came sufficiently close to the reality of the fighting and saw the enormous toll paid in blood, they had to deal with these atrocities just as did the hundreds of thousands of other men and women who as soldiers, nurses or civilians were also witnesses of the horrors of this war.[45]

The role of royal heirs during the First World War cannot be understood, however, purely in terms of such human and individual experience. A further dimension is also evident in the Prince of Wales's entry for 29 September 1915 – the young captain had arrived with his own driver and been accompanied by the division commander. After the events of 29 September became known, King George's private secretary promptly wrote to Lord Cavan on behalf of His Majesty, calling on the commander to consider very carefully when and where the young prince would visit the front. In short: in war as in his normal life, the heir to the throne enjoyed privileges that made his experience fundamentally different from the fate of his fellow soldiers. 'Your Life, so precious to your country', the king's private secretary, Lord Stamfordham, wrote to him, was to be specially protected – unlike the lives of untold soldiers. This extraordinary

---

[45] *A King's Story*, p. 114.

treatment made it difficult, however, for future monarchs to use the war as an opportunity to demonstrate the military prowess, acceptance of hardship and personal courage that would buttress their claims to power and privilege. Yet precisely such examples were urgently needed when rulers and governments were appealing to their peoples to make the ultimate sacrifice. With millions of men called upon to fight 'for King and Country', the monarchical system and its most prominent representatives would need to prove themselves worthy of the devotion demanded of their subjects. Contemporary propaganda sought to convince its audience that such was undoubtedly the case. 'As in the olden days, the German princes too are drawn into the struggle as soldiers, who each, from the place assigned to him according to age and rank, look death in the eye like the last musketeer', claimed a German text from 1915. 'History has never before seen this for any state, that such an array of princes rush to arms, including themselves entirely without question in the general conscription.'[46]

In truth, the wartime achievements of the royal houses in the First World War were far less heroic than such celebratory prose would suggest. Lothar Machtan's examination of the military contributions of the German princes during the war yields a fairly sobering conclusion. The brutal reality of the war, he writes, revealed most of the German monarchs as 'living tin soldiers' and idlers on the battlefield, all too ready to limit their contribution to peering through a scissor scope, unnecessary parleys far from the front, and occasional visits to a field hospital. Certainly, there were a few noteworthy exceptions to this rule. Prince Ernst II of Saxony-Altenburg and Prince Adolf of Schaumburg-Lippe had fairly earned their good reputations as commanding officers, and a number of royal heirs – Crown Prince Wilhelm of Prussia, Crown Prince Rupprecht of Bavaria and Duke Albrecht of Württemberg held high command, although with varying degrees of success.[47] Also actively engaged were Crown Prince and Regent Alexander, as supreme commander of the Serbian forces, and the Austrian archduke and later emperor Karl, who was promoted to lieutenant field marshal and would command troops in the Italian and Romanian theatres of war. Prince Leopold, the thirteen-year-old son of the King of the Belgians, served as

---

[46] Ibid., pp. 115, 119; Heather Jones, 'The Nature of Kingship in First World War Britain', in Matthew Glencross, Judith Rowbotham and Michael D. Kandiah (eds.), *The Windsor Dynasty: 1910 to the Present* (London, 2016), pp. 195–216; Lothar Machtan, *Die Abdankung. Wie Deutschlands gekrönte Häupter aus der Geschichte fielen* (Berlin, 2008), p. 93.

[47] Machtan, *Die Abdankung*, pp. 92–107.

a private in 1915 and even came under fire, while the British heir, Prince Edward, performed various tasks in France, Italy and the Middle East.[48]

The active military engagement of heirs to the throne – whether or not it had much effect – was part of a broader task faced by royal houses during the First World War. Heather Jones has noted that 'The British royal family was central to both the practical mobilisation of the war effort and the cultural belief systems that underpinned contemporary British mentalities', and that royal role was not limited to the British Isles. In leading their country in a time of war, the monarch and the members of the monarch's family were defending not just the fatherland but also their own position within the country's political structures and cultural as well as emotional configurations. The spectrum of monarchical activities ranged from actual military command and political leadership – as in the case of the Belgian king Albert I – to multifarious ceremonial and benevolent activities, such as investitures, appeals for donations and visits to the troops and to hospitals.[49]

Everywhere monarchs' activity was visibly intertwined with the fate of their subjects and the success of their military forces, whose leadership they had claimed and celebrated under the auspices of the constitutional state for a century. This connection continued during a time of extreme crisis and bloody sacrifice. It is therefore hardly surprising that the failure of the total war effort – in other words, defeat – delivered a fatal blow to the structures of leadership that were ultimately held responsible. That failure was not the only reason why the First World War brought the monarchical century to a close. In driving the process of dynastic nationalisation, in other words the identification of the ruling house with the nation that it ruled, to new heights, the war severed the ties between closely related princely families. The familial solidarity that had transgressed the boundaries of the state lost all political significance when the armies of the imperial cousins in London, Berlin and Saint Petersburg lined up against each other in 1914.[50]

---

[48] Stephen Graham, *Alexander of Jugoslavia: Strong Man of the Balkans* (London, 1938), pp. 82–94; Eva Demmerle, *Kaiser Karl I. 'Selig, die Frieden stiften …'. Die Biographie*, 2nd edn (Vienna, 2005), pp. 84–91; Yury Winterberg and Sonya Winterberg, *Kleine Hände im Großen Krieg. Kinderschicksale im Ersten Weltkrieg* (Berlin, 2014), pp. 196–197.

[49] Jones, 'The Nature of Kingship in First World War Britain', p. 195.

[50] Gustaaf Janssens, 'Die belgische Monarchie und Albert I. Ritterkönig und Friedensfürst?', in Martin Wrede (ed.), *Die Inszenierung der heroischen Monarchie. Frühneuzeitliches Königtum zwischen ritterlichem Erbe und militärischer Herausforderung* (Munich, 2014), pp. 409–437; Frank-Lothar Kroll, 'Zwischen europäischem Bewußtsein und nationaler Identität. Legitimationsstrategien monarchischer Eliten in Europa des 19. und 20. Jahrhunderts', in Hans-Christof Kraus and Thomas Nicklas (eds.), *Geschichte der Politik. Alte und neue Wege* (Munich, 2007), pp. 353–374; Hartmut Pogge von Strandmann, 'Nationalisierungsdruck und Namensänderung in England. Das

No royal heir would have been more aware of the fact that the age of transnational royal clans had come to an end than the Prince of Wales. Just twelve months before the outbreak of the war, he had joyfully roamed in his car from one German royal court to another, and in September 1915, he narrowly avoided being blown to smithereens by a German shell, along with his car and his driver. Two further crown princes – the oldest son of the German emperor and Crown Prince Rupprecht from the House of Wittelsbach, both of whom held high commands in the German army – would witness the downfall of their own dynasties on the battlefield. Here we consider how the militarisation of the monarchy in the nineteenth century dictated the nature and results of their wartime service and how these heirs to the throne contributed to the various fates that awaited their thrones after 1918.

**

On 29 May 1919, Prince Edward, the heir to the British throne, was made a Freeman of the City of London. In the magnificent Guildhall, he expressed his gratitude for this honour and paid tribute to the troops from London who had served during the war. 'Mr Chamberlain, in his very kind reference to me, spoke of the periods which I spent at the Front', commented the prince towards the end of his speech. 'The part I played was, I fear, a very insignificant one, but from one point of view I shall never regret my periods of service overseas. In those four years I mixed with men. In those four years I found my manhood. When I think of the future, and the heavy responsibilities which may fall to my lot, I feel that the experience gained since 1914 will stand me in good stead.'[51] The scene contains much that is revealing about the military service of the heir to the British throne and how it was received by the British public: his reticence about having his military engagement celebrated; the maturing of the young heir to the throne into a new manliness in the midst of his wartime comrades; and finally the widespread knowledge of his time with the military, which would continue to determine how the prince was viewed for years after the war.

When the war broke out, King George recorded apprehensively in his diary that he had asked God to protect the life of his son Bertie. The king mentioned only Prince Albert (Bertie), his younger son, born in 1895, who at the time was serving as an officer on board the warship *HMS Collingwood*, but that should not be taken as a sign that he was indifferent

Ende der Großfamilie europäischer Dynastien', in Gerhard A. Ritter und Peter Wende (eds.), *Rivalität und Partnerschaft. Studien zu den deutsch–britischen Beziehungen im 19. und 20. Jahrhundert* (Paderborn, 1999), pp. 69–91.
[51] *Speeches by H.R H. The Prince of Wales 1912–1926* (London, 1927), p. 7.

to the fate of his first-born. Evidently, it simply did not occur to him that the heir to the throne would be exposed to any real danger. For the Prince of Wales, however, the sparing of his person was anything but reason for celebration. 'I am as good as heartbroken to think that I am totally devoid of any job whatsoever and have not the faintest chance of being able to serve my country. I have to stay at home with the women and the children, a passenger of the worst description!! Here I am in this bloody gt palace, doing nothing but attend meals', he wrote to his brother on 5 August, adding, 'Surely a man of 20 has higher things to hope for? But I haven't apparently!'[52]

Things were soon to look up for Edward. Only a few days later, and at his own request, the young man, who had only undertaken a short training course with the Life Guards so far, was given a commission in the Grenadier Guards. With great zeal, he threw himself into the life of an 'ordinary officer', trained with passion and immediately identified with his regiment. When his unit went to the continent in October 1914, he was deeply hurt to be transferred to another battalion, which remained in London. He made every effort to ensure he would soon be sent to the combat zone, even presenting his case to the Minister of War, Lord Kitchener. After a wait of several weeks, in November 1914 the prince received permission to switch to the staff of the Supreme Commander of the British forces in France, Field Marshal Sir John French.[53]

While he was attached to the British headquarters on the continent, Edward's frustrations only continued. 'I will try to keep him well occupied and as far from shells as possible', General William Lambton, the Field Marshal's military secretary had promised the king. But this promise could be kept only in part. While the future king was certainly spared any real danger, he could hardly be usefully employed. As inexperienced as he was highborn, the lieutenant could be given little meaningful work. He could not be expected to perform the basic tasks of an adjutant, but he lacked the skills for the more demanding work of a member of the general staff. Edward was left greatly troubled. Above all, he was discomforted that so many men – and officers from his Guards regiment in particular – were exposed to great danger on a daily basis, were injured or even killed, while he was denied and spared it all. He badgered his superiors and his father to allow him to be deployed in a more practical capacity, but even after he was transferred to the newly formed Guards Division, efforts continued to keep him out of harm's way. He was permitted no more than

[52] Philip Ziegler, *King Edward VIII: The Official Biography* (London, 1990), p. 49.
[53] Ibid., pp. 49–53.

occasional inspections at the front, visits to field hospitals and assignments such as the interrogation of German prisoners of war.[54]

In the spring of 1916 the heir to the throne, now promoted to captain, was sent to the Middle East, where his presence was intended to lift the spirits of the British, Australian and New Zealand troops in Egypt. Here too his efforts were not directly related to the fighting; instead, he became a tourist and carried out public relations work: he travelled to the legendary city of Khartoum, in Sudan, where, in January 1885, after a ten-month siege, the British general Charles George Gordon had been killed by rebels, promptly turning him into a martyr and hero back home in Britain. A visit to Cairo, a trip on the Nile and an outing to the Egyptian antiquities were also on the programme. Above all, however, Edward was to bolster the mood amongst the troops, and the fit and youthful prince did this outstandingly well. Although, as his letters and diary entries show, he abhorred public attention and ceremony, he developed the ability to appear affable and appealing to those around him, and he won the hearts of the soldiers. The mood amongst the men at the Suez Canal, recorded a report written after the prince's departure in May 1916, had improved decisively with the visit of the heir to the throne.[55]

Edward returned to France via Italy, where he met King Vittorio Emanuele III but again had no opportunity to be actively involved in the fighting. In France the established pattern continued: he unhesitatingly carried out unimportant and sometimes less than dignified tasks, largely in the safer zone far behind the front. Thus, for example, he once stood in the rain for hours to direct traffic at the western entry to a French city. He showed great discipline adhering to a strict exercise regime in order to remain physically fit, and he always asked for more meaningful and riskier tasks. On occasion, he dared to advance into more dangerous sections of the front on his own initiative, but each time he was soundly ordered back. In the autumn of 1917, he was transferred to Italy. A few months later, in May 1918, he took part in the official festivities in Rome that marked the third anniversary of the Italian entry into the war. Here again the heir to the throne was given ceremonial tasks that he performed adeptly. Edward spent the last weeks of the war in France, where he applied himself in particular to attending to the soldiers from the British dominions of Canada and Australia and to Britain's allies from the USA.[56]

[54] Ibid., p. 54.   [55] Ibid., pp. 68–73.
[56] Heather Jones, 'A Prince in the Trenches? Edward VIII and the First World War', in Frank Lorenz Müller and Heidi Mehrkens (eds.), *Sons and Heirs: Succession and Political Culture in Nineteenth-Century Europe* (Basingstoke, 2016), pp. 236–241; Ziegler, *King Edward VIII*, pp. 73–84.

When the war ended in November 1918, Prince Edward had served for a full four years in various roles and had a realistic understanding of the suffering of the soldiers and the destruction of the war. That he had been given so little opportunity to make decisions or to participate directly in the fighting could suggest that his wartime experience was relatively insignificant. After all, he was never promoted beyond the rank of captain. That interpretation would be incorrect. Edward had been changed by these years: he had, as he later declared, become a man amongst men. It was evident even at the beginning of the war that the young heir had internalised a concept of masculinity that was closely associated with an ability to fight – he had complained to his brother that as a non-combatant he would be required to stay at home with the 'wives and children'. While at university, his fellow students had teased him for his delicate appearance, his shyness and the amount of time he spent with his tutor Henry Hansell. Prince and tutor were dubbed 'Hansel and Gretel' and Edward was on occasion called 'Little Pretty'.[57] It is therefore all the more understandable that the surprisingly youthful-looking heir found it important to assert his status as a grown man by proving himself in war. And yet precisely this was made impossible by his position, which left him profoundly disappointed with his time in the army.

If he could not prove his manliness in battle and demonstrate the courage of a hero, then he would have to perform and prove that masculinity during the war in different ways. He did so principally by demonstrating his physicality – with an athletic fitness, acquired on long bike tours and through running and marching, and with a hedonistic enjoyment of a sexuality first discovered during the war, which was associated with visits to brothels in Paris and numerous love affairs with women who were not of his social class. His sexual adventures, which were kept hidden from the general public, began in the arms of a French prostitute named Paulette, who had been made available to him by his army companions in 1916. During this period, the prince began to talk about women, and also more generally, using a language that was highly aggressive, sometimes obscene and often coarse, which he also applied – evidently in an effort to suggest the manly grittiness of the trenches – to the enemy, unloved superiors, incompetent politicians and supposedly uncivilised Italians.[58]

This internal and external toughening-up enabled Edward to interact on a more intimate level with the soldiers whose wellbeing evidently

[57] Genevieve Parkurst, *A King in the Making: An Authentic Story of Edward, Seventeenth Prince of Wales* (New York and London, 1925), pp. 122–123.

[58] Ziegler, *King Edward VIII*, pp. 53–54, 88–105; Jones, 'A Prince in the Trenches?', pp. 241–242.

mattered greatly to him. The picture that emerged was of a prince who suffered with his fellow soldiers and spoke up on their behalf, an image that was of great use to the monarchy. Soon anecdotes were circulating of the prince driving exhausted soldiers to their accommodation unrecognised, sleeping on the floor in order that others might have his camp bed, serving incognito as a bike messenger, or participating in a mud-caked game of soccer. Rightly or wrongly, soldiers perceived Edward as a man who bravely shared the dangers to which they themselves were exposed. Scenes like the one depicted in Figure 25 were seen as characteristic of his service. Writing to his parents, a private in the Coldstream Guards recounted how 'only last night he passed me when the German shells were coming over'. These depictions climaxed in a very well known, although not entirely verifiable, incident during a visit to a field hospital. Edward was said to have noticed that one patient was hidden behind a curtain. On asking about the case, he was told that this soldier had been so hideously disfigured by his injuries that no one could be expected to

Figure 25. For Edward, the youthful Prince of Wales, the First World War marked a deep caesura: 'In those four years I mixed with men', he would later declare. 'In those four years I found my manhood.' The Print Collector/Alamy Stock Photo.

look at him. The prince, it was said, then approached the bed where the injured man was lying and kissed him. Years later the scene was still being vaunted by the hospital chaplain, who commented, 'Remember, men have gone to heaven for less. Never can we forget that action.'[59]

However frustrating the war may have been for Prince Edward, the stories surrounding this king-in-waiting illustrate that the British monarchy was able to contribute effectively to the nation's war effort. And the opposite was also true: the war was useful to the monarchy and its future. In the course of these four years, King George performed about 1,000 visits to the troops, field hospitals, factories and dockyards, while Queen Mary contributed great energy and much time to the image of the monarchy through her indefatigable charitable work. The dynasty also benefited from having the wartime service of the heir to the throne portrayed by a sympathetic press in the proper light.[60]

'The nation deeply appreciates the implied sacrifice of the King in thus consenting to the eager desire of his eldest son to bear his part in the war', declared the *Evening Standard* as early as November 1914. 'No stronger link between Sovereign and subjects could be forged than this of comradeship on the battlefield.' The *Pall Mall Gazette* could foresee a day when British men would say, 'My KING and I fought together for freedom and for right.' The press praised Edward for not desiring special treatment and for often mixing unrecognised with regular soldiers. The feedback from other sources was also favourable. After the prince visited Canadian troops, a colonel wrote that Edward 'had been the best force in real Empire building that it was possible for Great Britain to have because he absolutely won the hearts of the many he came in contact with'. The troops had found, he continued, that 'he was every inch the gentleman and the sportsman, so simple, so charming and so genuine'. The response from Buckingham Place was immediate. Whereas in 1914 the prince had had to beg to be sent to France, in spring 1918 the king was almost angry when he realised his son was still in London when a German offensive had begun: 'Good God! Are you still here? Why aren't you back with your Corps?', he was said to have snapped. It was not right, he insisted, that Edward should remain in London while the British lines were being broken and the army stood with its back to the wall, 'I left immediately', the prince continued in his memoirs.[61]

[59] Ziegler, *King Edward VIII*, p. 55; Heather Jones, *For King and Country: The British Monarchy and the First World War* (Cambridge, 2021), p. 162; Genevieve Parkhurst, *A King in the Making*, pp. 144–148; Basil Maine, *Prinz von Wales. König Eduard VIII. Eine Biographie* (Berlin, 1936), pp. 21–22.

[60] Kenneth Rose, *King George V* (London, 1983), p. 179.

[61] Jones, 'A Prince in the Trenches?', pp. 234, 236; Ziegler, *King Edward VIII*, p. 84; *A King's Story*, p. 121.

When the war was over, the heir to the throne and the royal house whose future he embodied could conclude that it had gone well. In the eyes of the public, the delicate-looking student who during his time at Oxford had been mocked as overly feminine had grown into a seasoned warrior who could cope with hardship and had shown real courage. The Prince of Wales, as Heather Jones reminds us, had become 'an integral part of the moral economy of wartime, serving as a constant illustration of the ways in which the royal family were participating in the national sacrifice that total war entailed'. He thus buttressed the popularity of a dynasty at the head of a victorious nation. Within the royal house, the future king would continue for many years to represent the generation of war veterans. In 1923, for example, he attended the unveiling of a memorial to the London policemen who had been killed in the war. The speaker addressed the royal heir directly: 'A large proportion of these men were Reservists in His Majesty's Guards with which Division, Sir, you served for so many months. You will therefore specially appreciate the valour of those who fell and it is quite possible that you may have been actually present on occasions when those casualties occurred, for it is within the lively recollection of all of us who are here present that you served almost continuously with the Armed Forces of the Crown during the War.'[62]

*

The example of Prussian–German Crown Prince Wilhelm, however, tells us that several years of military service were not alone sufficient to turn an heir to the throne into a promising resource for the dynasty. Unlike his British cousin, Wilhelm did not have to make do with the lower rank that enabled Edward to develop a rapport with the troops but kept him at a clear distance from strategic decision-making. Instead, Crown Prince Wilhelm sought to fulfil the traditional demands on a Hohenzollern prince by performing, or at least appearing to perform, the part of a senior commander. In doing so, he damaged not just his own reputation but also that of the crown.

When the world learnt of the assassination of Archduke Franz Ferdinand, heir to the Austrian throne, and his wife, Sophie, Crown Prince Wilhelm, the eldest son of Emperor Wilhelm II, was relaxing at the Baltic resort town of Zoppot, not far from the city of Danzig. The crown prince's response to the shocking news was characteristic: he rushed to ensure he could play a few more games of tennis with a number of young ladies before the official declaration of a period of

---

[62] Ted Powell, *King Edward VIII: An American Life* (Oxford, 2018), p. 15; Jones, 'A Prince in the Trenches?', p. 243; Jones, *For King and Country*, p. 159.

mourning would deprive him of this pleasure. The public were well used to such capers by the heir to the throne, who was a notorious dandy and lothario. The press repeatedly mocked his half-hearted military service with a regiment of Hussars stationed at Danzig, which was frequently interrupted by his penchant for sporting and automobile-related pursuits. His training in strategy undertaken in spring 1914 with the General Staff in Berlin had also been little more than an act. In late 1913, Wilhelm's superior officer, the universally revered August von Mackensen, had not minced his words in an official evaluation of the crown prince: Wilhelm, he recorded, could 'in every respect be harder on himself. The demands of duty were not unconditionally and self-evidently prioritised over personal desires and inclinations; concentrated and demanding thinking is avoided all too readily. His imperial and royal highness's development towards being a more senior commander is thus inhibited.'[63]

When war broke out in August 1914, the thirty-two-year-old princely colonel proved unusually ambitious, which, if we are to believe Wilhelm's memoirs, was largely fuelled by dynastic traditions and legends. 'In my final mobilisation assignment, I was designated commander of the 1st Guards Infantry Division, and I looked forward to leading such experienced elite troops should it come to war. But I also held within me an understandable desire to play my part in a higher position, following the example of my forefathers.' In line with this princely braggadocio, when the war broke out, the Chief of the General Staff, Helmuth von Moltke, suggested that Wilhelm be given command of the Fifth Army. 'And thus history was maintained', the crown prince declared in his memoirs, 'for in the wars of 1866 and 1870–1871, Crown Prince Friedrich Wilhelm of Prussia, at a relatively young age, had led the army against the enemy.' However, the decision-makers appear to have been well aware that Wilhelm had even less of what it takes to shoulder such responsibility than had his grandfather, Friedrich III. The emperor, who did not necessarily hold his tongue when it came to criticism of his son, was very clear with Wilhelm, in the presence of the Imperial Chancellor, Minister of War and Naval Secretary, when the prince was given this appointment, 'I have entrusted you with supreme command of the Fifth Army. You are

---

[63] Katherine Anne Lerman, 'Wilhelm's War: A Hohenzollern in Conflict 1914–1918', in Frank Lorenz Müller and Heidi Mehrkens (eds.), *Sons and Heirs: Succession and Political Culture in Nineteenth-Century Europe* (Basingstoke, 2016), p. 247; Klaus W. Jonas, *Der Kronprinz Wilhelm* (Frankfurt am Main, 1962), pp. 102–103, 120–121; Helmut Ries, *Kronprinz Wilhelm* (Hamburg, Berlin and Bonn, 2001), p. 132.

being assigned Lieutenant General Schmidt von Knobelsdorf as Chief of the General Staff. You must do what he advises.'[64]

General Josef Count Stürgkh, the Austro-Hungarian delegate to the German General Staff, viewed this astonishing promotion of a man with few qualifications for the job as the product of a dynastic and political calculation: 'The heirs to the thrones of Bavaria and Württemberg, admittedly older and with a higher rank as generals, were army commanders; on that count the heir to the German imperial crown could not be left to trail behind them. And the crown prince would have been hard put to find a better means of increasing his own popularity and securing the foundations of the Hohenzollern throne than by leading his future subjects to victory at the head of an army and sharing with them in the dangers of war.' The radiant image of 'Our Fritz', the hero who returned home in glory from France, may have proved very alluring. Stürgkh pointed, though, to two conditions for achieving both personal popularity and monarchical consolidation: victory and shared danger. If these conditions were not met, then the outcome might prove very much the opposite of what had been intended. In proposing this reckless heir, for whom Mackensen had already attested 'an unsuppressed tendency to believe he knows better', for such an important command, the Prussian monarchy was playing with fire.[65]

Initially the gamble seemed to be paying off. The soldiers of the Fifth Army were victorious at Longwy, near the French–Belgian border, in late August 1914. 'The behaviour of the troops was exemplary, with even the reserves fighting splendidly', the crown prince reported to his father. The emperor was enthusiastic and immediately decorated his son: 'I congratulate you on your first victory, which with the help of God you have achieved so beautifully. I am awarding you the Iron Cross Second and First Class. Greet your brave troops with my thanks and with the thanks of the fatherland. Well done, I am proud of you. Your loyal father Wilhelm.' The emperor seemed genuine in his praise. When, during a discussion at the end of August 1914, he celebrated his son's military achievements, the Chief of the Military Cabinet, Moritz von Lyncker, interjected 'Knobelsdorf, Your Majesty', reminding everyone who was in fact responsible. A witness reported that the proud father would hear none of it. 'At this the emperor bridled and declared this two-day battle to be a capital achievement by the distinguished gentleman and so on.' That response was entirely understandable, for the attribution of this early

---

[64] Kronprinz Wilhelm, *Meine Erinnerungen an Deutschlands Heldenkampf* (Berlin, 1923), pp. 3–4.

[65] Jonas, *Der Kronprinz Wilhelm*, p. 126; Ries, *Kronprinz Wilhelm*, p. 133.

success to the crown prince was a gift for monarchical propaganda: more than a million postcards were printed to celebrate the triumph at Longwy and many additional photographs of the royal heir flooded the market in the fatherland.[66]

Wilhelm was frequently associated with the less than subtle slogan *Immer feste druff!* (Always at full whack!), which could be traced back to an utterance by the crown prince in 1913. In 1914, the phrase would serve as the title of a 'humourous–patriotic song of war' by David Kunhart. At the time, the ditty concocted by this former volunteer soldier from the 'great era of 1870–1871' was 'to be performed with enthusiasm', but today its many stanzas induce nothing but embarrassment. The refrain of this dubious piece ran as follows: 'Crown Prince Wilhelm, at full whack / Kick the Frenchies in the back / Hit that filthy mob / Thwack! Right in the gob!' And there was more. On 1 October 1914, Berlin's Theater am Nollendorfplatz delighted its patrons with a new 'patriotic' musical comedy in four acts by Hermann Haller and Willi Wolf, with music by Walter Kollo. 'Always at Full Whack!', the title of this cultural jewel, capitalised on the crown prince's now widely known maxim. In Berlin alone, the play was performed more than 800 times and proved a major success.[67]

In retrospect it seems an irony of fate that early in the war the monarchy banked on the crown prince to ensure its popularity, for at the end of the conflict the heir to the throne was one of the most hated men in the German leadership. Four years after the victory at Longwy, the battle cry 'Always at full whack' served as the title of an anti-German pamphlet published in Paris. Alongside a caricature showing the heir to the imperial throne on top of a pile of skulls was written 'Just recently I asked a mother, "German mother, what does your son say about the full-whack-prince?" "My son lost both legs at Verdun, but the crown prince never came under fire, for the crown prince was always behind the front, out of harm's way."' In the end, the repudiation of the heir to the throne was greater still than the rejection of his father, and even the few voices that spoke up in favour of maintaining the German monarchy in the autumn of 1918 did not want Crown Prince Wilhelm. 'The firm can and must be preserved', declared Friedrich Ebert, leader of the Social Democrats, when speaking

---

[66] Walter Görlitz (ed.), *Regierte der Kaiser? Kriegstagebücher, Aufzeichnungen und Briefe des Chefs des Marine-Kabinetts Admiral Georg Alexander von Müller 1914–1918*, 2nd edn (Berlin and Frankfurt am Main, 1959), pp. 51–52.

[67] David Kunhardt, *Kronprinz Wilhelm, feste druff!: Humoristisch-vaterländisches Kriegslied* (Berlin, 1914); Eva Krivanec, *Kriegsbühnen. Theater im Ersten Weltkrieg. Berlin, Lissabon, Paris und Wien* (Bielefeld, 2012), p. 117.

about the monarchy in late October 1918, 'but not in the person of the crown prince: he is truly and justifiably unpopular.'[68]

The memoirs with which the former German crown prince turned to the Germans from his Dutch exile in 1922 reveal that he was fully aware of the principal reasons for his lack of popularity. In collaboration with the writer and former war reporter Karl Rosner, Wilhelm took up each complaint in turn and sought to refute them all: the accusation that he had remained committed to victory at any cost for too long, his identification with the massive and pointless bloodshed at Verdun, and his inappropriate exuberance, which seemed almost obscene when compared with the suffering of the soldiers and the gravity of the situation.[69] The former crown prince pointed out that in a memorandum dated as early as 1915 he had made the case for a negotiated peace and that he had constantly argued against 'mistaken and overly optimistically assessments'. The full-whack-prince would not rid himself so easily of his reputation as a proponent and prolonger of the war, though. '"But"', many will object here, "certainly more than once, in public and to the troops specifically, the crown prince professed and demanded, orally and in writing, a will to win and confidence about winning"', Wilhelm continued in his memoirs. 'And indeed, I did do that!', he conceded, adding defiantly, 'and thus I did my duty as an army commander and a soldier'. That as a 'politically minded man' he might have had other views that he kept to himself carried almost no weight in the public's assessment of his actions, and on that point he could do little. In the minds of the German public, the most damaging aspect was the crown prince's association with the Battle of Verdun, infamously known as the 'Blood Mill'. Wilhelm was fully aware of the toxic impact of the suggestion that he 'was responsible for the heavy losses and ultimate failure at Verdun' and he did everything he could to destroy what he termed this 'fraudulent tale'.[70]

It was evident that the crown prince could not have made such weighty decisions on his own, but it proved all but impossible for him to distance himself from the Battle of Verdun. Operation Judgement (*Operation*

---

[68] 'Immer feste druff!' (propaganda flyer, Paris, 1918), http://digital.staatsbibliothek-berlin.de/werkansicht?PPN=PPN767871014&PHYSID=PHYS_0001&DMDID=DMDLOG_0001 (accessed 19 April 2017); Jonas, *Der Kronprinz Wilhelm*, p. 127; Lerman, 'Wilhelm's War', pp. 248, 250; Wolfram Pyta, 'Die Kunst des rechtzeitigen Thronverzichts. Neue Einsichten zur Überlebenschance der parlamentarischen Monarchie in Deutschland im Herbst 1918', in Patrick Merziger, Rudolf Stöber, Esther-Beate Körber and Jürgen Michael Schulz (eds.), *Geschichte, Öffentlichkeit, Kommunikation. Festschrift für Bernd Sösemann zum 65. Geburtstag* (Stuttgart, 2010), p. 367.

[69] Karl Rosner (ed.), *Erinnerungen des Kronprinzen Wilhelm. Aus den Aufzeichnungen, Dokumenten, Tagebüchern und Gesprächen* (Stuttgart, 1922), pp. 168–169, 201ff., 209ff.

[70] Ibid., pp. 168–169.

Gericht) of February 1916, the major offensive at Verdun, was indeed partly a product of the desire to give the heir to the German imperial throne an opportunity to win glory as a military commander. In military circles, the attack on this stronghold, which lay within the section of the front occupied by Crown Prince Wilhelm's Fifth Army, was understood as a campaign *ad maiorem Kronprinz gloriam* (for the greater glory of the crown prince). Highly symbolic details such as the battle cry 'Hurrah Crown Prince' and the attack order signed by Wilhelm were additional elements that tied the reputation of the heir to the outcome of this battle. To make matters worse, Wilhelm's relationship with his chief of staff, Konstantin Schmidt von Knobelsdorf, who had operational command on the battlefield, was very strained, with the crown prince happily using the general as a shield and scapegoat. The waters were also muddied by Wilhelm's somewhat ambiguous attitude towards the battle, which in the end had cost the lives of more than 300,000 German and French soldiers. In his extensive war reminiscences, published in 1923, Wilhelm described his 'longing to be on the move again with my magnificent troops', which 'made him inwardly happy'. Although he professed to early doubts about whether the offensive was sensible, up until July 1916 he clung to hope of victory. Even in his memoirs, published in 1922, in which he sought to minimise his responsibility for the course of the battle, he could not resist the temptation of pointing to 'the over-whelming successes of the first three days', when 'in storming forward, miracles of bravery' had been accomplished. Only later, he recorded, would exhaustion and the lack of reserve troops deny Germany 'the prize of victory'. Then, he wrote, he had recognised 'that it would not be possible to break through the tenacious defence' and had 'invested everything in halting the attack'. He took credit for ending the attack and declared in the same breath – not without pride – that 'seventy-five French divisions ... were crushed in the hell's cauldron of Verdun'.[71]

In the light of this attitude, which was contradictory even when recalled retrospectively, Verdun remained a strong argument for opponents of the crown prince and the monarchy. It was not coincidental that the French pamphlet 'Always at Full Whack!' appealed to the 'warriors of the crown prince's battles, all you who participated in the great murder' and summoned the soldiers into battle against the 'imperial idiots' and the 'crowned bloody tyrants'. This attack was made all the more trenchant by its repeated references to the crown prince's refusal to share the

---

[71] Lerman, 'Wilhelm's War', pp. 250–252; Machtan, *Die Abdankung*, pp. 102–103; Olaf Jessen, *Verdun 1916. Die Urschlacht des Jahrhunderts* (Munich, 2014), pp. 92–93, 232–233, 318–319; Rosner (ed.), *Erinnerungen des Kronprinzen Wilhelm*, pp. 204–206; Kronprinz Wilhelm, *Meine Erinnerungen an Deutschlands Heldenkampf*, p. 160.

dangers faced by the soldiers, to his absence from the battlefield, his undeserved honours and his excessively dapper uniform. It thus brought up a sore point that was also a cause of concern for the empire's political and military leadership: the impression of frivolity, even in the midst of an ominous situation, created by the crown prince's lifestyle during the war. His superficiality was noted not just by outsiders. 'The crown prince for breakfast', recorded the chief of the Naval Cabinet on 7 April 1918, 'One joke after the next. Of the grave situation at the front, not a trace to be seen.'[72]

Between the victory at Longwy in August 1914 and the beginning of the attack on Verdun in February 1916, the crown prince had largely disappeared from public view. Like his father, who complained in November 1914 that the General Staff no longer told him anything and that he was confined to drinking tea, sawing wood and taking walks, the crown prince also lived in the shadow of events. Accommodated very comfortably near Stenay, in the chateau at Tilleul, with its park, tennis court and air-raid shelter, Wilhelm had little to do. Each morning he was given a short report, but thereafter his time was his own. On occasion, he would receive his father, who liked to come to lunch on account of the renown of the cook at the chateau. Forbidden to visit the front, the heir to the throne raced back and forth through the communications zone in his bright red car, to which he had attached a horseshoe for good luck. As can also be seen in Figure 26, he appeared to be in the best of moods, such that his constant laughter ultimately became a signature feature that increasingly struck observers as inappropriate. Picking up on the title of a novel by Victor Hugo, the French civilian population called him *l'homme qui rit*, the man who laughs. The pieces came together to form an unfavourable picture overall – of the prince, dressed for the hunt, riding crop in hand and surrounded by his hounds, greeting soldiers returning from the front with a smile and on occasion tossing them cigarettes.[73]

The heir to the throne palpably found visits to field hospitals and other forms of care for the troops increasingly insufferable and therefore preferred to dedicate himself to sporting activities – tennis and riding – and more or less discrete love affairs with French women. Wilhelm's schoolfriend Gustav Steinbömer described the crown prince's behaviour with a sardonic candour: 'The younger female population soon demonstrated their interest in multiple ways, coming up to their windows, standing at

---

[72] Görlitz (ed.), *Regierte der Kaiser?*, p. 369.
[73] Epkenhans, 'Das Ende eines Zeitalters', pp. 69–70; Lerman, 'Wilhelm's War', pp. 252–255; Jonas, *Der Kronprinz Wilhelm*, p. 153.

Figure 26. Sporty, sharply dressed and forever smiling: 'Our Crown Prince at War' soon turned into a public relations nightmare for the German authorities. Author's private collection.

their doors, nodding and waving. Then he had the car stop, began to chat with some nice girl or lovely young woman. The next time, the visit would be longer. He knew where he had liked a pretty child. He got out and sat himself down.' A young flower seller from Stenay distinguished herself so greatly in her tender care of the heir to the throne that she was soon the bearer of the soubriquet 'Crown Princess'. The behaviour of the commander of the Fifth Army was cause for outrage in military circles, and soon wild rumours – fuelled by allied propaganda – were doing the rounds in Germany. In the winter of 1916, it was whispered, the married crown prince had secretly absented himself from his troops to luxuriate for two weeks in the arms of a lover.[74]

Even though this tale was groundless – Wilhelm had actually been convalescing in hospital after a light bout of typhus – worries about the reputation of the heir to the throne were still so great that the Supreme Army Command took up the issue. In early April 1917, Field Marshal Paul von Hindenburg wrote to a high-ranking military commander that it was 'unseemly' for 'the future bearer of the imperial crown' to be blamed for the failed attack on Verdun and the setbacks east of the River Meuse. Hindenburg also took a stand against the 'fatuous rumours about the private life of His Imperial Highness the Crown Prince'. When such suggestions reached the ears of the officers, they were to contradict them, to protect the reputation of the senior commander of the 'Army Group German Crown Prince', the position to which the heir to the throne had been promoted in November 1916. A further form of damage limitation was the publication of the lavishly illustrated volume *Unser Kronprinz im Felde* (*Our Crown Prince at War*) by August Scherl, a major publishing company. The work contained numerous paintings and drawings by the war artist Wilhelm Pape and was furnished with an introduction by the war reporter Karl Rosner, with whom Wilhelm would later cooperate in penning his memoirs. In the introduction, dated March 1918, Rosner celebrated the spirit of the crown prince, which for years had been expressed day after day 'in his overabundant work as commander of the formidable military forces subordinate to him and in his actions as a warm-hearted human being who cares for the wellbeing of every individual man'. Every day anew, according to the author, the 'man in the trenches' sees 'that the crown prince has a heart and mind for every smallest concern, that in his concern for the whole he never forgets the individual'. As if to substantiate his words, they were followed by numerous large-format prints depicting telling scenes from life at war for the future people's emperor: the crown prince as he transported a seriously injured man to the hospital in his own car; the crown prince as he distributed gifts to the troops; the crown prince at a hospital bedside: the crown prince in the trenches; the crown prince conversing with Field Marshal von Hindenburg.[75]

The propagandistic efforts of Rosner and Pape had little measurable impact, and Hindenburg's appeal bore no fruit either. According to a report for Supreme Headquarters dated 1 February 1918, the mood

---

[74] Jessen, *Verdun 1916*, p. 75; Jonas, *Der Kronprinz Wilhelm*, pp. 153–156.
[75] Jonas, *Der Kronprinz Wilhelm*, p. 155; *Unser Kronprinz im Felde. Gemälde und Skizzen von Wilhelm Pape, Kriegsmaler im Großen Hauptquartier* (Berlin, 1918).

amongst the people and in the army was set irreversibly against Wilhelm, for which, amongst other things, the 'many imprudences' of the crown prince were to blame, having led to rumours about his 'very lively dealings with French women'. According to individuals who had contact with the heir to the throne, these rumours were not without merit, the report noted. A scandal had occurred recently, it continued, when Wilhelm had arranged to have an oil painting made of an attractive French woman with whom he was in a relationship. Thereupon the woman had also made herself available to the artist, which had incensed the crown prince. 'Such stories spread like wildfire through the trenches', the report summarised, where, it drily concluded, their impact was 'by no means conducive to the preservation of the state'. Things would have to improve and the 'duties of the heir to the German imperial crown and the crown of Prussia' must be made clear to the crown prince.[76]

The events of autumn 1918 would demonstrate, however, that the crowns no longer had a future in Germany. The increasingly hated emperor, who was held responsible by a war-wearied and embittered population for the disastrous course of the war and blamed for the delay in concluding a peace, had dug a grave for the monarchical state. His oldest son was seen not as part of the solution but as part of the problem. Shipping magnate Albert Ballin reported to the chief of the Naval Cabinet in October 1918, 'The crown prince would be decisively rejected not just by [US President] Wilson, but also by the German people.' On 9 November 1918, the day on which Imperial Chancellor Max von Baden announced on his own authority that the emperor had abdicated, the crown prince made his inadequacies evident yet again. He arrived late for the decisive meeting at the headquarters at Spa and left before the gathering had ended, to return to the woman who had been the reason for his delayed arrival that morning. His actions were not without consequence. Immediately after the emperor had crossed the border into Holland and begun his exile on 10 November 1918, the crown prince was informed by the War Ministry in Berlin that he had been relieved of his military command.

There was little resistance to his dismissal amongst the officer corps. Having discussed the situation with other high-ranking officers, Albrecht von Thaer, a colonel in the General Staff, recorded in his diary that Wilhelm, 'as a result of his wilfulness and more specifically his often-lacking sense of duty had too greatly corrupted his position in the nation and with the people . . . that he might remain eligible in such a situation for the monarchical succession'. Even a private return to Germany – for

[76] Jonas, *Der Kronprinz Wilhelm*, p. 156.

example to the castle of Oels, not far from Breslau, which the crown prince had inherited in 1888 – seemed not without risk. The diplomat Ernst zu Rantzau believed that the peasants there would beat him to death.[77]

Crown Prince Wilhelm followed his father into exile in the Netherlands on 12 November 1918 – not least so that he could avoid living together with his wife again. There he promptly began to cast his actions in a more favourable light. In his discharge letter addressed to Field Marshal von Hindenburg he defended himself against 'many iniquitous voices that have always sought to make me appear a warmonger and reactionary'. He claimed that he would never have resisted 'the liberal reconfiguration of our political system'. Wilhelm's final military order also had a markedly political character: 'The Army Group has not been vanquished by weapons', he stated, declaring that he had belonged 'for four long years fully and with all his heart to my loyal troops'. With his sights set firmly on a possible re-establishment of the Hohenzollern monarchy, even after his renunciation of the throne on 1 December 1918 the crown prince did not cease his efforts in the cause of his rehabilitation.[78]

In his memoirs, Wilhelm directly addressed the most damaging of the accusations against him and whether he really was 'the laughing murderer of Verdun'. He took the bull by the horns: 'Yes, and yes again. In my younger years I liked to laugh and I was never one to mope or cocoon myself', he declared defiantly. 'And during the war, despite all the bitter afflictions, I never fully forgot how to laugh . . . I know that as a result at the time I was badly faulted on occasion in my homeland, and perhaps also in the combat zone: the crown prince always looks so amused – he certainly is not taking matters very seriously.' Even at a distance of several years, he could not bring himself to apply any sincere self-criticism. His response tended instead to be condescending. 'You dear and dutiful pundits and smart alecs, so what did you know anyway?' During the war, he had had just one concern, he noted, and that was 'the men entrusted to me who stood on the battlelines'. To encourage them in difficult times, he had laughed and broadcast his good mood. 'Thus it was with the laughing', the exiled former crown prince drew a line under the matter, while at the same time providing further evidence of his incorrigibility: 'Yes, and while I'm on the matter anyway, another acknowledgement – I can still do it today!'[79]

---

[77] Görlitz (ed.), *Regierte der Kaiser?*, p. 428; Jonas, *Der Kronprinz Wilhelm*, pp. 161–164; Lerman, 'Wilhelm's War', p. 258.

[78] Jonas, *Der Kronprinz Wilhelm*, p. 165.

[79] Rosner (ed.), *Erinnerungen des Kronprinzen Wilhelm*, pp. 209–212.

This mix of scant self-awareness and a lack of earnestness scuppered Wilhelm's plans for a future on the Hohenzollern throne. Although after 1923 he was able to return to Germany, there, according to the historian Stephan Malinowski, he belonged 'neither to the political elite in his land nor to the intellectual elite of his estate'. His ultra-nationalist and fascist sympathies would eventually cause Wilhelm to draw close to the Nazi Party and led to an informal, if abortive, agreement with Hitler. All in all, during the interwar years the former crown prince remained a largely insignificant and marginal figure, for whom the possibility of a genuine restoration of the monarchy never unfolded. Even before the First World War, there had been severe doubts within informed circles about the competence of the heir to the throne, who even then was understood to be at the reactionary end of the political spectrum. 'Just be careful not to shoot the emperor', Foreign Secretary Alfred von Kiderlen-Waechter had joked to a friend who had been invited to hunt with Wilhelm II, 'he who is next is even worse.' His assessment would be confirmed by the war and the performance of the heir to the throne, whose public image degenerated from the soldierly full-whack-prince to the womanising man-who-laughed. The crown prince's need to emulate his ancestors and to go to war while holding an imposing position contributed decisively to bringing the age of the militarised monarchy in Prussia–Germany to an end.[80]

*

It is remarkable how often leadership in the First World War was at least nominally in the hands of future kings. From late summer 1916, the German forces on the Western Front were divided into three groups, each of which was commanded by a royal heir. Alongside the central 'Army Group German Crown Prince' and the more southerly 'Army Group Duke Albrecht', which was under the command of the Württemberg heir to the throne, the 'Army Group Crown Prince Rupprecht' operated on the northern section of the front, commanded by the heir to the Bavarian throne. In the light of the common fate of these troops – defeat in autumn 1918 – and of their commanders – the disappearance of the crowns of Prussia, Württemberg and Bavaria in the November Revolution – we may readily assume an automatic development here: the reputation and prospects of a royal heir who carries highly visible military responsibilities are irreparably damaged by defeat in the war. Yet the case of the Bavarian Crown Prince Rupprecht, especially when set against the performance of Crown Prince Wilhelm of Prussia,

---

[80] Stephan Malinowksi, 'Der braune Kronprinz', in *Zeit-Online*, www.zeit.de/2015/33/ho henzollern-kronprinz-nationalsozialismus-adolf-hitler (2015) (accessed 21 April 2017); Görlitz (ed.), *Regierte der Kaiser?*, p. 97.

suggests that, while the outcome in each instance was so similar, intriguing nuances were part of the process.

In early August 1914, when the German High Command gathered in Munich, the Inspector General of the Bavarian troops, Prince Rupprecht, who held the rank of colonel general, was appointed commander-in-chief of the Sixth Army, which largely comprised the Bavarian army corps. The forty-five-year-old son of the king of Bavaria had reached the pinnacle of his long and ambitious military career. In 1886, at age seventeen, the prince had been appointed a second lieutenant in the Infantry Lifeguards. After completing his basic military training and serving for two years in this elite unit, he was assigned to the 3rd Field Artillery Regiment in 1888, where he served for one more year before beginning his university studies in Munich and Berlin. From the summer semester of 1891, he supplemented his studies with lectures at the Bavarian War Academy. In the autumn of 1891, he became a first lieutenant with the 1st Heavy Cavalry Regiment, where he remained for the next four years. In 1893–1894 the prince attended courses that served as training for the General Staff. Having returned to the infantry, Rupprecht was promoted to colonel in 1899 and assumed command of the 2nd Infantry Regiment. From there, the royal heir's career advanced rapidly: in 1900 he commanded a brigade in Bamberg as a major general, and just six years later, as *General der Infanterie*, he was at the head of the Bavarian army corps. Finally, in early 1913 he achieved the rank of Inspector General of the Fourth Army Inspectorate, which meant he would be designated supreme commander should the troops be mobilised. Rupprecht had achieved this final advancement in part by threatening otherwise to resign his commissions.[81]

As was usual for royal soldiers, the crown prince had experienced a dizzying career. But he was clearly much more qualified and his personality better suited for command of first an army and subsequently an army group than was his Prussian counterpart. For Crown Prince Rupprecht, who like the Prince of Wales and Crown Prince Wilhelm was actively engaged with military matters throughout the war, these years were an opportunity to render a service to the monarchical system as a whole and to the specific cause of the Kingdom of Bavaria. He distinguished himself in several ways: through the successes of the troops he commanded, through his informed and methodical style of leadership, through his realistic assessment of the situation and through his consistent emphasis

[81] Dieter J. Weiß, *Kronprinz Rupprecht von Bayern. Eine politische Biografie* (Regensburg, 2007), pp. 45–55, 96; Dieter Storz, 'Kronprinz Rupprecht von Bayern – dynastische Heerführung im Massenkrieg', in Winfried Heinemann and Markus Pöhlmann (eds.), *Monarchen und ihr Militär* (Potsdam, 2010), p. 45; Jonathan Boff, *Haig's Enemy: Crown Prince Rupprecht and Germany's War on the Western Front* (Oxford, 2018), pp. 11–16.

on the interests of his Bavarian homeland. Notwithstanding these strengths, the Bavarian heir, whose own dreams for the future died alongside those of the other German princes in November 1918, can by no means be acquitted of the failings of the German leadership in the First World War. Above all, there was Rupprecht's relatively brief advocacy of annexations, which were to be achieved through a German victory and would benefit Bavaria in particular. In this, he was part of the less-than-glorious discussion of war aims in which a number of German princes participated. Despite this blunder, even the critically inclined historian Lothar Machtan has entered the wartime service of the Bavarian crown prince as a credit on the balance sheet giving account of the ruling princely houses' military performance.[82]

Assisted by a Bavarian chief of staff, Major General Konrad Krafft von Dellmensingen, Rupprecht took command of the Sixth Army, which was largely composed of Bavarian troops and was deployed in Lorraine and the Vosges at the beginning of the war. Initially its role was entirely defensive, but on 19 August, Rupprecht, on his own initiative, ordered the troops to attack the French lines, which the following day brought him victory in the Battle of Lorraine. Like Crown Prince Wilhelm after the Battle of Longwy, Rupprecht was celebrated as a triumphant hero.

Following the usual pattern, Emperor Wilhelm sent Rupprecht the Iron Cross First and Second Class, 'With you, I thank God for this magnificent victory', he informed the Wittelsbach prince. Following the battle at Lorraine, a postcard bearing the title 'The King's Gratitude' circulated in Bavaria. Under portraits of King Ludwig III and Crown Prince Rupprecht, garlanded with laurel and oak leaves, could be read the words 'I am proud that, at the head of his brave troops, my son has achieved such stunning successes.' The Bavarian press contained extensive reports of Rupprecht's triumph. Biographical articles informed readers about the life of the new Bavarian national hero, who had become famous throughout the empire overnight. The royal cabinet in Munich received numerous adulatory cards sent by soldiers declaring their loyalty to the ruling house. In next to no time an enterprising fine-art dealer in Munich, C. Andelfinger & Cie, offered postcards for sale specifically for this purpose. Even outside Bavaria, Rupprecht was celebrated. Patriotic rallies were held in Berlin and Dresden. In 1915, a commemorative medal bearing Rupprecht's countenance was struck to recall the triumph. Years later, the Battle of Lorraine, designated 'the first great German victory', was particularly prominent in the lavish *Bayernbuch vom Weltkriege* (*Bavarian Book of the World War*), a two-volume 'popular book'

[82] Machtan, *Die Abdankung*, p. 99.

(*Volksbuch*) published in 1930 to celebrate the Bavarian soldiers' contribution to the war. The author, Rupprecht's former Chief of Staff Krafft von Dellmensingen, was full of praise: 'In strategic terms, the crown prince was able to achieve the valuable result that the German army command was relieved of its worry about the army's southern flank and had been given the freedom to utilise the majority of the forces that had been deployed in Lorraine in other locations in the cause of bringing about the great victory against the French–English army.'[83]

The elated mood after the battle was interrupted by tragic news that only heightened sympathies for the widowed heir to the Bavarian throne: on 27 August 1914, Rupprecht's oldest son, the thirteen-year-old Hereditary Prince Luitpold, died unexpectedly of polio. The whole nation joined the royal house in mourning the much-loved boy, whose funeral had to take place without his father, for Rupprecht's presence on the front was indispensable. What most helped him deal with the grief, the crown prince wrote to his father in early September, was 'relentless work'. The death of his son nevertheless profoundly affected the much-afflicted prince, who before the war had already lost his wife Marie Gabriele, his daughter Irmingard and his younger son Rudolf. Major General Karl von Wenniger, who saw Rupprecht in person during these days, found that the 'poor man' looked terrible.[84]

Soon after, the Sixth Army was redeployed to northern France. Here, as a result of the failure of the original German strategy, a deadlocked war of attrition soon took shape. Without a decisive breakthrough, the colossal loss of men and materiel over the course of the following months and years produced no real result for either side. The circumstances required continual attempts to foster loyalty to the dynasty. Thus, in January 1915, the seventieth birthday of the Bavarian king Ludwig III was marked on the Western Front. The *Augsburger Postzeitung* reported for its readers back home in Bavaria on a large parade at the crown prince's headquarters in Lille: 'Crown Prince Rupprecht gave a brief speech, to which his troops responded with a rousing "Long live the king!".' In a published letter to his father, Rupprecht praised Ludwig's 'fruitful and untiring activities as ruler' and expressed his delight at the jubilation of a 'grateful and devoted' people. German war propaganda fully exploited every commendable military action involving the crown prince. After

---

[83] Konrad Krafft von Dellmensingen (ed.), *Das Bayernbuch vom Weltkriege 1914–1918. Ein Volksbuch*, vol. 1 (Stuttgart, 1930), pp. 32–33; Weiß, *Kronprinz Rupprecht von Bayern*, pp. 96–108; Stefan März, *Das Haus Wittelsbach im Ersten Weltkrieg. Chance und Zusammenbruch monarchischer Herrschaft* (Regensburg, 2013), pp. 173–179; Boff, *Haig's Enemy*, pp. 23–24.

[84] März, *Das Haus Wittelsbach im Ersten Weltkrieg*, pp. 179–180; Boff, *Haig's Enemy*, p. 27.

Rupprecht had led a successful defence against British attacks in Artois in autumn 1915, he was graced with the honorary title of 'Victor of Arras and La Bassée'. The following summer, King Ludwig III promoted his son to the rank of Bavarian Field Marshal. Here was another opportunity to burnish the dynastic legend: the day on which his advancement was announced, 23 July 1916, was the fiftieth anniversary of King Ludwig's wounding at Helmstadt.[85]

The crown prince was aware that such opportunities, along with the Bavarian king's numerous visits to the front, were effective not just in lifting the mood amongst the soldiers but also in strengthening their loyalty. He was convinced, he informed his father's adjutant general, 'that His Majesty's visits, which are always greeted with great joy by the Bavarian troops, contribute wonderfully to preserving and fortifying a Bavarian national sentiment and allegiance to the royal house of Bavaria'. He also contributed personally: while attending a parade in May 1917 he asked that all officers who had fought with him at Arras be presented to him: 'Because of this I too have shaken hands with royalty', wrote a delighted Kurt Kreiter, a volunteer soldier from Germersheim in the Palatinate, to his fiancée.[86]

At the end of August 1916, Rupprecht took command of the newly formed 'Army Group Crown Prince Rupprecht'. On his departure from the Sixth Army, Rupprecht sent praise to its 'commanders and troops'. While he also welcomed the replacement of the hated Erich von Falkenhayn as chief of the Supreme Army Command by Paul von Hindenburg and Erich Ludendorff, he was not at all happy. Leopold Krafft von Dellmensingen, a diplomat serving in the crown prince's headquarters, reported to the Bavarian Minister President that 'under the impact of the vast battles and the naturally very severe losses' the heir to the throne found himself 'in a very serious mood'. That sentiment was in accord with Rupprecht's increasing scepticism about the chances of a German victory. By late 1915 at the latest, he had recognised that a military victory was very unlikely. Thereafter he advocated internally for efforts to secure a negotiated peace. To that end, he accepted the need to forgo any annexations; at most, ran his sober assessment, the empire could hope to retain its possessions as of 1914. In January 1917, given the severely limited supply of foodstuffs within the German Empire and Austria-Hungary, Rupprecht described it as the best option 'to make peace as soon as possible, no matter how hard the enemy's terms may

---

[85] Weiß, *Kronprinz Rupprecht von Bayern*, pp. 109–110, 116; März, *Das Haus Wittelsbach im Ersten Weltkrieg*, pp. 181–186, 250.

[86] März, *Das Haus Wittelsbach im Ersten Weltkrieg*, p. 257.

be, for they are not going to be any better when we are close to starving to death'. He even reckoned on relinquishing parts of Alsace-Lorraine. It was now impossible for the war to end in victory, the crown prince wrote to his father in February 1918, even before the start of the great German spring offensive. His realistic assessment, which despite his efforts did not carry the day, earned him repeated accusations of pessimism. Unlike other high-ranking officers, Rupprecht could afford to hold such unpopular views – and occasionally clash with the Supreme Army Command – because of his dynastic position. As Dieter Storz has noted, removing a 'Prince-General' was practically impossible.[87]

Rupprecht's later realism was in marked contrast to the ambitious war aims that he had championed until mid 1915. In December 1914, in a letter to his father, whose expansionist goals he still shared at this point, he had reflected on an increase in Bavarian territory after the end of the war. He believed an expansion of the second-largest federal state to be absolutely necessary to secure the survival of German federalism. His eye was on 'lower Alsace with Strasbourg, along with a part of Lorraine that borders on the Palatinate'. Its rich coal reserves made acquiring territory in the Saar basin very desirable, he noted. Rupprecht was considering more than just the reassignment of part of Alsace-Lorraine, which lay within the empire. In the spring of 1915, he looked beyond the German borders. In April, he addressed the future of Belgium in an extensive memorandum and wrote in favour of a reallocation of its territory. The crown prince made a case for pushing the German border westwards, after the annexation of Belgium, Luxembourg, the Netherlands and parts of northern France. The Channel coast and the most significant strongholds in northern France would thus fall into German hands. Rupprecht's vision had the newly formed regions become states within the German Empire, which would then acquire a looser, more clearly federal character. The relative curtailment of Prussian dominance that would result could only benefit Bavaria's autonomy and strengthen both the country and its dynasty.[88]

If we accept Dieter Storz's suggestion that Rupprecht's real war aim was to reinforce Bavaria's position, then we should also add that the crown prince's struggle on behalf of Bavarian interests was not just a matter of Wittelsbach self-preservation, but was also intended to thwart

---

[87] Ibid., pp. 319–320; Boff, *Haig's Enemy*, p. 208; Kronprinz Rupprecht, *Mein Kriegstagebuch*, ed. Eugen von Frauenholz, vol. 2 (Berlin, 1929), p. 91; Storz, 'Kronprinz Rupprecht von Bayern', pp. 52–53.

[88] Weiß, *Kronprinz Rupprecht von Bayern*, pp. 129–134; Karl-Heinz Janßen, *Macht und Verblendung. Kriegszielpolitik der deutschen Bundesstaaten 1914–1918* (Göttingen, 1963), pp. 61–65.

any damage that might be done to the monarchy more broadly. 'If the federal princes as a result of the decrease in their influence also were to lose respect amongst their subjects', argued Rupprecht to his father in July 1915, the inevitable result would be 'a weakening of the monarchical idea, which would surely seem highly undesirable to the emperor in the light of what would follow'. Yet, only a few weeks later – probably as a result of a discussion with the less-than-confident Imperial Chancellor, Theobald von Bethmann Hollweg, on 13 October 1915 – the crown prince had completely changed his views of where the war might end. As the historian Karl-Heinz Janßen pithily noted, the staunch advocate of a dictated peace had become the equally staunch proponent of a negotiated peace.[89]

Along with his – largely unsuccessful – efforts to lobby the military and political leadership of the empire along these lines, Crown Prince Rupprecht subsequently dedicated himself to his responsibilities as a military commander with a grim determination and conscientiousness. In so doing, he distinguished himself through his great professionalism and sense of duty. His extensive and highly detailed war diary – the three-volume version published in 1929 runs to more than 1,300 pages – makes evident that he certainly did not limit himself to high-level issues or representational tasks. As was confirmed by the Prussian lieutenant general Hermann von Kuhl, who replaced Krafft von Dellmensingen as Rupprecht's chief of staff in November 1915, the crown prince had a 'sound knowledge and mastery of the army's circumstances, both broadly and in detail' and also a 'remarkably good perception and great understanding of operational situations'. Observers praised the calm working atmosphere at Rupprecht's headquarters and the prince's diligence. His public image – captured here in Figure 27 – was that of a serious, earnest man. The Bavarian heir inspected the soldiers fighting at the front in person, repeatedly putting himself in danger on the battlefield. Even critical observers such as the Bavarian lieutenant general Nikolaus Ritter von Endres had to admit that the crown prince was popular amongst his soldiers.[90]

Rupprecht carried out his duties against the background of a gathering political storm that he regarded as increasingly threatening. This applied not just to the ceasefire he sought but also to internal political upheavals. His own analysis suggested that, together with the huge burdens placed on the people by the increasingly futile war, the suspension of German

---

[89] Storz, 'Kronprinz Rupprecht von Bayern', p. 54; Janßen, *Macht und Verblendung*, pp. 69–72, 85–87; Kronprinz Rupprecht, *Mein Kriegstagebuch*, vol. 1, pp. 395–396.

[90] Kronprinz Rupprecht, *Mein Kriegstagebuch*; Storz, 'Kronprinz Rupprecht von Bayern', p. 51; Weiß, *Kronprinz Rupprecht von Bayern*, pp. 124–125; Boff, *Haig's Enemy*, pp. 108–113.

In ungeahnter Größe offenbart sich der innere Wert unseres Volkes: opferwilliger Sinn in der Heimat, Heldentum im Felde.

Figure 27. His serious and professional demeanour marked out Crown Prince Rupprecht of Bavaria as a very different personality from his flippant Prussian counterpart. He emerged from the war as a respected individual. Author's private collection.

federalism in favour of military and political centralisation threatened a dangerous outcome. 'For Bavaria in particular, where the middle class is quite numerous, the situation is becoming catastrophic', he wrote to the Bavarian Minister President in July 1917. 'The members of this estate, the vast majority of whom were previously well-disposed to the monarchy, are now in part even more anti-monarchy than the Social Democrats, for they blame the government for their misfortune. [...] The government is accused of acquiescing to Berlin in everything, and an increasing number support the view that, since Berlin has taken the lead on everything, our government is now nothing more than unnecessary ballast. And what is more, in the other federal states the anti-monarchical mood is even worse.' Although the Wittelsbach prince was mainly critical of the German emperor's blunders and inaction and had doubts about the survival of Hohenzollern rule, by 1917 he had to acknowledge that even in his Bavarian homeland there were revolutionary, anti-monarchical efforts afoot.[91]

Rupprecht's Cassandra-like warnings came to nothing, and the crown prince was left to look on helplessly from the collapsing Western Front as the Wittelsbach monarchy itself became the first victim of the

[91] Weiß, *Kronprinz Rupprecht von Bayern*, p. 158.

revolutionary movement. With the emperor's refusal to abdicate and thereby clear the path for a negotiated peace, the revolutionary movement throughout Germany adopted a strongly anti-monarchical character. In Munich, the elderly King Ludwig III and his family fled from the royal residence in the late evening of 7 November 1918, and soon after their departure the Social Democrat Kurt Eisner proclaimed the Free State of Bavaria. Rupprecht learned of these events in Brussels on the morning of 8 November. Two days later, he protested in an official declaration at the 'political upheaval, which has been initiated by a minority, without the involvement of the legislative authorities and the majority of the Bavarian citizens in the army and the homeland'. After the signing of the armistice on 11 November, the former crown prince made his way, incognito and with a forged passport, via the neutral Netherlands back to Bavaria, where he arrived only at the end of the month, after an adventurous journey. The new Bavarian government allowed him to remain, but he was unable to achieve any political influence. Having lost his position, his income and even his home, he had to flee abruptly to Austria when the short-lived Munich Soviet Republic (*Räterepublik*) was proclaimed in April 1919. Only at the end of the year did he find a permanent residence in Berchtesgaden. As the crown prince's biographer, Dieter J. Weiß, summed up, where once Rupprecht's life had been dominated by the constant activity of the commander of an Army Group, now, surplus to requirements, he fell into a void.[92]

The letters that Rupprecht sent to his family during these days show that he combined an unsparing analysis of the reasons for the revolution with a stoic acceptance of events. 'What events since my last letter!', he wrote at the beginning of December to his father. 'I am surprised only at the timing; that it would happen had been my concern for a long time. In my letters I had taken the liberty of repeatedly noting that the bow was too tightly strung – and now it is broken.' He was even more explicit when he wrote to his aunt Theresa: 'How often did I not [...] warn Papa and implore him to object energetically in Berlin, for it was clear that it could not go on thus, but then I was seen as alarmist! I admit that for me the months from March to November, time spent anticipating the approaching collapse, were worse than the collapse itself! Better an end in horror than horror without end.'[93]

---

[92] Ibid., pp. 163–179; Dieter J. Weiß, 'Kronprinz Rupprecht von Bayern (1869–1955). Thronprätendent in einer Republik', in Frank-Lothar Kroll and Dieter J. Weiß (eds.), *Inszenierung oder Legitimität. Die Monarchie in Europa im 19. und 20. Jahrhundert. Ein deutsch–englischer Vergleich* (Berlin, 2015), p. 156.

[93] März, *Das Haus Wittelsbach im Ersten Weltkrieg*, pp. 512–513.

Because he adopted this attitude, and not least because of his military service during the war, Rupprecht's reputation in the period after the war was much more favourable than that of the former Prussian crown prince. His high standing would continue to burden Rupprecht's relationship with his father, which had been tense for some time. The former king feared that his popular son might supplant him in his claims to the throne, and therefore held tight to his position as head of the family. In the light of Ludwig III's unpopularity, concrete plans for the restoration of the Wittelsbach monarchy could take shape only after his death, in October 1921. While Rupprecht was amenable to the idea, he adamantly opposed any notion of a putsch. He insisted that the kingdom could be restored only through constitutional means, at the request of the government and the people. Although a monarchical movement would later take shape around the person of the former crown prince, that call never came.[94]

***

The militarisation of the constitutional monarchies over the course of the long nineteenth century reached its climax in the First World War. For generations the crowned heads of Europe and their families had posed and dressed as the military leaders they fancied themselves to be. Now, under the most challenging conditions imaginable, they had to attempt to meet the expectations they had aroused. The beginning of what would soon prove to be total war and the collapse of transnational family solidarity amongst interrelated dynasties caused cataclysmic changes. At the same time, some continuities within the militarised monarchies persisted. With various levels of success, the participating monarchies sought to serve their countries as supreme commanders and fathers of their nations – entirely in line with the role they had performed for decades.

Hardly any crowned head succeeded as well as the Belgian king Albert I, who was the only constitutional monarch who actually led his country militarily and politically. 'The tragic test that was the war', observed Flemish politician Frans Van Cauwelaert in 1934, after Albert's death, 'added to a crown already adorned with honesty, integrity and goodness the red crown jewel of flawless heroism.' And the tireless engagement of the British royal couple on behalf of the troops, the war wounded and their families had, according to historian Heather Jones, 'the corollary of making the monarchy appear approachable and human, at a moment in history when industrial warfare had made battle faceless, mechanical and anonymous'. The king's actions were in effect an 'antidote to the modern

---

[94] Ibid., p. 513; Weiß, 'Kronprinz Rupprecht von Bayern', p. 157; Boff, *Haig's Enemy*, pp. 247–253.

terrors of Great War anonymity'. The decision of the Italian king, Vittorio Emanuele III, to go to the front, where he had no influence on the conduct of the war but for more than three years visited the troops and encouraged optimism, also met with approval. By joining his soldiers, the British ambassador judged, the king had 'enormously strengthened his position and [was] now the most popular man in Italy'. Although there were widespread complaints about the monarch's weak leadership in governmental and military circles, patriotic propaganda was able to per-petuate the image of the Soldier King (*Re Soldato*), the Infantrymen's Infantryman (*Il Fante dei Fanti*) and Italy's First Soldier (*Primo Soldato d'Italia*). After the unexpectedly felicitous – considering the country's military performance – outcome of the war, the monarch was even cele-brated as the victorious realiser of the national mission. 'It was he, the third Emanuele, Vittorio the Victor, who achieved the greatest fulfilment and saw Italy at last encircled by the boundaries that Dante and Mazzini had predicted and invoked', enthused the Italian author Annibale Grasselli Barni even as late as 1922.[95]

In other places, the monarchs were less successful. The aged Austrian emperor, Franz Joseph, practically cemented into his daily routine, was no longer able to adapt to the new circumstances. After the war broke out, he never left Vienna again, remaining in the city until his death in November 1916. Shielded by a circle of similarly superannuated advisers, he lost any immediate contact with the external world beyond daily reports, audiences and presentations. Manfried Rauchensteiner has noted that, in the years immediately before his death, Franz Joseph spent thousands of hours in this geriatric setting. The absence of the monarchical head was not mitigated by the presence of the heir to the throne, the young Archduke Karl. Despite his various military and polit-ical deployments, Karl's appearances during the war, Rauchensteiner has observed, tended to be episodic and conveyed superficiality and imma-turity rather than intelligence and determination.[96]

The German emperor Wilhelm proved even less able to meet the demands of the moment. Entirely out of his depth, the man designated

---

[95] Janssens, 'Die belgische Monarchie und Albert I.', p. 409; Jones, 'The Nature of Kingship in First World War Britain', p. 213; Romano Bracalini, *Il re 'vittorioso'. La vita, il regno e l'esilio di Vittorio Emanuele III* (Milan, 1980), pp. 85–99; Denis Mack Smith, *Italy and Its Monarchy* (New Haven, CT and London, 1989), pp. 220, 223–224, 242; Robertson, *Victor Emmanuel III*, pp. 113–134; Annibale Grasselli Barni, *Vittorio Emanuele Terzo* (Piacenza, 1922), p. 95.

[96] Manfried Rauchensteiner, *Der Erste Weltkrieg und das Ende der Habsburgermonarchie 1914–1918* (Vienna, Cologne and Weimar, 2013), pp. 655, 665; Michaela Vocelka and Karl Vocelka, *Franz Joseph I. Kaiser von Österreich und König von Ungarn, 1830–1916* (Munich, 2015), pp. 357–358; Demmerle, *Kaiser Karl I.*, pp. 84–87.

'supreme commander' was soon forced into the background by his generals. With little to do, the emperor could have thrown himself into the role of the benevolent father of the nation – much like his cousin George V – but he lacked the inclination to do so. For his safety, during his carefully staged visits to the front he never advanced any further than the rear area. These events, which involved music and parades, were often irksome for the soldiers and certainly had little to do with their everyday experience of war. Moreover, the emperor was also living out his need for amusement to an extent that was unacceptable even to those around him. As Wilhelm was leaving headquarters to visit an art exhibition in Frankfurt, the Chief of the Military Cabinet could no longer contain himself: 'I informed him in the strongest of terms of his responsibilities towards his starving and suffering people. All hell broke loose between us, which ended when he ran out inveighing loudly and angrily and forcefully slammed the door with a crash', wrote Moritz von Lyncker to his wife in May 1917. Because of Wilhelm's attitude even opulent propaganda productions such as the 450-page volume *Der Kaiser im Felde* (*The Emperor at War*), published in 1916, proved largely futile. Its lacklustre recitation of imperial appearances and formulaic orations would hardly have made for edifying reading for soldiers at the front, for whom the volume was primarily intended. It was therefore not at all surprising that, when the tide eventually turned against Germany, the emperor, who was held responsible for the impending defeat and the prolongation of the war, quickly became a hate figure.[97]

The world war placed extraordinary demands not only on monarchs but also on those of their sons who were of an age to serve in the military. They had largely enjoyed somewhat fabulous military careers and were committed to the widely held belief in the nexus of manliness and the will to fight. As such, heirs to the throne would inevitably have to join the hundreds of thousands of other men who were expected to don battle fatigues and do their duty for their country. As the wartime experiences of Prince Edward, Crown Prince Wilhelm and Crown Prince Rupprecht demonstrate clearly, they shared in these expectations. Edward believed that a cloud hung over his manliness when he was not permitted to experience the dangers and deprivations of the soldiers. Crown Prince Wilhelm was under the spell of a dynastic legend that recounted how his grandfather had advanced from crown prince to war hero. Crown Prince Rupprecht saw his war service as an opportunity to counter Bavaria's Prussian tutelage, just as his father had done fifty years earlier at Helmstadt. During the world war, the tried and

[97] John C. G. Röhl, *Wilhelm II: Into the Abyss of War and Exile 1900–1941* (Cambridge, 2014), pp. 1131–1134.

tested instrumentalisation of the military for political ends was intensified, with heirs to the throne providing a particular focus. The name and image of the ruler-to-be were found everywhere – in the press and in propaganda, within illustrated books, on commemorative medals and at visits to the troops – in an effort to strengthen the subjects' willingness to do battle and reinforce their loyalty to the king.

The heirs to the throne were hardly able to meet the expectations invested in them, neither within the narrowly focused military sphere nor in terms of their propagandistic impact. How they were perceived depended more than ever on their characters and their personal aptitudes. Prince Edward grasped what it was to live a Spartan existence and to convey to the simple soldier a sense of solidarity with comrades; he was also able to satisfy the urges of his powerful sex drive more discreetly than was Crown Prince Wilhelm. In the case of the Hohenzollern prince, his penchant for a flashy uniform and a ritzy lifestyle and his propensity for a flippant smugness did considerable damage, for such personal weaknesses were intensified by mechanisms anchored in each monarchical system. On the German side, dynastic considerations greatly impacted significant personnel decisions during the war. Dynastic pride ensured that Crown Prince Wilhelm was granted his 'understandable wish' to emulate his grandfather and have command of an army. The Hohenzollern prince had no intention of taking a back seat to the princely army commanders from the kingdoms of Württemberg and Bavaria. Thus Crown Prince Wilhelm wittingly ended up in a dire situation in which his indisputable inability to live up to the demands of his military role clashed with his responsibility for everything formally under his command. To the rousing battle cry 'Hurrah for the Crown Prince', his self-inflicted fate ran its course.

The case of the heir to the imperial throne was thus very different from that of the Prince of Wales, whose duties in a war that he began as a lieutenant and ended as a captain were far less ambitious, and also from that of the more competent Crown Prince Rupprecht. Crown Prince Wilhelm violated a condition that each royal heir within a constitutional monarchy was absolutely bound to respect: his performance in the world war had made it almost impossible for his future subjects to believe that militarily, politically or in terms of his character he would ever be able to carry out the duties of a monarch appropriately. To make matters worse, the breach happened precisely as he was leading an army in the midst of a war, so in a moment of existential significance and with maximum visibility. As defeat in war caused the imperial regime to falter, Crown Prince Wilhelm helped ensure that the question of whether it would remain viable – and with it the monarchies in the German federal states – was met with a resounding *no*.

For the victorious monarchies, which emerged from the world war even stronger than before, the events between 1914 and 1918 also formed a caesura. The memory of the massive scale of the deaths at the Somme, on the Isonzo or at Passchendaele meant that it was now impossible for that merry military *oompah, oompah* to continue unchanged, with the monarchy as drum major. A new age needed a new symbolism, one that could supplement the previously cultivated tradition of monarchical and militaristic self-representation. In the years after the war the Belgian king Albert I attended events held throughout the country to honour the military and civilian victims of the war, always appearing in uniform, and thus sought to keep alive the memory of the suffering and the heroism of the Belgian people. In Great Britain, at the suggestion of King George V, on 11 November 1919 Armistice Day was marked with a two-minute silence at 11 a.m., precisely the moment at which the guns had fallen silent, establishing a tradition that has persisted to this day. The following year, the king unveiled the Cenotaph in Whitehall (Figure 28), an austere and

Figure 28. In the heart of London, on the steps of the austere Cenotaph, the British royal family would stage a very different kind of military leadership: monarchy as the representative of a mourning and grateful nation. Topical Press Agency/Stringer/Getty Images.

imposing monument erected to honour the fallen. Each year from then on, from its steps the king would lead the nation in a ceremony remembering the dead. As we have seen, Prince Edward, who was both heir to the throne and a veteran who had served in the war, could support his father both constructively and authentically in this highly symbolic duty.[98]

It was not given to everyone to be able to recast the role of monarchy so sensitively and so skilfully. For many other monarchs much remained as it always had been, even in exile. Amongst the many items of furniture that Wilhelm II arranged to have sent from Berlin to Huis Doorn, his new residence in Holland, one particular treasure was deemed indispensable: the desk chair equipped with a saddle.

[98] Janssens, 'Die belgische Monarchie und Albert I.', p. 430; Adrian Gregory, *The Silence of Memory: Armistice Day, 1919–1946* (Oxford, 1994); David Cannadine, 'War and Death: Grief and Mourning in Modern Britain', in Joachim Whaley (ed.), *Mirrors of Mortality: Studies in the Social History of Death* (London, 1981), pp. 219–226.

Conclusion

As the First World War was reaching its end, the crowned heads of Germany were staring into the abyss. The fateful course of the war and, in particular, the leadership provided by Emperor Wilhelm II during these difficult years did not bode well. The end of all of Germany's monarchies hung in the air. In October 1918, Grand Duke Friedrich August, who had ruled his half million Oldenburg subjects since 1900, uttered a grim prophecy on behalf of his fellow princes: 'We are in no doubt that the emperor has ruined the empire, that he will be sent packing and that we will share his fate. Wilhelm will bring us down, to that we have resigned ourselves.' For his part, Grand Duke Ernst Ludwig of Hesse did not attribute the guilt for what occurred in November 1918 wholly to the emperor. He reckoned that the German monarchs shared the blame: 'They were swept aside leaving nothing behind because they were complete nonentities', he would later record in his memoirs. 'They did not even understand that one must move with the times if one does not wish for the times to pass one by in the end.'[1]

Events at the close of the First World War seemed to confirm both views. The misery of the war and the experience of defeat did indeed lead to the widescale demise of the crowns of Germany and Austria, which had survived so remarkably since the revolutionary upheaval of the late eighteenth century. With the tragedy of the war, the monarchical century reached its endpoint. Now a new age was dawning, an era that would be characterised by republicanism and dictatorship. The end of European monarchy was not limited to the German-speaking lands. In Russia, Tsar Nicholas II had already been forced to abdicate in February 1917 and, in the following year, revolutionaries murdered him and all the members of his immediate family. Between December 1919 and October 1922, the Turkish sultanate was also gradually eliminated.

[1] Michael Horn, 'Zwischen Abdankung und Absetzung. Das Ende der Herrschaft der Bundesfürsten des Deutschen Reichs im November 1918', in Susan Richter und Dirk Dirbach (eds.), *Thronverzicht. Die Abdankung in Monarchien vom Mittelalter bis in die Neuzeit* (Cologne, Weimar and Vienna, 2010), pp. 267, 277.

The demise of Europe's four great empires was by no means the end of the de-monarchification of the continent. In 1923, dictator Miguel Primo de Rivera seized power from Alfonso XIII, the Spanish king, and eight years later Spain's short-lived Second Republic was proclaimed. The young constitutional monarchy in Yugoslavia became a royal dictatorship in 1929. After the German invasion in 1941, King Peter II fled into exile, where he abdicated four years later. In June 1946, the Italian monarchy fell after the majority of Italians had voted in a referendum in favour of the republic. In 1946 and 1947, 'People's Republics' replaced the monarchical systems in Bulgaria and Romania. In 1973, after decades of severe crisis, the monarchy was also abolished in Greece. Long before the 'short twentieth century' – the decades from the outbreak of the First World War to the dissolution of the Soviet Union – would come to an end, the once almost ubiquitous European phenomenon of monarchy had shrunk to become a relatively rare exception, found primarily on the north-western edge of the continent.[2]

The demise of the monarchies was a protracted process, but the fatal blow fell in the autumn of 1918. Not only did the imperial and royal monarchies of Austria-Hungary and Prussia–Germany disappear during these November days but with them went the princely rulers of twenty-one further German territories – from the grand-duchy of Mecklenburg-Strelitz to the kingdom of Bavaria, from the principality of Waldeck to the duchy of Saxony-Meiningen. This collapse of monarchical regimes unfolded with remarkable speed. King Ludwig III of Bavaria was the first to go, fleeing from his Munich palace in the night of 7/8 November 1918 accompanied by his family and equipped only with a box of cigars; the party first made for the Chiemgau region in the Bavarian Alps and then crossed the border to Austria. The abdication of the German emperor, Wilhelm II, was proclaimed on 9 November, and, by 10 November, the former ruler was crossing the border into the Netherlands, where he would spend the remainder of his long life in exile. Days later, the Austrian emperor, Karl, signed a document in which he renounced 'all claims to the business of state'. Thereafter, the German monarchies fell like dominoes. By the time Prince Günther von Schwarzburg-Sondershausen, the last to go, relinquished his position

---

[2] Eric Hobsbawm, *The Age of Extremes: The Short Twentieth Century, 1914–1991* (London, 1994), p. 5. On this theme see also Benjamin Hasselhorn, 'Das Monarchiesterben 1914–1945. Ein Siegeszug der Demokratie?', in Benjamin Hasselhorn and Marc von Knorring (eds.), *Vom Olymp zum Boulevard. Die europäischen Monarchien von 1815 bis heute – Verlierer der Geschichte?* (Berlin, 2018), pp. 47–60.

on 25 November 1918, a centuries-old monarchical landscape had been permanently eradicated in just a little over two weeks.[3] The collapse was not just breathtakingly fast but also surprisingly subdued, indeed almost incidental and fortunately largely bloodless. Rulers whose dynasties had in some instances resided in their ancestral lands for hundreds of years responded to the protests and to the demands of the freshly constituted workers' and soldiers' councils by shrugging their shoulders and striking their colours. Nothing illustrated the blasé and dispassionate attitude of those who abdicated better than the petulant words of farewell supposedly pronounced by the last Saxon king, Friedrich August III, on 13 November 1918: 'Well, now you can look after your mess without me.' Those who might have been expected to come to the aid of the crowned heads did nothing: 'Not a single Guards officer was ready to be sliced up for the sake of the king of Prussia', the historian Karl-Heinz Janßen dryly observed. No chamberlain attempted to stop the course of events, no court preacher risked life and limb to protect a dynasty. But the rejoicing was also limited. Apart from the hated German emperor, whose abandoned palace in Berlin was occupied and – somewhat hesitantly – plundered by workers' and soldiers' councils, hardly a single monarch engendered a particularly impassioned loathing. Even as they were being deposed, several rulers – Grand Duke Ernst Ludwig of Hesse, for example, or King Wilhelm II of Württemberg – were viewed with a bittersweet affection. After abdicating, most monarchs could still move about freely and unhindered in the lands they had once ruled. The lingering sympathies aroused by the genial former king of Saxony, Friedrich August III, provided material for many a tale. The king was said to have responded to one enthusiastic crowd with the words 'Well, what a fine lot of republicans you are!'[4]

For some historians, the speed and apparent ease with which dozens of constitutional monarchies succumbed after the First World War show that this governmental model had long since become untenable and dysfunctional. At the conclusion of a persistent and multi-faceted erosion

---

[3] For this and the following paragraph, see Lothar Machtan, *Die Abdankung. Wie Deutschlands gekrönte Häupter aus der Geschichte fielen* (Berlin, 2008); Helmut Neuhaus, 'Das Ende der Monarchien in Deutschland 1918', in *Historisches Jahrbuch* 111 (1991), pp. 102–136; Fritz Wecker, *Unsere Landesväter. Wie sie gingen, wo sie blieben* (Berlin, 1928).

[4] Frank Lorenz Müller, *Royal Heirs in Imperial Germany: The Future of Monarchy in Nineteenth-Century Bavaria, Saxony and Württemberg* (London, 2017), pp. 2–5; Karl-Heinz Janßen, 'Der Untergang der Monarchie in Deutschland', in Hellmuth Rößler (ed.), *Weltwende 1917. Monarchie – Weltrevolution – Demokratie* (Göttingen, 1965), p. 104; Ingo Materna, 'Schloß und Schloßbezirk in der Revolution 1918/19', in Wolfgang Ribbe (ed.), *Schloß und Schloßbezirk in der Mitte Berlins. Das Zentrum der Stadt als politischer und gesellschaftlicher Ort* (Berlin, 2005), pp. 139–147; *Ihr seid mir scheene Republikaner. Anekdoten aus der sächsischen Geschichte* (Berlin, 2006), p. 58.

of monarchical legitimacy stood, they propose, a regime of stubborn mediocrities who should have been got rid of much earlier. Nowhere across the German lands, Lothar Machtan summarised, had it proved possible to develop a new form of monarchy, even a prototype that might have generated a viable alternative to the self-obsessed 'autocratic media emperor'. Trapped in their 'bizarre political way of life', none of the monarchs, he states, had shown the ability to accommodate themselves voluntarily to the inexorable modernisation of state and society. They were unable to grasp that they would only be able to save themselves by fusing democracy with popular kingship (*Volkskönigtum*).[5]

This sombre depiction of Germany's constitutional monarchy appears justified by the nature of those monarchies that survived intact, in some instances even strengthened, after the First World War and throughout the years that followed. According to the political scientist Karl Loewenstein, all of the survivors – the crowns of Great Britain, Belgium, the Netherlands, Luxembourg, Denmark, Norway and Sweden – were 'parliamentary monarchies'. In this configuration, popular sovereignty and the monarchical principle could exist alongside each other, since adherence to the latter was simply an empty courtesy, with the monarchical rulers commanding no political decision-making powers. Loewenstein noted that in these monarchies actual political power had long been exercised by parliament, which had, when there was any doubt, consistently acted to reduce the royal prerogative even further. According to this reading, the conclusion of the First World War stands as the endpoint of the monarchical age in two respects: first, the constitutional monarchies of Central Europe which were still committed to the coexistence and interplay of crown and parliament as the two organs of the state had proved incapable of reform and were swept aside; secondly, in the constitutional monarchies that did survive, respect for the crown amounted to nothing more than polite lip service.[6]

Yet when we recall the role played by Europe's royal heirs in the reconfiguration and preservation of the monarchical system throughout the nineteenth century, this interpretation is not without its problems. For one thing, it stresses differences between the monarchies that perished and those that survived at the expense of

---

[5] Ernst Wolfgang Böckenförde, 'Das Ende der Monarchie', in Kurt G. A. Jeserich, Hans Pohl and Georg-Christoph von Unruh (eds.), *Deutsche Verwaltungsgeschichte*, vol. 4 (Stuttgart, 1985), pp. 2–9; Lothar Machtan, 'Deutschlands gekrönter Herrscherstand am Vorabend des Ersten Weltkriegs. Ein Inspektionsbericht zur Funktionstüchtigkeit des deutschen Monarchiemodells', in *Zeitschrift für Geschichtswissenschaft* 58 (2010), pp. 229, 238–239.

[6] Karl Loewenstein, *Die Monarchie im Modernen Staat* (Frankfurt am Main, 1952), pp. 27, 43.

acknowledging Europe-wide similarities and convergences. Moreover, by asserting the alleged rigidity and stasis of the constitutional, non-parliamentary monarchies, this reading ignores rather too readily that they also underwent a constant process of modification and a quiet accommodation to contemporary circumstances.

To start with, conveyed as they were via the upbringing, responsibilities and portrayal of those next-in-line, the future prospects which Europe's constitutional monarchies proffered to their people were remarkably similar across the board. Monarchies – and not just Loewenstein's 'parliamentary' monarchies – displayed a willingness to embrace an increasingly narrow interpretation of the constitutionally defined powers of the ruler who would exercise his or her functions within the law, in cooperation with elected assemblies and under the gaze of the public. In this context, reactionary heirs such as Archduke Franz Ferdinand or the German crown prince Wilhelm serve as exceptions. Their lack of popularity and controversial reputations confirmed a general rule that princes had to accept and herald constitutional progress. This rule had firmly established itself in the course of the nineteenth century – and not just west of the River Rhine. To be sure, by 1914, Europe's monarchies had not all reached the same milestones along this trajectory. The crowns of Prussia or Austria still commanded much more hard power than those of Britain or of the Netherlands; and the inverse can be said for these countries' respective parliaments. As the 'Century of Restorations' was drawing to its close, though, the direction of the monarchies' travel was clear across the continent.

The muted and composed removal of the German monarchs in autumn 1918 can therefore be seen in a different light. Notwithstanding all the emphasis on upholding the monarchical principle, respect for the ruler's prerogatives had long amounted to little more than adherence to a traditional courtesy even in many German-speaking countries. The abolition of the monarchies was therefore a discourteous act, but it no longer implied a fundamental upheaval in the political order. This was even more the case, given that in most monarchies a parliamentary system had been hurriedly introduced at the end of the war. The removal of the crowns could therefore proceed relatively peaceably. Even before then, a blurring of the line between monarchical and republican–presidential systems had seemed conceivable in some places, as the Social Democrat leader Wilhelm Keil had insinuated in his well-known article marking the Silver Jubilee of King Wilhelm II of Württemberg: 'Should a republic replace the monarchy in Württemberg tomorrow', Weil had declared in October 1916, 'if the decision fell to all the men and women who are citizens of the state, no candidate would be more likely than the present king to be placed at the head of the state.' For this monarch, Keil continued, had not stood in the way of the 'development of the constitution' but had actually supported it. As Volker Sellin has observed, in the nineteenth century the monarchical principle and democratic principle had begun to converge, even to the extent that Social Democrats could talk of a king as president.[7]

Keil was neither the first nor the only German Social Democrat politician to imagine a shared future for Social Democracy and constitutional monarchy. In the years before the First World War, several Social Democrat authors considered what it might mean for monarchy to turn into popular kingship. 'Monarchy is not as bad as you make it out to be', Keil had quoted from August Bebel's speech to the Socialist Congress held in Amsterdam in 1904, adding that Social Democrats were certainly not enthusiastic about a 'bourgeois republic'. One had only to look beyond the borders of Germany to find alternatives. In an article that appeared in the monthly *Sozialistische Monatshefte* in 1906, the Norwegian socialist Olav Kringen had described the monarchy in his homeland as 'a more modern institution than the conservative republic'. Although he had been an American citizen for ten years, Kringen wrote, he would unhesitatingly opt for the Norwegian monarchy over the American republic. Yes, in principle, the republic was the better solution, but he saw 'no need to deploy republican theories, and even less republican propaganda, in a land in which the monarchy had to keep in step with the democratisation of its institutions'. For men such as Keil the decisive issue was not the question of monarchy or republic. He was more concerned about the transformation of the social foundations that determined the lives of the people. Indeed, as the Socialist Reichstag deputy Ludwig Quessel explained in 1909, the members of his party called themselves 'not social republicans, but social democrats' and could wholeheartedly welcome the 'development towards a democratic monarchy' that was also in progress in Germany. 'The democratic interest', Quessel declared three years later, 'commands us to follow the path of parliamentarianism that runs also into the imperial palace.'[8]

---

[7] *Schwäbische Tagwacht* of 5 October 1916; Volker Sellin, *Das Jahrhundert der Restaurationen* (Munich, 2014), pp. 139–140; Frank Lorenz Müller, 'Symptomatisch für den Niedergang des Bismarck-Reiches? Die leise Entkrönung der kleineren deutschen Königreiche im November 1918', in Holger Afflerbach and Ulrich Lappenküper (eds.), *1918 – Das Ende des Bismarck-Reiches?* (Paderborn, 2021), pp. 79–99.

[8] Olav Kringen, 'Monarchie oder Republik?', in *Sozialistische Monatshefte* 10 (1906), p. 66; Ludwig Quessel, 'Sind wir Republikaner?', in *Sozialistische Monatshefte* 13 (1909), p. 1262; Ludwig Quessel, 'Sozialdemokratie und Monarchie', in *Sozialistische Monatshefte* 16 (1912), p. 275.

That contemporaries who were anything but prone to unquestioning monarchical devotion could speak in such terms suggests that the differences, although undoubtedly real, that separated 'parliamentary' monarchies from their constitutional counterparts should not be overstated. Evidently, observers in many quarters entertained a credible expectation that sooner or later forms of what Quessel had described as 'democratic monarchy' would prevail – and that this would happen not only in the west and north of the European continent where parliamentary monarchies could be found, but even in locations as seemingly inauspicious as the palace of the German emperor.

This broad, European-wide convergence came at the end of a long and varied process of change, its pace differing from country to country. There can certainly be no talk of a 'democratic monarchy' in Prussia, Bavaria, Saxony or Piedmont at the beginning of the nineteenth century. It should also be noted, though, that, at that time, the monarchical systems that were taking shape following the introduction of constitutions in Great Britain, the Netherlands and Belgium also stood at the beginning of a process of change that would continue throughout the century. In 1834, King William IV of England still dismissed the liberal cabinet of Lord Melbourne even though it had a parliamentary majority. His successor, Queen Victoria, was convinced that the rights of the crown were hers as gift from God, and, in the early phase of her reign, she and her husband, Prince Albert, claimed an active part in the government for the crown. Leopold I, who had become King of the Belgians following the revolution of 1830, acted in a similar fashion: he took personal command of the business of state and acknowledged the authority of his ministers only in that they were 'ministers of the king'. In 1840, King Willem I of the Netherlands preferred to abdicate rather than bow to parliamentary control of his government.[9]

All European monarchies had to confront the process of change that the French Revolution had set in motion. That they generally succeeded in doing so for decade after decade forms an integral element of any comprehensive portrait of the age. First, they had to master the transition from absolute to constitutional rule. As soon as constitutions had been introduced, constitutional monarchies had to reorientate themselves in response to the pull of democracy. Here, Great Britain led the way for almost all of Europe. Many of the traditional functions that had been

[9] Ian Newbould, 'William IV and the Dismissal of the Whigs, 1834', in *Canadian Journal of History* 11 (1976), pp. 311–330; David Cannadine, 'The Last Hanoverian Sovereign? The Victorian Monarchy in Historical Perspective, 1688–1888', in A. L. Beier, David Cannadine and James M. Rosenheim (eds.), *The First Modern Society: Essays in English History in Honour of Lawrence Stone* (Cambridge, 1989), pp. 140–141, 144.

exercised by monarchical rulers in the ancient world, the Middle Ages or the early modern period – those of 'god, governor and general' – were now, in the nineteenth century, taken on by other individuals and institutions. It was increasingly evident, David Cannadine has further noted, 'that modern monarchy is about doing new things, finding new functions, and creating new rationales for its continued existence in societies no longer rural, religious and hierarchical [...] but instead urban, secular and democratic'.[10]

By picking up the gauntlet and throwing themselves into performing specific monarchical functions, the royal dynasties were able to stand their ground through the generations. The spectrum of possibilities available to them reached from impartial moderating to forming a collective identity, from upholding tradition to leading the nation. To this end, while always preserving characteristic partial identities, the monarchies had to adapt constantly, holding out a latent promise to accommodate the ever-changing political, social and cultural needs of the age. In large parts of European society, this pledge fostered a willingness not just to tolerate this form of monarchical rule but even to champion it. Here a psychological factor also came into play, described by Lothar Machtan for the German context but applicable throughout much of Europe: many people were content to support the idea of monarchy because they admired the power of the crowned heads to counter the banality of human existence by bringing 'glamour and poetry' to everyday life on certain occasions, and even to 'smother it with pomp'.[11]

The ability of monarchies to adapt and to perform certain functions, as well as their capacity for delivering consolation and entertainment, constitute only one side of the equation, though. They should not be credited with an abundance of initiative or creative drive. As David Cannadine has concluded for Britain, in the course of the nineteenth century, monarchies were increasingly more likely to be 'responding to events than initiating them, presiding over a period of time but not dominating it'.[12] At the same time – and this is a significant part of the overall picture – the importance of persistent and reactionary elements of monarchical rule must not be underestimated either: the tradition of a high-aristocratic way of life, an unworldly dynastic self-perception, the symbiotic relationship of the crown with often reactionary elites and the frequent efforts to delay

---

[10] David Cannadine, 'From Biography to History: Writing the Modern British Monarchy', in *Historical Research* 77 (2004), pp. 293–294, 303.
[11] Machtan, 'Deutschlands gekrönter Herrscherstand am Vorabend des Ersten Weltkriegs', p. 240.
[12] Cannadine, 'From Biography to History', p. 298.

a reconfiguration of the political system in a parliamentary or democratic direction.

By standing for both continuity and change, the process of succession, that is, the transfer of power to another member of the dynasty, and especially the individual heirs themselves contributed decisively to monarchical self-preservation. They did so within the narrowly defined political arena, where the monarchical system profited from the handing-over to a new generation. Crown princes tended to be at least somewhat more liberal than their predecessors and – thanks to their upbringing – they were more able to adapt to the demands of their age. Such was particularly the case when it came to their willingness to accept the written and unwritten limitations on the constitutionally determined remit of the ruler. Evident political differences between monarch and successor reconciled contemporaries who sought change from the status quo; the innovations for which they longed seemed to be only deferred and would occur when, inevitably, the throne changed hands. Seen in this light, political tensions between generations – however burdensome they were for the participants themselves – were not necessarily a disadvantage for the monarchical system. Both the loyal heir and the oppositional crown prince buttressed the system – each in their own way.

Royal heirs also helped the monarchies to hold their own beyond the narrowly conceived political domain. Their carefully staged and media-savvy appearances, which captured the attention and interest of the public, enabled them to accumulate the soft power that attracted large parts of the population to the various monarchies. The relationship with their future subjects was initiated by the creation of an emotional attachment to the princely child; it continued with the presentation of the heirs' exemplary attitude towards first their parents and subsequently their spouse and children. Additionally, the public learned of the thorough preparation of the future ruler at school, at university and in the institutions of the state, and no opportunity was missed to portray his philanthropic beneficence and commitment to cultural endeavours as well as his military prowess. All this allowed even less-than-progressive heirs to acquire a modern and approachable image – quite irrespective of their actual political views. The schooling of Crown Prince Wilhelm, for example, was carefully aligned with contemporary expectations, while the depiction of his wedding in 1905 as a love match bolstered his image, as did his avid support for the still-young sport of football.

Essentially, the personal, familial and public parameters of the lives of Europe's future rulers overlapped significantly, and the central demands they faced were largely consistent across Europe. A highly visible, well-nigh impeccable private life was a prerequisite for a successful heir.

Additionally, he had to be willing and able to acquire a suitable education and to display a never-tiring geniality. In Great Britain or Prussia, in Italy or the Netherlands – everywhere did heirs find themselves facing the fundamental challenge of the non-simultaneity of the simultaneous, whether in relation to their reigning predecessors, in their marriages, during their time at school and with the military, or generally in public. Dynastic claims were rooted in immutability, timelessness and exceptionalism, and heirs to the throne had to fall in line publicly with reverence-inspiring monarchical traditions, both those which were genuinely ancient and those invented much more recently.[13] At the same time, however, they had to impress the contemporary public by acting in accord with the standards of the day, ensuring their behaviour was impeccable when measured against modern 'bourgeois' criteria of proficiency and morality. The portrayal and activities of the heirs and the implicit promise they embodied meant that the modernisation of the monarchical system was more than just a suggestion, although its realisation was gradual and elements of the monarchical principle were retained.

The succession therefore offered the monarchies a welcome and recurring opportunity for (re)invention, accommodation and adjustment. They could fashion their political brand on the person of the heir according to the preferences and requirements of the specific market in which they had to operate and thus preserve the monarchy's position. Just as crustaceans shed and replace their outer shell so that they can thrive, monarchies used the recurring process of succession as a transformative opportunity. A clearly recognisable political organism could thus survive while adapting constantly to new contexts.

For the European monarchies of the nineteenth century, the change that came with succession was therefore not simply unavoidable – it was also needed and useful. Yet, the accession of a new ruler was always a moment of vulnerability and insecurity. Whether the ambitious goals associated with this transition would be met depended not just on current structures and prevailing trends but also, and above all, on a person who had been raised to this important position purely as the result of an accident of birth. The individual's strengths and weaknesses, his or her character traits and personal preferences and at times even the blows of fate thus played a disproportionately significant role in political systems based on hereditary monarchy. Occasionally a blue-blooded genetic problem was part of the mix, as described in 1891 in remarkably candid terms by Georg Hinzpeter, tutor of the last German emperor: 'the physiological fact [. . .] that the members of all ruling houses tend to suffer from

---

[13] Eric Hobsbawm und Terence Ranger (eds.), *The Invention of Tradition* (London, 1983).

a certain physical and emotional depression of their vital energies'.[14] A languid and lethargic heir like the British Prince Eddy, who died prematurely, or a hedonist and dandy like Crown Prince Wilhelm or an incorrigibly gruff personality like Archduke Franz Ferdinand could endanger the system. On occasion misfortune or tragedy might cause a monarchy to falter – we need think only of the accidental death of Ferdinand Philippe d'Orléans in 1842 or the shocking end of Crown Prince Rudolf in January 1889.

And yet these tragic individual cases did not present the greatest risk. The threat to the existence of the monarchical system at times of extreme political strain was far greater. The monarchies found themselves in just such a situation at the end of the long nineteenth century, when the crowned heads declared war on one another, and their heirs, the personification of the future of these monarchical nations, led their subjects onto the battlefields of the First World War. A Social Darwinist and militarily inflected age saw this clash as 'God's test by war' and, for anyone who failed that ultimate trial, their claims to rule were over.[15] In the moment of defeat, the prince's position at the head of a nation at arms – precisely the most visible, most valued and most deeply rooted ideal of royal self-affirmation in the nineteenth century – was fatal.

The long and on the whole successful late flowering of monarchy found its dramatic end in the mass demise of the monarchies of Europe after the First World War, to whose outbreak this form of government had made a regrettable contribution. Even in the midst of profound change, monarchy had successfully persisted throughout the nineteenth century. It had not just survived the modernisation of the European continent but had even shaped that process. The century that followed the Congress of Vienna was relatively peaceful in Europe, but this monarchical era ended when societies throughout great parts of Europe experienced the trauma of defeat in what was the most horrific war in human history to date. The evident inability of monarchical rulers of these warring nations to perform their most ancient of duties had profoundly delegitimised the form of government they represented and the elites that supported it. In France, this mechanism had already brought the monarchical age to an end in 1870. Precisely because of the central significance of military spectacle in the staging of the rule of Napoleon III, explains Matthew Truesdell, a lost war could only have catastrophic results. 'This style of leadership, this "playing soldier", was bound to be most effective when combined with

---

[14] Hinzpeter Denkschrift, 1891 (Geheimes Staatsarchiv Preußischer Kulturbesitz, 1. HA, Rep 76 I, Sektion 1, Nr. 125).

[15] Harold Frazer Wyatt, 'God's Test by War', in *The Nineteenth Century and After* 69 (1911), pp. 591–606.

military victory and was entirely incompatible with military defeat such as that of Sedan.'[16] What the Battle of Sedan had been for France, the First World War would be for Europe's defeated monarchies.

This conclusion contains a double irony. Monarchical propaganda celebrated war precisely as the particular domain of princes. *Ultima ratio regis* – 'the final argument of kings' – ran the inscription displayed proudly and menacingly on Spanish, French and Prussian cannons. But now it was war that swept away the crowns. It was the Archduke Franz Ferdinand, perhaps the most prominent exception to the rule that heirs to the throne had to change with the times, who was killed by a Serbian terrorist on 28 June 1914, along with his wife. The man who died at Sarajevo presented an anachronistic problem, an heir with neo-absolutist inclinations who defiantly refused to make any effort to charm his way into soft power. Many Austrian contemporaries, recorded the jurist and politician Josef Redlich in his diary at the time, 'saw in the end of the archduke and his wife a happy providential act for Austria'. Now at last, with its new heir, Archduke Karl, young, likeable and conciliatory, the Danubian Monarchy seemed to have given itself the opportunity to change. That transformation would never come to pass, though, for the shots fired at Sarajevo had sparked the war that would bring a bloody end to the monarchical century.[17]

Thus the story of the princely heirs as the future of Europe's monarchies was concluded. It had begun in January 1793 in Paris with the execution of a French king on the scaffold, and it came to a similarly bloody end, in June 1914 in Sarajevo, with the murder of a ruler-in-waiting.

[16] Matthew Truesdell, *Spectacular Politics: Louis-Napoleon Bonaparte and the 'Fête Imperiale'*, *1849–1870* (New York and Oxford, 1997), p. 155.

[17] Michaela Vocelka and Karl Vocelka, *Franz Joseph I. Kaiser von Österreich und König von Ungarn, 1830–1916* (Munich, 2015), p. 344.

Appendix: List of Rulers and Heirs

	Lived	Reigned	Title
Austria-Hungary			
Franz I	1768–1835	1804–1835	emperor
Ferdinand I	1793–1875	1835–1848	emperor
Franz Joseph I	1830–1916	1848–1916	emperor
Rudolf	1858–1889		crown prince
Franz Ferdinand	1863–1914		archduke
Karl I	1887–1922	1916–1918	emperor
Bavaria			
Maximilian I Joseph	1756–1825	1806–1825	king
Ludwig I	1786–1868	1825–1848	king
Maximilian II	1811–1864	1848–1864	king
Ludwig II	1845–1886	1864–1886	king, declared incompetent
Otto I	1848–1916		king, declared incompetent
Luitpold	1821–1912	1886–1912	prince regent
Ludwig III	1845–1921	1912–1913	prince regent
		1913–1918	king
Rupprecht	1869–1955		crown prince
Belgium			
Leopold I	1790–1865	1831–1865	king
Leopold II	1835–1909	1865–1909	king
Albert I	1875–1934	1909–1934	king
Leopold III	1901–1983	1934–1951	king

	Lived	Reigned	Title
Denmark			
Christian XIII	1786–1848	1839–1848	king
Frederik VII	1808–1863	1848–1863	king
Christian IX	1818–1906	1863–1906	king
Frederik VIII	1843–1912	1906–1912	king
Christian X	1870–1947	1912–1947	king
France			
Louis XVI	1754–1793	1774–1792	king
Napoleon I	1769–1821	1804–1814	emperor
Louis XVIII	1755–1824	1814–1824	king
Charles X	1757–1836	1824–1830	king
Louis Philippe I	1773–1850	1830–1848	king
Ferdinand Philippe, duke of Orléans	1810–1842		royal prince
Napoleon III	1808–1873	1852–1870	emperor
Napoleon	1856–1879		prince imperial
Great Britain			
George III	1738–1820	1760–1811/1820	king
George IV	1762–1830	1811/1820–1830	king
William IV	1765–1837	1830–1837	king
Victoria	1819–1901	1837–1901	empress and queen
Edward VII	1841–1910	1901–1910	emperor and king
Albert Victor	1864–1892		prince
George V	1865–1936	1910–1936	emperor and king
Edward VIII	1894–1972	1936	emperor and king
Greece			
Otto I	1815–1867	1832–1862	king
Geórgios I	1845–1913	1863–1913	king
Konstantínos I	1868–1923	1913–1917 and 1920–1922	king
Italy (Piedmont-Savoy)			
Vittorio Emanuele II	1820–1878	1849–1878	king
Umberto	1844–1900	1878–1900	king
Vittorio Emanuele III	1869–1947	1900–1946	king

	Lived	Reigned	Title
Netherlands			
Willem I	1772–1843	1813–1840	king
Willem II	1792–1849	1840–1849	king
Willem III	1817–1890	1849–1890	king
Wilhelmina	1880–1962	1890/1898–1949	queen
Norway			
Haakon VII	1872–1957	1905–1957	king
Olav V	1903–1991	1957–1991	king
Prussia–Germany			
Friedrich Wilhelm III	1770–1840	1797–1840	king
Friedrich Wilhelm IV	1795–1861	1840–1858/1861	king
Wilhelm I	1858–1870	1858–1861	prince regent
		1858–1870	king
		1871–1888	emperor and king
Friedrich III	1831–1888	1888	emperor and king
Wilhelm II	1859–1941	1888–1918	emperor and king
Wilhelm	1882–1951		crown prince
Saxony			
Johann I	1801–1873	1854–1873	king
Albert I	1828–1902	1873–1902	king
Georg I	1832–1904	1902–1904	king
Friedrich August III	1865–1932	1904–1918	king
Georg	1893–1943		crown prince
Sweden–Norway[a]			
Karl XIV Johann	1763–1844	1818–1843	king
Oscar I	1799–1859	1844–1859	king
Karl XV	1826–1872	1859–1872	king
Oscar II	1829–1907	1872–1907	king
Gustav V	1858–1950	1907–1950	king

[a] The union of the crowns of Sweden and Norway ended in 1905.

	Lived	Reigned	Title
Spain			
Ferdinand VII	1784–1833	1808 and 1813–1833	king
Isabella II	1830–1904	1833/1843–1868/1870	queen
Alfonso XII	1857–1885	1874–1885	king
Alfonso XIII	1886–1941	1902–1931	king
Württemberg			
Wilhelm I	1781–1864	1816–1864	king
Karl I	1823–1891	1864–1891	king
Wilhelm II	1848–1921	1891–1918	king
Albrecht	1865–1939		duke

Bibliography

A King's Story: The Memoirs of the Duke of Windsor, New York 1951
Amicis, Edmondo De, *The Heart of a Boy (Cuore)*, trans. G. Mantellini, New York 1895, www.google.co.uk/books/edition/The_Heart_of_a_Boy/e21KAAAAIA AJ?hl=en&gbpv=1 (accessed 1 June 2022)
Anon. [E. Schweizer], *Wilhelm II. König von Württemberg. Ein Lebensbild*, Ludwigsburg 1891
Antonetti, Guy, *Louis-Philippe*, Paris 1994
Arnstein, Walter, 'The Warrior Queen: Reflections on Queen Victoria and Her World', in *Albion* 30 (1998), pp. 1–28
Avenarius, Ferdinand, 'Unsere Fürsten und wir', in *Der Kunstwart* 23, 13 (April 1910), pp. 1–11
Bagehot, Walter, *The English Constitution*, ed. Paul Smith, Cambridge 2001
Banerjee, Milinda, 'Ocular Sovereignty, Acclamatory Rulership and Political Communication: Visits of Princes of Wales to Bengal', in Frank Lorenz Müller and Heidi Mehrkens (eds.), *Royal Heirs and the Uses of Soft Power in Nineteenth-Century Europe*, London 2016, pp. 81–100
Bartoschek, Gerd (ed.), *Preußisch korrekt – berlinisch gewitzt. Der Maler Franz Krüger 1797–1857* (exhibition catalogue), Berlin 2007
Behrman, Cynthia, *Victorian Myths of the Sea*, Athens, OH 1977
Bei Kronprinzens. Aus dem Familienleben des Kronprinzenhauses, Berlin c. 1914
Bell, Duncan, 'The Idea of a Patriot Queen? The Monarchy, the Constitution and the Iconographic Order of Greater Britain, 1860–1900', in *The Journal of Imperial and Commonwealth History* 34 (2006), pp. 3–22
Benson, Arthur C., and Viscount Esher (eds.), *The Letters of Queen Victoria*, vols. 1 and 2, London 1908 and 1911
Bentley, Michael, 'Power and Authority in the Late Victorian and Edwardian Court', in Andrzej Olechnowicz (ed.), *The Monarchy and the British Nation, 1780 to the Present*, Cambridge 2007, pp. 163–187
Biesendahl, Karl, *König Wilhelm II. von Württemberg. Ein Fürstenbild. Dem deutschen Volke und Heere zugeeignet*, Rathenow n.d. (1891)
Bismarck, Otto von, *Werke in Auswahl*, ed. Gustav Adolf Rein, vol. 2, Darmstadt 1963
Bled, Jean-Paul, *Franz Ferdinand. Der eigensinnige Thronfolger*, Vienna 2013
Bled, Jean-Paul, *Franz Joseph. 'Der letzte Monarch der alten Schule'*, Vienna 1988
Bled, Jean-Paul, 'La cour de François-Joseph', in Karl F. Werner (ed.), *Hof, Kultur und Politik im 19. Jahrhundert*, Bonn 1985, pp. 169–182

Bled, Jean-Paul, *Rodolphe et Mayerling*, Paris 1989

Blumenfeld, R. D., *R. D. B.'s Diary 1887–1914*, London 1930

Böckenförde, Ernst Wolfgang, 'Das Ende der Monarchie', in Kurt G. A. Jeserich, Hans Pohl and Georg-Christoph von Unruh (eds.), *Deutsche Verwaltungsgeschichte*, vol. 4, Stuttgart 1985, pp. 2–9

Bösch, Frank, *Mediengeschichte. Vom asiatischen Buchdruck zum Fernsehen*, Frankfurt am Main and New York 2011

Bösch, Frank, *Öffentliche Geheimnisse. Skandale, Politik und Medien im Kaiserreich und Großbritannien, 1880–1914*, Munich 2009

Boff, Jonathan, *Haig's Enemy: Crown Prince Rupprecht and Germany's War on the Western Front*, Oxford 2018

Bogdanor, Vernon, *The Monarchy and the Constitution*, Oxford 1995

Boldt, Hans, 'Der Föderalismus im Deutschen Kaiserreich als Verfassungsproblem', in Helmut Rumpler (ed.), *Innere Staatsbildung und gesellschaftliche Modernisierung in Österreich und Deutschland 1867/71–1914*, Vienna and Munich 1991

Bordin, Giorgio, and Laura Polo D'Ambrosio, *Medicine in Art*, Los Angeles, CA 2010

Bornewasser, Hans A., 'König Wilhelm I.', in Coenraad A. Tamse (ed.), *Nassau und Oranien. Statthalter und Könige der Niederlande*, Göttingen and Zurich 1985, pp. 213–255

Bornewasser, Hans A., 'König Wilhelm II.', in Coenraad A. Tamse (ed.), *Nassau und Oranien. Statthalter und Könige der Niederlande*, Göttingen and Zurich 1985, pp. 256–288

Borutta, Manuel, 'Repräsentation, Subversion und Spiel. Die kulturelle Praxis nationaler Feste in Berlin und Rom, 1870/71 und 1895', in Ulrike von Hirschhausen and Jörn Leonhard (eds.), *Nationalismen in Europa. West- und Osteuropa im Vergleich*, Göttingen 2007, pp. 243–266

Bosbach, Franz (ed.), *Die Studien des Prinzen Albert an der Universität Bonn, 1837–1838*, Berlin and New York 2010

Boyd, Carolyn P., 'El rey-soldado. Alfonso XIII y el ejercito', in Javier Moreno Luzón (ed.), *Alfonso XIII. Un politico en el trono*, Madrid 2003, pp. 213–238

Bracalini, Romano, *Il re 'vittorioso'. La vita, il regno e l'esilio di Vittorio Emanuele III*, Milan 1980

Bracalini, Romano, *La regina Margherita*, Milan 1983

Brice, Catherine, 'Königin Margherita (1851–1926). "Der einzige Mann im Hause Savoyen"', in Regina Schulte (ed.), *Der Körper der Königin. Geschlecht und Herrschaft in der höfischen Welt seit 1500*, Frankfurt am Main 2002

Brice, Catherine, *Monarchie et identité nationale en Italie (1861–1900)*, Paris 2010

Brooks, Sidney, 'The King of Italy', in *The North American Review* 176, 555 (February 1903), pp. 246–253

Bruch, Rüdiger vom, 'Kaiser und Bürger. Wilhelminismus als Ausdruck kulturellen Umbruchs um 1900', in Rüdiger vom Bruch, *Bürgerlichkeit, Staat und Kultur im Kaiserreich. Ausgewählte Aufsätze*, Stuttgart 2015, pp. 25–51

Brunner, Otto, 'Vom Gottesgnadentum zum monarchischen Prinzip. Der Weg der europäischen Monarchie seit dem hohen Mittelalter', in *Das Königtum*.

Seine geistigen und rechtlichen Grundlagen, Lindau and Constance 1956, pp. 293–303

Budde, Gunilla, *Blütezeit des Bürgertums. Bürgerlichkeit im 19. Jahrhundert*, Darmstadt 2009

Bülow, Bernhard Fürst von, *Denkwürdigkeiten*, vol. 4, Berlin 1931

Büschel, Hubertus, *Untertanenliebe. Der Kult um deutsche Monarchen 1770–1830*, Göttingen 2007

Burdiel, Isabel, *Isabel II. Una biografía (1830–1904)*, 3rd edn, Madrid 2011

Burke, Peter, *Die Inszenierung des Sonnenkönigs*, Berlin 1993

Cannadine, David, 'From Biography to History: Writing the Modern British Monarchy', in *Historical Research* 77 (2004), pp. 289–312

Cannadine, David, *Ornamentalism: How the British Saw Their Empire*, London 2001

Cannadine, David, 'The Last Hanoverian Sovereign? The Victorian Monarchy in Historical Perspective, 1688–1888', in A. L. Beier, David Cannadine and James M. Rosenheim (eds.), *The First Modern Society: Essays in English History in Honour of Lawrence Stone*, Cambridge 1989, pp. 127–165

Cannadine, David, 'War and Death: Grief and Mourning in Modern Britain', in Joachim Whaley (ed.), *Mirrors of Mortality: Studies in the Social History of Death*, London 1981, pp. 219–226

Casalegno, Carlo, *La regina Margherita*, Bologna 2001

Cerny, Heimo (ed.), *Die Jugend-Tagebücher Franz Josephs (1843–1848). Ungekürzte kommentierte Textedition*, Vienna 2003

Clark, Christopher, 'Fathers and Sons in the History of the Hohenzollern Dynasty', in Frank Lorenz Müller and Heidi Mehrkens (eds.), *Sons and Heirs: Succession and Political Culture in Nineteenth-Century Europe*, Basingstoke 2016, pp. 19–37

Clark, Martin, *Modern Italy 1871–1982*, London 1984

Colenbrander, H. T. (ed.), *Gedenkstukken der algemeene geschiedenis van Nederland van 1795 tot 1840*, part 10, vol. 3, The Hague 1920, http://resources .huygens.knaw.nl/gedenkstukken (accessed 30 November 2016)

Colley, Linda, 'The Apotheosis of George III: Loyalty, Royalty and the British Nation 1760–1820', in *Past & Present* 102 (1984), pp. 94–129

Collingham, H. A. C., *The July Monarchy: A Political History of France 1830–1848*, London and New York 1988

Colombo, Paolo, 'In consenso spezzato. La legittimazione militare di Vittorio Emanuele II', in Elena Fontanella (ed.), *Vittorio Emanuele II. Il Re Galantuomo*, Turin 2010, pp. 66–73

Cook, Andrew, *Prince Eddy: The King Britain Never Had*, Stroud 2006

Cornwell, Bernard, *Waterloo: The History of Four Days, Three Armies and Three Battles*, London 2014

Daum, Werner, Peter Brandt, Martin Kirsch and Arthur Schlegelmilch (eds.), *Handbuch der europäischen Verfassungsgeschichte im 19. Jahrhundert. Institutionen und Rechtspraxis im gesellschaftlichen Wandel*, vol. 2: *1815–1847*, Bonn 2012

Demmerle, Eva, *Kaiser Karl I. 'Selig, die Frieden stiften …'. Die Biographie*, 2nd edn, Vienna 2005

Deneckere, Gita, 'The Impossible Neutrality of the Speech from the Throne: A Ritual between National Unity and Political Dispute. Belgium, 1831–1918', in Jeroen Deploige and Gita Deneckere (eds.), *Mystifying the Monarch: Studies on Discourse, Power, and History*, Amsterdam 2006, pp. 208–209

Deutscher Geschichtskalender, founded by Karl Wippermann, vol. 2, Leipzig 1913

Dizionario del Risorgimento Nazionale, vol. IV: *Le persone*, Milan 1937

Dollinger, Heinz, 'Das Leitbild des Bürgerkönigtums in der europäischen Monarchie des 19. Jahrhunderts', in Karl F. Werner (ed.), *Hof, Kultur und Politik im 19. Jahrhundert*, Bonn 1985, pp. 325–363

Duggan, Christopher, 'Francesco Crispi, the Problem of the Monarchy, and the Origins of Italian Nationalism', in *Journal of Modern Italian Studies* 15, 3 (2010), pp. 336–353

Duggan, Christopher, *The Force of Destiny: A History of Italy since 1796*, London 2007

Dumont, Georges-Henri, *Léopold II*, Paris 1990

Dunn, Susan, 'Camus and Louis XVI: An Elegy for the Martyred King', in *The French Review* 62 (1989), pp. 1032–1014

Dunn, Susan, *The Deaths of Louis XVI: Regicide and the French Political Imagination*, Princeton, NJ 1994

Eggert, Hans, and Rainer Kubatzki, *Friedrich August III. Lebensbilder, Briefe, Testamente*, Meißen 2007

Epkenhans, Michael, 'Das Ende eines Zeitalters. Europäische Monarchen und ihre Armeen im Ersten Weltkrieg', in Winfried Heinemann and Markus Pöhlmann (eds.), *Monarchen und ihr Militär*, Potsdam 2010, pp. 59–74

Evans, Richard J., *The Pursuit of Power: Europe, 1815–1914*, London 2016

Eysinga, Sicco Ernst Willem Roorda van, *Uit het leven van Koning Gorilla*, The Hague 1888

Felix, Julius [Kronprinz Rudolf], 'Oesterreich-Ungarn und seine Alliancen. Offener Brief an S. M. Kaiser Franz Joseph I.', in Kronprinz Rudolf, '*Majestät, ich warne Sie ...*'. *Geheime und private Schriften*, ed. Brigitte Hamann, Vienna 1979, pp. 190–227

Fellmann, Walter, *Sachsens letzter König. Friedrich August III.*, Berlin and Leipzig 1992

Fetting, Martina, *Zum Selbstverständnis der letzten deutschen Monarchen. Normverletzung und Legitimationsstrategien zwischen Gottesgnadentum und Medienrevolution*, Frankfurt am Main 2013

Feuerstein-Praßer, Karin, *Augusta. Kaiserin und Preußin*, 2nd edn, Munich and Zurich 2011

Findeisen, Jörg-Peter, *Die schwedische Monarchie. Von den Vikingerherrschern zu den modernen Monarchen*, vol. 2, Kiel 2010

Findeisen, Jörg-Peter, *Jean Baptiste Bernadotte. Revolutionsgeneral, Marschall Napoleons, König von Schweden und Norwegen*, Gernsbach 2010

Fischer, Paul David, *Italien und die Italiener. Betrachtungen und Studien über die politischen, wirthschaftlichen und sozialen Zustände Italiens*, 2nd edn, Berlin 1901

Forster, J. M., *Ludwig. Königlicher Prinz von Bayern*, Munich 1894

Forster, J. M., *Prinz Ludwig von Bayern. Biographie und Reden Sr. Königl. Hoheit des Prinzen Ludwigs von Bayern*, Munich 1897

Förster, Stig, *Der doppelte Militarismus. Die deutsche Heeresrüstungspolitik zwischen Status-Quo-Sicherung und Aggression, 1890–1913*, Stuttgart 1985

Franz, Eckart G. (ed.), *Erinnertes. Aufzeichnungen des letzten Großherzogs Ernst Ludwig von Hessen und bei Rhein*, Darmstadt 1983

Franz, Georg, *Erzherzog Franz Ferdinand und die Pläne zur Reform der Habsburger Monarchie*, Brünn [Brno], Munich and Vienna 1943

Franzel, Emil, *Franz Ferdinand d'Este. Leitbild einer konservativen Revolution*, Vienna and Munich 1964

Frevert, Ute, 'Das jakobinische Modell. Allgemeine Wehrpflicht und Nationsbildung in Preußen-Deutschland', in Ute Frevert (ed.), *Militär und Gesellschaft im 19. und 20. Jahrhundert*, Stuttgart 1997, pp. 17–47

Frevert, Ute, 'Das Militär als "Schule der Männlichkeit". Erwartungen, Angebote, Erfahrungen im 19. Jahrhundert', in Ute Frevert (ed.), *Militär und Gesellschaft im 19. und 20. Jahrhundert*, Stuttgart 1997, pp. 145–173

Fricke, Dieter, and Kurt Finker, 'Kyffhäuser-Bund der Deutschen Landeskriegerverbände (KB) 1900–1943', in Dieter Fricke (ed.), *Die bürgerlichen Parteien in Deutschland. Handbuch der Geschichte der bürgerlichen Parteien und anderer bürgerlicher Interessenorganisationen vom Vormärz bis zum Jahre 1945*, vol. 2, Leipzig 1970, pp. 296–312

Friske, Tobias, *Staatsform Monarchie. Was unterscheidet eine Monarchie heute noch von einer Republik?*, Freiburg 2007, https://freidok.uni-freiburg.de/data/3325 (accessed 10 August 2017)

Fulford, Roger (ed.), *Beloved Mama: Private Correspondence of Queen Victoria and the German Crown Princess, 1878–1885*, London 1981

Geisthövel, Alexa, 'Den Monarchen im Blick. Wilhelm I. in der illustrierten Familienpresse', in Habbo Knoch and Daniel Morat (eds.), *Kommunikation als Beobachtung. Medienwandel und Gesellschaftsbilder 1880–1960*, Munich 2003, pp. 59–80

Geisthövel, Alexa, 'Wilhelm I. am "historischen Eckfenster". Zur Sichtbarkeit des Monarchen in der zweiten Hälfte des 19. Jahrhunderts', in Jan Andres, Alexa Geisthövel and Matthias Schwengelbeck (eds.), *Die Sinnlichkeit der Macht. Herrschaft und Repräsentation seit der Frühen Neuzeit*, Frankfurt am Main 2005, pp. 163–185

Gigliozzi, Giovanni, *Le regine d'Italia*, Rome 1997

Giloi, Eva, 'Copyrighting the Kaiser: Publicity, Piracy and the Right to Wilhelm II's Image', in *Central European History* 45 (2012), pp. 407–451

Giloi, Eva, *Monarchy, Myth, and Material Culture in Germany 1750–1950*, Cambridge 2011

Goldstein, Erik, 'Royal Ambassadors: Monarchical Public Diplomacy and the United States', in Frank Lorenz Müller and Heidi Mehrkens (eds.), *Royal Heirs and the Uses of Soft Power in Nineteenth-Century Europe*, London 2016, pp. 63–80

Gollwitzer, Heinz, 'Die Endphase der Monarchie in Deutschland', in Heinz Gollwitzer, *Weltpolitik und deutsche Geschichte*, ed. Hans-Christof Kraus, Göttingen 2008, pp. 367–369

Gollwitzer, Heinz, 'Fürst und Volk. Betrachtungen zur Selbstbehauptung des bayerischen Herrscherhauses im 19. und 20. Jahrhundert', in *Zeitschrift für bayerische Landesgeschichte* 50 (1987), pp. 723–747

Gollwitzer, Heinz, *Ludwig I. von Bayern. Eine politische Biographie*, Munich 1997

Goltz, Colmar von der, *Léon Gambetta und seine Armeen*, Berlin 1877

Gordon, Peter, and Denis Lawton, *Royal Education: Past, Present and Future*, 2nd edn, London and Portland, OH 2003

Gordon, Sophie, 'Travels with a Camera: The Prince of Wales, Photography and the Mobile Court', in Frank Lorenz Müller and Heidi Mehrkens (eds.), *Sons and Heirs: Succession and Political Culture in Nineteenth-Century Europe*, Basingstoke 2016, pp. 92–108

Görlitz, Walter (ed.), *Regierte der Kaiser? Kriegstagebücher, Aufzeichnungen und Briefe des Chefs des Marine-Kabinetts Admiral Georg Alexander von Müller 1914–1918*, 2nd edn, Berlin and Frankfurt am Main 1959

Gosewinkel, Dieter, and Johannes Masing (eds.), *Die Verfassungen in Europa 1789–1949*, Munich 2006

Gottwald, Dorothee, *Fürstenrecht und Staatsrecht im 19. Jahrhundert. Eine wissenschaftsgeschichtliche Studie*, Frankfurt am Main 2009

Graham, Stephen, *Alexander of Jugoslavia: Strong Man of the Balkans*, London 1938

Grases i Riera, José, *Memoria del anteproyecto de monumento que ha de erigirse en Madrid a la gloria del Rey Don Alfonso XII, el Pacificador*, Madrid 1901

Grasselli Barni, Annibale, *Vittorio Emanuele Terzo*, Piacenza 1922

Gregory, Adrian, *The Silence of Memory: Armistice Day, 1919–1946*, Oxford 1994

Greve, Tim, *Haakon VII. Menneske og monark*, Oslo 1980

Grey, Charles, *The Early Years of His Royal Highness the Prince Consort*, London 1868

Grotke, Kelly L., and Markus J. Prutsch (eds.), *Constitutionalism, Legitimacy, and Power*, Oxford 2014

Grunwald, G., 'Fürstenerziehung', in Ernst Roloff (ed.), *Lexikon der Pädagogik*, vol. 2, Freiburg im Breisgau 1913

Häfner, Heinz, *Ein König wird beseitigt. Ludwig II. von Bayern*, Munich 2008

Hall, N. John, *Max Beerbohm Caricatures*, New Haven, CT and London 1997

Hamann, Brigitte, 'Der Wiener Hof und die Hofgesellschaft in der zweiten Hälfte des 19. Jahrhunderts', in Karl Möckl (ed.), *Hof und Hofgesellschaft in den deutschen Staaten im 19. und beginnenden 20. Jahrhundert*, Boppard am Rhein 1990, pp. 61–78

Hamann, Brigitte, *Elisabeth. Kaiserin wider Willen*, 4th edn, Munich 2014

Hamann, Brigitte, 'Erzherzog Albrecht – Die graue Eminenz des Habsburgerhofes. Hinweise auf einen unterschätzten Politiker', in Isabella Ackerl, Walter Hummelburger and Hans Mommsen (eds.), *Politik und Gesellschaft im alten und neuen Österreich. Festschrift für Rudolf Neck zum 60. Geburtstag*, vol. 1, Munich 1981, pp. 32–43

Hamann, Brigitte, *Kronprinz Rudolf. Ein Leben*, Vienna 2006

Hamilton, W. Mark, *The Nation and the Navy: Methods and Organization of British Navalist Propaganda, 1889–1914*, London 1986

Handbuch der deutschen Bildungsgeschichte, vol. 3, ed. Karl-Ernst Jeismann and Peter Lundgreen, Munich 1987

Handbuch der deutschen Bildungsgeschichte, vol. 4, ed. Christa Berg, Munich 1991

Hanham, Andrew, 'The Leicester House Faction', www.historyofparliamenton
line.org/periods/hanoverians/leicester-house-faction (accessed 10 May 2017)
Hannig, Alma, 'Archduke Ferdinand: An Uncharming Prince?', in Frank
Lorenz Müller and Heidi Mehrkens (eds.), *Royal Heirs and the Uses of Soft
Power in Nineteenth-Century Europe*, London 2016, pp. 139–160
Hannig, Alma, *Franz Ferdinand. Die Biografie*, Vienna 2013
Hardman, John, *Louis XVI*, New Haven, CT and London 1993, pp. 231–233
Hasselhorn, Benjamin, 'Das Monarchiesterben 1914–1945. Ein Siegeszug der
Demokratie?', in Benjamin Hasselhorn and Marc von Knorring (eds.), *Vom
Olymp zum Boulevard. Die europäischen Monarchien von 1815 bis heute – Verlierer
der Geschichte?*, Berlin 2018, pp. 47–60
Hasselhorn, Benjamin, and Marc von Knorring (eds.), *Vom Olymp zum
Boulevard. Die europäischen Monarchien von 1815 bis heute – Verlierer der
Geschichte?*, Berlin 2018
Hauser, Kaspar [Kurt Tucholsky], *Unser Militär!* (1919), www.textlog.de/tucho
lsky-unser-militaer.html (accessed 20 March 2017)
Herzogin Viktoria Luise, *Ein Leben als Tochter des Kaisers*, Göttingen 1965
Hettling, Manfred, and Stefan-Ludwig Hoffmann (eds.), Der bürgerliche
Wertehimmel. *Innenansichten des 19. Jahrhunderts*, Göttingen 2000
Hibbert, Christopher, *Edward VII: A Portrait*, London 1976
Hillard, Gustav [Gustav Steinbömer], *Herren und Narren der Welt*, Munich 1954
Hintze, Otto, *Die Hohenzollern und ihr Werk 1415–1915. Fünfhundert Jahre
vaterländische Geschichte*, 5th edn, Berlin 1915
Hobsbawm, Eric, *The Age of Capital: 1848–1875*, London 1975
Hobsbawm, Eric, *The Age of Empire: 1875–1914*, London 1987
Hobsbawm, Eric, *The Age of Extremes: The Short Twentieth Century, 1914–1991*,
London 1994
Hobsbawm, Eric, *The Age of Revolution: Europe 1789–1848*, London 1962
Hobsbawm, Eric, and Terence Ranger (eds.), *The Invention of Tradition*, London
1983
Holaas, Odd, *Norge under Haakon VII, 1905–1945*, Oslo 1976
Holstein, Friedrich von, *Die geheimen Papiere Friedrich von Holsteins*, ed.
Norman Rich and M. H. Fisher, German edition by Werner Frauendienst,
vol. 2, Göttingen 1957
Holsten, Hennig, and Daniel Schönpflug, 'Widersprüche eines dynastischen
Gipfeltreffens im Jahr 1913', in Ute Daniel and Christian K. Frey (eds.), *Die
preußisch-welfische Hochzeit 1913. Das dynastische Europa in seinem letzten
Friedensjahr*, Braunschweig 2016, pp. 50–68
Horn, Michael, 'Zwischen Abdankung und Absetzung. Das Ende der Herrschaft
der Bundesfürsten des Deutschen Reichs im November 1918', in
Susan Richter and Dirk Dirbach (eds.), *Thronverzicht. Die Abdankung in
Monarchien vom Mittelalter bis in die Neuzeit*, Cologne, Weimar and Vienna
2010, pp. 267–290
Houben, Hubert, *Kaiser Friedrich II. (1194–1250). Herrscher, Mensch und Mythos*,
Stuttgart 2008
Huber, Ernst Rudolf, *Deutsche Verfassungsgeschichte*, vol. 3, Stuttgart 1963

Huch, Gaby, *Zwischen Ehrenpforte und Inkognito. Preußische Könige auf Reisen. Quellen zur Repräsentation der Monarchie zwischen 1797 und 1871*, vol. 1, Berlin 2016

Hureau, Joëlle, *L'espoir brisé. Le duc d'Orléans 1810–1842*, Paris 1995

Hundert Jahre Erziehung der Jugend auf Schloß Plön. Eine Festschrift, Plön 1968

Ihr seid mir scheene Republikaner. Anekdoten aus der sächsischen Geschichte, Berlin 2006

Im Dienste Preußens. Wer erzog Prinzen zu Königen?, Berlin 2001

Im Lichte neuer Quellen. Wilhelm II. – der letzte König von Württemberg (exhibition catalogue), ed. Albrecht Ernst, Stuttgart 2015

'Immer feste druff!' (propaganda flyer, Paris 1918), http://digital.staatsbibliothek-berlin.de/werkansicht?PPN=PPN767871014&PHYSID=PHYS_0001&DMD ID=DMDLOG_0001 (accessed 19 April 2017)

Isaksen, Trond Norén, 'The Power of Presence: Crafting a Norwegian Identity for the Bernadotte Heirs', in Frank Lorenz Müller and Heidi Mehrkens (eds.), *Royal Heirs and the Uses of Soft Power in Nineteenth-Century Europe*, London 2016, pp. 103–121

Janssens, Gustaaf, 'Die belgische Monarchie und Albert I. Ritterkönig und Friedensfürst?', in Martin Wrede (ed.), *Die Inszenierung der heroischen Monarchie. Frühneuzeitliches Königtum zwischen ritterlichem Erbe und militärischer Herausforderung*, Munich 2014, pp. 409–437

Janßen, Karl-Heinz, 'Der Untergang der Monarchie in Deutschland', in Hellmuth Rößler (ed.), *Weltwende 1917. Monarchie – Weltrevolution – Demokratie*, Göttingen 1965

Janßen, Karl-Heinz, *Macht und Verblendung. Kriegszielpolitik der deutschen Bundesstaaten 1914–1918*, Göttingen 1963

Jensen, Olaf, and Winfried Steffani, 'Königreich Dänemark', in Winfried Steffani (ed.), *Regierungsmehrheit und Opposition in den Staaten der EG*, Opladen 1991

Jessen, Olaf, *Verdun 1916. Urschlacht des Jahrhunderts*, Munich 2014

Jonas, Klaus W., *Der Kronprinz Wilhelm*, Frankfurt am Main 1962

Jones, Heather, 'A Prince in the Trenches? Edward VIII and the First World War', in Frank Lorenz Müller and Heidi Mehrkens (eds.), *Sons and Heirs: Succession and Political Culture in Nineteenth-Century Europe*, Basingstoke 2016, pp. 229–246

Jones, Heather, *For King and Country: The British Monarchy and the First World War*, Cambridge 2021

Jones, Heather, 'The Nature of Kingship in First World War Britain', in Matthew Glencross, Judith Rowbotham and Michael D. Kandiah (eds.), *The Windsor Dynasty: 1910 to the Present*, London 2016, pp. 195–216

Kaiser Friedrich III., *Das Kriegstagebuch von 1870/71*, ed. Heinrich Otto Meisner, Leipzig and Berlin 1926

Kaiser Wilhelm II., *Aus meinem Leben, 1859–1888*, 4th edn, Berlin and Leipzig 1927

Kann, Robert A., 'Groß-Österreich', in Robert A. Kann, *Erzherzog Franz Ferdinand Studien*, Munich 1976

Kaul, Chandrika, 'Monarchical Display and the Politics of Empire: Princes of Wales and India 1870–1920s', in *Twentieth Century British History* 17, 4 (2006), pp. 464–488

Kebbel, T. E. (ed.), *Selected Speeches of the Late Right Honourable the Earl of Beaconsfield*, vol. II, London 1882, p. 528

Keßler, Johannes, *Ich schwöre mir ewige Jugend*, Leipzig 1935

Kirsch, Martin, 'Die Funktionalisierung des Monarchen im 19. Jahrhundert im europäischen Vergleich', in Stefan Fisch, Florence Gauzy and Chantal Metzger (eds.), *Machtstrukturen im Staat in Deutschland und Frankreich*, Stuttgart 2007, pp. 82–98

Kirsch, Martin, *Monarch und Parlament im 19. Jahrhundert. Der monarchische Konstitutionalismus als europäischer Verfassungstyp – Frankreich im Vergleich*, Göttingen 1999

Kirschstein, Jörg, *KaiserKinder. Die Familie Wilhelms II. in Fotografien*, Göttingen 2011

Kirschstein, Jörg, 'Kaisertochter und Welfenprinz. Die glanzvolle Hochzeit von Victoria Luise und Ernst August im Jahr 1913', in Stiftung Residenzschloss Braunschweig (ed.), *Europas letztes Rendezvous. Die Hochzeit von Victoria Luise und Ernst August*, Braunschweig 2013, pp. 14–55

Koch, Jeroen, 'The King as Father, Orangism and the Uses of a Hero: King William I of the Netherlands and the Prince of Orange, 1815–1840', in Frank Lorenz Müller and Heidi Mehrkens (eds.), *Royal Heirs and the Uses of Soft Power in Nineteenth-Century Europe*, London 2016, pp. 263–280

König Friedrich August III. Von Sachsen. Ein Lebensbild zusammengestellt nach dem 'Kameraden', Dresden 1905

Körner, Axel, 'Heirs and Their Wives: Setting the Scene for Umbertian Italy', in Frank Lorenz Müller and Heidi Mehrkens (eds.), *Sons and Heirs: Succession and Political Culture in Nineteenth-Century Europe*, Basingstoke 2016, pp. 38–52

Körner, Axel, *Politics of Culture in Liberal Italy: From Unification to Fascism*, London 2009

Körner, Hans-Michael, 'Die Monarchie im 19. Jahrhundert. Zwischen Nostalgie und wissenschaftlichem Diskurs', in Winfried Müller and Martina Schattkowsky (eds.), *Zwischen Tradition und Modernität. König Johann von Sachsen 1801–1873*, Leipzig 2004, pp. 26–27

Kohlrausch, Martin, *Der Monarch im Skandal. Die Logik der Massenmedien und die Transformation der wilhelminischen Monarchie*, Berlin 2005

Kohlrausch, Martin, 'Die höfische Gesellschaft und ihre Feinde. Monarchie und Öffentlichkeit in Großbritannien und Deutschland um 1900', in *Neue Politische Literatur* 47 (2002), 450–466

Kohlrausch, Martin, 'Zwischen Tradition und Innovation. Das Hofzeremoniell der wilhelminischen Monarchie', in Andreas Biefang, Michael Epkenhans and Klaus Tenfelde (eds.), *Das politische Zeremoniell im Deutschen Kaiserreich 1871–1918*, Düsseldorf 2008, pp. 31–51

Kohut, Thomas A., *Wilhelm II and the Germans: A Study in Leadership*, Oxford 1991

Kosztolányi, Desző, *Kornél Esti: A Novel*, trans. Bernard Adams, New York 2011

Krafft von Dellmensingen, Konrad (ed.), *Das Bayernbuch vom Weltkriege 1914–1918. Ein Volksbuch*, vol. 1, Stuttgart 1930

Kraus, Karl, 'Franz Ferdinand und die Talente', in *Die Fackel* 400–403 (10 July 1914), pp. 1–4, www.textlog.de/39154.html (accessed 29 May 2022)

Kringen, Olav, 'Monarchie oder Republik?', in *Sozialistische Monatshefte* 10 (1906), pp. 64–68

Krivanec, Eva, *Kriegsbühnen. Theater im Ersten Weltkrieg. Berlin, Lissabon, Paris und Wien*, Bielefeld 2012

Kroll, Frank-Lothar, 'Die Idee eines sozialen Königtums im 19. Jahrhundert', in Frank-Lothar Kroll and Dieter J. Weiß (eds.), *Inszenierung oder Legitimität. Die Monarchie in Europa im 19. und 20. Jahrhundert. Ein deutsch–englischer Vergleich*, Berlin 2015, pp. 111–140

Kroll, Frank-Lothar, 'Monarchen als Gelehrte. Zum Typus des "homme de lettres" in den deutschen Fürstenstaaten des 19. Jahrhunderts', in Sächsische Schlösserverwaltung and Staatlicher Schlossbetrieb Schloss Weesenstein (eds.), *König Johann von Sachsen. Zwischen zwei Welten*, Halle an der Saale 2001, pp. 135–140

Kroll, Frank-Lothar, 'Zwischen europäischem Bewußtsein und nationaler Identität. Legitimationsstrategien monarchischer Eliten des 19. und frühen 20. Jahrhunderts', in Hans-Christof Kraus and Thomas Nicklas (eds.), *Geschichte der Politik. Alte und neue Wege*, Munich 2007, pp. 353–374

Kronenbitter, Günter, 'The Opposition of the Archdukes: Rudolf, Franz Ferdinand and the Late Habsburg Monarchy', in Frank Lorenz Müller and Heidi Mehrkens (eds.), *Sons and Heirs: Succession and Political Culture in Nineteenth-Century Europe*, Basingstoke 2016, pp. 211–225

Kronprinz Rupprecht, *Mein Kriegstagebuch*, ed. Eugen von Frauenholz, 3 vols., Berlin 1929

Kronprinz Wilhelm, *Meine Erinnerungen an Deutschlands Heldenkampf*, Berlin 1923

Kunhardt, David, *Kronprinz Wilhelm, feste druff!: Humoristisch-vaterländisches Kriegslied*, Berlin 1914

Lampedusa, Giuseppe Tomasi di, *The Leopard*, trans. Archibald Colquhoun, New York 1960

Langewiesche, Dieter, 'Die Monarchie im Europa des bürgerlichen Jahrhunderts. Das Königreich Württemberg', in Landesmuseum Württemberg (ed.), *Monarchie und Moderne*, Stuttgart 2006, pp. 25–37

Langewiesche, Dieter, *Die Monarchie im Jahrhundert Europas. Selbstbehauptung durch Wandel im 19. Jahrhundert*, Heidelberg 2013

Langewiesche, Dieter, 'Nation, Nationalismus, Nationalstaat. Forschungsstand und Forschungsperspektiven', in *Neue Politische Literatur* 40 (1995), pp. 205–210

Langewiesche, Dieter, 'Nationalismus im 19. und 20. Jahrhundert. Zwischen Partizipation und Aggression', in Dieter Langewiesche, *Nation, Nationalismus, Nationalstaat in Deutschland und Europa*, Munich 2000, pp. 35–54

Laureys, Veronique, 'Les princes de Belgique au Sénat', in Veronique Laureys (ed.), *L'histoire du Sénat de Belgique de 1831 à 1995*, Brussels 1999, pp. 292–309

Lee, Sir Sidney, *King Edward VII: A Biography*, vol. 1, London 1925

Lerman, Katherine Anne, 'Wilhelm's War: A Hohenzollern in Conflict 1914–1918', in Frank Lorenz Müller and Heidi Mehrkens (eds.), *Sons and Heirs: Succession and Political Culture in Nineteenth-Century Europe*, Basingstoke 2016, pp. 247–262

Levsen, Sonja, 'Gemeinschaft, Männlichkeit und Krieg. Militarismus in englischen Colleges und deutschen Studentenverbindungen am Vorabend des Ersten Weltkrieges', in Christian Jansen (ed.), *Der Bürger als Soldat. Die Militarisierung europäischer Gesellschaften im langen 19. Jahrhundert. Ein internationaler Vergleich*, Essen 2004, pp. 230–246

Liliencron, Detlev von, *Die Musik kommt* (1883), www.projekt-gutenberg.org/liliencr/gedichte/chap028.html (accessed 10 May 2022)

Lipparini, Lilla (ed.), *Lettere fra la regina Margherita e Marco Minghetti*, Milan 1955

Loewenstein, Karl, *Die Monarchie im modernen Staat*, Frankfurt am Main 1952

Lorenz, Angelika, *Das deutsche Familienbild in der Malerei des 19. Jahrhunderts*, Darmstadt 1985

Luh, Jürgen, *Der Große. Friedrich II. von Preußen*, 2nd edn, Munich 2011

Luzón, Javier Moreno, 'Alfonso *el Regenerador*. Monarquía escénica e imaginario nacionalista español, en perspectiva comparada (1902–1913)', in *Hispania* LXXIII (2013), pp. 319–348

Lyden, Anne M., *A Royal Passion: Queen Victoria and Photography*, Los Angeles, CA 2014

Machiavelli, Niccolò, *The Prince*, trans. W. K. Marriott, www.gutenberg.org/files/1232/1232-h/1232-h.htm (accessed 9 May 2022)

Machtan, Lothar, 'Deutschlands gekrönter Herrscherstand am Vorabend des Ersten Weltkriegs. Ein Inspektionsbericht zur Funktionstüchtigkeit des deutschen Monarchiemodells', in *Zeitschrift für Geschichtswissenschaft* 58 (2010), pp. 222–242

Machtan, Lothar, *Die Abdankung. Wie Deutschlands gekrönte Häupter aus der Geschichte fielen*, Berlin 2008

Mack Smith, Denis, *Italy and Its Monarchy*, New Haven, CT and London 1989

Maine, Basil, *Prinz von Wales. König Eduard VIII. Eine Biographie*, Berlin 1936

Magnus, Philip, *King Edward the Seventh*, London 1964

Mann, Thomas, *Königliche Hoheit*, Berlin 1909, www.gutenberg.org/files/35328/35328-h/35328-h.htm (accessed 25 November 2016)

Mansel, Philip, *The Court of France 1789–1830*, Cambridge 1988

Marchi, Maria Christina, 'Margherita: Italy's First Heir', AHRC Project *Heirs to the Throne in the Constitutional Monarchies of Nineteenth-Century Europe (1815–1914)*, 'Heir of the Month' (February 2014), http://heirstothethrone-project.net/?page_id=843 (accessed 27 January 2017)

Marchi, Maria Christina, *The Heirs to the Savoia Throne and the Construction of 'Italianità', 1860–1890*, London 2022

Marchi, Maria-Christina, 'Morandi's Italian Job: Nationalising Italy's First Heir', AHRC Project *Heirs to the Throne in the Constitutional Monarchies of Nineteenth-Century Europe (1815–1914)*, 'Heir of the Month' (June 2014), http://heirstothethrone-project.net/?page_id=1039 (accessed 17 February 2017)

Marchi, Maria-Christina, 'Princes on the Road', AHRC Project *Heirs to the Throne in the Constitutional Monarchies of Nineteenth-Century Europe (1815–1914)*, 'Heir of the Month' (May 2015), http://heirstothethrone-project.net/?page_id=1548 (accessed 30 June 2017)

Marchi, Maria-Christina, 'The Royal Shop Window: Royal Heirs and the Monarchy in Post-Risorgimento Italy, 1860–1878', in Frank Lorenz Müller and Heidi Mehrkens (eds.), *Royal Heirs and the Uses of Soft Power in Nineteenth-Century Europe*, London 2016, pp. 23–44

März, Stefan, *Das Haus Wittelsbach im Ersten Weltkrieg. Chance und Zusammenbruch monarchischer Herrschaft*, Regensburg 2013

März, Stefan, *Ludwig III. Bayerns letzter König*, Regensburg 2014

Massenbach, Christian von, *Fürsten-Erziehung in repräsentativen Verfassungen*, 2nd edn, Heidelberg 1817

Materna, Ingo, 'Schloß und Schloßbezirk in der Revolution 1918/19', in Wolfgang Ribbe (ed.), *Schloß und Schloßbezirk in der Mitte Berlins. Das Zentrum der Stadt als politischer und gesellschaftlicher Ort*, Berlin 2005, pp. 139–147

Maurenbrecher, Romeo, *Grundsätze des heutigen deutschen Staatsrechts*, 2nd edn, Frankfurt am Main 1843

May, Otto, *Deutsch sein heißt treu sein. Ansichtskarten als Spiegel von Mentalität und Untertanenerziehung in der Wilhelminischen Ära (1888–1918)*, Hildesheim 1998

Mayer, Kathrin, *Mythos und Monument. Die Sprache der Denkmäler im Gründungsmythos des italienischen Nationalstaates 1870–1915*, Cologne 2004

Mehrkens, Heidi, 'The Impossible Task of Replacing a Model Heir: The Death of Ferdinand-Philippe d'Orléans and the "New France"', in Frank Lorenz Müller and Heidi Mehrkens (eds.), *Sons and Heirs: Succession and Political Culture in Nineteenth-Century Europe*, Basingstoke 2016, pp. 196–210

Mehrkens, Heidi, 'The Prince, the President and the Cholera', AHRC Project *Heirs to the Throne in the Constitutional Monarchies of Nineteenth-Century Europe (1815–1914)*, 'Heir of the Month' (January 2014), http://heirstothethrone-project.net/?page_id=768 (accessed 7 July 2017)

Mergen, Simone, *Monarchiejubiläen im 19. Jahrhundert. Die Entdeckung des historischen Jubiläums für den monarchischen Kult in Sachsen und Bayern*, Leipzig 2005

Metzsch, W. von, *Friedrich August III. König von Sachsen. Ein Lebensbild*, Berlin 1906

Meyer, Jean, *L'éducation des princes du XVe au XIXe siècle*, Paris 2004, pp. 205–240

Meyer Forsting, Richard, 'Isabel II: Niña de la libertad', AHRC Project *Heirs to the Throne in the Constitutional Monarchies of Nineteenth-Century Europe (1815–1914)*, 'Heir of the Month' (March 2014), http://heirstothethrone-project.net/?page_id=900 (accessed 22 June 2017)

Meyer Forsting, Richard, *Raising Heirs to the Throne in Nineteenth-Century Spain: The Education of the Constitutional Monarch*, London 2018

Meyer Forsting, Richard, 'The Importance of Looking the Part: Heirs and Male Aesthetics in Nineteenth-Century Spain', in Frank Lorenz Müller and Heidi Mehrkens (eds.), *Royal Heirs and the Uses of Soft Power in Nineteenth-Century Europe*, London 2016, pp. 181–200

Mittheilungen über die Verhandlungen des außerordentlichen Landtags, II. Kammer, 2. Sitzung, 5 July 1902, https://digital.slub-dresden.de/werkansicht/dlf/11504/49 (accessed 18 January 2017)

Mittheilungen über die Verhandlungen des Landtags, I. Kammer, 10. Sitzung, 1 January 1914, http://digital.slub-dresden.de/id20028367Z/190 (accessed 18 November 2016)

Mittheilungen über die Verhandlungen des Landtags, II. Kammer, 3. Sitzung, 18 November 1891, http://digital.slub-dresden.de/id20028419Z/35 (accessed 9 May 2022)

Möckl, Karl, 'Hof und Hofgesellschaft in den deutschen Staaten im 19. und beginnenden 20. Jahrhundert. Einleitende Bemerkungen', in Karl Möckl (ed.), *Hof und Hofgesellschaft in den deutschen Staaten im 19. und beginnenden 20. Jahrhundert*, Boppard am Rhein 1990, pp. 7–15

Møller, Jes Fabricius, 'Die Domestizierung der Monarchien', in Benjamin Hasselhorn und Marc von Knorring (eds.), *Vom Olymp zum Boulevard. Die europäischen Monarchien von 1815 bis heute – Verlierer der Geschichte?*, Berlin 2018, pp. 35–45

Møller, Jes Fabricius, 'Domesticating a German Heir to the Danish Throne', in Frank Lorenz Müller und Heidi Mehrkens (eds.), *Sons and Heirs: Succession and Political Culture in Nineteenth-Century Europe*, Basingstoke 2016, pp. 129–146

Morandi, Luigi, *Come fu educato Vittorio Emanuele III*, Turin 1901

Morgenstern, Ulf, *Lehrjahre eines neo-absoluten Monarchen. Kaiser Wilhelm II. als Kasseler Abiturient im Spiegel eines unbekannten Aufsatzheftes*, Friedrichsruh 2011

Müller, Frank Lorenz, '"Distant from the Court and All of Its Influences": The German Crown Prince at the *Prinzenschule* in Plön', AHRC Project *Heirs to the Throne in the Constitutional Monarchies of Nineteenth-Century Europe (1815–1914)*, 'Heir of the Month' (January 2015), http://heirstothethrone-project.net/?page_id=1349 (accessed 24 February 2017)

Müller, Frank Lorenz, '"Frau Deines Mannes, Tochter Deiner Mutter". Victoria und das Scheitern einer Mission', in Jürgen Luh and Julia Klein (eds.), *Perspektivweitung – Frauen und Männer machen Geschichte. Beiträge des zweiten Colloquiums in der Reihe 'Kulturgeschichte Preußens – Colloquien' vom 10. und 11. Oktober 2014*, https://perspectivia.net//publikationen/kultgep-colloquien/2/mueller_scheitern (2016) (accessed 23 May 2017)

Müller, Frank Lorenz, 'Ludwig of Bavaria and Helmstadt: The Heroic Memory of an Unmilitary Prince', AHRC Project *Heirs to the Throne in the Constitutional Monarchies of Nineteenth-Century Europe (1815–1914)*, 'Heir of the Month' (July 2016), http://heirstothethrone-project.net/?page_id=2512 (accessed 28 March 2017)

Müller, Frank Lorenz, *Our Fritz: Emperor Frederick III and the Political Culture of Imperial Germany*, Cambridge, MA 2011

Müller, Frank Lorenz, *Royal Heirs in Imperial Germany: The Future of Monarchy in Nineteenth-Century Bavaria, Saxony and Württemberg*, London 2017

Müller, Frank Lorenz, 'Stabilizing a "Great Historical System" in the Nineteenth Century? Royal Heirs and Succession in an Age of Monarchy', in Frank Lorenz Müller and Heidi Mehrkens (eds.), *Sons and Heirs: Succession and Political Culture in Nineteenth-Century Europe*, Basingstoke 2016, pp. 1–16

Müller, Frank Lorenz, 'Symptomatisch für den Niedergang des Bismarck-Reiches? Die leise Entkrönung der kleineren deutschen Königreiche im November 1918', in Holger Afflerbach and Ulrich Lappenküper (eds.), *1918 – Das Ende des Bismarck-Reiches?* Paderborn 2021, pp. 79–99

Müller, Frank Lorenz, '"Winning Their Trust and Affection": Royal Heirs and the Uses of Soft Power in Nineteenth-Century Europe', in Frank Lorenz Müller and Heidi Mehrkens (eds.), *Royal Heirs and the Uses of Soft Power in Nineteenth-Century Europe*, London 2016, pp. 1–19

Müller, Frank Lorenz and Heidi Mehrkens (eds.), *Royal Heirs and the Uses of Soft Power in Nineteenth-Century Europe*, London 2016

Müller, Frank Lorenz and Heidi Mehrkens (eds.), *Sons and Heirs: Succession and Political Culture in Nineteenth-Century Europe*, Basingstoke 2016

Müller, Karl Alexander von, *Aus Gärten der Vergangenheit. Erinnerungen 1882–1914*, Stuttgart 1951

Münkler, Herfried 'Die Visibilität der Macht und Strategien der Machtvisualisierung', in Gerhard Göhler (ed.), *Macht der Öffentlichkeit – Öffentlichkeit der Macht*, Baden-Baden 1995, pp. 213–230

Naumann, Friedrich, *Demokratie und Kaisertum. Ein Handbuch für innere Politik*, Berlin 1900

Naumann, Friedrich, 'Monarchie und Demokratie' (1912), in Friedrich Naumann, *Werke*, vol. 2, Cologne and Opladen 1964, pp. 439–444

Netzer, Hans-Joachim, *Albert von Sachsen-Coburg und Gotha. Ein deutscher Prinz in England*, Munich 1988

Neuhaus, Helmut, 'Das Ende der Monarchien in Deutschland 1918', in *Historisches Jahrbuch* 111 (1991), pp. 102–136

Neumeister, Sebastian, 'Philalethes – König Johann als Dante-Übersetzer', in Winfried Müller and Martina Schattkowsky (eds.), *Zwischen Tradition und Modernität. König Johann von Sachsen 1801–1873*, Leipzig 2004, pp. 203–216

Newbould, Ian, 'William IV and the Dismissal of the Whigs, 1834', in *Canadian Journal of History* 11 (1976), pp. 311–330

Nicolson, Harold, *King George the Fifth: His Life and Reign*, New York 1953

Nye, Joseph S., Jr, 'The Infant Prince George Is a Source of Real-World Power', in *Financial Times* 24 July 2013, www.ft.com/content/0bd55672-f482-11e2-a62e-00144feabdc0 (accessed 1 June 2017)

Nye, Joseph S., Jr, *Soft Power: The Means to Success in World Politics*, New York 2004

O'Connor, Adrian, 'Between Monarch and Monarchy: The Education of the Dauphin and Revolutionary Politics, 1790–1791', in *French History* 27, 2 (2013), pp. 176–201

Osterhammel, Jürgen, *The Transformation of the World: A Global History of the Nineteenth Century*, Princeton, NJ 2014

Otte, Wulf, 'Zwischen Welfenstolz und Preußenmacht. Die braunschweigische Thronfolgefrage 1866–1918', in Meike Buck, Maik Ohnezeit and Heike Pöppelmann (eds.), *1919 – Herrliche moderne Zeiten?*, Braunschweig 2013, pp. 52–60

Pope-Hennessy, James, *Queen Mary: The Official Biography*, with an introduction by Hugo Vickers, London 2019

Pope-Hennessy, James, *The Quest for Queen Mary*, ed. Hugo Vickers, London 2018

Palmer, Robert R., *The Age of the Democratic Revolution: A Political History of Europe and America, 1760–1800*, 2 vols., Princeton, NJ 1959 and 1964

Parkhurst, Genevieve, *A King in the Making: An Authentic Story of Edward, Seventeenth Prince of Wales*, New York and London 1925

Pascal, Adrien, *Vie militaire, politique et privée de Son Altesse Royale monseigneur le duc d'Orléans*, Paris 1842

Paulmann, Johannes, 'Peripatetische Herrschaft, Deutungskontrolle und Konsum. Zur Theatralität in der europäischen Politik vor 1914', in *Geschichte in Wissenschaft und Unterricht* 53 (2002), pp. 444–461

Paulmann, Johannes, *Pomp und Politik. Monarchenbegegnungen in Europa zwischen Ancien Régime und Erstem Weltkrieg*, Paderborn 2000

Paulucci, Paolo, *Alla corte di Re Umberto. Diario segreto*, Milan 1986

Persson, Fabian, *Survival and Revival in Sweden's Court and Monarchy, 1718–1930*, London 2020

Pflanze, Otto, *Bismarck and the Development of Germany*, vol. 1, Princeton, NJ 1990

Plunkett, John, *Queen Victoria: First Media Monarch*, Oxford 2003

Pogge von Strandmann, Hartmut, 'Nationalisierungsdruck und Namensänderung in England. Das Ende der Großfamilie europäischer Dynastien', in Gerhard A. Ritter and Peter Wende (eds.), *Rivalität und Partnerschaft. Studien zu den deutsch–britischen Beziehungen im 19. und 20. Jahrhundert*, Paderborn 1999, pp. 69–91

Polland, Imke, 'How to *Fashion* the Popularity of the British Monarchy: Alexandra, Princess of Wales and the Attraction of Attire', in Frank Lorenz Müller and Heidi Mehrkens (eds.), *Royal Heirs and the Uses of Soft Power in Nineteenth-Century Europe*, London 2016, pp. 201–221

Porciani, Ilaria, 'Der Krieg als ambivalenter italienischer Gründungsmythos – Siege und Niederlagen', in Nikolaus Buschmann and Dieter Langewiesche (eds.), *Der Krieg in den Gründungsmythen europäischer Nationen und den USA*, Frankfurt am Main and New York 2003, pp. 193–212

Powell, Ted, *King Edward VIII: An American Life*, Oxford 2018

Price, Munro, *The Perilous Crown: France between Revolutions, 1814–1848*, Basingstoke and Oxford 2007

Price, Roger, *The French Second Empire: An Anatomy of Political Power*, Cambridge 2001

'Prinzenerziehung', in K. A. Schmid (ed.), *Encyklopädie des gesammten Erziehungs- und Unterrichtswesens*, vol. 6, Gotha 1867

Prittwitz und Gaffron, Ferdinand von, *Die Königlichen Hausgesetze in Preußen* (dissertation), Leipzig 1908

Prochaska, Frank, *Royal Bounty: The Making of a Welfare Monarchy*, New Haven, CT and London 1995

Prochaska, Frank, 'The Crowned Republic and the Rise of the Welfare Monarchy', in Frank-Lothar Kroll and Dieter J. Weiß (eds.), *Inszenierung oder Legitimität. Die Monarchie in Europa im 19. und 20. Jahrhundert. Ein deutsch–englischer Vergleich*, Berlin 2015, pp. 141–150

Pyta, Wolfram, 'Die Kunst des rechtzeitigen Thronverzichts. Neue Einsichten zur Überlebenschance der parlamentarischen Monarchie in Deutschland im Herbst 1918', in Patrick Merziger, Rudolf Stöber, Esther-Beate Körber and Jürgen Michael Schulz (eds.), *Geschichte, Öffentlichkeit, Kommunikation. Festschrift für Bernd Sösemenn zum 65. Geburtstag*, Stuttgart 2010, pp. 363–381

Quataert, Jean, *Staging Philanthropy: Patriotic Women and the National Imagination in Dynastic Germany 1813–1916*, Ann Arbor, MI 2001

Quessel, Ludwig, 'Sind wir Republikaner?', in *Sozialistische Monatshefte* 13 (1909), pp. 1254–1262

Quessel, Ludwig, 'Sozialdemokratie und Monarchie', in *Sozialistische Monatshefte* 16 (1912), pp. 271–275

Radforth, Ian, *Royal Spectacle: The 1860 Visit of the Prince of Wales to Canada and the United States*, Toronto 2004

Rauchensteiner, Manfried, *Der Erste Weltkrieg und das Ende der Habsburgermonarchie 1914–1918*, Vienna, Cologne and Weimar 2013

Reidelbach, Hans, *Ludwig. Prinz von Bayern. Ein Lebens- und Charakterbild*, Munich 1905

Requate, Jörg, 'Einleitung', in Jörg Requate (ed.), *Das 19. Jahrhundert als Mediengesellschaft*, Munich 2009, pp. 7–18

Requate, Jörg, 'Kennzeichen der deutschen Mediengesellschaft des 19. Jahrhunderts', in Jörg Requate (ed.), *Das 19. Jahrhundert als Mediengesellschaft*, Munich 2009, pp. 30–42

Requate, Jörg, 'Politischer Massemarkt und nationale Öffentlichkeiten – Die Entstehung einer "vierten Gewalt"? Deutschland, England und Frankreich im Vergleich', in Martin Kirsch, Anne G. Kosfeld and Pierangelo Schiera (eds.), *Der Verfassungsstaat vor der Herausforderung der Massengesellschaft. Konstitutionalismus um 1900 im europäischen Vergleich*, Berlin 2002, pp. 145–168

Retallack, James, 'Obrigkeitsstaat und politischer Massenmarkt', in Sven Oliver Müller and Cornelius Torp (eds.), *Das Deutsche Kaiserreich in der Kontroverse*, Göttingen 2009, pp. 121–135

Riall, Lucy, 'Men at War: Masculinity and Military Ideals in the Risorgimento', in Silvana Patriarca and Lucy Riall (eds.), *The Risorgimento Revisited: Nationalism and Culture in Nineteenth-Century Italy*, Basingstoke 2012, pp. 152–170

Richards, Thomas, *The Commodity Culture of Victorian England: Advertising and Spectacle, 1851–1914*, London 1990

Richter, B., *Kleine Episoden und Charakterzüge aus dem Leben unseres Kaisers Friedrich III.*, Reudnitz and Leipzig 1888

Ridley, Jane, *Bertie: A Life of Edward VII*, London 2012

Ridley, Jane, 'Bertie Prince of Wales: Prince Hal and the Widow of Windsor', in Frank Lorenz Müller and Heidi Mehrkens (eds.), *Royal Heirs and the Uses of Soft Power in Nineteenth-Century Europe*, London 2016, pp. 123–138

Ridley, Jane, *Victoria: Queen, Matriarch, Empress*, London 2015

Ries, Helmut, *Kronprinz Wilhelm*, Hamburg, Berlin and Bonn 2001

Riotte, Torsten, 'Nach "Pomp und Politik". Neue Ansätze in der Historiographie zum regierenden Hochadel im 19. Jahrhundert', in *Neue Politische Literatur* 59 (2014), pp. 209–228

Robertson, Alexander, *Victor Emmanuel III: King of Italy*, London 1925

Röhl, John C. G. (ed.), *Philipp Eulenburgs politische Korrespondenz*, vol. 2, Boppard am Rhein 1979

Röhl, John C. G., *The Kaiser and His Court: Wilhelm II and the Government of Germany*, Cambridge 1994

Röhl, John C. G., *Young Wilhelm: The Kaiser's Early Life, 1859–1888*, Cambridge 1998

Röhl, John C. G., *Wilhelm II: Into the Abyss of War and Exile 1900–1941*, Cambridge 2014

Röhl, John C. G., *Wilhelm II: The Kaiser's Personal Monarchy, 1888–1900*, Cambridge 2004

Röschner, Matthias, 'Förderer und Protektor. Die Rolle Ludwigs III. in der Gründungs-und Aufbauphase des Deutschen Museums', in Ulrike Leutheusser and Hermann Rumschöttel (eds.), *König Ludwig III. und das Ende der Monarchie in Bayern*, Munich 2014, pp. 127–144

Roon, Albrecht von, *Denkwürdigkeiten aus dem Leben des Generalfeldmarschalls Kriegsminister Grafen von Roon*, vol. 1, 4th edn, Breslau 1897 [1892]

Rose, Kenneth, *King George V*, London 1983

Rosner, Karl (ed.), *Erinnerungen des Kronprinzen Wilhelm. Aus den Aufzeichnungen, Dokumenten, Tagebüchern und Gesprächen*, Stuttgart 1922

Rüger, Jan, *The Great Naval Game: Britain and Germany in the Age of Empire*, Cambridge 2007

Rundquist, Angela, 'Pompe en noir et blanc. Présentation officielle des dames à la cour de Suède', in *Actes de la Recherche en Sciences Sociales* 110 (December 1995), pp. 65–76

Salazar, Fanny Zampini, *Margherita of Savoy: First Queen of Italy. Her Life and Times*, London 1914

Sanson, Henri, *Tagebücher der Henker von Paris*, vol. 1, www.projekt-gutenberg.org/sanson/henker1/chap012.html (accessed 10 May 2022)

Schama, Simon, 'The Domestication of Majesty: Royal Family Portraiture, 1650–1850', in *The Journal of Interdisciplinary History* 17 (1986), pp. 155–183

Schieder, Theodor, *Staatensystem als Vormacht der Welt, 1848–1918*, Berlin 1986

Schindler, Hermann, *König Friedrich August III. von Sachsen: Ein Lebens- und Charakterbild*, Dresden 1906/1916

Schlögl, Rudolf, *Alter Glaube und moderne Welt. Europäisches Christentum im Umbruch 1750–1850*, Frankfurt am Main 2013

Schmidt, Hans-Joachim, 'Fürstenspiegel', in *Historisches Lexikon Bayerns* (2011), www.historisches-lexikon-bayerns.de/Lexikon/F%C3%BCrstenspiegel (accessed 6 February 2017)

Schneider, Louis, 'Der Prinz von Preußen. Zum 1. Januar 1857', in *Der Soldatenfreund* 24 (December 1856), pp. 1–136

Schneider, Miriam, 'A "Sporting Hermes": Crown Prince Constantine and the Ancient Heritage of Modern Greece', in Frank Lorenz Müller and Heidi Mehrkens (eds.), *Royal Heirs and the Uses of Soft Power in Nineteenth-Century Europe*, London 2016, pp. 243–261

Schneider, Miriam, 'The Prussian Duke of Sparta', AHRC Project *Heirs to the Throne in the Constitutional Monarchies of Nineteenth-Century Europe (1815–1914)*,

'Heir of the Month' (March 2015), http://heirstothethrone-project.net/?page_id=1467 (accessed 5 July 2017)

Schneider, Miriam, *The 'Sailor Prince' in the Age of Empire: Creating a Monarchical Brand in Nineteenth-Century Europe*, London 2017

Schneider, Miriam, *Who should educate the Prince of Wales? Eine Debatte im viktorianischen England*, BA thesis, Universität Bayreuth 2009

Schneider, Reinhold, *Die Hohenzollern*, 2nd edn, Cologne 1953

Schöbel, Anja, *Monarchie und Öffentlichkeit. Zur Inszenierung der deutschen Bundesfürsten 1848–1918*, Cologne, Weimar and Vienna 2017

Schönpflug, Daniel, *Die Heiraten der Hohenzollern. Verwandtschaft, Politik und Ritual in Europa 1640–1918*, Göttingen 2013

Schönpflug, Daniel, 'Heirs before the Altar: Hohenzollern Marriages in a Bourgeois Age', in Frank Lorenz Müller and Heidi Mehrkens (eds.), *Sons and Heirs: Succession and Political Culture in Nineteenth-Century Europe*, Basingstoke 2016, pp. 53–71

Schulze, Hagen, *Staat und Nation in der europäischen Geschichte*, Munich 1994

Schulze, Hermann, *Die Hausgesetze der regierenden deutschen Fürstenhäuser*, vol. 1, Jena 1862

Schulze, Hermann, *Die Hausgesetze der regierenden deutschen Fürstenhäuser*, vol. 3, Jena 1883

Schulze-Wegener, Guntram, *Wilhelm I. Deutscher Kaiser – König von Preußen – Nationaler Mythos*, Hamburg and Bonn 2015

Sellin, Volker, *Das Jahrhundert der Restaurationen*, Munich 2014

Sellin, Volker, 'Die Erfindung des monarchischen Prinzips. Jacques-Claude Beugnots Präambel zur *Charte Constitutionelle*', in Armin Heinen and Dietmar Hüsen (eds.), *Tour de France. Eine historische Rundreise. Festschrift für Rainer Hudemann*, Stuttgart 2008, pp. 489–497

Sellin, Volker, 'Die Nationalisierung der Monarchie', in Benjamin Hasselhorn and Marc von Knorring (eds.), *Vom Olymp zum Boulevard. Die europäischen Monarchien von 1815 bis heute – Verlierer der Geschichte?*, Berlin 2018, pp. 241–253

Sellin, Volker, *Gewalt und Legitimität. Die europäische Monarchie im Zeitalter der Revolutionen*, Munich 2011

Sellin, Volker, 'Restorations and Constitutions', in Kelly L. Grotke and Markus J. Prutsch (eds.), *Constitutionalism, Legitimacy, and Power*, Oxford 2014, pp. 84–103

Sheehan, James J., *Where Have All the Soldiers Gone? The Transformation of Modern Europe*, New York 2008

Smith, Jeffrey R., 'The Monarchy versus the Nation: The Festive Year 1913 in Wilhelmine Germany', in *German Studies Review* 23 (2000), pp. 257–274

Smith, William H. C., *Napoleon III: The Pursuit of Prestige*, London 1991

Snow, Nancy, and Philip Taylor (eds.), *Routledge Handbook of Public Diplomacy*, London 2009

Speeches by H.R.H. The Prince of Wales 1912–1926, London 1927

Spellman, W. M., *Monarchies 1000–2000*, London 2001

Stagl, Justin, 'Einleitung', in Justin Stagl (ed.), *Ein Erzherzog reist. Beiträge zur Weltreise Franz Ferdinands*, Salzburg 2001, pp. 3–8

Stecher, Richard, *König Friedrich August III. von Sachsen. Ein Lebensbild*, Dresden 1905

Sterkenburgh, Frederik Frank, 'Narrating Prince Wilhelm of Prussia: Commemorative Biography as Monarchical Politics of Memory', in Frank Lorenz Müller and Heidi Mehrkens (eds.), *Royal Heirs and the Uses of Soft Power in Nineteenth-Century Europe*, London 2016, pp. 281–301

Stickler, Matthias, 'Dynastie, Armee, Parlament. Probleme staatlicher Integrationspolitik im 19. Jahrhundert', in Winfried Müller and Martina Schattkowsky (eds.), *Zwischen Tradition und Modernität. König Johann von Sachsen 1801–1873*, Leipzig 2004, pp. 109–140

Storz, Dieter, 'Kronprinz Rupprecht von Bayern – dynastische Heerführung im Massenkrieg', in Winfried Heinemann and Markus Pöhlmann (eds.), *Monarchen und ihr Militär*, Potsdam 2010, pp. 45–57

Tamse, Coen A., 'Die niederländische Monarchie', in Horst Lademacher and Walter Mühlhausen (eds.), *Freiheitsstreben. Demokratie. Emanzipation. Aufsätze zur politischen Kultur in Deutschland und den Niederlanden*, Münster and Hamburg 1993, pp. 107–138

Tamse, Coenraad A., 'König Wilhelm III. und Sophie', in Coenraad A. Tamse (ed.), *Nassau und Oranien. Staathalter und Könige der Niederlande*, Göttingen and Zurich 1985, pp. 308–328

Telesko, Werner, *Geschichtsraum Österreich. Die Habsburger und ihre Geschichte in der bildenden Kunst des 19. Jahrhunderts*, Vienna 2006, pp. 282–286

Thoma, Ludwig, 'Ein kranker König' (1907), in Ludwig Thoma, *Gesammelte Werke*, vol. 1, Munich 1968

Thompson, Andrew, 'Fathers and Sons: Intergenerational Conflict in the Early Hanoverian Monarchy', lecture given at Hampton Court in 2013 (unpublished manuscript)

Thompson, J. M. (ed.), *English Witnesses of the French Revolution*, Oxford 1938, pp. 227–231

Toskana, Luise von, *Mein Lebensweg*, Berlin 1926

Travaini, Lucia, *Storia di una passione. Vittorio Emanuele III e le monete*, 2nd edn, Rome 2005

Truesdell, Matthew, *Spectacular Politics: Louis-Napoleon Bonaparte and the 'Fête Imperiale', 1849–1870*, New York and Oxford 1997

Turner, E. S., *The Court of St James's*, New York 1959

Ungari, Andrea, 'The Role of the Monarchy in the War in Libya', in Luca Micheletta and Andrea Ungari (eds.), *The Libyan War 1911–1912*, Cambridge 2013, pp. 15–38

Unowsky, Daniel, *The Pomp and Politics of Patriotism: Imperial Celebrations in Habsburg Austria, 1848–1916*, West Lafayette, IN 2005

Unser Kronprinz im Felde. Gemälde und Skizzen von Wilhelm Paper, Kriegsmaler im Großen Hauptquartier, Berlin 1918

Urbach, Karina, 'Die inszenierte Idylle. Legitimationsstrategien Queen Victorias und Prinz Alberts', in Frank-Lothar Kroll and Dieter J. Weiß (eds.), *Inszenierung oder Legitimität. Die Monarchie in Europa im 19. und 20. Jahrhundert. Ein deutsch–englischer Vergleich*, Berlin 2015, pp. 23–33

Urbach, Karina, *Queen Victoria. Eine Biographie*, Munich 2011

Vacaresco, Hélène [Elena Văcărescu], *Kings and Queens I Have Known*, New York 1904

Vallone, Lynne, *Becoming Victoria*, New Haven, CT and London 2001

Vierhaus, Rudolf (ed.), *Das Tagebuch der Baronin Spitzemberg, geb. Freiin v. Varnbüler. Aufzeichnungen aus der Hofgesellschaft des Hohenzollernreiches*, 3rd edn, Göttingen 1963

Villa, Valentina, 'An Italian Heir for the New Century: Vittorio Emanuele, Prince of Naples', in Frank Lorenz Müller and Heidi Mehrkens (eds.), *Sons and Heirs: Succession and Political Culture in Nineteenth-Century Europe*, Basingstoke 2016, pp. 160–175

Vincent, James Edmund, *His Royal Highness Duke of Clarence and Avondale: A Memoir*, London 1893

Vocelka, Karl, and Lynne Heller, *Die private Welt der Habsburger. Leben und Alltag einer Familie*, Graz 1998

Vocelka, Michaela, and Karl Vocelka, *Franz Joseph I. Kaiser von Österreich und König von Ungarn, 1830–1916*, Munich 2015

Vogel, Jakob, 'Der "Folkloremilitärismus" und seine zeitgenössische Kritik – Deutschland und Frankreich 1871–1914', in Wolfram Wette (ed.), *Militarismus in Deutschland 1871 bis 1945*, Münster 1999, pp. 277–292

Vogel, Jakob, '"En revenant de la revue". Militärfolklore und Folkloremilitarismus in Deutschland und Frankreich 1871–1914', in *Österreichische Zeitschrift für Geschichtswissenschaft* 9 (1998), pp. 9–30

Vogel, Jakob, *Nationen im Gleichschritt. Der Kult der 'Nation in Waffen' in Deutschland und Frankreich, 1871–1914*, Göttingen 1997

Vogel, Juliane, *Elisabeth von Österreich. Momente aus dem Leben einer Kunstfigur*, Frankfurt am Main 1998

Wagner, Yvonne, *Prinzenerziehung in der 2. Hälfte des 19. Jahrhunderts. Zum Bildungsverhalten des preußisch–deutschen Hofes im gesellschaftlichen Wandel*, Frankfurt am Main, 1995

Watanabe-O'Kelly, Helen, *Projecting Imperial Power: New Nineteenth-Century Emperors and the Public Sphere*, Oxford 2021

Wawro, Geoffrey, *The Austro-Prussian War: Austria's War with Prussia and Italy 1866*, Cambridge 1996

Wecker, Fritz, *Unsere Landesväter. Wie sie gingen, wo sie blieben*, Berlin 1928.

Weigand, Katharina, 'Der gelehrte Monarch und die Kulturpolitik. Johann von Sachsen und Maximilian II. von Bayern im Vergleich', in Winfried Müller and Martina Schattkowsky (eds.), *Zwischen Tradition und Modernität. König Johann von Sachsen 1801–1873*, Leipzig 2004, pp. 189–202

Weigand, Katharina, 'Die konstitutionelle Monarchie im 19. Jahrhundert im Spannungsfeld von Krone und Staat, Macht und Amt', in Wolfgang Wiese and Katrin Rössler (eds.), *Repräsentation im Wandel*, Ostfildern 2008, pp. 36–37

Weis, Eberhard, *Der Durchbruch des Bürgertums. 1776–1847*, Berlin 1990

Weiß, Dieter J., 'Kronprinz Rupprecht von Bayern (1869–1955). Thronprätendent in einer Republik', in Frank-Lothar Kroll and Dieter J. Weiß (eds.), *Inszenierung oder Legitimität. Die Monarchie in Europa im 19. und 20. Jahrhundert. Ein deutsch–englischer Vergleich*, Berlin 2015, pp. 153–167

Weiß, Dieter J., *Kronprinz Rupprecht von Bayern. Eine politische Biografie*, Regensburg 2007

Weissensteiner, Friedrich, *Franz Ferdinand. Der verhinderte Herrscher*, Vienna 2007

Weissensteiner, Friedrich, *Große Herrscher des Hauses Habsburg. 700 Jahre europäische Geschichte*, Munich 1997

Werner, Karl F., 'Fürst und Hof im 19. Jahrhundert. Abgesang oder Spätblüte', in Karl Ferdinand Werner (ed.), *Hof, Kultur und Politik im 19. Jahrhundert*, Bonn, 1985, pp. 1–53

Who Should Educate the Prince of Wales?, London 1843

Widestadt, Kristina, 'Pressing the Centre of Attention: Three Royal Weddings and a Media Myth', in Mats Jönsson and Patrik Lundell (eds.), *Media and Monarchy in Sweden*, Göteborg 2009, pp. 47–58

Wienfort, Monika, 'Dynastic Heritage and Bourgeois Morals: Monarchy and Family in the Nineteenth Century', in Frank Lorenz Müller and Heidi Mehrkens (eds.), *Royal Heirs and the Uses of Soft Power in Nineteenth-Century Europe*, London 2016, pp. 163–179

Wienfort, Monika, *Verliebt, Verlobt, Verheiratet. Eine Geschichte der Ehe seit der Romantik*, Munich 2014

Williams, Kate, *Becoming Queen*, London 2009

Williamson, Samuel R., Jr, 'Influence, Power, and the Policy Process: The Case of Franz Ferdinand, 1906–1914', in *The Historical Journal* 17 (1974), pp. 417–434

Willman, Anni, *Der gelernte König. Wilhelm II. von Württemberg. Ein Porträt in Geschichten*, Stuttgart 2007

Wilson, A. N., *Prince Albert: The Man Who Saved the Monarchy*, London 2019

Wilson, A. N., *Victoria: A Life*, New York 2014

Windt, Franziska, 'Majestätische Bilderflut. Die Kaiser in der Photographie', in Generaldirektion der Stiftung Preußische Schlösser und Gärten Berlin-Brandenburg (ed.), *Die Kaiser und die Macht der Medien*, Berlin 2005, pp. 67–77

Winkelhofer, Martina, *Eine feine Gesellschaft. Europas Königs- und Kaiserhäuser im Spiegel ihrer Skandale*, Vienna 2014

Winterberg, Yury and Sonya Winterberg, *Kleine Hände im Großen Krieg. Kinderschicksale im Ersten Weltkrieg*, Berlin 2014

Witzleben, E. von, *Adolf von Deines. Lebensbild, 1845–1911*, Berlin 1913

Wolf, Friedrich August, *Darstellung der Alterthumswissenschaften*, ed. F. W. Hoffmann, Leipzig 1833

Wortman, Richard S., *Scenarios of Power: Myth and Ceremony in Russian Monarchy*, vol. 2, Princeton, NJ 2000

Wrede, Martin, 'Einleitung. Die Inszenierung der mehr oder weniger heroischen Monarchie. Zu Rittern und Feldherren, Kriegsherren und Schauspielern', in Martin Wrede (ed.), *Die Inszenierung der heroischen Monarchie. Frühneuzeitliches Königtum zwischen ritterlichem Erbe und militärischer Herausforderung*, Munich 2014, pp. 8–39

Wyatt, Harold Fraser, 'God's Text by War', in *The Nineteenth Century and After* 69 (1911), pp. 591–606

Zanten, Jeroen van, *Koning Willem II, 1792–1849*, Amsterdam 2013

Ziegler, Philip, *King Edward VIII: The Official Biography*, London 1990
Zorn, Philipp, 'Erinnerungen an den deutschen Kronprinzen', in *Deutsche Revue* 46, 4 (1921), pp. 207–210
Zweig, Stefan, *The World of Yesterday*, trans. Benjamin W. Huebsch and Helmut Rippinger, Lincoln, NE and London, 1964

Newspapers and Magazines

Allgemeine Rundschau
Allgemeine Zeitung
Augsburger Postzeitung
Bayern-Kurier
Berliner Tageblatt
Der Beobachter. Ein Volksblatt aus Schwaben
Der Deutsche
Der Sozialdemokrat
Die Jugend
Die Volkswacht
Die Zeit
Dresdener Rundschau
Dresdner Anzeiger
Dresdner Journal
Dresdner Nachrichten
Dresdner Neueste Nachrichten
El Imparcial
Herald Democrat
Illustreret Tidende
Journal des Débats Politiques et Littéraires
La America (Madrid)
Leipziger Volkszeitung
Leipziger Zeitung
Le Petit Parisien
L'Illustrazione Italiana
L'Opinione
Morning Post (London)
Münchener Tageblatt
Münchner Neueste Nachrichten
National-Zeitung
Neue Freie Presse (Vienna)
Neue Freie Volkszeitung
Neue Preußische Zeitung
Neues Tagblatt (Stuttgart)
New York Times
Norddeutsche Allgemeine Zeitung
Pall Mall Gazette
Politiken
Reynold's Newspaper

Rheinische Blätter
Sächsische Arbeiter-Zeitung
Sächsische Volkszeitung
Schwäbische Kronik
Schwäbische Tagwacht
Schwäbischer Merkur
Staats-Anzeiger für Württemberg
The Illustrated London News
The Manchester Guardian
The Standard (London)
The Times
Unterhaltungsblatt der Augsburger Postzeitung
Volksblatt
Volks-Zeitung
Vossische Zeitung

Online Sources and Websites

http://heirstothethrone-project.net
http://landtagsprotokolle.sachsendigital.de
http://news.bbc.co.uk
http://statuesmonumentsnpdc.pagesperso-orange.fr
http://thevictorianist.blogspot.de
https://en.wikipedia.org
https://onb.wg.picturemaxx.com
www.br.de
www.documentarchiv.de
www.hdbg.eu
www.heraldica.org
www.npg.org.uk
www.rct.uk
www.royalcourt.no
www.zeit.de
www.zeno.org

Index